S0-BAH-891

Physiology, Emotion & Psychosomatic Illness

*The Ciba Foundation for the promotion of international cooperation in
medical and chemical research is a scientific and educational charity established by
CIBA Limited – now CIBA-GEIGY Limited – of Basle. The Foundation operates
independently in London under English trust law.*

*Ciba Foundation Symposia are published in collaboration with
Associated Scientific Publishers (Elsevier Scientific Publishing Company, Excerpta Medica,
North-Holland Publishing Company) in Amsterdam.*

Associated Scientific Publishers, P.O. Box 1270, Amsterdam

Physiology, Emotion & Psychosomatic Illness

Ciba Foundation Symposium 8 (new series)

1972

Elsevier · Excerpta Medica · North-Holland
Associated Scientific Publishers · Amsterdam · London · New York

© *Copyright 1972 Ciba Foundation*

All rights reserved. No part of this publication may be reproduced or transmitted in any form or by any means, electronic or mechanical, including photocopying and recording, or by any information storage and retrieval system, without permission in writing from the publishers.

ISBN Excerpta Medica 90 219 4009 4
ISBN American Elsevier 0-444-10402-X

Library of Congress Catalog Card Number 72-93253

Published in 1972 by Associated Scientific Publishers, P.O. Box 3489, Amsterdam, and 52 Vanderbilt Avenue, New York, N. Y. 10017.

Suggested series entry for library catalogues: Ciba Foundation Symposia.

Ciba Foundation Symposium 8 (new series)

Printed in The Netherlands by Koninklijke Van Gorcum & Comp. N.V., Assen

Contents

Participants

Symposium on Physiology, Emotion and Psychosomatic Illness, held at the Ciba Foundation, London, 18th-20th April 1972

SIR DENIS HILL (*Chairman*)   Institute of Psychiatry, De Crespigny Park, Denmark Hill, London SE5 8AF

R. C. B. AITKEN   University Department of Psychiatry, Royal Edinburgh Hospital, Morningside Park, Edinburgh EH10 5HF

V. H. DENENBERG   Department of Biobehavioral Sciences, The College of Liberal Arts and Sciences, The University of Connecticut, Box U-154, Storrs, Conn. 06268, USA

K. W. DONALD   Department of Medicine, University of Edinburgh, The Royal Infirmary, Edinburgh EH3 9YW

G. L. ENGEL   Departments of Psychiatry and Medicine, University of Rochester, School of Medicine and Dentistry, 260 Crittenden Boulevard, Rochester, NY 14620, USA

ELZBIETA FONBERG   Department of Neurophysiology, Nencki Institute of Experimental Biology, 3 Pasteur Street, Warsaw 22, Poland

B. E. GINSBURG   Department of Biobehavioral Sciences, The College of Liberal Arts and Sciences, The University of Connecticut, Box U-154, Storrs, Conn. 06268, USA

J. A. GRAY   Department of Experimental Psychology, University of Oxford, South Parks Road, Oxford OX1 3PS

JOEL GRINKER   The Rockefeller University, New York, NY 10021, USA

J. P. HENRY   Department of Physiology, University of Southern California, 815 W 37th Street, Los Angeles, Cal. 90007, USA

R. A. HINDE   MRC Unit on the Development and Integration of Behaviour, University Sub-Department of Animal Behaviour, Madingley, Cambridge CB3 8AA

M. A. HOFER   Department of Psychiatry, Albert Einstein College of Medicine, Montefiore Hospital and Medical Center, 111 E 210th Street, Bronx, NY 10467, USA

M. H. LADER   Institute of Psychiatry, De Crespigny Park, Denmark Hill, London SE5 8AF

S. LEVINE   Department of Psychiatry, Stanford University School of Medicine, Stanford University Medical Center, Stanford, Cal. 94305, USA

J. C. NEMIAH   Department of Psychiatry, Harvard Medical School, Beth Israel Hospital, 330 Brookline Avenue, Boston, Mass. 02215, USA

F. REICHSMAN   State University of New York, Downstate Medical Center, Brooklyn, NY 11203, USA

M. L. RUTTER   Institute of Psychiatry, De Crespigny Park, Denmark Hill, London SE5 8AF

E. J. SACHAR   Department of Psychiatry, Albert Einstein College of Medicine, Montefiore Hospital and Medical Center, 111 E 210th Street, Bronx, NY 10467, USA

J. SANDLER   Institute of Psychiatry, De Crespigny Park, Denmark Hill, London SE5 8AF *and* The Hampstead Child-Therapy Clinic, 21 Maresfield Gardens, London NW3

P. E. SIFNEOS   Department of Psychiatry, Harvard Medical School, Beth Israel Hospital, 330 Brookline Avenue, Boston, Mass. 02215, USA

P. SLEIGHT*   Cardiac Department, The Radcliffe Infirmary, Oxford OX2 6HE

P. B. STOREY   Psychiatric Department, St. George's Hospital, Clare House, Blackshaw Road, Tooting, London SW17 OQT

G. TIBBLIN   Department of Medicine, University of Göteborg, Sahlgren's Hospital, 413 45 Göteborg, Sweden

J. M. WEISS   The Rockefeller University, New York, NY 10021, USA

O. H. WOLFF   Department of Child Health, Institute of Child Health, University of London, 30 Guilford Street, London WC1N 1EH

A. ZANCHETTI   Istituto di Ricerche Cardiovascolari dell'Università di Milano, Via F. Sforza 35, 20122 Milan, Italy

Editors: RUTH PORTER and JULIE KNIGHT

---

* Address until September 1973: Hallstrom Institute of Cardiology, University of Sydney, Royal Prince Alfred Hospital, Camperdown, New South Wales 2050, Australia.

Introduction

SIR DENIS HILL

Institute of Psychiatry, University of London

It has often been said that advances in medicine have been held up by lack of communication between the relevant people, particularly between non-clinical and clinical scientists working in different areas on different aspects of the same problem. It has also been said that non-clinical scientists may be unaware of, or only partially informed about, the problem as seen from the clinical point of view. Or it is said that the non-clinical scientist may be ignorant of the facts, relevant to his own work, which clinical medical investigations in a broad sense have revealed. On the other hand, clinical scientists may well ask how the new techniques devised in the laboratory can be applied to their own work, and when, as in this symposium, we are concerned with behaviour, it is evident that there are tremendous limitations on clinical science. We cannot manipulate man as we can an experimental animal. But there are now new techniques developed for the study of behaviour in smaller mammals, which have, we assume, the same sort of central nervous system and the same sort of physiology as we have, and these are leading to great advances and make this sort of symposium worthwhile now. The conditions under which such small mammals are subject to stress, noxious social pressures and the like, and the analysis of these situations and their consequences, are surely of the greatest importance and interest to clinicians.

The general objectives of this symposium are therefore to bring together clinical and non-clinical scientists working in fields relevant to the understanding of behavioural stress, and to provide the conditions which give maximum opportunity for free communication between us. It is important, if our objectives are to be reached, that each of us should be prepared to admit his ignorance as well as his knowledge. We should try to interpret ourselves to one another, and we should not be disturbed in asking or receiving seemingly naive questions.

This group is representative of scientists, clinical and non-clinical, who are working in the fields relevant to the topic; psychology, ethology and psycho-analysis are represented here, as well as physiology, neurophysiology and neuroendocrinology. On the clinical side we have physicians, psychiatrists and paediatricians. We shall first be concerned mainly with the theoretical aspect of our subject—the nature of emotion and of the emotional state, and looked at from more than one point of view. Then we move on to the mechanisms, both experiential and physiological, which are evident within the organization of the emotional state. We shall then discuss clinical phenomena and psycho-somatic medicine.

Concepts of emotion

R. A. HINDE

MRC Unit on the Development and Integration of Behaviour, Madingley, Cambridge

Abstract The concept of emotion is used in a variety of different ways by both scientists and laymen. The following usages are discussed: emotion as a category of input; as subjective experience; as a phase of a process; as a bodily state and/or intervening variable; and as a response. Discussion of the problems of emotion can only be meaningful if the dangers inherent in loose usage of the term are constantly borne in mind.

In a conference concerned with emotion one thing is certain—we shall not all use the term 'emotion' in the same way. From the start, therefore, it seems worthwhile to list briefly the principal ways in which the term and its derivatives are used, and to comment on some of the problems which arise. We shall see that the ways in which 'emotion' is used are not merely diverse but logically quite distinct, and yet all are concerned with an interrelated set of questions. The terminological confusion both results from and contributes to the difficulties of the problem.

EMOTION AS A CATEGORY OF INPUT

This is perhaps the most trivial usage. The most obvious case involves reference to 'emotional stimuli'—it is seldom stated whether this category of stimuli is to be defined in terms of the subjective feelings or the physiological state or the behaviour that they induce in the reactor, or in terms of the state of the individual presenting the stimuli. A similar ambiguity is associated with the term 'emotional deprivation'; has the individual concerned not been exposed to certain categories of behaviour in others, or has he not experienced certain subjective or physiological states? In the latter case, the distinction is clearly important, for not having experienced a certain internal state could be due either to absence of the appropriate input or to a failure to respond to it.

EMOTION AS SUBJECTIVE EXPERIENCE

In everyday speech 'emotion' is closely associated with subjective feelings (though usually not with sensations, such as headaches). Psychologists around the turn of the century used the term in a similar way: for James (1892) emotion was a 'tendency to feel' and for McDougall (1908) a generic term for the modes of affective experience. Today psychiatrists still use the term in a similar way: Davis (1957), for instance, equates it with 'feeling tone'. Often, however, emotions are restricted to a sub-class of feelings. For example:

(*a*) Formerly feeling was regarded as a more elementary process, emotion being 'a complex of feeling and sensation'. Woodworth (1938), though referring to this distinction as 'traditional', points out that it cannot be applied in practice. This use seems now to have disappeared.

(*b*) Others differentiate the mild feelings of pleasantness or unpleasantness that accompany sensory preferences from intense experiences such as grief, joy or anger, classifying only the latter as emotions. A similar distinction is used by some physiologists (e.g. Moruzzi 1969). It is also implied in dictionary definitions: *The Concise Oxford Dictionary* gives 'emotion: agitation of mind, feeling; excited mental state'. However it is of doubtful value to superimpose such a distinction on a continuum.

(*c*) Bowlby (1969) prefers to limit the term emotion to feelings or affects which are 'inherently connected with one or another form of action', such as love, hate, fear or hunger. These are distinguished from such feelings as sadness, pleasure or distress, which are not so obviously related to action. Again the distinction is clearly not absolute: if it were, how would we ever know that others felt sad or happy? The distinction becomes a little clearer if we limit the action to action oriented with respect to some object. (To call hunger an emotion seems to conflict with common usage, but this does not necessarily mean that Bowlby's distinction is not useful for causal analysis.)

The restrictions on the concept of emotion implied by common speech are in fact interesting to discuss but hard to pin down: certainly they are not based merely on intensity, for lassitude and fatigue are not called emotions however intense they may be. Attempts to draw a hard line between subjective feelings which are and are not to be called emotions would seem to be not very profitable.

If we accept this difficulty of definition, we can at least attempt to classify subjective feelings or emotions. We may characterize them:

(*a*) According to intensity, as indicated above. Often we use different words to signify successive ranges along an intensity continuum (e.g. fear, terror; anger, rage, fury).

(*b*) According to whether they are pleasant or unpleasant (can an emotion be neutral?).

(*c*) Into qualitative types. McDougall (1908) recognized a limited number of primary instincts—flight, repulsion, curiosity, pugnacity, self-abasement, self-assertion, the parental instinct and a few others. Associated with each of these was an emotion (respectively fear, disgust, wonder, anger, subjection, self-display and the tender emotion). In McDougall's view these primary emotions could combine to give complex emotions such as admiration or gratitude. Joy and sorrow, however, were not regarded as emotional states but as qualifications of the emotions they accompany. Since one criterion for a primary emotion was held to be the occurrence of similar phenomena in animals, an association with activity (c.f. Bowlby's later distinction, above) was relevant.

(*d*) According to their degree of relationship to an object. 'Love' and 'anger' are usually related to a particular object, while 'depression' and 'happiness' usually are not. Again, however, the distinction is not clear.

Although many psychologists have wrestled with these problems, recent research has passed them by unsolved; it remains the case that some subjective experiences are associated with fairly specific categories of behaviour (anger), others are apparently more general (excitement) and yet others are by common consent not regarded as emotions at all. Furthermore, there are no necessary relations between the characteristics listed above: some but not all emotions become increasingly unpleasant with intensity, and emotions may or may not be more intense or more pleasant if associated with a particular object.

With regard to the role of subjective feelings in behaviour, there are two distinct views. On the one hand, body and mind may be held to be separate but to interact in ways not yet understood: either subjective feelings may influence behaviour, or behaviour may influence subjective feelings (James-Langer theory), or both. Ryle (1949) has argued that the view that feelings cause behaviour derives from a covert and mistaken assumption that human body and mind belong to the same logical category: the result is that mind must be described in negative terms (not in space, not observable etc.). When emotion words are used in an apparently causal sense in everyday speech they are, in Ryle's view, being used merely to describe reasons or dispositions. Ryle regards a statement of the type 'Jealousy made A hit B' as implying a reason why A hit B, or a disposition of A to hit B, rather than a cause. (Similarly, if we ask 'Why did the glass break?' a cause might be 'Because the stone hit it' and a reason 'Because the glass was brittle'.) To one interested in causal analysis, however, this merely evades the issue and it is necessary to turn to the correlated physiological state (in this case that accompanying jealousy) as *one* of the causes of the behaviour. It is in fact always profitable to treat behaviour as the consequence of a causal nexus rather than to attempt to identify a single cause for each response (Hanson 1955).

On the other hand there are those who treat subjective feelings as mere epiphenomena: while they may be correlated with particular physiological states, only behaviour and its physiological machinery are regarded as real. While such an approach is empirically justifiable and scientifically respectable, it is impossible to escape the view that it fails to do justice to the importance of subjective experience.

A compromise between these views is impossible. Some writers dismiss the mentalistic view as mere animism (e.g. Hebb 1949). Others prefer to remain agnostic, arguing that we must first concern ourselves with problems of neuro-physiology and behaviour which, however complex, seem possible to tackle with the tools we now have: perhaps this will yield a means for approaching the even more difficult problems of subjective experience. Others, especially clinicians, are forced to concern themselves with subjective phenomena and for the most part (but see below) ignore the logical difficulty.

In fact simple relationships between subjective feelings and behaviour are less common than might be expected, for two principal reasons—responses are not specific to particular subjective emotions but may be common to many; and one emotion (e.g. fear) can be expressed in several ways (e.g. freezing or fleeing). In addition, in interpreting the emotions of others from their be-haviour we often use evidence drawn from the context: thus in different contexts we may infer different emotions from closely similar patterns of be-haviour. It is thus pertinent to ask, for instance, how far does the gradual development of emotional expression in the child imply a synchronous develop-ment of (subjective) emotional states?

EMOTION AS A PHASE OF A PROCESS

While the experimental psychologist is usually able to bypass the problem of the causal role of subjective feelings, the psychotherapist cannot, since he is faced daily with the relations between feeling and behaviour. Bowlby (1969), following Langer (1967), regards feeling as a phase of a physiological process. Just as the redness of heated iron can be regarded as a phase of the iron itself, and not an entity distinct from the iron, so feeling can be regarded as a phase of a physiological process rather than a product of it. In Langer's view the problem is thus not one of how a non-physical feeling arises in a physical system, but of how the process may pass into a felt phase and out of it again.

Bowlby suggests that the processes involved are an individual's 'appraisals either of his own organismic states and urges to act or of the succession of environmental situations in which he finds himself'. These processes of appraisal may or may not be felt. They clearly play a causal role in behaviour; to suppose that the feelings which are phases of those processes do so would (in my view) be a category mistake.

EMOTION AS A BODILY STATE, INTERVENING VARIABLE AND/OR FACTOR IN BEHAVIOUR

Amongst scientists the commonest implication of the term 'emotion' concerns the internal state of the individual concerned. This can be independent of the status accorded to subjective feelings. If we regard them as the core of the concept of emotion, then the personal experience of each one of us indicates that particular categories of subjective feelings are correlated with particular bodily states, and the latter demand examination. If we choose to disregard subjective experience, our knowledge of the emotions of others depends on their behaviour: since consistencies in emotional behaviour must depend on consistencies in internal state, the internal state becomes a central issue.

In considering emotion as a state, we must differentiate states according to their persistence in time. In some contexts emotional state is associated closely with a particular type of response and is thought of as lasting only as long as the behaviour. In others it refers to a state of longer duration (mood) involving a proneness to respond in particular (emotional) ways either spontaneously or given adequate stimulation. The term 'emotionality' usually refers to permanent characteristics of the individual manifest by 'emotional' behaviour in particular situations; it has been applied especially to the behaviour (defecation and locomotion) of rodents in an open field situation (Whimbey & Denenberg 1967). We must also note that 'emotional' may imply a state associated either with a relatively constant high level of certain types of behaviour or with marked oscillations in that behaviour.

If we neglect subjective feelings, then emotion words stand for variables postulated in association with particular patterns of response probabilities in the individual's behaviour. For instance, a man is called angry when he is scowling and is likely to punch, kick, yell etc., but unlikely to sleep, feed or smile. It is important to recognize that each emotion is related to many types of behaviour; thus in terms of response probabilities, at least, emotions are likely to be multidimensional and therefore not easily measurable along a single scale.

Clearly, with the postulation of a variable associated with particular patterns

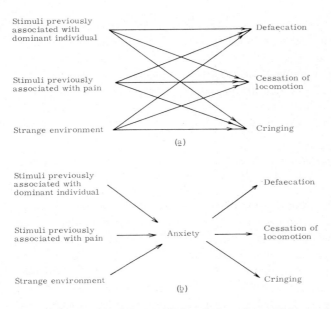

Fig. 1. Relationships between (*a*) three independent variables and three dependent variables; (*b*) three independent variables, one intervening variable and three dependent variables.

of response probabilities, the notion of causation is not far away. Sometimes emotions are used as intervening variables to link a number of response probabilities and a number of causal factors in a manner similar to that in which drive is used by many experimental psychologists. Adapting an example given by Miller (1959), Fig. 1 shows how three types of treatment (independent variables) may produce three types of effect (dependent variables) on an animal. If we are to understand the relationship between each type of treatment and each symptom, it would be necessary to establish nine relationships. Considerable economy could be achieved if we could postulate an intervening variable, 'anxiety', for we should then have to establish only three relationships between the independent variables and the intervening variable and three between the intervening variable and the dependent variables. Clearly the degree of economy will depend on (*a*) the number of independent and dependent variables considered and (*b*) the extent of the correlation between the dependent variables. The intervening variable will be valuable just so long as we are interested in the degree to which the dependent variables correlate, and will cease to be so when we focus on their divergence. At a less sophisticated level this is the way in which we use many 'emotion' words in everyday speech.

An intervening variable need carry no physiological implications. It becomes valuable at more than a behavioural level if it leads to the study of particular physiological mechanisms which mediate the behaviour under consideration. Neural structures are said to be causally involved if they show changes in activity which occur simultaneously with or (better) precede subjective feelings or emotional behaviour, or (better still) if direct stimulation of those structures induces either the feelings or the behaviour.

When emotional states are considered as causal to behaviour they may be regarded either as specific to particular categories of behaviour or as more or less general. Here again are parallels to the use of 'drive' in experimental psychology. 'Emotion' used in a specifically causal sense is often associated with studies of mechanisms in the hypothalamus and limbic system underlying sexual, aggressive (etc.) behaviour. In a more general sense emotion is associated with activation theories (e.g. Lindsley 1951; Schlosberg 1954), especially with those that stress energy mobilization (e.g. Duffy 1962), and with studies of the brainstem reticular system. In this context, however, it must be stressed that the physiological indices of activation show much less correlation with each other than traditional activation theory demands (e.g. Lacey et al. 1963; see also Bartoshuk 1972, and other chapters in Kling & Riggs 1972).

Whether emotions are thought of as specific to particular categories of behaviour or in more general terms, the causal relations proposed may be of several types:

(a) The emotion may be thought of as energizing behaviour directly. The effect may be considered as more or less general, as in Darwin's (1872) principle of 'direct nervous discharge', or specific to particular types of behaviour, as when Berkowitz (1962) describes anger as an emotional state which, in the presence of a suitable cue, instigates aggressive responses. In either case, the dependence of the behaviour on the emotion (or emotional state) is not a function of the consequences of the behaviour.

(b) The emotion may be thought of as a positively or negatively reinforcing event, on the grounds that organisms tend to repeat actions which terminate unpleasant emotional states or produce pleasant ones. Here 'pleasant' and 'unpleasant' are either used to imply subjective feelings or defined operationally in terms of their consequences on the behaviour. On this view fear, for instance, can become an acquired drive, in the sense that an animal will learn a response which reduces it.

(c) Closely related to the last, emotions can be thought of as goals or positive incentives (hedonism). For instance, much of the entertainment industry depends on a willingness to pay in order to experience emotion. Conversely, the avoidance of emotion may serve as a goal.

(d) Emotions are sometimes said to have a modulating influence on behaviour—

we work well if we are happy, clumsily if we are angry. Positive effects are usually thought of as mediated by the physiological systems underlying arousal or activation (see above), disruptive ones by overactivity in the same systems or by interfering emotional responses dependent on other mechanisms. While some psychologists have regarded all emotions as disorganizing, others regard emotion as an organizing influence except either when it is extreme or when it conflicts with some other motivation (e.g. Leeper 1948). But such generalizations soon run into the difficulties inevitably associated with the looseness of the concept of emotion. Thus, how do we measure intensity? Is shyness to be called intense just because it has a disorganizing influence? In any case, in such cases causality is never proven. Does mild emotion facilitate behaviour, or *vice versa*? In conflict situations, is it the emotion or the conflict which produces the disorganization?

EMOTION AS A RESPONSE

'Emotion' is sometimes considered as a form of behaviour, though the label 'emotional behaviour' is often applied here. The responses involved are diverse:

(*a*) Sometimes 'emotional behaviour' is used co-extensively with 'motivated behaviour' (Bindra 1959), though others differentiate 'emotional behaviour' as being disorganized or lacking goal direction (e.g. Young 1943). Neither use is satisfactory: the former makes emotion almost co-extensive with behaviour and is thus a useless category, while the latter is clearly incorrect in that much behaviour that would commonly be called emotional is highly organized.

(*b*) Expressive movements, adapted in evolution for a signal function. These are the facial expressions of smiling, laughter, crying, anger and so on (Darwin 1872; van Hooff 1972; Argyle 1972). In animals they have been studied especially in the context of threat and courtship displays which occur in situations in which the animal is subject to conflicting tendencies (Cullen 1972; Thorpe 1972; Eibl-Eibesfeldt 1972). Not all such expressive movements are associated with conflict and not all would be considered as examples of emotional behaviour— for instance the movements which signal that a bird is about to fly.

(*c*) Movements adapted for use in situations of danger. Examples are Cannon's (1929) 'emergency reaction' and the various responses associated with fear, flight, fright etc. This category overlaps with the previous one and some responses included here may serve as signals even though not adapted to do so.

(*d*) Movements, postures etc. not apparently adapted (in an evolutionary sense) for any specific functional purpose, which occur under conditions of excitement—jumping up and down in joy, waving the arms about in frustration, and so on. These also may come to serve as signals.

(*e*) Absence of responding. Experimental psychologists sometimes use the 'conditioned emotional response' procedure, in which the change recorded is the interruption or diminution of ongoing behaviour by a stimulus previously associated with an aversive stimulus. Thus if rats, trained to press a bar for food until they are performing at a regular overall rate, are given periodic presentations of an auditory stimulus followed by an electric shock, the rate of bar-pressing during the auditory stimulus is reduced. It is presumed that 'emotional responses' elicited by the stimulus interfere with bar-pressing (Estes & Skinner 1941).

(*f*) We have seen that emotion may be held to affect behaviour by acting as a reinforcer—organisms tending to repeat behaviour which terminates negative emotional states or initiates positive ones. However, the term 'reinforcer' is usually applied to a stimulus which affects the emission of responses upon which it is contingent. Emotion, then, can be applied to responses consequent upon reinforcing stimuli (Weiskrantz 1968). On this view emotional behaviour can be used for specific responses to a reinforcing stimulus, and emotional state for a condition, similarly induced by a reinforcing stimulus, which may be manifest either through specific responses or by alterations in the probabilities of groups of responses. However, some of the responses to a reinforcing stimulus will operate on the stimulus (e.g. escape), while others will be elicited by it but have only a remote influence on the efficiency of those responses which do so operate (e.g. vasomotor changes). Weiskrantz prefers to consider only the latter as emotional behaviour.

It will be apparent that, while there is some behaviour which all would label as emotional (e.g. laughing, crying), beyond that there is little agreement. Furthermore, either the somatic or the autonomic nervous system may be involved, though the latter normally plays an important role.

CONCLUSION

To emphasize that an everyday word like 'emotion' is liable to be used loosely when taken over by scientists is of course an easy game to play. In mitigation, it must be said that we must beware of the pitfalls inherent in our terminology before progress can be made. And in avoiding them we must not at the same time skirt round the most difficult problems.

ACKNOWLEDGEMENTS

I am grateful to Ariane Etienne, N. K. Humphrey and Ruth Porter for their comments on an earlier draft.

References

ARGYLE, M. (1972) Non-verbal communication in human social interaction. In *Non-Verbal Communication* (Hinde, R. A., ed.), pp. 243-270, Cambridge University Press, London
BARTOSHUK, A. K. (1972) Motivation. In *Experimental Psychology* (Kling, J. W. & Riggs, L. A., eds.), pp. 793-846, Holt, Rinehart and Winston, New York
BERKOWITZ, L. (1962) *Aggression*, McGraw-Hill, New York
BINDRA, D. (1959) *Motivation*, Ronald Press, New York
BOWLBY, J. (1969) *Attachment and Loss*, vol. 1: *Attachment*, Hogarth Press, London
CANNON, W. B. (1929) *Bodily Changes in Pain, Hunger, Fear and Rage*, Appleton-Century, New York
CULLEN, J. M. (1972) Some principles of animal communication. In *Non-Verbal Communication* (Hinde, R. A., ed.), pp. 101-126, Cambridge University Press, London
DARWIN, C. (1872) *The Expression of the Emotions in Man and the Animals*, John Murray, London
DAVIS, D. R. (1957) *An Introduction to Psychopathology*, Oxford University Press, London
DUFFY, E. (1962) *Activation and Behavior*, Wiley, New York
EIBL-EIBESFELDT, I. (1972) Similarities and differences between cultures in expressive movements. In *Non-Verbal Communication* (Hinde, R. A., ed.), pp. 297-314, Cambridge University Press, London
ESTES, W. K. & SKINNER, B. F. (1941) Some quantitative properties of anxiety. *J. Exp. Psychol.* **29**, 390-400
HANSON, N. R. (1955) Causal chains. *Mind* **64**, 289-311
HEBB, D. O. (1949) *The Organization of Behavior*, Wiley, New York
HINDE, R. A. (ed.) (1972) *Non-Verbal Communication*, Cambridge University Press, London
HOOFF, J. A. R. A. M. VAN (1972) A comparative approach to the phylogeny of laughter and smiling. In *Non-Verbal Communication* (Hinde, R. A., ed.), pp. 209-242, Cambridge University Press, London
JAMES, W. (1892) *Textbook of Psychology*, Macmillan, London
KLING, J. W. & RIGGS, L. A. (eds.) (1972) *Experimental Psychology*, Holt, Rinehart and Winston, New York
LACEY, J. I., KAGAN, J., LACEY, B. C. & MOSS, H. A. (1963) The visceral level: situational determinants and behavioral correlates of autonomic response patterns. In *Expression of the Emotions in Man* (Knapp, P. H., ed.), pp. 161-196, International Universities Press, New York
LANGER, S. (1967) *Mind: an Essay on Human Feeling*, Johns Hopkins Press, Baltimore
LEEPER, R. W. (1948) A motivational theory of emotion to replace 'emotion as disorganized response'. *Psychol. Rev.* **55**, 5-21
LINDSLEY, D. B. (1951) Emotion. In *Handbook of Experimental Psychology* (Stevens, S. S., ed.), pp. 473-516, Wiley, New York
McDOUGALL, W. (1908) *An Introduction to Social Psychology*, Methuen, London
MILLER, N. E. (1959) Liberalization of basic S-R concepts. In *Psychology, a Study of a Science* (Koch, S., ed.), Study 1, vol. 2, pp. 196-292, McGraw-Hill, New York

MORUZZI, G. (1969) The emotional significance of the ascending reticular system. *Archs. Ital. Biol.* **96**, 17-28

RYLE, G. (1949) *The Concept of Mind*, Hutchinson, London

SCHLOSBERG, H. (1954) Three dimensions of emotion. *Psychol. Rev.* **61**, 81-88

THORPE, W. H. (1972) Vocal communication in birds. In *Non-Verbal Communication* (Hinde, R. A., ed.), pp. 153-176, Cambridge University Press, London

WEISKRANTZ, L. (1968) *Emotion in Analysis of Behavioral Change*, Harper and Row, New York

WHIMBEY, A. E. & DENENBERG, V. H. (1967) Two independent behavioral dimensions in open field performance. *J. Comp. Physiol. Psychol.* **63**, 500-504

WOODWORTH, R. S. (1938) *Experimental Psychology*, Holt, New York

YOUNG, P. T. (1943) *Emotion in Man and Animal*, Wiley, New York

[For discussion related to this pre-circulated paper see pp. 120-125.]

Emotions and physiology: an introduction

JOHN C. NEMIAH

Department of Psychiatry, Harvard Medical School, Beth Israel Hospital, Boston

Abstract In an attempt to provide observations that will form a starting point for the discussion of the relation between emotions and physiology, two clinica vignettes are presented, each of which manifests obvious, gross disturbances in psychological functioning. The first is a patient with a major hysterical dissociation resulting in an amnesia for an emotionally traumatic past event. The second is a patient with a history of rheumatoid arthritis and duodenal ulcer who appeared to be abnormally unresponsive to a painful life situation. Although both patients shared an apparent unawareness of emotional distress, further investigation revealed significant differences between them in regard to the nature of their memory and association systems, and to their capacity to experience emotions. The amnesic patient had a wide range of detailed memories and vivid emotions relating to the traumatic event that were generally dissociated from her awareness but available to conscious recall under special conditions. The patient with psychosomatic disease, although her memory for her painful life events was intact, remained incapable of experiencing or describing emotions and fantasies, or developing a significant network of associations concerning them. Speculations are advanced as to how these two highly different constellations of mental and behavioural phenomena can be related to specific underlying structural or functional neuronal differences.

In his lecture of December 22, 1891, delivered to the *beau monde* of Paris who attended his clinic at the Salpêtrière, Charcot commented as follows: 'We must not forget that psychology... forms a part of medicine, and that it is after all, at least for the most part, nothing but the physiology of the higher portions of the brain.' (Charcot 1893). As neurologists, Charcot and his followers kept one foot firmly planted on the functioning of the nervous system as they took a step with the other in the direction of the psychological phenomena of hysteria and related neurotic disorders. His dictum that psychology was 'nothing but physiology' could, however, be only a pious hope in view of the profound ignorance of the functioning of the 'higher portions of the brain' at the time when Charcot wrote—a hope, nonetheless, that reflected a long tradition among those who, over the centuries, had studied the vagaries of behaviour.

The earliest attempts to relate psychology to physiology are shrouded in the humoral mists of the past, and it is only within the last few decades that scientific knowledge of the physiology and pharmacology of the peripheral visceral components of emotion has reached a fair degree of sophistication. If our understanding of the anatomically more central and aetiologically more significant brain mechanisms underlying emotions has lagged behind, recent developments in the neurophysiology of the limbic system, in neuropharmacology, in developmental neurology, and in theories pertaining to learning have further stimulated our hopes of building bridges between clinical psychiatry and the basic sciences dealing with brain function.

In this regard the most important advances have been in our understanding of the neuropharmacology of mood, which has given clinicians an effective and widely applied therapeutic tool in the form of the tricyclic antidepressant drugs. More empirically, the phenothiazines have proved useful in treating other forms of psychosis, although the mechanisms underlying the symptoms are not clearly understood. These are, however, only beginnings in the direction of elucidating the brain mechanisms associated with psychopathology, and the clinician, especially when he is dealing with the more subtle aspects of psychiatric illness, usually frames his explanations in psychological concepts. Indeed, neurophysiological and neuropharmacological knowledge and constructs have generally not reached the degree of refinement achieved by psychological theory and are accordingly less helpful to the clinician in his daily work of caring for patients.

It is of interest that where it has been possible to make significant correlations between psychological and physiological phenomena (as in the disorders of mood) the psychological variables have been simple and obvious. A profound degree of depression, for example, is a psychological event much more clearly experienced by the depressed person, much more readily observed by the investigator, and to a much greater degree unidimensional than, say, the more subtle, less intensely felt emotions of hope, envy, pleasure, anxious expectation, pride, admiration etc. To one observing the profound changes in the behaviour and functioning of persons with severe depressions, it does not seem unreasonable to assume that there must be equally profound and extensive alterations in the underlying brain function—alterations that should be detectable, given the appropriate instruments for physiological measurement. It is perhaps not surprising, therefore, that it is in the area of mood disorders that the greatest amount of information about correlative brain processes has been accumulated. It should be noted that in the psychophysiological correlations derived from a study of mood, the physiological parameter consists of measurements of neurohumoral metabolites that point more to the biochemical mechanisms of action than to the localization and definition of the specific anatomical sites and structures within the brain that underlie the clinical observations. They tell us, that is, what neurochemical elements are altered, but little about the neuronal pathways that are involved in disturbances of mood.

Are there other psychological and clinical phenomena that are comparable in magnitude and sharpness of definition to the changes in mood found in clinical depression, and that will at the same time give us clues pointing to the anatomical configurations related to them? I believe that there are, and that, as with the phenomena of depression, they can be isolated and defined with sufficient precision to lead us to the creation of further possible bridges between physiology and emotion. Let us look at two areas that warrant attention as these are exemplified for us by two patients with clinical disorders—one with hysteria, the other with a psychosomatic illness.

The lecture by Charcot cited earlier was devoted to the description of the case of Madame D., who at age 34 was hospitalized at the Salpêtrière for a severe disturbance of memory. The onset of her illness occurred on August 28, 1891, some four months before Charcot's presentation. 'About four o'clock in the afternoon', writes Charcot, 'our patient had left a neighbour's house, where she was accustomed to work. She had been home about a quarter of an hour, when a stranger suddenly stuck his head in the door, which was open, and without more ado said to her: "Madame D..., get a bed ready. Your husband has died, and they are bringing him home now". You can imagine the emotion and anguish the poor woman must have felt. Her neighbours came running at her cries of despair, and she told them of the event I have just recounted to you.

'Before long a small crowd had collected at her house, and as they offered the usual consolations to the poor woman, one of them went off to get more information. He found her husband (alive and well) at his carpenter shop and brought him home. A neighbour, who saw him coming in the distance, had the inopportune idea of crying out: "There he comes". At these words, no doubt believing that they were actually bringing her dead husband, Madame D. fell into a nervous crisis...'

Thus began a long, interesting, and, for the patient, trying sequence of events. The acute 'nervous crisis' lasted two days. It was characterized by attacks of anxiety and episodic muscular writhings interspersed with periods of alterations of consciousness, during which the patient could not be aroused and experienced terrifying visual hallucinations referable to the event that had precipitated her disorder. At the end of two days she returned to normal consciousness but was then found to have a disturbance in memory manifested in two different forms of amnesia. In the first place, she exhibited a total retrograde amnesia extending backward in time to almost six weeks before the distressful episode of the hoax of her husband's death. Likewise she had no memory whatsoever of the painful precipitant itself or of the period of two days during which she had been in the hysterical delirium. Even more curious, however, was an *anterograde* amnesia that continuously affected her memory after she had regained normal consciousness: she had a persistent inability to remember any of the events that occurred from that point on for any longer than a minute or two. Her consciousness was a point of awareness moving along the time continuum, and she had apparently lost the capacity to lay down permanent memories of the events she was experiencing—not only the little happenings of everyday life but significant events as well, such as having been bitten by a mad dog which necessitated her going to Paris for a course of anti-rabies treatment, an episode that had occurred during the weeks following her delirium.

There was, however, a significant exception to this highly incapacitating disturbance in Madame D.'s memory. In the course of her hospitalization at the Salpêtrière it was noted by her wardmates that she talked in her sleep about many of the events which had occurred during the period covering both her retrograde and her anterograde amnesia. It appeared, therefore, that although they were not accessible to conscious awareness, the patient did have memories of recent occurrences, and she was hypnotized in order to explore this further. In the hypnotic state it was discovered that she had a detailed and vivid set of memories for everything that had happened during the entire extent of her period of amnesia.

Before I comment on these observations, let me give you a further clinical vignette by way of comparison and contrast. Mary B., a single woman in her middle thirties, suffered from rheumatoid arthritis and duodenal ulcer. The ulcer symptoms had begun during a period of serious personal disappointment. The man to whom she had been engaged during his absence in World War II had returned from the service a changed person. Although he continued to see her, he behaved as if the engagement had never existed and made no mention of their being married. Although perplexed and distressed by his apparent change of heart, she at no time questioned him about his behaviour or his intentions and finally quietly stopped seeing him. Furthermore, she made no mention of her quandary to her family, with whom she was living, nor did she reveal any feelings she may have had about the situation to a psychiatrist with whom she was in analysis for three years. As she said, 'If anything happened to me, I'd never discuss it with anybody. I'd just let it die, and that's it. I just keep it in'.

When I asked her to tell me about these events, she would not elaborate beyond the bare facts. Her associations were so meagre as to be almost non-existent, and she showed no emotional response to what sounded like a painful and difficult situation. When I pressed her to describe her feelings, she at length stated that she had been 'sad' and 'angry', but I could never get her to describe or talk meaningfully about what she had experienced. Let me give you from a tape-recorded interview a sample of her behaviour in this regard:

Doctor: I wonder what the feeling of sadness is that you have. Can you describe it?

Patient: No, I can't really. You don't mean my physical feeling?

Doctor: Are there physical feelings that go with the sadness? Do you feel it anywhere?

Patient: Oh, I have a sort of dead feeling.

Doctor: Yes—where?

Patient: Oh, right through my stomach. That's not a very full explanation.

Doctor: When you feel angry, do you feel that in any part of your body?

Patient: No. I can't say I do. I don't really know now. I guess I get warm.

Each of these patients falls into a different but major category of illness. Madame D. exhibits the symptoms of hysteria—a *psychoneurosis*, whereas Mary B. suffers from a *psychosomatic disorder*. They share one feature in common: each is confronted with the painfully stressful situation of the loss of a person they love. Each, however, responds to that loss with a strikingly different form of psychopathological behaviour. In psychological terms, we attribute those differences to the employment of different psychological defence mechanisms, the function of which is to protect the patient from experiencing the potentially overwhelming psychological pain inherently associated with loss.

Madame D. would, in psychological parlance, be described as employing the mechanism of *repression*—that is, she is forcing out of consciousness all of the memories and related feelings connected with the painful event, with the resulting symptom of amnesia. Although thus dissociated, the unconscious complex of mental phenomena retains the capacity to affect her conscious awareness in the form of hallucinations, dreams and the recall of the memories under hypnosis. To Mary B. would be assigned the use of the mechanism of the *denial* of the significance of the external events and of the feelings associated with them, and a concomitant *somatization* that results in a pathophysiological dysfunction of a bodily organ leading to an actual somatic lesion in the organ involved.

These psychological concepts help us to explain and to understand the mechanism of the development of clinically different symptoms and disease states. There is, however, nothing inherent in the concepts to tell us why one psychological defence mechanism should be employed in preference to another. Here, as a psychologically oriented clinician, I would ask: can information from the disciplines of neurophysiology and the other basic sciences add to our understanding? Are the differences in psychological mechanisms determined by differences in the related underlying structure of the brain and its functional pathways? These are the questions the clinician would put to those immersed in the basic, experimental sciences. Before allowing you to answer, let me make a few speculations of my own that may help us to focus our attention in our discussions.

Let us return to the two patients and compare Madame D. with Mary B.

In Madame D. there is at the beginning of her disorder a major alteration of consciousness, associated with a widespread discharge of affect: she is agitated, anxious, despairing and grief-stricken, and thrashes about with the wild movements of a hysterical seizure. This then gives way to a return to normal consciousness in which she manifests a severe disturbance in memory, characterized by the striking retrograde and anterograde amnesia I have described. It is to be noted, however, that beneath her waking consciousness (and normally unavailable to it) a rich network of associations is being formed that includes detailed memories of the events of the entire period of her amnesia before and after the traumatic event of her husband's alleged death. That event, indeed, appears to be the central focus around which the associations crystallize out away from her waking consciousness. This cluster of associations has a life of its own, removed from her voluntary recall, but giving evidence of its existence, as I have suggested, in her hallucinations and dreams, and in the hypnotic recall of her memories.

In Mary B. the situation is completely different. At no time does she show or appear to feel any real emotion, nor does she give evidence of any disturbance in memory. This was entirely intact for the events throughout her life, and in the interviews with her one could uncover no larger, more extended network of unconscious associations of the sort seen in Madame D. She remained at all times affectively flat, pale, colourless and unmoved, and her mental content maintained a persistent meagreness of associations, that generally dwelt on mundane daily events and were not apparently determined or directed by her seemingly distressing life events, even when in interviews her attention was vigorously focused on these and any possible emotional reaction she might have had in response to them. In this regard she was similar to many other patients with psychosomatic disorders, in whom months, even years of psychotherapy aimed at uncovering hidden affects and associated fantasies and memories, fail to disclose anything that was not on the surface in the first place. One seems to be dealing with a circumscribed unit of a disturbing life event matched with a dysfunction of an organ system without any associated, intermediate elaboration in the psychological realm of feelings, memories, associations or fantasies.

If from a theoretical point of view we were to imagine the kind of physical structure necessary to support Madame D.'s observed behavioural and psychological manifestations, we should have to postulate at least three things: first, a structure that would underlie her well-developed capacity for experiencing feeling, and secondly, a complex network of neuronal connections and pathways correlated with a similar richness in mental associations, the two in intimate communication to allow for their reciprocal action. These structures would, I suspect, be provided for in the limbic and cortical areas of the human brain. But, thirdly, we must explain her widespread and peculiar disturbance in memory. I am struck by the similarity of her anterograde amnesia to the memory disorder of patients with Korsakoff's syndrome. In each there is a perception of events, but at the same time there is a failure to register long-term memory traces so that the patient cannot recall those events after the passage of a very few seconds of time—with this significant difference: that in Madame D. the memories are found to exist when she is dreaming or in a state of hypnosis, phenomena not to be observed in Korsakoff patients. Could it be that the mamillary bodies and associated structures, damage to which leads to permanent memory loss in Korsakoff's syndrome, are also functionally involved in the amnesic phenomena to be observed in Madame D.—and perhaps also in the basic processes which we refer to psychologically as repression and unconscious mentation?

In the clinical behaviour of patients with psychosomatic disorders like Mary B., the standard psychological explanation, as I have indicated, invokes the mechanism of denial. It is assumed in this concept that the patient has the *potential* capacity to experience feelings, but that these are so stringently kept from conscious awareness and expression that the patient appears to the external observer to be almost totally devoid of normal human emotional responses.

Recently, Sifneos and I have questioned the adequacy of this explanation and the concepts behind it. In a recent study (Nemiah & Sifneos 1970) we reported our findings from an evaluation of the transcripts of nearly a hundred recorded interviews with 20 patients (8 women and 12 men) each with a current or past history of two or more of the following psychosomatic diseases: duodenal ulcer, ulcerative colitis, rheumatoid arthritis, asthma and atopic dermatitis. These were all patients, it should be emphasized, who had been interviewed as part of a study of specificity in psychosomatic illnesses some 15 years before either of us had developed doubts about the relevance of the usual psychodynamic formulations of psychosomatic disorders—doubts which could not, therefore, have influenced the content of their productions elicited during the interviews. In 16 of the 20 patients, two features characterized their psychological and behavioural functioning: (1) They seemed to have little or no vocabulary with which to describe feelings, nor did they appear to experience feelings in their bodies (e.g. muscular tension, 'butterflies in their stomach', a hollowness or emptiness in the chest or epigastrium) as do most people. (2) The content of their thought consisted of reflections on the minutiae of the trivial details of external events and actions. In these patients we could not find fantasies coloured by and expressive of inner drives and feelings; they did not, for example, have sexual daydreams, or imagine angry revenge, or dwell with longing on a lost object. Their thoughts appeared shallow, colourless, and lacking in the freedom, excursiveness and richness of intimate, personal associations that is characteristic of most of us.

These findings, and evidence from further investigations now being made by Dr Sifneos, suggest that psychosomatic patients differ from those suffering from neurotic or psychotic disorders, with their wealth of inner fantasies and their colourful expressiveness of feelings. We have been forced to wonder whether patients with psychosomatic illness *do*, in fact, have the potential capacity to experience and express feelings and fantasy at all, and we have therefore raised the question of whether the psychological concept of denial is an appropriate one to explain the facts, or whether the language of psychology is really germane to the phenomena.

As an alternative hypothesis, we would suggest that in these patients there is perhaps an absence, or at best only a rudimentary form, of the neural mechanisms that normally subserve the experience of feeling and of complex mental associations, and at the same time a lack or incompleteness of connections between these mechanisms to permit their mutual influence. Can this be correlated with the observable structure of the limbic system and the cortex in patients with psychosomatic disorders? Is there somehow a short-circuiting of neuronal discharges such that the perception of traumatic environmental events directly activates hypothalamic autonomic centres without being routed through the long circuits of higher nervous centres? If so, is this the result of hereditary influences on brain structure, or of a failure to develop adequate neuronal pathways as the infant interacts with a deficient human environment in the early phases of his growth after birth?

These are the observations. These are the questions. Let us hope that in our discussions we may arrive together at some of the answers.

References

CHARCOT, J. M. (1893) *Clinique des Maladies du Système Nerveux*, Vol. II, Félix Alcan, Paris
NEMIAH, J. C. & SIFNEOS, P. E. (1970) Affect and fantasy in patients with psychosomatic disorders. In *Modern Trends in Psychosomatic Medicine* (Hill, O. W., ed.), pp.26-34, Butterworths, London

Discussion

Hill: Did Madame D. completely recover? And has the anterograde amnesia described by Charcot and which you, I think rightly, describe as a Korsakoff type of learning defect, been established as a phenomenon of dissociative hysteria? I am not aware that such patients have been shown to have this capacity to learn but not to retain the information for more than a minute, which is the Korsakoff type of defect. It raises the question of whether Madame D. was suffering in fact from dissociative hysteria, unless there is other evidence that in this condition, which is relatively rare in peace-time and common in war, this observation can be made on patients who *do* recover.

Nemiah: I don't know whether this kind of amnesia is a part of dissociative hysteria, nor have I seen it described elsewhere. Charcot's clinical observations of patients were unusually full and exact, and from what he has told us about Madame D. there was no indication that she was suffering from brain disease. Her symptoms and course were in general entirely similar to several other of Charcot's patients with clearcut major dissociative states.

Madame D. was eventually taken into treatment by Dr Pierre Janet, who was then a student of Charcot's. Using hypnosis he was able to restore her memory to a considerable degree, although even at the end of eight months there were still gaps that caused her some disability. There is no record of her clinical course thereafter.

Gray: I was under the impression that the incidence of hysteria of this particular kind has declined considerably, in England and America at any rate, in the last 50 years. If this is correct, does it indicate anything about the disease, if one can call it that, or about the nature of psychiatric diagnosis over that period? Would one see this kind of case commonly, or at all, today?

Sachar: It depends very much on the social and cultural milieu. In New York City we see these disturbances most commonly in, for example, Puerto Rican patients who have recently arrived from rural areas of Puerto Rico. We are therefore impressed now with the relationship to a particular kind of cultural and social upbringing.

Henry: In the acute disintegration that you have described (*Sachar et al.* 1970) in the panic state that occurs in schizophrenia, are there any after-effects that suggest organic brain damage as a result of the sustained intense emotional state? In other words, could these patients get themselves into such a state of panic and emotional upheaval that they suffer organic damage with resulting disturbance in their neuroendocrine mechanisms, especially those controlling the release of catecholamines?

Sachar: I don't know any evidence for organic lesion of the central nervous system in schizophrenics. On the other hand, Meltzer has some evidence that in acute schizophrenic reactions (which Madame D. was apparently *not* suffering from) organic lesions are produced in the muscles (Meltzer & Engel 1970; Fishman *et al.* 1970). This has been confirmed by others. Lesions in the nervous system have never been demonstrated.

Dr Nemiah, since you are challenging some of our basic concepts, I wonder what reason we have for considering your patients with physical disorders such as duodenal ulcer and rheumatoid arthritis to have psychosomatic conditions? What evidence is there that these disorders are not like any other illness Mary B. might have suffered, but specifically related to her character and her ways of handling emotion? They have been described and put in the category of psychosomatic illness—that is, related to emotional status and psychological influences—but perhaps we ought to re-examine that question as well?

Donald: Could I add to that question? Did you have a control group of patients with definite organic disease, such as pneumonia and measles?

Nemiah: In the work I have presented here we had no controls. Several years ago, however, I had the opportunity to take part in a cooperative study (Stoeckle *et al.* 1961) of a group of coal miners from the hills of Kentucky and Pennsylvania with silicosis. Most of them were very similar to Mary B. and could generally be characterized as having no words for feelings.

Donald: Welsh miners might be very different in this respect!

Zanchetti: This is an important point to clarify at the beginning of the meeting. Should our attitude be that a group of psychosomatic illnesses does exist, or are we to discuss first whether there are psychosomatic illnesses, and then which are the psychosomatic illnesses, and what are the mechanisms through which the psyche can influence the body? There is no question, of course, that the two patients presented by Professor Nemiah had very different ways of reacting psychologically, and I don't doubt that the behaviour of Madame D. was correlated with psychic repressive mechanisms, but one could question whether the illness presented by Mary B. was really related to the denial mechanism.

Hill: I suggest that we do not attempt to discuss what are psychosomatic illnesses, or what the definition of psychosomatic illness is. We are concerned with the relationship between the emotional state, in psychological, physiological or chemical terms, and 'illness'. We shall not make much progress if we try to define psychosomatic illness, or discuss whether a duodenal ulcer is, and dermatitis is not, a psychosomatic illness. I think we should therefore try to stick to the observations, identify their reality, and discuss these.

Aitken: Professor Nemiah has suggested a connection between his observations and the mechanism concerned. I agree that it might not be very useful to discuss whether something is or is not psychosomatic illness, but connective tissue disorder is the second most common cause of time lost from work; chronic respiratory disease is the most common. Duodenal ulcer also has a high prevalence, though it may be decreasing. We do not know the prevalence of lack of feelings or of their denial, but clinical experience suggests that it is quite common. Therefore it should not be surprising when occasionally three common disorders occur in the same patient. It is unusual, and so we remember such a patient, but this does not tell us anything about the causality of one or other phenomenon. It does not follow that because disorders are sometimes associated they necessarily have a causal relationship.

Hill: To take up Professor Donald's point, I suppose that Professor Nemiah might be challenged with the fact that he didn't have a carefully matched control series for his patients with rheumatoid arthritis, taken from the same sociocultural and educational groups, matched for age and sex, and subjected to his examination for capacity to express feelings.

Nemiah: Perhaps I did not make it clear in my paper that I am challenging the concept of denial too, and that I am not convinced that a psychological explanation of the so-called psychosomatic disorders *is* an appropriate one. This is not necessarily to imply that these disorders are not a reaction to social and environmental stress, but that the underlying mechanisms of the production of symptoms are different from what one finds in a hysterical patient. I am also not sure that control subjects are relevant at this stage. We are now merely attempting to describe observable behavioural phenomena and to create an instrument to determine with reliability whether any given individual does or does not show alexithymic characteristics. The next step would be to apply it to a variety of populations to see whether the behaviour of patients with psychosomatic disorders does conform to our initial impressions, and, if so, whether to a significantly greater degree than matched controls.

Donald: One explanation could be that Madame D. started with a psychotic episode. You spoke about her evading the results of a sudden horrible experience. That horrible experience may have been her own hallucination that someone came and told her that her husband was dead. All this could have been internal to her. Mary B., on the other hand, was at no time psychotic. These two people were reacting differently to unfortunate events: an acute psychotic episode and the loss of a boyfriend. The latter event happens to many people, and there are variable reactions to it. I would not expect the two cases to start from the same place in any way.

Hill: These are two different phenomena, as Professor Nemiah emphasized. The case of classical hysteria is of great interest. Many patients, particularly in war situations, who later develop either dissociative or conversion hysteria (after the loss of a limb, for example), may in an acute battle situation or in acute disaster develop acute panic with anxiety and hallucinations (they would not necessarily be called psychotic), and then suddenly dip into conversion or dissociative hysteria.

Henry: Dr Nemiah and Dr Sifneos pointed out (1970) that their observations were stimulated by the earlier description of *la pensée opératoire* by Marty & de M'Uzan (1963). Thus two separate groups have been impressed that people with high blood pressure, peptic ulcer or rheumatoid arthritis often show an impaired capacity for fantasy and dream recall. In fact the condition would appear to be the reverse of the introverted state, which Jung (1933) describes as one in which the individual is responsive to such fantasy and dream activity. It has been suggested that a balance between the extraverted and introverted modes is needed.

Hill: The alleged mechanism of hysteria described by Freud was repression. The patient who develops conversion or dissociative hysteria is recognized classically by his *belle indifférence*—his calmness, his lack of emotion and feeling. What we would like to know is what is happening to his physiology.

Lader: The distinction between hysteria and psychosomatic illness is an artificial one, with many more similarities than differences. The natural history of hysterical disorder is rather variable, and one should distinguish between acute and chronic conversion hysteria. Acute hysterical episodes tend to occur in young girls with a histrionic personality. (I avoid using the term 'hysterical personality'!) They experience some psychological stress and develop one or more hysterical conversion symptoms. While they have these symptoms their autonomic measures (sweat gland activity and heart rate) are at low levels (Behrman & Levy 1970). These patients have a fairly good prognosis if they are treated vigorously. Patients with chronic symptoms of conversion hysteria, typically astasia–abasia, have a poor prognosis (Lader 1969). These patients have very high levels of autonomic activity (Lader & Sartorius 1968; Meares & Horvath 1972). Therefore it would be interesting to know the outcome for Madame D.

Hill: You are talking about conversion hysteria, which usually presents to the neurologists. Madame D. would be diagnosed now as a case of dissociative hysteria, I suppose.

Lader: My series contained only two patients with the dissociative state, and they were similar in physiological terms to those with other conversion symptoms.

Engel: One problem in a symposium of this kind is that we inescapably speak from our own areas of clinical experience. Dr Lader tells us that conversion symptoms are primarily neurological; I, working as an internist and psychiatrist, see neurological-type conversion symptoms infrequently. Much more often the conversion symptoms we see are pain, nausea, vomiting, dyspnoea, hyperventilation and the like, with pain by far the most prevalent. This is because these are the kinds of symptoms that lead the patient to see his family physician or an internist, but they are less readily identified as conversion by most internists and hence the patients are not referred for psychiatric consultation.

I have the same problem with Dr Nemiah's material. I don't question the reliability of his observations, but I do reject his use of the term 'psychosomatic illness' as applying to a particular group of diseases. Our experience studying unselected medical patients reveals that psychological factors may be involved in the precipitation and course of the widest variety of so-called somatic illnesses, from hepatitis to systemic lupus to leukaemia. Hence we would prefer to speak in terms of *psychosomatic factors* in disease rather than of 'psychosomatic diseases'. I discussed this perspective at the 1966 meeting of the Society for Psychosomatic Research (Engel 1967). But even if we confine our attention to Franz Alexander's 'holy seven' (peptic ulcer, asthma, rheumatoid arthritis, neurodermatitis, ulcerative colitis, hyperthyroidism, hypertension) as Dr Nemiah and Dr Sifneos did, my experience does not correspond with theirs. By no means all these patients have the difficulty in expressing emotion that they describe. I have seen patients who could describe their affects with great ease. Perhaps the difference reflects patient selection.

Finally, in your comparison between your two patients, Dr Nemiah, you didn't tell us what the settings and circumstances were in which Mary B.'s organic disease became activated. At what points in time and in relationship to what events and psychological experiences, reported and unreported, did the patient develop symptoms?

Nemiah: Two kinds of stresses were involved. In the first place, she suffered the loss of a long-standing relationship with her boyfriend, shortly after which her ulcer symptoms appeared. The arthritis began in a setting of strife with her family, in particular with her sister, by whom she felt victimized. In neither situation could she express the emotions of sadness or anger one would have expected her to feel, nor was she able adequately to describe to me what, if any, feelings she may have had.

Hill: A concept that has been common in the psychosomatic literature for some time is that these patients are unable to experience their emotions or respond to life events and relate to people in such a way as to get rid of feeling; rather they suffer it chronically in their bodies, with consequences of physical disease. If we were to consider this hypothesis we should need a great deal of evidence, which is not being presented here because that is not the objective of this symposium—we are concerned with mechanisms.

Ginsburg: Has anyone monitored patients who do not express their feelings verbally, taking physiological measures such as galvanic skin response, respiration or blood pressure, during these states, to see whether there are physiological expressions of affect even though there are no verbal expressions?

Engel: Weiner *et al.* (1962) compared cardiovascular responses in patients with peptic ulcer and hypertension. They found that whether or not the patient interacted with the experimenter was the variable determining physiological reactivity, not the nature of the disease.

Aitken: We have studied people with bronchial asthma, selected randomly from registers of diagnosed cases (Aitken *et al.* 1970; Zealley *et al.* 1971). We found virtually no difference in the distribution of psychopathology from that found in the general population (see pp. 375-380).

References

AITKEN, R. C. B., ZEALLEY, A. K. & ROSENTHAL, S. V. (1970) Some psychological and physiological considerations of breathlessness. In *Breathing: Hering-Breuer Centenary Symposium (Ciba Found. Symp.)*, pp. 253-273, Churchill, London

BEHRMAN, J. & LEVY, R. (1970) Neurophysiological studies on patients with hysterical disturbances of vision. *J. Psychosom. Res.* **14**, 187-194

ENGEL, G. L. (1967) The concept of psychosomatic disorder. *J. Psychosom. Res.* **11**, 3-9

FISHMAN, D. A., MELTZER, H. & POPPER, R. W. (1970) Disruption of myofibrils in skeletal muscle in acute psychotic patients. *Arch. Gen. Psychiatr.* **23**, 503-515

JUNG, C. G. (1933) *Psychological Types or the Psychology of Individuation* (Baynes, H. G., trans.), Kegan Paul, London

LADER, M. H. (1969) The effect of anxiety on response to treatment. *Aust. N.Z. J. Psychiatr.* **3**, 288-292

LADER, M. H. & SARTORIUS, N. (1968) Anxiety in patients with hysterical conversion symptoms. *J. Neurol. Neurosurg. Psychiatr.* **31**, 490-495

MARTY, P. & DE M'UZAN, M. (1963) La pensée opératoire. *Rev. Fr. Psychoanal.* **27**, suppl., 345-356

MEARES, R. & HORVATH, T. (1972) 'Acute' and 'chronic' hysteria. *Br. J. Psychiatr.* in press

MELTZER, H. & ENGEL, W. K. (1970) Histochemical abnormality of skeletal muscle in patients with acute psychoses. *Arch. Gen. Psychiatr.* **23**, 492-502

NEMIAH, J. C. & SIFNEOS, P. E. (1970) Affect and fantasy in patients with psychosomatic disorders. In *Modern Trends in Psychosomatic Medicine* (Hill, O. W., ed.), pp. 26-34, Appleton-Century-Crofts, New York

SACHAR, E. J., KANTER, S. S., BUIE, D., ENGLE, R. & MEHLMAN, R. (1970) Psychoendocrinology of ego disintegration. *Am. J. Psychiatr.* **126**, 1067-1078
STOECKLE, J. D., HARDY, H. L., KING, W. B., JR & NEMIAH, J. C. (1961) Respiratory disease
in U.S. soft-coal miners: clinical and etiological considerations. *J. Chronic Dis.* **15**,
887-905
WEINER, H., SINGER, M. T. & REISER, M. F. (1962) Cardiovascular responses and their
psychological correlates. I. A study in healthy young adults and patients with peptic
ulcer and hypertension. *Psychosom. Med.* **24**, 477-498
ZEALLEY, A. K., AITKEN, R. C. B. & ROSENTHAL, S. V. (1971) Personality and bronchial
asthma. *Proc. R. Soc. Med.* **64**, 825-829

The role of affects
in psychoanalytic theory

JOSEPH SANDLER

The Institute of Psychiatry and the Hampstead Child-Therapy Clinic, London

Abstract This paper is concerned with tracing some of the vicissitudes of the concept of affect in psychoanalytic theory, with presenting some of the difficulties which arise in relation to the concept because of the changes which have taken place in that theory, and with offering some tentative formulations which may be of both theoretical and clinical relevance.

Before 1897 the concept of affect was a crucial one in Freud's theory, being related to trauma on the one hand, and to the production of symptoms on the other. In the next phase of Freud's thinking affects were relatively neglected, but they were to some extent reinstated after 1923 (when Freud put forward the 'structural' model). This paper discusses some historical aspects of the current confusion with regard to affects in psychoanalytic theory, and the view is developed that the distinction between somatic changes and subjective experience is a necessary one, if the theoretical problems involved in emotions are to be clarified. The role played by conscious and unconscious feeling-states in psychological functioning will be discussed, as well as some aspects of the interaction between psychological processes and somatic disturbances.

As Robert Hinde points out (1972), the problem of terminology is an important one in this symposium. In the first part of what follows the term 'affect' will be used in a relatively broad sense, for reasons which I hope will become apparent. Later in this paper a differentiation will be made between the physical and somatic processes involved in emotional states on the one hand, and *feelings* on the other.

The most exhaustive treatment of the history of the psychoanalytic theory of affect has been given by Rapaport (1953). His scholarly paper is of substantial value, not only for its detailed exploration of the problems which surround the theory of affect, but also because it shows the degree of confusion and uncertainty which exists in connection with the place of the concept of affect in psychoanalytic theory. Rapaport found it convenient to divide the history of psychoanalysis into a number of phases, and it is possible to make use of this approach with benefit here. However, in my view, Rapaport unfortunately failed to clarify the conceptual problems sufficiently because of his adherence to a unitary theory of affect—that is, one which encompassed the physical, energic and experiential aspects within the same concept. A number of other authors (e.g. Brierley 1937; Lewin 1965; Jacobson 1953; Schur 1953) have addressed themselves to the same theoretical problems, and although feelings are frequently distinguished from instinctual drives and also from bodily changes in emotion, the single overall concept of affect has been maintained. As a consequence, the subject appears to remain as confused as ever. This is partly due to the tendency of psychoanalytic theorists to retain all previous formulations, discarding none, and to attempt to formulate theoretical propositions in a way which would be consistent with previously accepted formulations, especially those of Freud. Unfortunately it is often forgotten that Freud himself discarded certain of his own theories when he found them to be inadequate.

At this point an account of the major phases of development in Freud's own writings is appropriate. Freud was always aware that his psychological formulations and models were essentially theoretical constructs, to be adhered to as long as they proved useful, and to be modified as necessary. The account of the developmental phases in psychoanalysis which follows is based on a modification of Rapaport's description (1953).*

THE FIRST PHASE

Four years after qualifying in medicine, Freud visited Charcot in France and attended his demonstrations at the Salpêtrière for some months in 1885-1886. The patients demonstrated by Charcot could be made to lose their physical symptoms by psychological interventions, particularly suggestion and hypnosis. Freud was impressed by the link which the French had shown between the mental 'dissociation' induced by hypnosis, and the apparently similar dissociation between a conscious and unconscious part of the mind which seemed to occur in patients with hysterical symptoms. Freud was profoundly impressed by his experience with Charcot and this led him to the belief that mental disturbances could have psychological origins. He was later able to elaborate the notion of dissociation further in his theories of repression and defence.

---

* The description of the three phases in the development of Freud's psychoanalytic theories is taken in large part from a paper on the historical context and phases in the development of psychoanalysis (Sandler *et al.* 1972*a*).

On his return to Vienna Freud began a collaboration with Josef Breuer (Breuer & Freud 1893-1895) and was led to the conclusion that the patient's symptoms could be seen as the irruption, in a distorted form, of *charges of affect* which had been kept in a pent-up state, dissociated from consciousness. This dissociation was (contrary to the view of Charcot and Janet) regarded by him as an active process of *defence*. Freud also became convinced that the barrier between the conscious and unconscious parts of the mind occurred in normal as well as in neurotic subjects. Symptoms arose when the quantity of affective energy was too great to be absorbed in the normal way, and was forced to find some form of indirect expression. The pent-up or 'strangulated' affects were thought of as having been aroused by *real* traumatic experiences.* The memories associated with these emotions were not acceptable to the patient's moral and ethical standards and, being no longer under voluntary control once they had been repressed, found their concealed expression through, for example, being 'converted' into hysterical symptoms. Thus conversion hysteria (as well as the other psychoneuroses) was seen as a way in which traumatically induced affect could be 'discharged'. It is important to remember that in this phase Freud equated affect with energy, and saw psychoneurotic symptoms as being brought about by the need for the mind to rid itself of abnormally large quantities of such affective energy (to restore 'constancy'). From the point of view of therapy, the central aim was to release such emotions by bringing them (and the associated memories) into consciousness, with subsequent abreaction or catharsis, and a resulting assimilation into consciousness of those mental contents which had previously been rejected.

It is evident that in the first phase the concept of affect played a central role in psychoanalytic theory. The evocation of a 'charge of affect' by traumatic experiences was thought to be an essential step in the development of pathology (particularly hysteria and obsessional neurosis). If the affect could be dealt with in 'normal' ways ('wearing away', 'discharge' through associative pathways etc.), pathology would not ensue. In this phase the arousal of affective energy was thought of as being predominantly in response to external stimulation, although charges of affect could also arise from the internal needs of the individual. An abnormally strong charge of energy could be a direct result of

---

* This was regarded as true of the psychoneuroses, but Freud also considered conditions (in the first phase) which were thought to be due to 'pent-up' affective energy which had accumulated for reasons other than psychological traumas. Typical of these was the 'anxiety neurosis', thought to be a manifestation of undischarged affective excitation due to sexual frustrations of one sort or another. The 'anxiety neurosis' was not, at that time, thought to be a psychoneurosis, but rather an 'actual' (in German *Aktual*, meaning 'current' or 'present-day') neurosis.

early sexual trauma, or an emotional reaction (of disgust, anxiety, guilt etc.) to the later revival of early sexual memories. The model of the 'mental apparatus' in this phase was a very simple one, and no theoretical distinction was made between feelings and 'charges of energy'.

THE SECOND PHASE

This phase lasted from 1897 until the publication of *The Ego and the Id* (Freud 1923). Freud's orientation now shifted completely from an emphasis on *real* traumatic experiences to instinctual drives arising from within. His change of viewpoint was a consequence of his realization that the memories which had been uncovered in his work with hysterical patients were often not real memories, but rather memories of early fantasies. His own self-analysis also played a significant part in his change of viewpoint. At the beginning of this phase he was paying special attention to the analysis of his own and his patients' dreams, and found dream analysis to be the most useful way of conducting psychoanalytic exploration. In his substantial work on dreams (1900) he put forward a new conceptual framework which was to form the basis for the theories of the second phase. This has come to be known as the topographical model of the mind. In 1901 he published the results of his studies on 'symptomatic acts' (such as slips of the tongue), seeing them as expressions of unconscious instinctual wishes. In 1905 he elaborated further the so-called 'instinct', or more properly, the *drive* (Freud used the German word *Trieb*) theory of psychoanalysis. Instinctual drives were seen as the basis for a whole range of sexual (and later, aggressive) wishes in childhood and adult life. Psychoanalysis was now unequivocally a drive psychology. Although in the first phase Freud had concentrated on adaptation to events in the external world, his orientation and interests now shifted to the way in which the person adapts to internal forces.

In the first phase, Freud had differentiated between conscious and unconscious aspects of the mind, and this distinction is elaborated in the topographical model. He now described two main sorts of unconsciousness. The first was characteristic of the processes in the system *Unconscious*, the reservoir of instinctual wishes which, if they were allowed to emerge to the surface, would constitute a threat to consciousness. The strivings in the Unconscious were regarded as being constantly propelled towards 'discharge', but being only allowed to reach consciousness and motility in a disguised and censored form. The second sort of unconsciousness was that which was attributed to the system *Preconscious*, conceived of as containing knowledge, thoughts and memories which were not defended against and which could enter consciousness relatively freely. The contents of the Preconscious were utilized by instinctual wishes for purposes of disguise, in their path from the depths to the surface. The instinctual wishes in the system Unconscious were thought to represent infantile sexual impulses derived from all the phases of the child's psychosexual development. A review of the changes which Freud made in his theory of instinctual drives during the second phase is given in the classical work by Bibring (1941).

The system Unconscious was regarded as being characterized by a primitive mode of functioning which Freud referred to as the *primary process*. Logical and formal relations between elements in the Unconscious are regarded as absent, and simple rules of primitive association apply. Drives and wishes in the Unconscious function according to what Freud termed the *pleasure principle*— that is, they seek discharge, gratification and relief of painful tension at all costs. The systems Preconscious and Conscious were considered as being in direct opposition to this. Here secondary processes—logic, reason and the knowledge of external reality, as well as conscious ideals and standards of conduct—predominate. In contrast to the Unconscious, the other two systems attempt to follow what Freud called the *reality principle* (1911)—that is, to take anticipated consequences into account.

In 1914 Freud introduced the concept of *narcissism* in an attempt to clarify the problem of the person's relation to his love objects and to himself in both normal and pathological states. Here Freud was also concerned with the formation of ideals, on the basis of the parents as models, and introduced the concept of the ego ideal, adumbrating the later concept of the superego. In all his discussions of self- and object-love descriptions of feelings are given, but the theoretical discussion is couched in terms of the disposition of 'libidinal energy'.

In all this the concept of 'energy' was taken over from the first phase, although it was now seen as instinctual energy, rather than as a 'charge' of affect. Ideas and feelings, as well as emotional tensions within the body, were seen predominantly as *drive-derivatives*. Affects were no longer regarded as main motivators in behaviour, but rather as secondary and surface manifestations of drive impulses finding their way from the depths of the system Unconscious. Thus, for example, anxiety was regarded as transformed 'libido' (the term given to the energy of the sexual drives—aggression was added to the instinctual drives relatively late in the second phase, and no specific term was coined for aggressive energy).

The pleasure (or pleasure–unpleasure) principle related to the tendency of the apparatus to experience tension (or to be in a state of tension) when instinctual drives were aroused, and to experience a reduction of tension (with associated pleasure) when the drives were gratified ('discharged'). Although Freud's formulations during this phase were often couched in affective experiential terms (e.g. pleasure–unpleasure), affects were relatively neglected, and the theoretical model was formulated predominantly in terms of energic tensions. The homeostatic 'pleasure principle' was little different from the 'principle of constancy' which Freud had adopted from Fechner in the first phase. Although Freud described many different feeling-states, in his theoretical explanations we find, for example, that 'to love' becomes 'to cathect (invest) with libido', etc. Feelings were all explained in terms of the vicissitudes of charges of libidinal energy.

THE THIRD PHASE

In this phase, beginning with the publication of *The Ego and the Id* (1923) and *Inhibitions, Symptoms and Anxiety* (1926), a major theoretical shift occurred. Freud now put forward his *structural* theory in order to deal with certain inconsistencies which had begun to be apparent in his view of the mental apparatus and its functioning. While he introduced this theory in 1923 partly in order to postulate the existence of an unconscious sense of guilt, it can be added that his formulations during the second phase in regard to narcissism and the clinical conditions of melancholia, paranoia and hypochondriasis, all contributed to the strain imposed on the explanatory potential of the topographical model.

In the structural theory Freud put forward a model which represented a three-fold division of the mental apparatus into major *structures:* the *id, ego* and *superego.*

The *id* corresponds approximately to what had been encompassed by the Unconscious in the second phase. It can be conceived of as the area containing primitive instinctual drives, dominated by the pleasure principle, and functioning according to the primary process. During development a portion of the id is modified, under the influence of the child's interaction with the external world, to become the *ego.* The primary function of this latter agency is that of self-preservation and the acquisition of means whereby a simultaneous adaptation to the demands of the id and of reality can be attained. It gains the function of delaying and controlling instinctual 'discharge', using a variety of mechanisms, including the mechanisms of defence. The third agency, the *superego,* was seen as a sort of internal precipitate of the child's early conflicts, especially in relation to his parents. The superego is regarded as the vehicle of the conscience and of the individual's ideals, and functions predominantly outside consciousness, as does a large part of the ego and all of the id. Consciousness was now seen as a 'sense organ' of the ego, and the latter structure was described as an organization attempting to serve three masters at one time—the id, the superego and the external world. Anxiety could be aroused by threats from any one of these three sources. Instead of anxiety being regarded as the way in which a threatening instinctual wish showed itself in consciousness (by means of a 'transformation' of libido), it was now seen as an affective signal, a response of the ego (1926), indicating the likely occurrence of a danger situation which, in turn, indicated the possibility of the ego being traumatically overwhelmed.

In the third phase the ego was seen as essentially a problem-solving apparatus and the importance attached to it as an organization with strength and forces of its own gradually increased.

Although Freud now put the *experiencing* of affects into the mental structure which he called the ego, he still made no formal theoretical distinction between the somatic aspects of emotion—which were still seen as drive-derivatives—and associated feeling-states. The energy concept, which can be traced back to the first phase, and which was retained in an altered form in the second phase, still remained as an essential part of psychoanalytic theory in the third phase. The ego was seen as operating with 'desexualized' energy, originating in the id, as well as possessing energies of its own. In this phase psychoanalysis was left with a muddled situation with regard to affects. On the one hand, the distinction between energies and affects, between instinctual and affective 'tensions', was not made. Although clinical psychoanalytic work operated via the understanding of affects as well as of ideas, theoretical explanations still focused on the hypothetical drives and their vicissitudes (Freud pointed out that the instinctual drives were never directly observable but were explanatory constructs). On the other hand, the introduction of the new theory of anxiety implied that a feeling —anxiety—could act as a *signal*, mobilizing adaptive and defensive behaviour on the part of the ego; and, moreover, that it could occur outside consciousness.

By pointing out, in 1926, that anxiety or fear could also arise as a consequence of the perception of dangers in the real world (i.e. not only because of the threatening nature of drive-linked impulses) Freud took a fundamental step in divorcing affects from drives. Unfortunately he never pursued this differentiation and for many, if not most psychoanalysts, affects are still seen as secondary drive manifestations, and as a form of psychic energy, a view which has remained more or less unmodified for three-quarters of a century. Attempts to reconcile new ideas about affects with the theory of energy disposition and energy transformation have resulted in, at times, the most tortuous theoretical acrobatics.

In what follows an outline will be given of a view of affects which may perhaps go some way towards solving certain of the difficulties surrounding this topic in psychoanalytic theory. However, before proceeding further, it may be useful to discuss one of the basic hypotheses of psychoanalysis, i.e. the existence of a 'mental apparatus'. The account which follows is based, in large part, on a discussion of the basic assumptions in psychoanalytic psychology given elsewhere (Sandler *et al.* 1972*b*).

THE MENTAL APPARATUS

The assumption of a mental apparatus implies the existence of a stable, or relatively stable, psychological organization in the individual. Although psychological processes can be assumed to be a function of the nervous system, psychoanalysis supposes, for the purposes of its theories, that psychological phenomena can be conceptualized as involving a psychological 'apparatus'. This concept parallels, in effect, the physiologist's concepts of the cardio-vascular, nervous, digestive and other bodily systems. It is an added 'system' which is a psychological rather than an organic one, although it is influenced by and has effects on the other systems. From the psychoanalytic viewpoint psychology can be regarded as including the study of the mental apparatus and its functioning, just as physiology, anatomy and biochemistry study the physical systems and their functions. The notion of a mental apparatus carries the implication of processes involving psychological 'structures'—psychological organizations with a slow rate of change—but the field of psychoanalytic psychology includes not only behaviour in terms of psychological structures and functions, but also the study of subjective experience.

The mental apparatus is regarded as relatively simple early in life, increasing in complexity as time goes on. Thus the apparatus is capable of modification, and its development is a function both of maturation and of the external and internal forces acting on the mental apparatus, and the responses which subserve psychological adaptation.

In this context the term 'adaptation' is related to the assumption that the apparatus functions (among other things) to maintain a 'steady state' (comparable to the physiological notion of homeostasis), in the face of constant disturbances of that hypothetical state. Such disturbances may arise from outside the individual, as well as from within. In the first phase the major source of disequilibrium was regarded as the external environment, but in the second phase the major source of disturbance was thought to be stimuli arising from the instinctual drives. In the third phase the external world was again given a place as a major source of disturbance of psychological homeostasis, and the apparatus was seen as having to cope with disruptions of the notional 'steady state' arising from the drives, from the external world, from the super-ego, and from within the ego itself. Processes of adaptation in turn bring about changes in the structure and in the mode of functioning of the mental apparatus. It should be noted that this approach to adaptation is radically different from that which emphasizes adaptation to the social environment only. From the psychoanalytic standpoint even the grossest self-destructive behaviour, completely maladaptive from a social point of view, can be considered to be the outcome of attempts at psychological adaptation.

The progressive development of the mental apparatus can be regarded as a consequence of the interaction between an individual's biological tendencies and his external environment. The high degree of complexity of the apparatus reached in the human is probably related to his capacity to make decisions, including decisions which take into account the long-term effect of his actions. The apparatus can be considered to be a psychological system which functions as a superordinate system controlling (primarily by means of evaluation, delay and facilitation) the automatic innate and learned psychological responses of the individual (Sandler & Joffe 1969). It has as its main function adaptation to all the inputs into it, from inside the body and from outside, and to forces arising from within the apparatus itself. In what follows I shall suggest that the relation of such adaptation to affect, and in particular to *feeling-states*, is a crucial one.

While both the bodily changes occurring in emotion and qualities of *feeling* have been subsumed under the heading of *affect*, and while physiological processes may be associated with feelings, it is important to distinguish between the two. The neurohumoral and metabolically caused changes in the body, commonly referred to as emotions, can be regarded as biologically based adaptive bodily responses to disturbances of physiological homeostasis, and can be thought of as having various functions in regard to the mobilization of responses, to preparation for 'fight' and 'flight', and so on. They can be initiated by psychological cues, and consideration of the actual physiological processes involved can safely be left in the hands of other contributors to this symposium, who will doubtless discuss aspects of them in detail.

As far as the mental apparatus is concerned, the only information on which judgments can be made is *experiential*. Although maturational and physical factors play an important part, the full development of the apparatus and its progressive modification is based firmly on its relation to experiential input. The child's progressive control over himself and over the external world depends entirely on the contents of experience. While these contents must be rudimentary at first, the sensations, feelings, images and ideas progressively experienced by the child gradually become differentiated as he builds up what might be called his *representational world* (Sandler 1962; Sandler & Rosenblatt 1962). The actions of the child, more or less automatic at first, alter his experiential feedback, and it is the interaction between subjective experience and the mental representations of action which is critical in the progressive development of the mental apparatus. I should like to emphasize that although physical events may give rise to various types of subjective experience (ultimately via processes in the nervous system), all the apparatus can 'know' are the contents of subjective experience. This applies even in regard to the 'real world', which is never known *in itself*—only experiential representations are known. And it follows that the control of reality is in essence the control of the subjective experience which we assume to be a representation of that reality. Even the 'purest' scientist, with the most sophisticated instruments, is working with experiential reflections of reality. From this we can go on to say that the function of the mental apparatus is to deal with changes in the realm of experience, to handle mental contents, whether these arise from perception, memory, the imagination or any other source. These contents are both the input and output data to which the mental apparatus adapts, even though the apparatus itself can be considered to be a function of the nervous system.

In order for experiential content to be assessed it must have *significance* and *meaning*, and I should like to suggest that such meaning and significance is closely related to feeling-states, even though these may be restricted to the merest trace in the form of a feeling-signal of one sort or another. The crudest forms of such meanings (which we assume to exist in the very young infant) are pleasure and pain, 'nice' and 'nasty', comfort and discomfort. Naturally such 'meanings' become progressively refined as development proceeds, but it is likely that even the most abstract experiential content only has significance for the mental apparatus through a connection with some form of feeling-signal. The behaviour of the child and the functioning of the mental apparatus is guided by the feeling-states and feeling-signals embedded in its experience. While this is usually referred to as the pleasure principle (or 'pleasure–unpleasure principle'), it is clear that this 'principle' has a number of different aspects to it. One of these refers to needs, drives and the bodily changes associated with these, and this aspect of the 'pleasure principle' is connected with the regulation of bodily homeostasis, particularly in relation to distur-bances brought about by instinctual drives. However, there is another aspect, relevant to the present discussion (Sandler & Joffe 1969):

"In the realm of experience we have the aspect of changes in feeling-state which accompany states of drive tension and discharge, changes which can be broadly subsumed under the headings of pleasure and unpleasure. In the very young infant there is a close correlation between these two aspects of the pleasure principle, a correlation which has major survival value for the individual. The regulation of feelings aroused by drive stimuli and those which accompany drive-reducing activities normally succeeds in bringing about the regulation of the drives themselves. However, feelings reflect more than the state of the drives, and gradually become attached to the ideational content reflecting the self and the outer world. Stimuli from the outer world affect the feeling-state increasingly as development progresses, although the instinctual drives always remain the main sources of disruption of the individual's feeling-state.

"In addition, a gradual differentiation of feelings occurs with development. Perhaps even from the beginning, there must be a difference between the sensual pleasures which accompany drive discharge and the feelings of satisfaction which follow such discharge. There is also possibly a subjective distinction from early on between the unpleasure of instinctual tension and pain (*Schmerz*) arising from other sources. Post-discharge satisfaction can be conceptualized as well-being, and we can regard this as a positive feeling-state rather than being a mere absence of feeling... Feelings become differentiated during development, often becoming remote from primitive drive-related experiences, and are increasingly linked with ideational content.

"As feelings differentiate, one type of feeling comes to play a major role in the regulation of experience; indeed, to such a degree that its maintenance above a minimum level (when it falls or threatens to fall below that level) becomes the dominant criterion in determining the activity of the psychic apparatus. This is the feeling of *safety* which can be regarded as being generated by smooth and integrated functioning of the apparatus as a whole (including its drive-discharge aspects). The gaining of pleasure will, as the suffering of our neurotic patients testifies, be sacrificed in the interests of maintaining or attaining a minimum level of safety feeling (Sandler 1960).

"Any experience of anxiety or feeling of disorganization lowers the level of safety feeling and indeed we may see the development of types of activity which at first sight seem to be inappropriate and unadaptive, but which are in fact adaptive in that they are aimed at restoring some minimum level of safety feeling. Included in this are, for example, some of the stereotyped and bizarre forms of behaviour shown by psychotics, who attempt in this way to control their activities in order to obtain a higher degree of what we may call perceptual security. They have to create a stable perceptual situation by hiding in a corner, clutching a doll or repeating a ritual, and must avoid activity which would lead to disorganized activity or the experience of loss of safety feeling.

"The need to maintain a feeling of safety (which is quite different from pleasure in direct instinctual gratification, though it may or may not accompany it) is of enormous importance in adaptation in general. The conflict between the need to maintain safety and the need to gain pleasure is possibly a forerunner of neurotic conflict in general. An activity which leads to pleasure may be inhibited if it lowers the level of safety feeling. The feeling of anxiety, when it acts as a signal to the apparatus, must be accompanied by a drop in the level of safety feeling. Different individuals will vary in the degree to which drive impulses or external factors affect their safety feeling level, and the whole history of the individual enters into determining this (as probably also do constitutional factors).

"The view of adaptation taken here implies that experiences are constantly being aroused which disrupt the person's basic feeling-state, and that the aim, function or purpose of adaptation is to maintain a basic stability of the central feeling-state. Of course the individual will allow his immediate impulses to proceed if these lead to pleasure, but only if at the same time they do not radically lower the safety level, or lead to unpleasure or threatened unpleasure. If, as the impulse proceeds, there is a signal of danger, then his psychic apparatus is activated to apply the appropriate psychological structures in order to change the content of the realm of experience into a form which is safer, even if it means giving up direct instinctual gratifications. Thus, whatever he becomes conscious of, or what he finally actually does, is related to this regulatory criterion. The structures which he uses may be the ordinary perceptual or cognitive structures aimed at the avoidance of perceptual or cognitive 'dissonance', or they may be the employment of defence mechanisms in such degree that neurotic or even psychotic disturbances ensue (as in the massive use of projection in paranoid illness).

"Kohler (1964) and others have shown that it is 'things of action' which are first organized in the child's perceptual world. We can take this further by suggesting that the whole development of knowledge of the 'world' is created through the link between the ideo-motor experiential representations and feeling-states. Even the highest form of symbolic representation is only meaningful, and indeed is only created, through its direct or indirect link with feelings. In this sense there is no such thing as a purely cognitive or intellectual process. A successful mathematical manipulation is associated with feelings of 'rightness', and these in turn have links with feelings of safety, of 'good' feelings, of mastery and of 'function pleasure' (Bühler).

"The apparatus is thus continually engaging in processes of problem-solving, and in all of this its basic problems relate to the regulation of feelings. In this context we can speak of an *economics of feeling-states*; the solution which is acceptable to the apparatus is one which represents the best possible compromise at any one time (and with the particular resources of the individual) between the various 'good' and 'bad' feelings which it may experience or anticipate. It is clear that to speak of 'signal anxiety' is not enough. We have to include signals of anticipated sensual gratification, safety, pain and possibly others. An economic point of view is thus essential to this model, but it is insufficient at this level of conceptualization to put it in terms of the distribution of quantities of energy... ...The 'reality principle' falls into place here (in line with Freud's view of it as an extension of the pleasure principle). It represents the taking into account of reality (as it is known or anticipated by the individual). To ignore it usually arouses a signal of anxiety or some other unpleasurable feeling; to take it into account usually provides an anticipated pleasure *or a feeling of safety*, or both. Thus present and future reality are only taken into account on a 'here-and-now' feeling basis. If, for one reason or another, it is more economical for the individual not to take reality into account—for example, if being aware of reality increases the sum total of unpleasant or threatening feelings and *lowers* the feeling of safety to an intolerable degree, he may adapt by finding a 'pathological' solution of one sort or another".

We can thus take the view that the mental apparatus functions to maintain a *feeling-homeostasis*. Normally this is 'in step' with the maintenance of bodily homeostasis. By this is meant that the restoration of a feeling-homeostasis (with its associated feeling of safety and well-being) is perfectly correlated with the restoration of homeostasis in the physical systems of the body. The infant who is hungry has a bodily need, with corresponding physiological disequilibrium, and through sucking at the breast temporarily does away with the need, with equilibrium being restored. At the same time we may say that he experiences a feeling of unpleasure as a consequence of the bodily need, obtains a form of sensual pleasure through the act of sucking, and experiences a feeling of well-being after the feed.*

It has been pointed out elsewhere (Sandler & Joffe 1969) that "In the assessment of the contents of the experiential field a process of rapid *scanning* of the field by the apparatus is involved, and we can make use of the concept of a scanning function which operates to guide the apparatus to some sort of action. Such action includes the organization of experience arising from stimuli from

---

* It has been suggested that a psychoanalytic learning theory can be written in terms of the reinforcing action of changes in feeling-states (Sandler & Joffe 1968).

the outside world as well as experience prompted by drive stimuli. This scanning function is the internal sense organ of the apparatus. It is part of the non-experiential realm, but a major part of its function is to scan the material of the experiential realm *before it reaches consciousness*".

From the point of view put forward in the present paper it would follow that the prime motivators, *from the point of view of the mental apparatus*, are changes in feeling-states. While drives, needs, emotional forces and other influences arising from within the body are highly important in determining behaviour, from the point of view of psychological functioning, they exert their effect *through changes in feelings*. The same is true for stimuli arising from the external world. This approach removes feelings from their total conceptual tie to the instinctual drives alone, and gives them a central position in psycho-analytic psychology.

It should be noted that it has been found necessary to postulate the somewhat paradoxical notion of *unconscious* feelings (or their equivalent), and that the mental apparatus (or the part of it which is usually referred to as the ego) can scan its field of experiential input and associated feeling signals extremely rapidly before experience is permitted to enter consciousness. If the experience carries with it a threat that consciousness might be overwhelmed by painful sensations, the mechanisms of defence may be called into play to *alter* the content of experience before the content is allowed access to consciousness.

The experiential field contains perceptual, memory, and imaginative products, as well as symbolic representations. These include, as a significant aspect, representations of self and of objects, and of the interaction between these. In addition, ideal or 'wished-for' states of the self are included, and the discrepancy between an 'actual' or 'present' state (as represented experientially) and an 'ideal' or 'wished-for' state may be accompanied by a painful feeling experience. In general we can say that the ideational content of the experiential field is embedded in a matrix of feelings, and these feelings are the essential basis upon which the nature and direction of the adaptive action of the mental apparatus is taken.

Although normally the mental apparatus and the physical apparatuses function 'in step', and the regulation of homeostasis in the realm of the body goes parallel with the regulation of feeling-homeostasis in the mental apparatus, the possibility exists for the two to get 'out of step'. Mental conflict may, for example, cause the mental apparatus to find an adaptive solution which restores a feeling of safety, at the same time interfering with normal physiological affective regulatory processes—that is, preventing so-called affective discharge. If we assume that an aggressive impulse causes affective changes in the body, or that a person has an unconscious reaction of rage against an irritating or threatening figure, the mental apparatus may (because of, say, guilt feelings) prevent the activity which would normally restore physiological affective homeostasis. The body may, as a consequence, remain in a state of chronic physiological imbalance because of the defensive activity of the mental apparatus. The person may consciously *feel* well, but may, for example, have an elevated blood pressure or other changes which, in the course of time, may lead to irreversible organic changes in the body. To put it another way: because of guilt or anxiety the mental apparatus may find a solution which restores a feeling-homeostasis, but does so at the expense of physiological adaptation. The body is thrown out of balance, so to speak, because the normal behavioural processes which lead to the disappearance of temporary and normal affective states are not permitted to take place. This leads to abnormal chronic affective physiological states, which may in turn lead to organic pathology. This is one possible pathway for the development of certain forms of psychosomatic disturbance.

References

BIBRING, E. (1941) The development and problems of the theory of instincts. *Int. J. Psycho-Anal.* 22, 102

BREUER, J. & FREUD, S. (1893-1895) *Studies on Hysteria.* Standard Edition, 2, Hogarth Press, London

BRIERLEY, M. (1937) Affects in theory and practice. *Int. J. Psycho-Anal.* 18, 256

FREUD, S. (1900) *The Interpretation of Dreams.* Standard Edition, 4 and 5, Hogarth Press, London

FREUD, S. (1901) *The Psychopathology of Everyday Life.* Standard Edition, 6, Hogarth Press, London

FREUD, S. (1905) *Three Essays on the Theory of Sexuality.* Standard Edition, 7, Hogarth Press, London

FREUD, S. (1911) Formulations on the Two Principles of Mental Functioning. Standard Edition, 12, Hogarth Press, London

FREUD, S. (1914) *On Narcissism: an Introduction.* Standard Edition, 14, Hogarth Press, London

FREUD, S. (1923) *The Ego and the Id.* Standard Edition, 19, Hogarth Press, London

FREUD, S. (1926) *Inhibitions, Symptoms and Anxiety.* Standard Edition, 20, Hogarth Press, London

HINDE, R. A. (1972) This volume, pp. 1-13

JACOBSON, E. (1953) The affects and their pleasure-unpleasure qualities in relation to the psychic discharge processes. In *Drives, Affects, Behavior*, vol. I (Loewenstein, R. M., ed.), International Universities Press, New York

KOHLER, I. (1964) *The Formation and Transformation of the Perceptual World.* International Universities Press, New York

LEWIN, B. (1965) Reflections on affect. In *Drives, Affects, Behavior*, vol. II (Schur, M., ed.), International Universities Press, New York

RAPAPORT, D. (1953) On the psychoanalytic theory of affects. *Int. J. Psycho-Anal.* 34, 177

SANDLER, J. (1960) The background of safety. *Int. J. Psycho-Anal.* **41**, 352

SANDLER, J. (1962) Psychology and psychoanalysis. *Br. J. Med. Psychol.* **35**, 91

SANDLER, J., DARE, C. & HOLDER, A. (1972*a*) Frames of reference in psychoanalytic psychology: II. The historical context and phases in the development of psychoanalysis. *Br. J. Med. Psychol.* **45**, 133-142

SANDLER, J., DARE, C. & HOLDER, A. (1972*b*) Frames of reference in psychoanalytic psychology: III. A note on the basic assumptions. *Br. J. Med. Psychol.* **45**, 143-147

SANDLER, J. & JOFFE, W. G. (1968): Psychoanalytic psychology and learning theory. In *The Role of Learning in Psychotherapy (Ciba Found. Symp.)*, pp. 274-287, Churchill, London

SANDLER, J. & JOFFE, W. G. (1969) Towards a basic psychoanalytic model. *Int. J. Psycho-Anal.* **50**, 79

SANDLER, J. & ROSENBLATT, B. (1962) The concept of the representational world. *Psychoanal. Study Child.* **17**, 128

SCHUR, M. (1953) The ego in anxiety. In *Drives, Affects, Behavior*, vol. I (Loewenstein, R. M., ed.), International Universities Press, New York

Discussion

Hill: Dr Sandler has conceptualized a mental and a physical apparatus and has said that the mental apparatus is a product of neural activity, which I imagine we would all accept. Nevertheless, in the light of Professor Hinde's paper (pp. 1-13), there are logical difficulties about the possibility of the mental apparatus getting 'out of step' with the physical apparatus, if the mental apparatus is the expression of nervous system function. Professor Hinde pointed out the dangers of the category mistake to which Gilbert Ryle first drew our attention, showing that psychophysical dualism, the mind–body concept with the interaction of immaterial mind and material body, doesn't make logical sense, and that the idea of affects, as psychological phenomena, causing changes in neuronal systems or *vice versa*, doesn't make logical sense either. In trying to understand Dr Sandler's proposition we should perhaps clarify the nature of his 'mental apparatus' and the relationship between it and the 'physical apparatus'.

Hinde: My paper arose out of the feeling that any symposium on emotion was likely to be dogged by the differences in the way in which the word was used. I tried to set out the different types of use in an effort to clarify my own thinking. I agree with you, Sir Denis, about the difficulty one gets in when one conceives of a mental apparatus and a physical apparatus that can get out of step with each other.

Gray: I took it that Dr Sandler was saying that what he calls 'the mental apparatus' affects bodily functions *outside* the central nervous system, such as the cardiovascular or gastrointestinal systems. In that case his mental apparatus can easily be regarded as some subset of systems within the CNS. If he was saying that, I don't see the problem.

Sandler: I think we need to realize that different functions *within* the nervous system can be in conflict. For example, a child who is stimulated to rage by the activities of a parent, and is at the same time frightened by the thought of losing that parent (or by the threat of withdrawal of that parent's affection), may begin to check his expressions of aggression and perhaps his feelings of anger as well. This occurs via representations (in perception or in thought) of the parent, and via feeling-states associated with those representations. Controlling systems are built up through development and learning. Such controlling systems would represent aspects of the mental apparatus. The child's immediate, innate tendency might be to react with rage and aggression, but he may control this tendency in order to preserve a feeling of well-being and safety or feelings of comfort through feeling loved. The imposition of controls occurs through the rapid scanning and evaluation of his feeling-states, and through his anticipation of what might happen if he allowed himself to act in a more spontaneous manner. This can lead to a state of conflict *within the mental apparatus.* The child may then suffer from the effects of what is (wrongly) called 'undischarged' emotion, which remains as a source of disequilibrium in the bodily apparatus because of the child's fear of what the actions that would restore equilibrium in the bodily apparatus would do to his mental state. This is what I meant by the mental apparatus being 'out of step' with the physical one.

Hill: So the 'getting out of step' is between two parts of the nervous system; and you are suggesting that in such a situation of conflict, the physiological changes which occur in the body persist in relation to the state of feeling or affect and are not related to the behaviour the child might undertake to remove the threatening situation?

Sandler: Ideally mental and physical functioning are 'in step', but a situation might arise in which the child is so frightened by the thought of the particular physical activity that he doesn't permit it to occur and so the whole bodily equilibrium may be thrown 'out of step' with the mental apparatus.

Denenberg: The direction of the meeting so far reminds me very much of introductory psychology textbooks, where the chapter headings go 'learning', 'perception', 'motivation', 'emotions'. The chapter on 'emotions' invariably begins with a marvellous case history; then the current *argot* of neurophysiology is produced, with the implications of causal mechanisms, followed by some experimental data to make everything respectable; the idea is to convince the student that emotions are understood. I am afraid that this is going to happen here, because I cannot see how what I have heard so far relates to what I am doing as an experimental psychologist, studying emotional behaviour with animals and obtaining quantitative data. Unless we can find some common meeting ground in terms of definitions, of measurements and of procedures, we may be talking past each other in this symposium.

Hill: One of the objectives of this meeting is to find common ground between the phenomena described by physicians and psychiatrists—that is, through clinical observations on patients—and the quite different phenomena observed by psychological and biological scientists.

Hinde: On this question of the meaning of the terms used by Dr Sandler, it could be taken that he implied that in the early phases of psychoanalytic theory there was a one-to-one relation between drives and emotions and there were thought to be about as many emotions as there were drives. When he came to current views, or his own views, he talked of feeling-states, positive or negative, as the primary motivators. Are feeling-states the same sorts of thing as emotions, and are they the same in number as emotions, or are they a different kind of thing altogether?

Sandler: The problem that psychoanalysis has had about emotion is exactly the same problem as psychologists have had, and I agree that we need to clarify our terms. Initially in psychoanalytic theory, a number of simple affects were linked with the state of the instinctual drives but no one-to-one correspondence between affect and drive was implied; in addition, anxiety was seen as an affect, and no distinction was made between feelings and bodily changes. Whether we refer to the total as 'affect' or as 'emotion' is something we need to decide, and Professor Hinde explained some of the difficulties in his paper. I think that feeling-states can become extremely complex. During development a whole hierarchy of feeling-states is built up, with the occurrence, at the most sophisticated levels, of such states as aesthetic pleasure. Basically the infant has feelings of erotic pleasure (for example, when sucking at the breast), feelings of painful tension and discomfort, and feelings of well-being and safety, which are not the same as the erotic pleasures but which are associated with the feelings one assumes that the infant experiences *after* being fed. During development the child may get into conflict between the types of feeling he is striving to obtain or maintain, and he may accordingly give up the obtaining of erotic pleasure in order to preserve his own feeling of safety.

These feeling-states are not active agents but rather signals. I don't think that they are exactly correlated with the drives; they are probably, in the adult, more complicated than the drives. I think that the more complex civilization becomes, the more finely differentiated such feeling-states become.

We get into great difficulties when we lump feelings, bodily states and drives under the general heading of 'emotion'. We have to differentiate between relatively basic emotions such as anger, excitement or anxiety, which may represent a basic set of psychophysiological units or concepts, and the whole realm of feeling-states which are developmentally associated with the former but which in the course of time become more and more differentiated psychologically.

Hill: By 'erotic', do you mean 'sensual'—that is, proceeding from the body?

Sandler: I mean those feelings which are sensorily 'nice'. The infant can't locate these feelings until much later, although they may stem from bodily stimulation. Only later does he associate these experiences with his perception of certain behavioural patterns of his own and of others, especially the caretaking mother.

Sachar: We are talking about emotions as being routed in two ways, first, toward subjective awareness (I think this is where Dr Sandler tends to use the term 'affect') and second, toward a physiological representation in other systems, through autonomic, endocrine and other pathways, and that's where Dr Sandler tends to use the term 'emotion', attempting to comprise the physiological as well as the psychological subjective awareness. What occurs in certain pathological states may be not so much a getting 'out of step' as a re-routing within the nervous system. Perhaps normally impulses are simultaneously discharged along two pathways, say, toward mental representation and physiological representation. In certain other circumstances, Dr Sandler is suggesting that there may be a re-routing in which the somatic representation is the primary form of discharge.

Engel: Rather than thinking in terms of mental and physical apparatuses getting 'out of step' or of 're-routing' within the nervous system, I find it more useful to think in terms of the capability of the mental apparatus and higher CNS as the supraordinate systems to process input from within and from without and to regulate bodily processes accordingly. When such input cannot be handled by mental processes alone, bodily systems are increasingly implicated, including emergency reactions controlled through limbic and other lower circuits. This can be studied developmentally. Thus, when we compared gastric secretory correlations of behaviour in two children with gastric fistulas, one between 15 and 20 months and the other between $4\frac{1}{2}$ and 5 years of age, we noted that whenever the younger child, Monica, who was physically retarded and had no speech as yet, was interacting actively with the experimenter who was aspirating the gastric juice from the fistula, her fasting stomach secreted acid actively. This was true whether her relationship at the time was pleasurable or unpleasurable—she could be angry and fussing, or she could be delighted and enjoying herself. On the other hand, when she withdrew and ceased to relate to the experimenter, the gastric secretion virtually ceased (Engel *et al.*

1956). In other words, fasting gastric secretion closely reflected the degree of engagement with persons in her environment.

Now, what happened with the four-year-old, Doris, who not only had speech at her command but also had a correspondingly greater capacity to relate and express herself in psychological terms? Dr Sandler referred to the development of a mental apparatus and in Doris I think we can see what he is speaking about. When she was relating effectively and comfortably with the experimenter, her fasting gastric secretion, in contrast to Monica's, remained relatively low. But when she was having difficulty in relating to him, for whatever reason, gastric secretion tended to increase. This was as true when the difficulty was subtle, for example when she couldn't understand him because he spoke in too rapid or complex a fashion, as when she was irritated or anxious (Engel *et al.* 1971). In other words, the strict correlation between secretion and degree of relating noted in the infant no longer held true. We suggest that by four years sufficient autonomy of mental functioning, or higher CNS functioning, had been achieved, so that gastric secretion as a physiological response was no longer an integral part of the bodily response activated in the course of relating to people. In the young infant gastric activity is very intimately involved in object relating, presumably because feeding is an early and repetitive activity involved in establishing the bond between infant and mother. At this early stage of infancy the fact that another person (mother) is regularly associated with feeding links the gastric secretory response to object-relating activities. But with maturation of the mental apparatus, particularly the development of speech and other modalities of relating, this link loses its potency unless or until the relationship is disturbed, in which circumstances regression to the earlier link between gastric secretion and relating may occur. The relative autonomy is lost and the previously utilized bodily system, gastric activity, is again activated. It is as if when Doris could not relate effectively by mental means alone she regressed to the oral organization of her earlier infancy when gastric secretory activity was a physiological concomitant of object relating.

To bring this into the context of psychosomatic disturbance, I would say that such an increase in gastric secretion in itself is of no pathogenic significance. It might become pathogenic if it interacted at the tissue level or the cellular level with some other pre-existing local vulnerability so as to lead to some localized organic process, such as an ulcer; or if multiple factors operated simultaneously at the tissue level. In other words, the 'getting out of step' may not be within the nervous system or between the nervous and mental systems; it may occur at the end organ. Only in this way can we account for the wide variety of somatic disorders the onsets of which appear to be facilitated by psychological disturbances. The specificity rests in the periphery.

Gray: Surely both types of mechanism might be operating in different kinds of disorders—either peripheral or central nervous mechanisms might be 'out of step'?

Nemiah: The inference from Dr Engel's observations on his two children with fistulas is that in the course of development neuronal pathways arise that allow for autonomy in the higher levels of the CNS. Let us assume that for some reason (perhaps because of lack of adequate environmental stimuli) a child does not develop these pathways (or, in Dr Denenberg's terms, does not learn) and consequently as an adult has only the kinds of pathways he had as an infant, so that the only way he can respond is with his body. This may give rise to the kind of problem one sees with the 'psychosomatic' patient. He has not learned the more elaborate kinds of social interaction patterns that, say, the hysterical patient has.

Engel: I would still question the wisdom of assuming that 'psychosomatic disorder' has primarily a neurogenic or psychogenic causation, though obvious psychological and neurobiological processes are contributory. Rather I contend that the so-called classic psychosomatic disorders, such as peptic ulcer, asthma or colitis, are not different from other organic illnesses such as pneumonia, leukaemia or cancer. They involve peripheral or tissue vulnerabilities of one sort or another and an interaction between influences that may originate psychologically, through the nervous system and its outflow, and the end organ, whatever it may be. The mechanisms of interaction are still unknown. The neural factor might be neurohumoral or it might involve direct neural action on the end organ but it is only one factor of many. For example, the old idea that activation of peptic ulcer is directly related to neurogenically (psychically) mediated increase in the secretion of gastric acid has not been confirmed; the patient with peptic ulcer has a high secretion of gastric acid whether his ulcer is active or not. Hence a psychogenic or neurogenic increase in gastric secretion cannot be *the* factor responsible for peptic ulcer activation (Mirsky 1958). 'Psychosomatic' disorders are based on complex interrelationships involving vulnerable peripheral systems. I would otherwise accept Dr Nemiah's point, but I would add that given the premise that this particular person is somatically vulnerable (which may be determined genetically, as in diabetes, or by previous experience), and given the kind of psychological development that he describes, such a person may be even more vulnerable by virtue of being less able to cope with life stresses by effective mental mechanisms. Hence the vulnerable end organ is more often or more severely subjected to physiological effects secondary to the failure of mental mechanisms. This is what I tried to exemplify by citing the gastric secretory changes in Doris when she couldn't cope with the experimenter, though I would emphasize that in Doris such increase in gastric secretion had no pathogenic effects; this is only an illustration. The goal of psychotherapy would be to improve the individual's ability to cope and thereby to reduce the frequency and intensity of psychophysiological reactions that may interact unfavourably with the pre-existing local vulnerability.

Wolff: A word of warning: it is dangerous to draw firm conclusions about changes occurring during development from a study of two children, one of whom was studied at the age of 15-20 months and the other at four years.

Engel: I fully accept that. But gastric fistula cases, especially in childhood, are rare. These are the only two children that have ever been studied in this fashion. Indeed only with a fistula can one obtain enough samples of gastric juice to permit meaningful correlations to be established by statistical means. I hope others will find and study more cases, for we need more data to follow this up.

Storey: One might expect a low incidence of psychosomatic disorders in psychiatrists, who tend to be introverted as a group and are accustomed to express emotions in words. Is this the case?

Engel: No. I know colleagues, including analysts, who have hypertension, peptic ulcer, ulcerative colitis and so forth. They also get pneumonia, myocardial infarctions and cancer. The notion of psychogenesis implicit in the question is oversimplified and therefore untenable.

Sandler: I think that psychoanalysts as well as other psychologists and physicians have their share of psychosomatic disorder, certainly not less than average. This may be partly related to the tendency to intellectualize and therefore to keep emotions at bay. Although fantasies may come into scientific discussions, there is a phase in development when the child has to learn to separate his intellectual control of the world from his being swamped with feelings, and perhaps this is hypertrophied in the scientist so that the somatic aspects of emotion are thrown out of balance, because of the need for intellectual control.

Donald: May I take up Dr Sandler's concept of feeling-homeostasis? The idea that the mind is seeking a happy state of safe pleasure to me is rather unreal; and even if it were so, the brain must be extraordinarily fast moving and changing in order to achieve this, with all these instincts coming in and problems impinging from the outside world. One even suspects that the brain is doing the opposite and that, to some, guilt, anguish and even danger give pleasure at times.

Sandler: To say simply that 'the mind is seeking a happy state of safe pleasure' does indeed sound rather unreal. Nevertheless, if the point of view is put in less condensed form it may not sound quite like that. What I have suggested is that the mental apparatus will function (particularly in response to demands from the drives) to reduce unpleasure, including the unpleasure related to tensions arising from various sources, and where possible, to gain pleasure. However, to use Freud's concept, the pleasure–unpleasure principle is modified when the safety of the organism is threatened, and such a threat can only come about through the medium of *feeling-signals* which herald a drop in safety-feeling or, in conjunction with the trial actions which constitute thought, an increase in such feelings. Normally the control over one's environment and over one's own self is adequate for a sufficient background feeling of safety to be generated; but this is not always the case. Where safety is threatened beyond a certain degree, behaviour which might otherwise lead to pleasurable gratification may be inhibited. My essential point is that there exists an economics of feeling-states, and it is on the basis of the rapid scanning of feeling-signals that 'meaning' is attached to thoughts, perceptions, and indeed to all mental representations.

Professor Donald suggests that the brain must be extraordinarily fast-moving in order for such processes to go on outside consciousness. I think that this is so, and one only need think of the way in which perceptual input is organized into formed percepts, with all the apperceptions and modifications which take place through the involvement of perceptual structures (both inherent and acquired), and the tremendous speed at which such organization occurs, in order to appreciate the rapidity with which the internal scanning to which I have referred can take place.

Certainly in some people guilt, anguish and danger give pleasure at times. Apart from the fact that suffering may yield a concealed sexual masochistic pleasure, a whole range of gratifications arise from conforming to an ideal which one (consciously or unconsciously) holds up to oneself. The wall-of-death rider may be gaining a tremendous feeling of omnipotent control, sufficient for him to risk his own life; and there are many other causes, I believe, for people to look for suffering, or to expose themselves to it, quite apart from any pleasure in pain. There can even be an element of safety-seeking in so-called masochistic behaviour, where the pain is accepted as the price for having, for example, a fantasied close relationship with the mother (Sandler 1960; Sandler & Rosenblatt 1962).

Hofer: One property of homeostatic systems fits well with what Dr Sandler is saying. Homeostasis does not always consist of keeping a given level in all conditions. For example, when somebody is exposed to prolonged heat stress, the system of priorities in central neural regulation conserves temperature regulation at the expense of water and electrolyte balance. The person becomes severely dehydrated and finally dies through failure of homeostasis in one system, while balance is maintained in the other system. There are some patients who for reasons of peripheral end organ failure develop heat stroke because they don't sweat. They tend to defend water balance at the expense of temperature regulation and become hyperthermic, to the point of becoming psychotic, with temperatures as high as 108°, on a very hot day. In the same way we should be able to conceive of the mental apparatus as having a system of priorities, within a homeostatic organization. Such a model, in the physiological realm, might help us to build a bridge between mental experience and bodily function.

Gray: In my own terms, I would see Dr Sandler's 'mental apparatus' as systems for the control of behaviour. Do you mean anything different from that?

Sandler: I mean exactly that, but I would include the control of subjective experience as an essential intermediary.

Hinde: Dr Sandler, you spoke earlier (p. 48) about a hierarchy of feeling-states and implied that aesthetic feelings were at the top, but then you talked about the differentiation of feelings in the adult organism from more basic ones and discussed the feeling-states that one supposes an infant has. Now, these must be inferred from behaviour, and therefore the feeling-states imputed to an infant must be closely linked to its behaviour. I am not clear whether in the adult organism, when the differentiation of feeling-states has supposedly taken place, the different feeling-states are all thought to be associated with different types of behaviour or whether they are thought to have acquired independence from behaviour.

Sandler: I think that there is a general tendency to underestimate feelings because they are linked so much with intangibles and are so difficult to measure and assess, particularly in infancy. Experimentalists tend to talk much more about physical changes, whereas to the clinician feelings are extremely important. My suggestion is that the decisions which the individual makes are intimately related to his scanning of feelings. I would assume that the infant experiences feelings, closely tied to his behaviour, and that as he gains some control over his own behaviour, this control is directed by him on the basis of the feeling-consequences of his behaviour.

As far as structures are concerned, there is a whole body of psychological as well as psychoanalytic literature (see, for example, Greenfield & Lewis 1965) relating to the concept of structures as organizations which develop in the course of experience being elaborations of existing biological structures and apparatuses. They constitute a superordinate psychological controlling system. The mental apparatus is developed, as Dr Gray has pointed out, for controlling and also facilitating certain types of behaviour. It also functions to judge whether the behaviour is 'successful' or not, in terms of the feedback of experience, including feeling-states.

Feelings are, of course, strongly linked with behaviour. When I suggested that aesthetic feelings are one of the highest forms in a hierarchy of feelings this was an attempt to illustrate the view that more differentiated and subtle feelings develop during the individual's experience. Naturally, other feelings besides aesthetic ones can be assumed to arise from more primitive ones during individual development. The infant has, I believe, very crude feelings, but so has the adult. He may not permit himself to experience these consciously, and the need to control such feelings may cause his bodily systems to get 'out of step' (to use this obviously bad phrase) with his mental apparatus.

By 'out of step' I mean the following sort of situation. Imagine that I have an angry response to something that someone has said: my training, the standards imposed on me from inside and from outside, may lead me to defend against experiencing the feelings associated with the anger. Nevertheless, the bodily changes connected with being angry would still occur (and I might notice these). If I had a psychosomatic symptom which was in some way a somatic consequence of being angry (I think that such symptoms *do* exist) I might notice that I was experiencing that symptom, without being aware of the feeling aspect (the *feeling* of rage) which is defended against. This is what I meant by the controlling, delaying apparatus getting out of step with the physical systems. It could probably be better put in other ways.

Levine: One has to consider a hierarchy of what is available to an organism. We recently did a series of studies (Conner *et al.* 1971) looking at various aspects of the adrenocortical system in rats after fighting. We used shock-induced fighting. The rats in the control group were given exactly the same amount of shock as those which fought. At the end of the session plasma concentrations of ACTH were measured. To our surprise, the ACTH concentrations in the rats that were fighting were much lower than those of the animals that were shocked. Both animals have essentially the same aversive stimulus, but what is available to the paired animals is a response system which is not available to the isolated, shocked animal. The active response seems to take over in terms of modulating the physiological response to the same stimulus, so there is a hierarchy of responses which depends on what the animal has available in order to cope with the environment. If a behavioural response is available certain neurohormones are not elaborated that are produced when that response is no longer available. One can only talk about a hierarchy when a choice of responses is available to the organism.

Sandler: I am not surprised by the lower concentrations of ACTH in the rats who are free to fight, because these rats are not out of step in the sense in which I have used the term. They are not in a state of fear or conflict. They can use a response which is based on their biologically given and on their learned responses. Those rats are not in as great a state of stress, so to speak, as the rats who don't know what decision to make, or who don't know whether, if they behave in a certain way, a painful experience will ensue or not, and are thus overwhelmed with anxiety. Professor Levine's observations are not inconsistent with the view I put forward.

Sifneos: I would like to know more about the connection between language and feeling; such knowledge may help us to understand better the second case described by Dr Nemiah. At what stage does a child learn to label his emotions, and to differentiate between such states as for example being cold, taking a hot bath and calling that pleasant, and being hot, taking a hot bath and calling that unpleasant? Is it possible to have feelings without language?

Sandler: I think there are feelings before language and that the child can experience the difference between a cold and hot bath before he has words. One cannot prove what the child actually feels and can only show that he reacts, but I would say that the child can differentiate feelings subjectively very much earlier than he can put names to them.

References

CONNER, R. L., VERNIKOS-DANELLIS, J. & LEVINE, S. (1971) Stress, fighting and neuro-endocrine function. *Nature (Lond.)* **234**, 564-566

ENGEL, G. L., REICHSMAN, F. & SEGAL, H. (1956) A study of an infant with a gastric fistula. Behavior and the rate of total hydrochloric acid secretion. *Psychosom. Med.* **18**, 374-398

ENGEL, G. L., REICHSMAN, F. & ANDERSON, D. (1971) Behavior and gastric secretion. III. Cognitive development and gastric secretion in children with gastric fistula (abstract). *Psychosom. Med.* **33**, 472

GREENFIELD, N. S. & LEWIS, W. C. (1965) *Psychoanalysis and Current Biological Thought*, University of Wisconsin Press, Madison & Milwaukee

MIRSKY, J. A. (1958) Physiologic and social determinants in the etiology of duodenal ulcer. *Am. J. Digest. Dis.* **3**, 285-314

SANDLER, J. (1960) The background of safety. *Int. J. Psycho-Anal.* **41**, 352

SANDLER, J. & ROSENBLATT, B. (1962) The concept of the representational world. *Psychoanal. Study Child.* **17**, 128

Conservation-withdrawal:
a primary regulatory process
for organismic homeostasis

GEORGE L. ENGEL and ARTHUR H. SCHMALE

Departments of Medicine and Psychiatry, University of Rochester, School of Medicine and Dentistry, Rochester, New York

Abstract Relative immobility, quiescence and unresponsiveness to environmental input together constitute a behavioural triad that occurs periodically and aperiodically among virtually every species of animal. We propose the term *conservation–withdrawal* to designate the underlying somatic homeostatic processes from which many regulatory variants adaptive for different species have evolved. In this paper we discuss the phylogenesis and ontogenesis of the conservation–withdrawal reaction with particular reference to the circumstances under which this pattern is evoked. We suggest that conservation–withdrawal encompasses the regulatory processes responsible for periodic rest and restitution and that these same processes also mediate shorter or longer episodes of unresponsiveness and arrest of activity at times or under circumstances where interaction with the environment has become impossible or unavailing. Distinctions are drawn between conservation–withdrawal as a primary biological process and the psychological patterns which may be expressive of, derivative from or reactive to conservation–withdrawal.

What we propose to discuss under the heading 'conservation–withdrawal' belongs in the category of a new look at some familiar behavioural phenomena, namely the triad of relative immobility, quiescence and unresponsiveness to environmental input, a behaviour noted periodically and aperiodically among virtually every species of animal. The term *conservation–withdrawal* is being used to refer to biological threshold mechanisms whereby survival of the organism is supported by processes of disengagement and inactivity *vis à vis* the external environment. This is a response which may be invoked either when input becomes excessive and beyond the organism's capacity actively to cope or when available input becomes inadequate to meet needs. The biological goal of conservation–withdrawal is to conserve resources and to assure the autonomy of the organism until environmental conditions are once again more compatible. We postulate that such regulatory mechanisms for protection against environmental extremes characterize all forms of life and we place them at one end of an activity–inactivity continuum of the homeostatic processes serving survival. We assume such systems operate at every level of organismic complexity and that in higher organisms the nervous system progressively assumes chaperonage over these functions.

This is not a new concept. For example, Hoagland wrote as follows in 1928: 'It may be said that in general an animal can react in one of two ways to stimuli which tend to influence its behaviour. The animal may respond positively to the stimulating object by making appropriate adjustments, such as of attack or retreat, or manipulative movements; or it may react in a second way which has been surprisingly overlooked by most students of animal behaviour: it may cease all movements and remain quiescent even in the presence of violently disturbing factors. This phenomenon is strikingly demonstrated by a great variety of forms ranging from planarians to man' (Hoagland 1928). Hoagland did not suggest a term to designate this class of behaviour which he discussed in relationship to behaviours variously called by others 'animal hypnosis', 'cataplexy', 'playing possum', 'death feint', and 'tonic immobility', among other terms. Our interest in such behaviour was first stimulated by observing its abrupt occurrence in the infant, Monica, when confronted by a stranger (Engel & Reichsman 1956). Not aware of Hoagland's earlier statement, we first formulated the concept as follows: 'We suggest that there are two basic modes of response of living cells or organisms to changes in the dynamic steady state. The first is represented by irritability phenomena, the tendency of living organisms or cells to respond to internal or external changes by *activity*. This activity has as its objective the restoration of a dynamic steady state which is achieved through internal rearrangements or alterations in relation to the environment. We think of this as dependent on available energy... The second response, which comes about when energy sources are depleted, threatened with depletion, or for some reason unavailable, involves a reduction in activity, a husbanding of energy, and may include metabolic rearrangements or structural changes which insulate against the environment (e.g., encystment) or reduce metabolic requirements (e.g., hibernation). If this response fails, exhaustion or death may eventually ensue. These fundamental biologic patterns acquire mental representations and come to constitute basic ego mechanisms' (Engel & Reichsman 1956, p. 446). Originally we used the term 'depression–withdrawal'; subsequently 'conservation–withdrawal' was introduced to refer to the biological system involved and to avoid confusion with the more psychological term 'depression' (Engel 1962, 1965, 1970; Schmale 1972*a*,*b*).

Since this original observation on Monica the Rochester group has been much concerned with considering the relationship between conservation–withdrawal, as a biological frame of reference, and various psychological phenomena such as helplessness, hopelessness, giving up, and depression (Schmale 1964; Schmale & Engel 1967; Engel 1968). We have used a phylogenetic and an ontogenetic perspective which postulates that there are biological anlagen intrinsic to the development of the nervous system which antedate and influence subsequent psychological development. We have been particularly interested in how conservation–withdrawal, as such a basic biological anlage serving survival, may be reflected in the behaviour and psychological experience of man (Engel 1962).

MONICA: THE FIRST OBSERVATION

In 1953 while studying the gastric secretion of an infant with a gastric fistula between her 15th and 21st month, we were astonished to observe a most unusual but stereotyped behaviour (Engel & Reichsman 1956). On each occasion that a stranger came into her view, Monica ceased all movement and averted her gaze (Fig. 1). If several glances in the next half minute or so confirmed his continued presence her arms and legs slowly sank with gravity and remained thereafter entirely motionless. Over the next several minutes her eyes appeared no longer to be focused, so that at times she seemed to be staring past or through the stranger. Then the lids would begin to fall, perhaps fluttering open a few times in the next few minutes, and within 10–15 minutes she would have quietly drifted off to what appeared to be sleep. This occurred even though she may have only shortly before awakened from a long sleep. Such a sleep-like state could last from a few minutes to as long as two to three hours and was as deep as that which occurred spontaneously in the laboratory on other occasions, as evidenced by the fact that aspiration of gastric juice through the fistula, a procedure to which she was thoroughly accustomed, could proceed without overt reaction on her part. On the other hand, unexpected stimuli such as noises or jarring might transiently alert her, sometimes even evoking a little cry. Only during the later phase of such a period might some mouthing or sucking movements appear but even these were infrequent in comparison to their occurrence during spontaneous sleep. Should she wake and find the stranger still present she would immediately close her eyes and resume the sleep-like state. Only when she found him no longer there, or in his place a familiar person, would she once again begin actively to re-engage with the environment, usually with a cry of recognition and eager looking and reaching toward the friend.

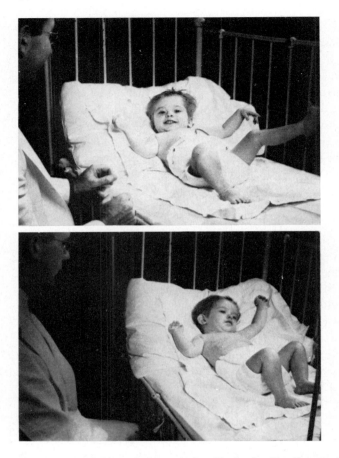

FIG. 1. *Top:* Monica relating actively with the familiar doctor. *Below:* In the presence of the stranger she lies motionless, her head and eyes averted, her limbs having fallen with gravity. (From Engel *et al.* 1956, with permission of the American Psychosomatic Society.)

During this withdrawal reaction gastric secretion ceased and became unresponsive to histamine stimulation while heart rate and respiration remained unchanged or slowed slightly (Engel *et al.* 1956).

Several factors no doubt contributed to the readiness with which this reaction was elicited in Monica. One was the pronounced limitation of mobility imposed by her physical underdevelopment, for at age 20 months, when the reaction was at its height, she was still unable to sit herself up, much less walk.

Also, from her sixth month onwards, her depressed mother repeatedly ignored Monica's crying and fed her through a fistula at her own convenience.

Ultimately, by the end of her first year, she had become a relatively withdrawn unresponsive baby. We postulate that Monica literally learned to bypass the active crying response when repeated experience revealed that it no longer brought relief. Rather than exhaust her already depleted resources, she instead fell back on the more economical conservation–withdrawal reaction, thereby conserving energy and reducing attention to the disturbing environmental input with which she no longer had any active means to cope. Cessation of gastric secretion may be seen as part of the physiological reorganization predicated on expectation of no nutritional input from the environment, just as the muscular hypotonia reflected no expectation of effective motor engagement with the environment. This bypassing of the more active reaction was evident not only in the general disposition toward lethargy, apathy and impoverishment of movement which generally characterized her upon admission, and which we referred to as a 'depression of infancy', but also in the distinctive response to the stranger which persisted long after recovery from this more global reaction. In brief, in this child the threshold for elicitation of conservation–withdrawal-type responses had been markedly lowered and the circumstances under which such responses occurred generalized to involve a variety of specific and nonspecific inputs.

Since Monica, we have had the opportunity to study other infants exhibiting such behaviour and to appreciate the extent to which in greater or lesser degrees it represents a ubiquitous response pattern in infancy (Spitz 1945; Peiper 1963).

PHYLOGENESIS OF CONSERVATION–WITHDRAWAL

Examples of inactivity in response to unfavourable environmental conditions abound in nature. Some of these reflect environmental periodicities, others the chance vicissitudes of the environment. The periodic patterns are in general correlation with the march of operating physical influences through the circadian cycles and the seasons. Throughout nature circadian rhythms are reflected in cycles of relative activity and inactivity, which reflect alternations between predominantly catabolic and anabolic phases. In the catabolic periods the organism expends energy, actively interacting with the environment to extract the elements essential for life. Alternating are anabolic periods in which there is relative detachment from the environment while the organism transforms the supplies previously taken in for repair, renewal and growth.

Variations in the conditions of the physical environment also influence activity. The amoeba, for example, responds to small changes in the surrounding medium by increasing or by changing the direction of its movements.

With an intense enough stimulus the amoeba contracts irregularly and ceases to move. If the acting agent is sufficiently powerful the organism may remain contracted until it dies; otherwise it usually soon resumes locomotion (Jennings 1906). A wide variety of patterns of dormancy, some, like hibernation, highly specialized, assure survival of organisms during periods of excessive heat, cold, moisture, dryness or other unfavourable environmental changes. What is common to all these reactions is inactivity and insulation against the environmental influence (Allee *et al.* 1949). Many organisms move away from exposed strata to a marginally safe environment, for example by making burrows in pond mud, where even homoiothermic animals may remain relatively quiet, except for periodic search for food until outside conditions once again improve. In lower organisms encystment would appear to be a general adjustment to any adverse condition, being brought about by low or high temperatures, lack of food, presence of an unfavourable concentration of waste products, or lack of oxygen (Allee *et al.* 1949, p. 38).

The same system is utilized in response to psychological and social changes as well. Examples abound in nature of immobility and lack of overt reactivity in a wide variety of situations directly or indirectly involving other organisms, such as threat or attack. Variously named ('animal hypnosis', 'sham death', 'tonic immobility'), this type of reaction has been noted across a host of species of vertebrates and invertebrates. As one ascends the phylogenetic scale the meaning of the provoking stimulus in terms of threat may become increasingly specific. Darwin was the first to ascribe survival advantage to this reaction by virtue of it rendering the organism less apparent or less interesting to predators (Darwin 1900, quoted by Ratner 1967). Thus many animals become quite immobile once the predator approaches within a certain distance and flight or fight are precluded (Ratner 1967). Specific physical characteristics of the near predator, such as the eye, may be a stimulus that evokes and prolongs the reaction (Gallup *et al.* 1971). Immobility once in the grasp of the predator may also have survival value if it invites a relaxation of the grip (Ratner & Thompson 1960).

The most effective means of inducing such an immobility reaction experimentally involve either restraint, particularly unfamiliar restraint, or sudden and intense or repetitive and monotonous stimulation (Ratner 1967). The reaction is marked not only by cessation of struggling and virtually total lack of movement but also by suppression or rapid habituation of the usual motor responses to such extremes of stimulation as electric shock, pin pricks, cutting, loud noises and bright lights. On the other hand, though not overtly reacting, the animal remains capable of detecting such stimuli, as evidenced by the autonomic responses that occur during such stimulation and by the fact that animals in such a state may nonetheless be aroused transiently in response to a novel stimulus even of very faint intensity (Ratner 1967). Wendt's immobilized monkey, for example, unresponsive to a variety of insults, nonetheless alerted in response to footsteps on the floor above (Wendt 1936).

Both in nature and in the laboratory animals have been conditioned or have learned to respond with an immobility reaction to a variety of stimuli. Merely the sight or touch of the restraining chair may elicit complete immobility in some monkeys (Foley 1938).

Most observations indicate that immobility-type reactions are most likely to develop when the animal has limited freedom of movement or can develop no effective responses to deal with the threat (Pavlov 1927; Overmier & Seligman 1967; Seligman & Maier 1967; Seligman 1968; Seligman & Maier 1968; Gellhorn 1967; Masserman & Pechtel 1953; Cook 1939; Gannt 1953; Liddell 1956). Thus monkeys exposed to a motivational conflict may sit for hours hunched and unresponsive, vocalizing infrequently. Some have been noted to become so indifferent to all stimuli that they could be scooped up unprotesting on the blade of a shovel (Masserman & Pechtel 1953).

Transient and prolonged immobility patterns also may occur when animals are separated from a companion or a group (Hediger 1955; Fiennes 1968; Yerkes & Yerkes 1929). The most pronounced responses are noted in some infant animals upon separation from the mother or in isolation (Harlow et al. 1971; Hinde & Spencer-Booth 1971; Kaufman & Rosenblum 1967). Fig. 2, taken from Kaufman & Rosenblum, demonstrates the response of a pigtail monkey infant a few days after its mother had been removed from the colony. The infant sits hunched up, almost rolled into a ball, with his head down between his legs, rarely moving except when actively displaced. Such movement as does take place often is extremely sluggish, social gestures or response to social invitation rarely occur, spontaneous play behaviour ceases, and the infant appears uninterested in and disengaged from the environment. The resemblance to behaviour displayed by Monica is striking.

Defeated animals may become inactive. Barnett, for example, describes defeated rats in confined colonies as displaying slow movements, drooping posture and bedraggled appearance (Barnett 1963). Indeed, the submissive posture of many animals, including invertebrates, includes suddenly becoming motionless, averting the gaze and lowering the head or trunk, and even lying supine (Darwin 1872; Lorenz 1952; Hinde 1970; Reese 1962; Grant & Mackintosh 1963; Ewing 1967; Barnett 1963).

In sum, a vast literature documents the widespread existence throughout nature of relative immobility, quiescence and reduced responsiveness as a fundamental modality for protection against a wide variety of dangers or

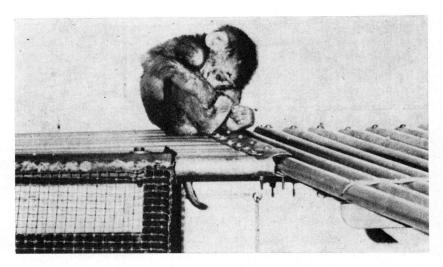

FIG. 2. An infant pigtail monkey two days after removal of its mother from the colony. (After Kaufman & Rosenblum 1967, with permission of the authors and of the American Psychosomatic Society.)

threats of danger from the physical or social environments. From the theoretical perspective we regard conservation–withdrawal as primarily serving an elemental survival function and specify as its identifying characteristics disengagement from active interaction with the environment, at both motor and perceptual levels, and husbanding of energy resources by reduction of activity and possibly metabolic rearrangements as well. This differentiates conservation–withdrawal type reactions from other patterns in which motor activity is suspended, as during periods of appraisal, concentration, scanning, listening, expectant waiting, silent vigilance, imminent flight or attack, or learned inhibition of motor activity (e.g. Bindra & Anchel 1963). Operational criteria remain to be delineated and some of the examples cited may well prove to have been improperly classified, but as extreme examples the behaviour of the monkeys described by Wendt (1936), Masserman & Pechtel (1953) and Kaufman & Rosenblum (1967) can be clearly differentiated from other immobility reactions commonly exhibited by monkeys, just as Monica's behaviour with a stranger was obviously very different from her motionless, silent watching of a child in the next crib or her quiet contemplative moods. On the other hand, as we shall discuss later (p. 70), we are less prepared to distinguish the quiet, reduced mobility associated with fatigue from conservation–withdrawal behaviour.

ONTOGENESIS OF CONSERVATION–WITHDRAWAL

The human infant clearly is equipped to respond with immobility and reduced awareness in circumstances of either understimulation or excessive stimulation. The crying fit is the prototype of the aroused, disturbed state and communicates to the environment that the infant is not capable within itself of alleviating or resolving its distress. Under ordinary circumstances crying ceases as the need, such as for food, sucking, or body contact, is met, whereupon the infant soon again quietens or lapses into sleep. But even when needs are not met crying does not necessarily go on indefinitely; the baby becomes quiet or returns to sleep long before exhaustion supervenes (Sullivan 1953; Engel & Reichsman 1956). Sometimes the crying fit can be abruptly ended and sleep-like quiet induced if the neonate is suddenly inverted or subjected to a quick falling motion, manoeuvres reminiscent of those used to provoke immobility reactions in animals (Peiper 1963, p. 506). Some neonates become lethargic and fall asleep during nursing if the nipple is withdrawn or becomes blocked (Ribble 1943; Fries & Woolf 1953). Infants in institutions, who are relatively understimulated compared to infants at home, are noted to be less active and to sleep excessively (Provence & Lipton 1962). With more pronounced social isolation and understimulation in institutions profound degrees of inactivity and withdrawal may be noted (Spitz 1945; Peiper 1963).

On the other hand intense stimulation, such as may occur with blood letting or minor surgical procedures without anaesthesia, such as circumcision, may induce sleep in neonates (Emde *et al.* 1971). Burton & Derbyshire (1958) described a one-year-old infant with secondary glaucoma who awoke, screamed in pain for over an hour and then abruptly fell into an unresponsive state from which he could not be aroused. When the eye was enucleated on the seventh day, without the need for anaesthesia, the child abruptly became normally alert and responsive.

CONSERVATION–WITHDRAWAL AND SLEEP

If conservation–withdrawal constitutes a homeostatic threshold mechanism to protect the organism against exhaustion, whether from inadequate supplies or overstimulation, it is difficult to escape the conclusion that sleep is part of the same mechanism. Certainly sleepiness and sleep are usual responses to such circumstances and the circadian cycles of activity and inactivity are, at least in higher animals, in fact cycles of wakefulness and sleep. Further, as we noted in Monica, the acute reaction commonly merges imperceptibly into sleep. Yet with Monica, it was also clear that whereas the inception of spontaneous sleep was always preceded by the usual panoply of presleep behaviour, such as yawning and stretching, no such behaviour was ever seen to precede her conservation–withdrawal sleep. This observation alone suggests that while conservation–withdrawal may be conducive to sleep, and may even share some of the neural systems mediating sleep, it would be premature simply to equate the two.

But even this is an oversimplification, for two different sleep states have now been identified, no rapid eye movement (NREM) or synchronized sleep and rapid eye movement (REM) or desynchronized sleep. Some have suggested that conservation–withdrawal is more related to NREM than REM sleep (Emde *et al.* 1971). In the adult NREM sleep appears to be responsive to the fatigue of the day-long vigil and activity, for it is concentrated in the first half of the night and increases after exercise and after sleep deprivation, particularly after deprivation of deep (NREM) sleep (Hobson 1968; Backland & Hartman 1970; Agnew *et al.* 1964; Webb & Agnew 1965). Also excessive sensory stimulation may even induce or increase NREM sleep in adults and in infants. Oswald experimentally induced NREM sleep among adult volunteers subjected to synchronized, rhythmic electric shocks, loud rhythmic music or strong flashing lights, even with the eyes glued open, while Emde demonstrated increased NREM sleep in neonates after the trauma of circumcision without anaesthesia (Oswald 1960; Emde *et al.* 1971).

It has also been suggested that homeostatic functions are served by an interplay between NREM and REM sleep, each fulfilling different restorative functions (Roffwarg *et al.* 1966; Dement 1969; Ephron & Carrington 1970; Snyder 1966; Zanchetti 1967; Mink *et al.* 1967; Freemon & Walter 1970; Hobson 1969*a,b*; Johnson & Sawyer 1971). In this view NREM sleep provides needed rest for bodily repair and growth and for those neural structures involved in slow or plastic activities, such as learning and memory, while REM sleep exerts a periodic restorative effect on cortical tonus in preparation for activation of the organism. Viewed from such a perspective the question of whether conservation–withdrawal is related more to NREM or REM sleep loses its cogency. Instead the NREM-REM cycles may be seen as constituting phylogenetically recent acquisitions linked together to serve the more complex homeostatic needs of the mammalian brain for both metabolic and tonic restoration alternately, while the resources of the body as a whole are being restored and husbanded. In this perspective conservation–withdrawal is seen as phylogenetically the older mechanism and as such initiates the processes required for reduction of overall energy expenditure and responsiveness to stimulation, including the NREM and REM sleep cycles in the higher animals with more complex nervous systems.

THE NEURAL ORGANIZATION SERVING CONSERVATION–WITHDRAWAL

The phylogenetic perspective which considers encystment, 'suspended animation' and various dormancy patterns of unicellular and lower organisms as primitive prototypes of conservation–withdrawal implies that these functions are taken over by and specialized within the nervous systems of the more complex organisms. These would include mechanisms for motor de-efferentation to reduce motor outflow and activity; for sensory de-afferentation to raise the threshold for ongoing input through sense receptors while maintaining receptivity to change in input; and for internal regulation in the face of reduction or interruption of sources of nutritional and sensory input for longer or shorter periods of time. Hess and Gellhorn developed the concept of the ergotropic and the trophotropic systems as reciprocal systems integrating dynamogenic and hypodynamic functions respectively (Hess 1957; Gellhorn 1967, 1970). Ergotropic effects are associated with arousal, wakefulness, increased muscle tone and activity, and environment-directed activity in general, while trophotropic effects are associated with the opposite. Indeed, Hess spoke of the trophotropic system as constituting a mechanism for 'protection against overstress'. Further, the nervous system provided the means whereby the organism can be forewarned of circumstances signifying danger of exhaustion. In this view conservation–withdrawal may be seen as involving an innate, or preformed, reaction pattern, the conditions for the activation of which may be subject to learning.

BEHAVIOURAL EXPRESSION AND EXPERIENCE OF CONSERVATION–WITHDRAWAL IN MAN

To summarize the thesis so far, we propose that conservation–withdrawal constitutes a phylogenetically ancient regulatory mechanism for maintaining homeostasis of the organism. How does conservation–withdrawal manifest itself as behaviour and experience in man? We suggest that behavioural expressions of varying degrees of conservation–withdrawal are commonplace and are responsible for familiar gestures, postures and facial expressions that may occur fleetingly in everyday life as well as in more sustained fashion in the course of mood changes and during illness, somatic as well as emotional. The underlying impetus for their elicitation is 'giving up', a conscious or unconscious psychic appraisal, if only fleetingly, of no solution, no response available.

The most evident outward manifestation of conservation–withdrawal in everyday life reflects a sudden or a sustained decrease in muscle tone, especially

FIG. 3. A woman coming for the first time upon the earthquake destruction that had literally eliminated all the familiar landmarks of her neighbourhood. Note how the jaw hangs slightly open, the hand supports the face, the shoulders are rounded and the hips and knees are flexed, all conveying the impression that she might slump to the ground were she to let herself go.

of anti-gravity muscles. The sagging face and slack jaw, often supported by the hand, the turned-down corners of the mouth, the rounding of the shoulders, the slumping forward, and the flexing of the knees are all typical motor responses of a person confronted with something for which at that moment he feels himself to have available no response or course of action, as may occur with an irretrievable loss, unacceptable news, an impossible dilemma, a profound disappointment; or in more general terms either a too intense input which

FIG. 4. The same earthquake scene. Note the common features of the stunned people, the jaw slack (or lips reactively pinched together), the hand to the face, supporting the chin. Some are holding on to or supporting each other; some hold themselves.

cannot be assimilated or a deficient input which indicates unavailability of supplies. Such a response can be fleeting or sustained, partial or massive. In its extreme form the person may literally sink to the ground in a heap while in its lesser expression the person may seek physical support, by leaning on or holding on to someone or to himself (Figs. 3 and 4).

Subjectively the typical bodily sensations accompanying such a reaction are weakness, fatigue and loss of energy. Everyday idiom vividly portrays this. 'The strength (energy) just drained out of me'. 'I didn't have an ounce of strength'. 'His jaw fell' (surprise). 'He sat slumped and dejected' (disappointment). 'It hit me like a ton of bricks'. 'I felt crushed'. Downcast, hangdog, down-in-the-mouth, dejected (literally, 'thrown down') and depressed (literally, 'pressed down') all convey the difficulty felt in maintaining the upright position and the accompanying awareness of the underlying motor inhibition.

From such examples of everyday occurrences can be generated a whole series of more pronounced or more prolonged behaviours of similar origin. These may reflect a continuation or a repetition of the central appraisal indicating 'no supplies or no solution available' or 'no action possible', an appraisal which may or may not in fact be in accord with reality. The net effect, however, may be manifest and felt as intermittent or sustained disinclination toward and reduction in muscular activity or exertion, diminished muscle tonus, slowing of movements, feelings of weakness and fatigue, constriction of attention to and interest in the environment and decline in active interpersonal relating behaviour. Ultimately sleepiness and increased sleeping or apathy and detachment may ensue. Such behaviours typically wax and wane, reflecting the waxing and waning of the conservation–withdrawal response with the periodic judgments of 'no solution' alternating either with renewed attempts to cope actively or with changes in environmental circumstances. The extreme of the unremitting pattern occurs under conditions of the most profound deprivation and constraint, as may occur among inmates in concentration or prisoner of war camps (Strassman *et al.* 1956). Equally profound but more transient reactions may be observed in response to disasters (Baker & Chapman 1962).

But conservation–withdrawal may also be activated in response to bodily processes, that is, to endogenous rhythms or enteroceptive inputs indicating the need for somatic conservation. We have already referred to the cycles of tiredness and sleepiness that recur regularly in a circadian rhythm, the built-in mechanism to assure renewal long before significant depletion of energy sources has occurred. Less appreciated, however, is the extent and frequency with which conservation–withdrawal may be activated by bodily processes associated with physical disease. Indeed, we suggest that the common so-called constitutional symptoms that regularly usher in or accompany many physical illnesses—that is, weakness, tiredness and fatigue, the urge to sit down, lie down or rest—are in fact of neurogenic origin. They are an expression of conservation–withdrawal invoked to protect the body and its components from uneconomical expenditure of resources in the face of real or threatened impairment of supplies consequent to the pathological processes, whatever they may be. Starvation is of course the prototypical situation calling for husbanding of energy; the appearance of the child victim of famine in Fig. 5 is remarkably similar to what we observed in Monica and other children and Kaufman and Rosenblum reported in the pigtail monkey (see Fig. 2).

As a central regulatory system responsive to both exteroceptive and enteroceptive inputs we also postulate signal or warning functions that forewarn the individual of a possible need to withdraw and conserve energy or that avert such a need by mobilizing available or present resources, coping devices, or defences. Many clinical data support such a formulation. One of the best documented is the longterm (now 20 year) follow-up of Monica, who in an impressively consistent fashion still displays a low threshold of response to

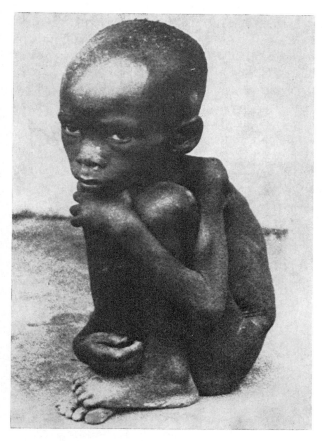

FIG. 5. A child victim of starvation.

situations reminiscent of those originally evocative of the conservation–withdrawal reaction. But now this response is minimized or averted by her ability quickly to mobilize behaviours that serve both to elicit help from the environment and to assure her that help is indeed always at hand. To a large extent many of these behaviours by now reflect character traits (Engel 1967, 1969).

CONSERVATION–WITHDRAWAL, GIVING UP AND DEPRESSION

Loose usage of the word 'depression' has contributed considerable confusion to which we have added our share. Clearly much of the difficulty in our own writings and in the literature may be ascribed to having confused frames of reference. Conservation–withdrawal, by definition, must be conceptualized in a biological frame of reference (Schmale 1972*a*). The term can be used to refer to the threshold mechanism *per se* or it can refer to the bodily, that is physiological and biochemical, processes associated with it, including manifest appearance and behaviour. We have already discussed the circumstances conducive to the induction of conservation–withdrawal and have pointed out that these may include psychological as well as physical events. But once we begin to consider the inner experience of the person in whom the conservation–withdrawal mechanism has been activated we are introducing another frame of reference, the psychological. We can deduce, but cannot document, the core subjective experience of conservation–withdrawal to include feelings of decreased strength, energy and interest in the outside world, that is, essentially, awareness of these body changes. When the conservation–withdrawal response has been triggered enteroceptively, as in the course of a physical illness or some pathophysiological process, some individuals may experience only these symptoms as the typical so-called constitutional symptoms accompanying illness.

On the other hand when the conservation–withdrawal response is triggered by a psychological or social event, including awareness of somatic disease, then the pathway involves first a psychological appraisal of 'giving up', with its concomitant affects of helplessness or hopelessness, which may then be followed or accompanied by conservation–withdrawal as the somatic response (Schmale 1972*a*). 'Giving up', a psychological response, may contribute feelings of 'depression' in the sense of 'blue', 'down in the dumps', 'discouraged', in addition to the conservation–withdrawal manifestations of fatigue, weakness, lack of energy and interest. Thus we differentiate between the subjective and manifest aspects of conservation–withdrawal on the one hand and the psychologically more elaborated expressions of 'giving up' on the other.

But we would also differentiate these non-specific 'depressive' manifestations of 'giving up' from the clinical syndromes of depression. These we consider to be psychologically more complex disorders of adaptation, some of which may involve distinctive neurobiological abnormalities as well (Schmale 1972*a,b*). Both conservation–withdrawal and 'giving up' manifestations may appear when the clinical syndromes of depression become ineffective as patterns of psychological adaptation, which may account for some of the confusion in differentiating these various depressive patterns. How and whether the neurochemical processes alleged to be involved in the syndromes of depression, particularly bipolar depression, are related to the conservation–withdrawal system remains to be seen, especially if individual vulnerability to depression proves to have a biochemical determinant. But until more is known in those areas it would seem prudent to consider that the so-called animal models of depression evoked by various types of social isolation are in fact models of conservation–withdrawal and thus are not strictly comparable to human depression (Senay 1966; McKinney *et al.* 1971).

ACKNOWLEDGEMENTS

This study was supported by U.S. Public Health Service Grants, MH 14151, MH 11668, MH 07228 and MH 7521. Dr Engel is a Career Research Awardee of the Public Health Service.

References

AGNEW, H. W., WILSE, M. A., WEBB, B. *et al.* (1964) The effects of stage four sleep deprivation. *Electroencephalogr. Clin. Neurophysiol.* **17**, 68-70

ALLEE, W. C., EMERSON, A. E., PARK, O., PARK, T. & SCHMIDT, K. P. (1949) *Principles of Animal Ecology*, Saunders, Philadelphia and London

BACKLAND, F. & HARTMAN, E. (1970) Sleep requirements and the characteristics of some sleepers. In *Sleep and Dreaming* (Hartman, E., ed.), pp. 33-43, Little, Brown, Boston

BAKER, G. W. & CHAPMAN, D. W. (eds.) (1962) *Man and Society in Disaster*, Basic Books, New York

BARNETT, S. A. (1963) *The Rat: A Study in Behavior*, Aldine, Chicago

BINDRA, D. & ANCHEL, H. (1963) Immobility as an avoidance response, and its disruption by drugs. *J. Exp. Anal. Behav.* **6** (2), 213-218

BURTON, I. & DERBYSHIRE, A. J. (1958) 'Sleeping fit' caused by excruciating pain in an infant. *A.M.A. J. Dis. Child.* **95**, 258-260

COOK, S. W. (1939) The production of 'experimental neurosis' in the white rat. *Psychosom. Med.* **1** (2), 293-308

DARWIN, C. (1872) *The Expression of the Emotions in Man and Animals*, Appleton, New York

DARWIN, C. (1900) A posthumous essay on instinct. In *Mental Evolution in Mammals* (Romanes, G. J., ed.), pp. 360-364, Appleton, New York

DEMENT, W. C. (1969) The biological role of REM sleep. In *Sleep: Physiology and Pathology* (Kales, A., ed.), pp. 245-265, Little, Brown, Boston

EMDE, R. N., HARMON, R. J., METCALF, D. *et al.* (1971) Stress and neonatal sleep. *Psychosom. Med.* **33** (6), 491-497

ENGEL, G. L. (1962) *Psychological Development in Health and Disease*, Saunders, Philadelphia

ENGEL, G. L. (1965) Clinical observation. The neglected basic method of medicine. *J. Am. Med. Assoc.* **192**, 849-852

ENGEL, G. L. (1967) Ego development following severe trauma in infancy: A 14 year study of a girl with gastric fistula and depression in infancy. *Bull. Assoc. Psychoanal. Med.* **6**, 57-61

ENGEL, G. L. (1968) A life setting conducive to illness. The giving up-given up complex. *Ann. Intern. Med.* **69**, 293-300

ENGEL, G. L. (1969) Ego development following severe trauma in infancy. *Bull. Phila. Assoc. Psychoanal.* **19**, 234-236

ENGEL, G. L. (1970) Nervousness and fatigue. In *Signs and Symptoms* (MacBryde, C. M. & Blacklow, R. S., eds.), pp. 632-649, Lippincott, Philadelphia

ENGEL, G. L. & REICHSMAN, F. (1956) Spontaneous and experimentally induced depressions in an infant with a gastric fistula. *J. Am. Psychoanal. Assoc.* **4**, 428-452

ENGEL, G. L., REICHSMAN, F. & SEGAL, H. L. (1956) A study of an infant with a gastric fistula. I. Behavior and the rate of total hydrochloric acid secretion. *Psychosom. Med.* **18**, 374-398

EPHRON, H. S. & CARRINGTON, P. (1970) On the functions of the sleep phases. In *Sleep and Dreaming* (Hartman, E., ed.), pp. 269-276, Little, Brown, Boston

EWING, L. S. (1967) Fighting and death from stress in a cockroach. *Science (Wash. D.C.)* **155**, 1035-1036

FIENNES, T. W. (1968) Ecological concepts of stress in relation to medical conditions in captive wild animals. *Proc. R. Soc. Med.* **61**, 161-162

FOLEY, J. P. (1938) Tonic immobility in the rhesus monkey *(Macaca mulatta)* induced by manipulation, immobilization, and experimental inversion of the visual field. *J. Comp. Physiol. Psychol.* **26**, 515-526

FREEMON, F. R. & WALTER, R. D. (1970) Electrical activity of human limbic system during sleep. *Compr. Psychiatr.* **11** (6), 544-551

FRIES, M. E. & WOOLF, P. J. (1953) Some hypotheses on the role of the congenital activity type in personality development. *Psychoanal. Study Child* **8**, 48-62

GALLUP, G. G., NASH, R. F. & ELLISON, A. L. (1971) Tonic immobility as a reaction to predation: Artificial eyes as a fear stimulus for chickens. *Psychon. Sci.* **23** (1B), 79-80

GANNT, W. H. (1953) Principles of nervous breakdown—schizokinesis and autokinesis. *Ann. N.Y. Acad. Sci.* **56**, 143-164

GELLHORN, E. (1967) *Principles of Autonomic-Somatic Integrations*, University of Minnesota Press, Minneapolis

GELLHORN, E. (1970) The emotions and the ergotropic and trophotropic systems. *Psychol. Forsch.* **34**, 48-94

GRANT, E. C. & MACKINTOSH, J. H. (1963) A comparison of the social postures of some common laboratory rodents. *Behaviour* **21**, 256-259

HARLOW, H. F., HARLOW, M. K. & SUOMI, S. J. (1971) From thought to therapy. Lessons from a primate laboratory. *Am. Sci.* **59** (5), 538-549

HEDIGER, H. (1955) *Studies of the Psychology and Behavior of Captive Animals in Zoos and Circuses*, Criterion Books, New York

HESS, W. R. (1957) *The Functional Organization of the Diencephalon*, Grune & Stratton, New York

HINDE, R. A. (1970) *Animal Behavior*, 2nd edn, McGraw-Hill, New York

HINDE, R. A. & SPENCER-BOOTH, Y. (1971) Effects of brief separation from mother on rhesus monkeys. *Science (Wash. D.C.)* **173**, 111-118

HOAGLAND, H. (1928) The mechanism of tonic immobility ('animal hypnosis'). *J. Gen. Psychol.* **1**, 426-447

HOBSON, J. A. (1968) Sleep after exercise. *Science (Wash. D.C.)* **162**, 1503-1505

HOBSON, J. A. (1969a) Sleep: physiologic aspects. *N. Engl. J. Med.* **281**, 1343-1345

HOBSON, J. A. (1969b) Sleep: biochemical aspects. *N. Engl. J. Med.* **281**, 1468-1470

JENNINGS, H. S. (1906) *Behavior of the Lower Organisms*, Macmillan, New York

JOHNSON, J. H. & SAWYER, C. H. (1971) Adrenal steroids and the maintenance of a circadian distribution of paradoxical sleep in rats. *Endocrinology* **89** (2), 507-512

KAUFMAN, I. C. & ROSENBLUM, L. A. (1967) The reaction to separation in infant monkeys: anaclitic depression and conservation-withdrawal. *Psychosom. Med.* **29**, 648-675

LIDDELL, H. S. (1956) *Emotional Hazards in Animals and Man*, Thomas, Springfield, Ill.

LORENZ, K. (1952) *King Solomon's Ring*, Thomas Cromwell, New York

MASSERMAN, J. H. & PECHTEL, C. (1953) Neurosis in monkeys: A preliminary report of experimental observations. *Ann. N.Y. Acad. Sci.* **56**, 253-265

MCKINNEY, W. T., SUOMI, S. J. & HARLOW, H. F. (1971) Depression in primates. *Am. J. Psychiatr.* **127** (10), 49-56

MINK, W. D., BEST, P. J. & OLDS, J. (1967) Neurons in paradoxical sleep and motivated behavior. *Science (Wash. D.C.)* **158**, 1335-1337

OSWALD, I. (1960) Falling asleep open-eyed during intense rhythmic stimulation. *Br. Med. J.* **1**, 1450-1455

OVERMIER, J. B. & SELIGMAN, M. E. P. (1967) Effects of inescapable shock upon subsequent escape and avoidance responding. *J. Comp. Physiol. Psychol.* **63** (1), 28-33

PAVLOV, I. P. (1927) *Conditioned Reflexes* (Anrep, G.V., trans.), Oxford University Press, London

PEIPER, A. (1963) *Cerebral Function in Infancy and Childhood*, Consultants Bureau, New York

PROVENCE, S. & LIPTON, R. C. (1962) *Infants in Institutions*, International Universities Press New York

RATNER, S. C. (1967) Comparative aspects of hypnosis. In *Handbook of Clinical and Experimental Hypnosis* (Gordon, J. E., ed.), pp. 550-587, Macmillan, New York

RATNER, S. C. & THOMPSON, R. W. (1960) Immobility reactions (fear) of domestic fowl as a function of age and prior experience. *Anim. Behav.* **8**, 186-191

REESE, E. S. (1962) Submissive posture as an adaptation to aggressive behavior in hermit crabs. *A. Tierpsychol.* **19**, 645-651

RIBBLE, M. A. (1943) *The Rights of Infants*, Columbia University Press, New York

ROFFWARG, H. P., MUZIO, J. N. & DEMENT, W. C. (1966) Ontogenetic development of the human sleep-dream cycle. *Science (Wash. D.C.)* **152**, 604-619

SCHMALE, A. H. (1964) A genetic view of affects with special reference to the genesis of helplessness and hopelessness. *Psychoanal. Study Child* **19**, 287-310

SCHMALE, A. H. (1972a) The adaptive role of depression in health and disease. *Am. Assoc. Adv. Sci. Publ.* (Senay, E., ed.), in press

SCHMALE, A. H. (1972b) Depression as affect, character style and symptom formation. In *Psychoanalysis and Contemporary Science*, vol. 1 (Holt, R., ed.), Macmillan, New York

SCHMALE, A. H. & ENGEL, G. L. (1967) The giving up-given up complex illustrated on film. *Arch. Gen. Psychiatr.* **17**, 135-145

SELIGMAN, M. E. P. (1968) Chronic fear produced by unpredictable electric shock. *J. Comp. Physiol. Psychol.* **66** (2), 402-411

SELIGMAN, M. E. P. & MAIER, S. F. (1967) Failure to escape traumatic shock. *J. Exp. Psychol.* **74** (1), 1-9

SELIGMAN, M. E. P. & MAIER, S. F. (1968) Alleviation of learned helplessness in the dog. *J. Abnorm. Psychol.* **73** (3), 256-262

SENAY, E. C. (1966) Toward an animal model of depression: a study of separation behavior in dogs. *J. Psychiatr. Res.* **4**, 65-71

SNYDER, F. (1966) Toward an evolutionary theory of dreaming. *Am. J. Psychiatr.* **123** (2), 121-142

SPITZ, R. (1945) Hospitalism. An inquiry into psychiatric conditions in early childhood. *Psychoanal. Study Child* **1**, 53-80

STRASSMAN, H. D., THALER, M. B. & SCHEIN, E. H. (1956) *Am. J. Psychiatr.* **112**, 998-1003

SULLIVAN, H. S. (1953) *The Interpersonal Theory of Psychiatry*, Norton, New York

WEBB, W. B. & AGNEW, H. W. (1965) Sleep: Effects of a restricted sleep regime. *Science (Wash. D.C.)* **150**, 1745-1746

WENDT, G. R. (1936) An interpretation of inhibition of conditioned reflexes as competition between reaction systems. *Psychol. Rev.* **43**, 258-281

YERKES, R. M. & YERKES, A. W. (1929) *The Great Apes: a study of anthropoid life*, Yale University Press, New Haven

ZANCHETTI, A. (1967) Brain stem mechanisms of sleep. *Anesthesiology* **28** (1), 81-99

Discussion

Levine: I understand the withdrawal part of the hypothesis but I don't understand the conservation part, because I don't know what is being conserved.

Engel: Conservation of energy can be achieved simply by reducing energy expenditure—that is, ceasing to be active when it serves no purpose. For example, Monica conserved energy when she stopped crying and fussing and remained quiet. The curled-up position sometimes assumed, both by animals and by people, suggests that it may also serve to conserve heat. In more long-term responses we might also expect to find evidence of metabolic rearrangements to allow the organism to use its own energy stores instead of requiring food from outside, especially when the reaction must be prolonged. The total cessation of gastric secretion, as observed in Monica, might reflect such a turning-off of the alimentary system, both to conserve energy and because ingestion is not going to be used for nutrition. Survival during encystment must call for profound reduction in energy utilization. Adolph (1971) has shown that newborn rats survive total oxygen lack by shifting to an anaerobic glycolytic mechanism to provide energy, including that needed for breathing. Regular breathing ceases but is replaced by periodic gasping at prolonged intervals, an effective device to save the energy that would have been expended fruitlessly by breathing in an anoxic environment while at the same time making it possible, by the gasp, to test whether oxygen has been restored to the atmosphere. Pretreatment with hypoxia greatly increases this anaerobic adaptation. To me, this demonstrates another aspect of the general capability of the organism to maintain homeostasis in the face of unavailability of supplies.

Levine: Monica is not a good example of conservation–withdrawal, because she has been *conditioned* not to cry; but you are postulating a phylogenetic mechanism which occurs in all animals and is innate and biological. There is an inconsistency here. If you place a rat in an open field and the rat freezes, do you consider this to be conservation–withdrawal? Its muscle tone does not suggest that it is relaxed; it may be extremely tense.

Engel: You are ignoring the other details of Monica's behaviour in dismissing it as due simply to her having been conditioned not to cry. That was only the first step, to learn that crying no longer brought a response from her mother, but it began when she was six months old and utterly helpless to tend to her own needs. What options did she have when she became hungry? She could have cried indefinitely, up to the point of literal exhaustion. But she did not. That is the whole point of the concept of conservation–withdrawal, that a regulatory mechanism exists to take care of such an eventuality. She not only stopped crying, she became inactive and fell back to sleep even though not fed. Where does conditioning come in? I would regard conservation–withdrawal as an unconditioned response to certain environmental situations significant of either excessive or deficient input with which the organism, for whatever reason, cannot cope. In Monica the circumstances in which the reaction could be provoked became generalized to many conditions (e.g. the stranger) which in most infants do not elicit such a response, mainly because they have success-fully used other responses. For Monica, exposure to a stranger represented but another input for which she had learned no more satisfactory response, and she had to fall back on the global emergency conservation–withdrawal response.

The rat freezing in an open field is not showing conservation–withdrawal. When we first observed the withdrawal reaction in Monica we wondered whether she was frozen with fear. Our main evidence against that was that muscle tone was markedly reduced, while heart rate and respiration were un-changed or slowed. Nor do I see conservation–withdrawal as the same as the 'stop' reaction described by Dr Gray (see pp. 95-116). On the other hand, the 'stop' reaction might be an initiating point, neurophysiologically speaking, for the conservation–withdrawal response. The animal can move in either direction: it may again become active in the sense of approach or flight–fight, or it may become inactive in the sense of conservation–withdrawal.

Levine: L. Rosenblum (personal communication) has shown that the isolated infant pigtail monkey, like the rhesus monkey, shows this withdrawal response but the bonnet monkey or squirrel monkey does not. How would your theory account for those so-called biological differences?

Engel: I see no contradiction here. As Kaufman and Rosenblum have pointed out, when the bonnet mother is removed from the group other adults provide mothering, which is not the case with the pigtail. Hence for the bonnet infant, removing the mother is not a sufficient or appropriate input for the conservation–withdrawal response. I assume there are species and genetic differences among animals in their propensity to develop this reaction, just as there are species and genetic differences in the tendency to show, say, flight or fight responses. Conservation–withdrawal is, so to speak, a second line of defence and therefore I would not expect it to be exhibited except under extreme or specialized conditions, unless generalized by learning as in Monica's case.

Storey: I have seen illustrations of immobile chickens and lizards; they were exposing their bellies and certainly not conserving energy. Nor was Monica conserving heat; her position was the opposite of curling up. And a chicken, paralysed by a hawk, appears from its very abnormal position to have high muscle tone.

Hinde: I don't doubt that conservation–withdrawal has a certain unity as a syndrome, and it must have some biological basis; but it seems unbiological to draw a similar symptom from animals as diverse as the amoeba and the human child and say that it is in some sense the same. You have classed together 'dormancy', in which there is a total shutting off of responsiveness to all stimuli, immobility in fear, in which the animal is highly responsive but immobile, and tonic immobility and sham death, where responsiveness is highly specific. These are diverse phenomena that happen to have the common symptom of immobility and to put them in the same basket is misleading. The evidence that conservation–withdrawal has a biological basis could be of a different type. It is conceivable that sound evidence could be found, and I am not quarrelling with your conclusion, but to use such heterogeneous examples as evidence weakens your case.

Gray: There might be a mechanism common to most *mammalian* species, say.

Denenberg: What evidence is there even for that? We are already speculating about a common mechanism but no one has described any mechanism at all. No one has mentioned a learning mechanism, which is a possibility. Dr Engel has taken a rather superficial behavioural observation—lack of movement—and used that to draw a very broad conclusion. I see no logical basis for this.

Weiss: I agree that with a symptom as general as immobility one can't really frame a hypothesis clearly until one can suggest a specific mechanism or some more specific definition of the concept. The basic symptom of immobility does not carry enough descriptive impact to carve out a distinct and testable hypothesis. In this particular case, it seems that one must specify some correlate, possibly below the level of skeletal-motor behaviour, before one can see how, for instance, the immobile reaction of a white rat when it's afraid is different from an animal which is playing dead, which again differs from an isolated pigtail monkey which looks depressed.

Engel: Immobility is a consistent feature of the behaviour of conservation–withdrawal but it is by no means the only feature. Nor am I suggesting that all varieties of immobility are the same and that they all represent conservation–withdrawal. But one should not expect the behavioural expression of conservation–withdrawal to be identical in all species, any more than one expects flight–fight patterns to be the same in different species. Species-specific differentiations of flight patterns are noted in animals according to whether they fly, run, dive or swim. What is common to all my examples is that the immobility and inactivity occur in response to major changes or threats of changes in environmental conditions and that the reaction can be seen as serving survival for the species. That the chicken or lizard appears rigid rather than limp is not to me sufficient grounds not to consider this pattern of behaviour to be a species-specific derivative of the basic conservation–withdrawal reaction.

Nor do I follow the argument that one cannot have an hypothesis without being first able to define the mechanism. And why must it be a 'learning mechanism'? I suggest that you can't know what mechanism to look at (or for) until you have a hypothesis. The hypothesis here is that conservation–withdrawal is a primary regulatory mechanism that is activated in certain circumstances. (From this one can begin to design studies of where learning and conditioning come into play.) When the organism has no active solution, it may go through a series of steps: one may be the 'stop' reaction; one may be watching and waiting, so to speak, to see what is going to happen; and the final one, if no active coping solution is possible, is conservation–withdrawal.

In looking back over phylogeny I was trying to tie in the global concept that virtually all animals go through cycles of activity and inactivity. These can be related respectively to periods in which the animal is actively engaging in and with the environment to extract something from it, and periods when the animal is less actively engaged with or even disengaged from the environment and its functioning more reflects internal processes. I am suggesting from this that in higher organisms an organization in the nervous system may have evolved to monitor these cycles of activity and inactivity and that this same CNS organization is also used in stress situations, the inactivity, disengagement and conservation of energy now being in the service of survival. The child that I discussed shows an example of a learning situation; she became conditioned to respond in this fashion to a variety of situations. Conditioning experiments in which the animal freezes may be a borderline area. Masserman & Pechtel (1953) described their monkeys in a situation of impossible conflict as ending up completely immobile and limp. I am suggesting that this is a basic response (conservation–withdrawal) which is different from both avoidance and fight and flight responses, and I carried this further to say that this has expression in man.

I think some of you are missing the point in that you are discussing conservation–withdrawal as though it were meant to refer only to a behaviour, whereas we are proposing it as a basic biological threshold mechanism meant to serve survival of the organism by disengagement and inactivity *vis à vis* the external environment. As such, manifest behaviour is but one expression, and one would expect species-typical variations and differentiations of such behaviour.

Henry: In a colony of mice that are free to interact, so that the behaviour is relatively normal but the mice cannot escape from a complex system, the subordinate mouse shows submissive behaviour. If a mouse or rat or tree shrew is introduced as an intruder into the situation, as Barnett (1963) and more recently von Holst (1972) have shown, the immobility becomes still more marked. There is no question from our experiments that the subordinate mouse shows much less activity than the dominant mouse. He remains isolated in one place and does not move around. One could say that he is conserving energy in the sense of biding his time, should an opportunity to escape arise.

Hinde: I concede that there may be an adaptive advantage in immobility in the presence of a stranger, because we know that movement in the presence of a predator or rival elicits attack. So I accept that the immobile child is showing an adaptive response. For the 'depressed' monkey, there may be some adaptive advantage in immobility. Superimposed on that are the thumb-sucking, self-hugging and hunched posture, which are possibly interpretable in terms of comfort through contact. The movements of the people in the earth-quake that Dr Engel illustrated again show some elements of a submissive gesture and it may be that there are *ontogenetic* relationships between such a gesture and the depressed postures in childhood. But that is a different sort of relationship from a phylogenetic one.

Levine: There is a basic problem about the meaning to be attached to a given response. If a rat is placed in an open field and is left there for an hour instead of the usual three minutes, it will first show severe immobility— that is, 'freezing'. It next shows a lot of exploratory behaviour. Eventually it stops exploring and simply lies quiet and immobile. Or consider a male rat which is permitted to show free copulatory behaviour; in between copu-lations, it will be immobile. Do we interpret immobility in the same way in each situation?

Engel: No. In conservation–withdrawal, immobility is combined with reduced muscle tone (at least in man), relative unresponsiveness and reduced, or restricted or specific, attention to the environment. In such circumstances it is logical to expect that components of submissive and self-comforting postures would derive from the same phylogenetic–ontogenetic roots as conservation–withdrawal. Hence I find Professor Hinde's comment to be in concord, not in opposition.

Levine: The criteria you mention exactly describe the post-copulatory rat, yet if you introduce a fresh female the rat will copulate immediately, so the im-mobility can't be explained as having the function of 'conserving sexual energy'.

Engel: Monica also responded immediately when a familiar person came in. Expenditure of energy and attention to the environment were in abeyance but she was quite capable of instantly mobilizing activity once the disturbing environmental situation passed. In fact, that capacity to switch from one pattern to another is precisely what led us to invoke the concept of a CNS mechanism which can be turned on or off as the occasion demands.

Zanchetti: I agree with Professor Engel that the conservation–withdrawal reaction shows more differences from than similarities to the 'stop' or passive avoidance behaviour that Dr Gray describes. The latter type of behaviour is exemplified by the reaction of an animal to an unconditioned aversive stimulus: the animal stops moving, but there is tension. The animal is ready to respond to the aversive conditioned stimulus which may follow. There are signs of sympathetic discharge. The withdrawal that Professor Engel described is more like the 'playing dead' behaviour of some mammals, such as the opossum and hedgehog, in dangerous situations. Indirect evidence from physiological experiments on cats by Folkow's group suggests that 'playing dead' behaviour may be connected with neural systems starting in the cingulate gyrus and relaying in the anterior hypothalamus. If those two regions are stimulated in the cat diffuse sympathetic inhibition occurs, affecting the heart rate and all vascular beds (Folkow *et al.* 1959; Löfving 1961). This system relays with the paramedial nucleus in the medulla, where afferent axons from the baro-receptors also enter the brain, so one system is potentiating the other (Löfving 1961; Hilton & Spyer 1968; R. Albertini & A. Zanchetti, unpublished findings). Unfortunately the opossum does not easily display the 'playing dead' reaction in the laboratory (B. Folkow, personal communication) so we can't yet study its cardiovascular manifestations directly.

Hofer: This discussion reflects the difference between the 'lumpers' and the 'splitters', and we all have our own bias! What worries me about Dr Engel's 'lumping' approach is the inclusion of reactions like sham death and tonic immobility of certain animals in the same conceptual category as the behaviour of Monica and of Dr Kaufman's monkeys. In tonic immobility in wild ground squirrels or chipmunks, although the heart rate is low, which might be said to be evidence of 'conservation', the respiratory rate is very high (Hofer 1970). These states, and more particularly sham death, are often terminated by sudden explosion into the most vigorous activity that I have seen in rodents. Often this occurs without stimulation from the environment: the latency of onset of the explosion into activity is random. One might even turn the concept round and see tonic immobility as a preparation for extraordinary activity rather than as the conservation of energy. I would guess that metabolic measures in such animals would be high rather than low; the animals may be gearing up rather than gearing down.

Tonic immobility, as seen in frogs and chickens, may have a lot to do with the vestibular apparatus and brainstem mechanisms which have very little to do with the social environment. Hoagland (1928) did some experiments in which a man was bent over very far forward and then flipped rapidly back. He adopts a position something like that of the chicken showing tonic immobility, and this probably occurs through a brainstem rather than a cortical process. Decortication in rats brings this response out; it is not seen in the intact adult rat, although it is present in young rats (McGraw & Klemm 1969). I would like to separate out these kinds of responses from Dr Engel's general concept.

Aitken: The difference between species has been emphasized. I declare myself to be a 'splitter', and it seems to me that differences in response between individuals often far exceed similarities. We know from observations of natural disasters the difficulties in finding a common theme. The diversities of emotional and behavioural responses are striking. For men under occupational stress, such as aircrew, an enormous diversity of response has been my experience (Aitken 1969, 1972). So too much should not be concluded from observations made on one child, as reported by Professor Engel.

Lader: Professor Hinde mentioned the possible adaptive value of the conservation–withdrawal reaction and Professor Engel regards it as an emergency adaptive mechanism. As an example, he showed illustrations of the behaviour and expressions of earthquake victims. But it can be argued that this ('giving up') response after an earthquake is *mal*adaptive: if outside relief measures do not reach an earthquake area within a few days, more people die of exposure and untreated wounds than die in the earthquake itself.

Sandler: I see the conservation–withdrawal reaction as a psychobiological response; that is, it is basically a biological response, but it can also occur as a response to psychological input. Professor Engel's human examples are mainly responses to an *evaluation* (through perception) of a particular painful situation —a strange doctor, a catastrophe; or a disaster with a lack of familiar landmarks. We see here a basic reaction to a psychological state characterized by a painful lack of safety through lack of familiarity, or by pain from some other source. The threshold for this reaction may be altered by fatigue or by the particular phase of some biological rhythm, but it is surely primarily a response to a psychological state, assessed by the mental apparatus. There appear to be different dimensions to the conservation–withdrawal response, but what is essentially being conserved is a feeling of safety through perceptual constancy.

Professor Engel clearly differentiated conservation–withdrawal from the clinical picture of depression. We should certainly not lump together all the descriptive pictures, although they may appear the same in different situations. This would be like putting together two quite different clinical syndromes, catatonic immobility and depressive retardation. Yet we know from clinical studies of people who have recovered from catatonia that part of the function of the response—the 'freezing'—was to maintain a perceptual constancy; they felt that any movement would lead to feelings of unsafety. I suggest that to Professor Engel's description of the psychological, subjective experience which goes with this picture, one should add the psychological situation to which this response *is* a response, namely the particular threat to the person's safety feelings—his feelings of unfamiliarity— and the resulting pain, coupled with a feeling of helplessness at not knowing what to do. This gives us a bridge to the clinical situation of depression. I see the depressive response as a basic psychobiological reaction to a situation of pain of one sort or another. We see it in physical disorders, where there is pain of somatic origin; and in malnutrition, where there is a general feeling of lack of pleasure. The picture of the malnourished child is exactly like Professor Engel's picture of Monica showing conservation–withdrawal.

Grinker: Our studies of the response of obese patients to weight reduction show that only certain patients, those with obesity of juvenile onset, show what might be called 'conservation' (see pp. 349-369). With weight reduction these patients show symptoms of depression, distortions in time perception indicative of a slowing of internal body rhythm, and fatigue—responses which are similar to those occurring in individuals of normal weight undergoing experimental starvation. Would that fit into your picture of conservation–withdrawal, Dr Engel? Using this analogy, we could say that these patients are defending their obese weight.

Engel: I would need more data to be sure, but certainly what you describe is consistent with conservation–withdrawal. If obesity is an equilibrium state metabolically and psychologically for the juvenile-onset obese person, enforced food restriction might initiate conservation–withdrawal as an adaptation to threat of starvation at a much lower threshold in this individual than in the non-obese person. As we pointed out (p. 70), starvation is a paradigm of a situation calling for conservation–withdrawal.

Sachar: I should like to take up the 'withdrawal' part of the syndrome and point out the complicated system that has been observed in man, from newborns to adults, for tuning in and tuning out stimuli, almost rhythmically. Anecdotally, we all find ourselves at times feeling that we have reached a saturation point, wanting to withdraw, to shut out, to cease to attend; needing to be off by ourselves. Daniel Stern (unpublished observations 1972) has studied the way the newborn child distributes his attention, from long gazes to short gazes, looking toward, looking away, and carefully and exquisitely regulating the amount of stimulation that he takes in through the visual system. If you are calling attention to a natural rhythm of life and saying that in certain situations this may be used massively and may involve other physiological mechanisms as well, one might pay attention to that dimension of human behaviour without necessarily having to look for analogies in animal behaviour.

Hill: Pavlov observed that when a dog was exposed to a repeated stimulus that had no consequences, either adverse or pleasant, it went to sleep.

Gray: The kind of conservation–withdrawal concept that Professor Engel is talking about would surely not include sleep as a result of long exposure to indifferent stimuli. If there is an analogy in Pavlov's experiments, it is with the dogs he described which are lively *until* they are put in the experimental stand and then fall asleep. Pavlov noted that this was dependent on the individual character of the dog and happened only to certain dogs (Teplov 1964).

Wolff: I find it difficult to see why Monica should drop off to sleep in the presence of a stranger of whom she is said to be frightened.

Engel: In these particular circumstances Monica drifted gradually into sleep, or at least a sleep-like state, after a fairly prolonged period of immobility; this was quite different from her usual falling asleep sequence. I suspect that the mechanism of conservation–withdrawal has a lot to do with sleep. After all, sleep is a very good example of a biological situation in which there is both conservation, in the sense of not expending energy, and withdrawal. I think that sleep may be the prototype of conservation–withdrawal and that it may be one place to start to look for mechanisms.

Hill: It may be relevant that the clinical syndrome of sleep paralysis is associated with immobility, relaxed muscle tone and reduced response to the environment. Cataplexy is another clinical syndrome that is closely associated with the sleep mechanism.

Sachar: We must be cautious about describing sleep as a state of conservation–withdrawal since certain stages of sleep, namely the rapid eye movement (REM) phases, are associated with intense psychophysiological activation. We should not oversimplify the situation.

References

ADOLPH, E. F. (1971) Physiological adaptation to hypoxia in newborn rats. *Am. J. Physiol.* **221**, 123-127

AITKEN, R. C. B. (1969) Prevalence of worry in normal aircrew. *Br. J. Med. Psychol.* **42**, 283-286

AITKEN, R. C. B. (1972) A study of anxiety assessment in aircrew. *Br. J. Soc. Clin. Psychol.* **11**, 44-51

BARNETT, S. A. (1963) *The Rat: A Study in Behavior*, pp. 202-203, Aldine, Chicago

FOLKOW, B., JOHANSSON, B. & ÖBERG, B. (1959) A hypothalamic structure with a marked inhibitory effect on tonic sympathetic activity. *Acta Physiol. Scand.* **47**, 262-270

HILTON, S. M. & SPYER, K. M. (1969) The hypothalamic depressor area and the baroreceptor reflex. *J. Physiol. (Lond.)* **200**, 107-108P

HOAGLAND, H. (1928) The mechanism of tonic immobility. *J. Gen. Psychol.* **1**, 426-447

HOFER, M. A. (1970) Cardiac and respiratory function during sudden prolonged immobility in wild rodents. *Psychosom. Med.* **32**, 633-647

LÖFVING, B. (1961) Cardiovascular adjustments induced from the rostral cingulate gyrus. *Acta Physiol. Scand.* **53**, Suppl. 184, 1-82

MCGRAW, C. P. & KLEMM, W. R. (1969) Mechanisms of the immobility reflex 'Animal Hypnosis'. III. Neocortical inhibition in rats. *Commun. Behav. Biol. A* **3**, 53-59

MASSERMAN, J. H. & PECHTEL, C. (1953) Neurosis in monkeys. A preliminary report of experimental observations. *Ann. N.Y. Acad. Sci.* **56**, 253-265

TEPLOV, B. M. (1964) in *Pavlov's Typology* (Gray, J. A., ed.), pp. 3-153, Pergamon Press, Oxford

VON HOLST, D. (1972) Renal failure as the cause of death in *Tupaia belangeri* (tree shrews) exposed to persistent social stress. *J. Comp. Physiol. Psychol.* **78**, 236-273

The structure of the emotions and the limbic system

JEFFREY A. GRAY

Department of Experimental Psychology, University of Oxford

Abstract The organization of the controlling systems for emotional behaviour is discussed in the light of data from experiments on learning and experiments in neuropsychology. It is proposed that the emotions represent states of the conceptual nervous system produced by reinforcing events or by stimuli which have in the subject's previous experience been followed by reinforcing events; that there are three major states of this kind in mammals (the data being drawn mainly from studies of rats, cats and dogs), one—the 'approach' system—mediating behavioural responses to signals of reward (or non-punishment), one—the 'behavioural inhibition' system—mediating responses to signals of punishment (or non-reward), and one—the 'fight/flight' system—mediating responses to unconditioned punishment (or non-reward); and that each of these states corresponds to activity in one of three sets of interlinked structures in the limbic system. Interrelations between these three systems are discussed.

A number of recent experiments on the 'behavioural inhibition' system are described. These experiments are concerned with the effects of sodium amylobarbitone (a drug believed to have a highly specific antagonism for the behavioural inhibition system) on the behaviour of rats in simple learning situations; with the effects of this and other drugs and a number of hormones on the threshold for driving the hippocampal theta rhythm by electrical stimulation of the medial septal area as a function of stimulation frequency; and with the difference between such 'theta-driving curves' obtained from male and female rats.

THE EMOTIONS IN ORDINARY LANGUAGE

It is not uncommon for the term 'emotion' to be dismissed in our textbooks as being no more than a chapter-heading. If so, it has usually been allotted to the wrong chapter; for, as we shall see, it is in the chapters on learning and physiology that a true theory of emotion has been rather stealthily ripening into maturity. Philosophers, too, have not been at all certain that there is a real area of discourse hidden behind the term 'emotion' and awaiting their techniques of analysis, though some kind of consensus appears to have developed—and this is in entire agreement with the conclusions we shall reach in this paper—that the emotion words have something to do with the appraisal of the objects which give rise to the emotional states as 'good' or 'bad' (e.g. Mischel 1969). Given all this doubt on the part of the experts, one would expect the layman to have great difficulty in understanding what emotions are all about. Yet I doubt whether anyone normally fluent in the use of the English language would have difficulty in deciding that 'fear', 'disappointment', 'hope' and 'anger', for example, are emotions, while 'hunger', 'thirst' or 'drowsiness' are not. So somewhere there is a reasonably clear distinction being drawn between states which are or are not emotional. A look at the use of what are presumably emotional states by learning theorists will, I think, enable us to see what that distinction is.

It is clear that, from the learning theorist's point of view, both emotions and 'drives' (as he would term 'hunger', 'thirst' and probably 'drowsiness') are hypothetical internal states of the organism—that is, states attributed to the conceptual nervous system (Hebb 1955). These states have to be invented in order to account for the fact that an organism's reactions to identical environmental inputs are not themselves invariant. If they were, the radical behaviourist programme of quietly describing stimulus–response relationships without recourse to theory or neuronal physiology would be a feasible one. As it is, we have to suppose that the variability inherent in the way organisms respond to their environments (assuming it is not totally random) reflects some systematic set of internal states which they may enter. The question, then, is: what differentiates those internal states we prefer to call 'drives' from those we prefer to call 'emotions'?

The answer, I think, is that drives are internal states which are principally caused by changes *internal* to the organism, while emotions are internal states which are principally caused by events *external* to the organism. Thus the states of hunger, thirst and drowsiness grow with the passage of time more or less independently of the environment in which the organism is placed, though it is true that they can be reversed or hindered in their development by environmental events (food, water or excessive stimulation for these three drives respectively). Fear, disappointment, hope and anger, on the other hand, are normally consequent upon the occurrence of particular kinds of environmental events. This analysis can be supported by a consideration of pathology. It is when drive states become dependent on specific environmental events, or alternatively cease to show the usual variation with time independently of environmental inputs, that we suspect illness: as in, say, the obese individuals described by Schachter (1967) or the condition of anorexia nervosa. Conversely, it is when emotional states arise with *no* precipitating environmental event that we smell pathology, as in 'free-floating' anxiety or 'endogenous' depression. Our vocabulary is particularly instructive in the case of erotic internal states. Sexual behaviour, from the point of view of this distinction between internal and external control, is a border-line case: it is about equally dependent on the internal milieu (hormonal status, in particular) and on appropriate external stimuli (optimally, those associated with a willing and attractive member of the opposite sex). In line with the distinction between internal and external causation of the typical drives and emotions, we do not, I think, regard 'feeling sexy' (where the emphasis is on internal causation) as an emotion, while we do so regard 'being in love' (where the emphasis is on a particular object in the environment).

Excursions into linguistic philosophy of this kind normally do no more than elucidate the use made of language; the distinctions uncovered need not correspond to distinctions which exist in reality, and only the latter are of interest to the behavioural scientist. However, in this case, the distinctions apparently made in ordinary language turn out to correspond rather well both to distinctions which have arisen in the theory of learning and to lines of demarcation within the neuroendocrine system. Moreover, as I claim elsewhere (Gray 1971b, 1972b, 1973), it is precisely individual differences in modes of emotional reaction to external stimuli which underlie the major dimensions of temperament and the major psychiatric syndromes. It is necessary, therefore, to obtain some idea of what distinguishes the emotional states from others, and ordinary language, on this occasion, appears to be based on some useful insights.

THE EMOTIONS AS DEDUCED FROM THE STUDY OF LEARNING

If the emotions are internal states elicited by external stimuli, what kinds of stimuli are these? The answer to this question is contained in the theory of the emotions which has grown out of the study of learning. This theory can trace its origins to a number of sources: Hull's (1952) and Spence's (1956) notions of the goal-gradient and incentive motivation; Estes & Skinner's (1941) work on the conditioned emotional response; Mowrer's (1947) and Miller's (1951) work on the role of fear in avoidance learning; Amsel's (1958) treatment of non-reward as eliciting 'frustration'; all culminating in Mowrer's (1960) important textbook. With this body of work behind us, it is possible to give a moderately simple definition of the emotions as '*those (hypothetical) states in the conceptual nervous system which are produced by reinforcing events or by stimuli which have in the subject's previous experience been followed by reinforcing events'*. Thus 'fear', in Miller's and Mowrer's use, is a hypothetical state in the conceptual nervous system elicited by stimuli previously followed by unconditioned punishing events; 'conditioned frustration', in Amsel's use, is the state produced by stimuli previously followed by frustrative non-reward (i.e. by the non-delivery of anticipated reward); and so on. Most of the theorists who have been responsible for developing this kind of approach to the emotions have espoused some kind of 'two-process learning theory' (e.g. Rescorla & Solomon 1967). In this kind of theory the emotional states are either innately elicited by unconditioned reinforcing events or may come to be elicited, as a result of classical Pavlovian conditioning by contiguity, by previously neutral stimuli. As a result of such classical conditioning, stimuli in the subject's environment acquire secondary reinforcing properties, either of an appetitive kind (eliciting approach behaviour) or of an aversive kind (eliciting withdrawal behaviour), and thus control the subject's instrumental behaviour by way of some kind of reinforcement principle. The details in which this general theoretical form is clothed vary somewhat from author to author; representative samples can be found in Mowrer's (1960) book, in Amsel's (1962) well-known paper in the *Psychological Review*, or in my own recent review of research on fear (Gray 1971*a*). For our present purposes the important information to abstract from this theoretical approach and from the experimental work to which it has given rise concerns *the number of distinguishable emotional states there are and the way in which each of them is organized*.

The first half of this question can be converted into the related question: how many distinguishable classes of reinforcing events and conditioned signals of reinforcing events are there? If we first consider the maximum possible number of such classes, on logical grounds, and then determine whether any of these classes ought, on empirical grounds, to be collapsed, we should be left with the number of actual distinguishable classes of reinforcing events—that is, of distinguishable emotional states.

In general terms, it would seem that reinforcing events can be first divided into the conditioned and the unconditioned variety; and that each of these can be divided into appetitive or aversive; and that each of these can be either presented (contingently upon some response or other) or withheld. This leads to the classification set out in Table 1.

There are grounds for believing, however, that this logical classification can indeed be reduced on empirical grounds. There is very good evidence, both from purely behavioural experiments and from experiments in physiological psychology, that the effects of signals of punishment and those of signals of frustrative non-reward are functionally identical and work through the same structures in the neuroendocrine system (Miller 1964; Wagner 1966; Gray

TABLE 1

Classification of reinforcing events

	Unconditioned		Conditioned	
Presentation	R	P	R	P
Omission or termination	$\bar{R}$	$\bar{P}$	$\bar{R}$	$\bar{P}$

R = reward; P = punishment

1967, 1970a, 1971a). There is much less evidence, though there is some (Olds & Olds 1965; Gray 1971a; Bull 1970; Grossen et al. 1969), in favour of a second simplifying hypothesis first proposed by Mowrer (1960; see also Gray 1971a, 1972a), that the effects of signals of reward and those of signals of 'relieving non-punishment' (i.e. the non-delivery of anticipated punishment, involved in active avoidance behaviour) are functionally and physiologically identical. We shall, however, proceed on the assumption that this hypothesis, too, is correct. We are thus left with two basic classes of signals of reinforcing events: signals of reward (including non-punishment) and signals of punishment (including non-reward), the former eliciting approach behaviour (including active avoidance, which is construed as approach to safety signals: see Gray 1971a) and the latter, behavioural inhibition or passive avoidance behaviour.

In considering the unconditioned reinforcing stimuli, we are placed in something of a dilemma. Common sense names no emotional state as being set up by, say, food or water (as distinct from stimuli signalling the availability of food or water, which common sense, with Mowrer [1960], is prepared to regard as eliciting 'hope'). Within learning theory, equally, this kind of stimulus is thought of as terminating internal states (namely, drives) rather than initiating them.

Furthermore, the forms of behaviour initiated by presentation of food, water and so on are quite diverse, depending on the particular stimulus presented (i.e. such consummatory acts as eating, drinking, copulation etc.), again in distinction to the forms of behaviour initiated by stimuli signalling availability of positive reinforcers, which all elicit similar forms of approach behaviour independently of the actual positive reinforcers signalled. Thus one would wish to exclude the states elicited by unconditioned positive reinforcers from the list of the emotions. On the other hand, the state or states elicited by presentation of unconditioned aversive stimuli, which typically give rise to fight or flight behaviour, are ones which we would equally strongly expect to find in a list of the emotions. It seems, then, that we have to depart from the tidy logical classification set out in Table 1 and include these, but not the states elicited by unconditioned positive reinforcers, among the emotions.

As in the case of signals of aversive events, we may pursue simplicity by grouping together unconditioned punishment and unconditioned frustrative non-reward, for there is evidence that these events are functionally equivalent in that both elicit a state in which the probability of aggressive behaviour (Ulrich 1967; Gallup 1965) or escape behaviour (Adelman & Maatsch 1956) is increased and behavioural vigour is also increased (Brown *et al.* 1951; Wagner 1963; Amsel & Roussel 1952).

What we may not do, however, is to collapse the states elicited by conditioned and unconditioned aversive events, although common sense (and learning theorists) often name both of them 'fear'. We may not do this because the behaviour patterns produced by unconditioned aversive events and stimuli warning of these are not only different but often diametrically opposed to each other. Thus, an electric shock applied to a rat causes a great increase in mobility (jumping, running etc.) and in vocalization (squealing). A conditioned stimulus (CS) regularly followed by such a shock, however, comes to elicit crouching and silence. Similarly, in human subjects, an electric shock produces an increase in heart rate, but a CS preceding the shock comes to elicit heart rate deceleration (Notterman *et al.* 1952; Obrist *et al.* 1965). Notice that this difference between the unconditioned response (UCR) to punishment and the conditioned response (CR) to signals of punishment is, as far as I know, the only exception to a weak form of the stimulus substitution theory of classical conditioning: namely, that any response change which is part of the CR, unless it was elicited by the CS before conditioning, is also elicited as a response change in the same direction, though not necessarily of the same magnitude, by the unconditioned stimulus (UCS). As I have argued elsewhere (Gray 1971a), this unusual exception to the laws of classical conditioning suggests that the rat—and probably mammals in general, since similar observations may be made in many other species—comes equipped with an innate set of responses, those involved in passive avoidance behaviour, but has to learn to which stimuli it must allocate this set of responses—namely, stimuli which have been followed by unconditioned punishments. The system governing this set of responses appears to be quite distinct from the one which governs responses to the unconditioned punishments themselves.

Thus, on the aversive side, we have, it seems, two emotional states, one elicited by unconditioned punishments and frustrative non-reward, the other by signals of punishment and signals of frustrative non-reward.

Within the former state, one might have expected to be able to distinguish between, on the one hand, an internal state corresponding to flight or *unconditioned* escape behaviour (as distinct from *learned* escape behaviour, which, like active avoidance behaviour, appears to involve predominantly the system which controls approach behaviour; see Gray 1971a) and, on the other hand, an internal state corresponding to aggressive behaviour, for both of these forms of behaviour may occur in response to unconditioned aversive stimuli. However, judging from the extensive work of Azrin and his associates (Ulrich 1967; Gray 1971a), the factor which determines whether fight or flight occurs in response to such stimuli does not lie in the nature of these stimuli themselves, but rather in other aspects of the environment in which they are presented. Roughly speaking, if escape is possible, the subject will try flight; if not, it will try fight.

It seems, then, that we should not split the emotional states elicited by aversive stimuli into more than two. Thus, *in toto*, the study of learning suggests the existence of three major emotional systems, which we may call the 'approach', 'stop' and 'fight/flight' systems, respectively (Table 2).

TABLE 2

Three major emotional systems

Emotional system	Reinforcing stimuli	Behaviour	Neural structures
Approach	Conditioned stimuli for R and $\bar{P}$	Approach learning; active avoidance; skilled escape; predatory aggression	Olds' reward system; especially septal area, medial forebrain bundle and lateral hypothalamus
Stop or behavioural inhibition	Conditioned stimuli for P and $\bar{R}$	Passive avoidance; extinction	Medial septal area, hippocampus, orbital frontal cortex, caudate nucleus
Fight/Flight	Unconditioned P and $\bar{R}$	Unconditioned escape; defensive aggression	Amygdala, stria terminalis, medial hypothalamus, central grey of midbrain

THE EMOTIONS AS DEDUCED FROM PHYSIOLOGICAL PSYCHOLOGY

Given the uncertainty which many scientists have felt as to the very existence of a field of study concerned with emotion, it may seem an act of striking boldness to conclude not only that such a field exists but also that there are three major emotions; especially when we consider that ordinary language, from which I have sought some support, recognizes the existence of a much greater number of distinct emotions. It is comforting, therefore, that a survey of studies in which emotional behaviour has been investigated as a function of

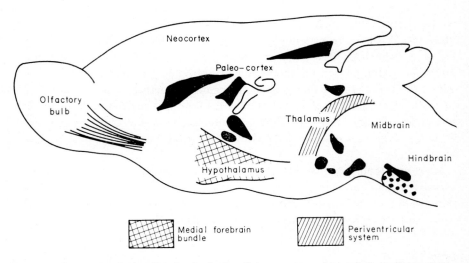

FIG. 1. The approach (medial forebrain bundle) system, as mapped by self-stimulation experiments in the rat by Olds & Olds (1965). The periventricular system consists of points at which stimulation is turned off by the rat; this area is also involved in the system mapped by de Molina & Hunsperger (1962) in the cat as mediating defensive aggression (Fig. 3).

a variety of interventions in the brains of experimental animals leads to the same conclusion, as well as putting a solid anatomico-physiological basis beneath each of our as yet free-floating emotional states. Since there are a number of available reviews (Grossman 1967; Deutsch & Deutsch 1966; Gray 1971a) of these studies, it will be sufficient here to summarize the main conclusions which can be drawn from existing data.

The first point of interest in these data is that the distinction we have drawn between, on the one hand, the emotions and, on the other, both drives and consummatory acts, is matched by major differences in the anatomical location of the structures governing emotional behaviour, drives and consummatory behaviour. The structures which are involved in the control of emotional behaviour lie predominantly in the forebrain, and particularly in the limbic system; the main controlling centres for drives and consummatory acts, in contrast, are predominantly located at the level of the hypothalamus and still lower in the midbrain. Some of the work reported by Olds & Olds (1965) strongly suggests that the medial hypothalamus is a kind of major meeting point at which forebrain emotional systems and hypothalamic drive mechanisms may influence each other (see Gray 1971a).

Within the domain of emotional behaviour, available data strongly point to the existence of three separate, though interacting, neural systems.

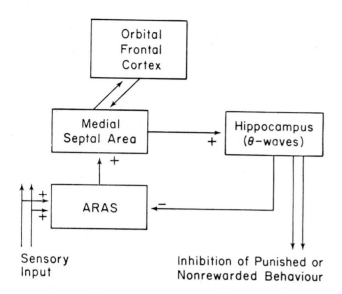

FIG. 2. The septo-hippocampal stop system. ARAS, ascending reticular activating system. (See Gray 1970a, 1972b.)

One of these has been described in most detail by the self-stimulation tech-nique introduced by Olds (Olds & Olds 1965), and it is rather clearly involved in the control of approach behaviour. Electrical stimulation of this system is found rewarding, in that the animal works to obtain it by whatever means is made available. The major focus of the self-stimulation phenomenon appears to lie in the medial forebrain bundle and the lateral hypothalamus; and more rostral points in the septal area, to which the medial forebrain bundle projects, also maintain high rates of responding (Fig. 1).

A second system is concerned with behavioural inhibition, and involves a series of interconnected structures (Fig. 2) including the hippocampus, the medial septal area, the orbital frontal cortex and the caudate nucleus (McCleary 1966; Douglas 1967; Butters & Rosvold 1968; Kimble 1969; Gray 1970a, b). Lesions in this system impair not only passive avoidance of shock but also extinction of appetitive behaviour and other behavioural responses to signals of frustrative non-reward, thus offering important support for the equation between signals of punishment and of frustrative non-reward made earlier on psychological grounds. The drug sodium amylobarbitone, which is known to block the behavioural effects of both signals of punishment and signals of frustrative non-reward (Miller 1964; Wagner 1966; Gray 1967; Ison & Rosen 1967), has been shown by Gray & Ball (1970) probably to exert these effects by way of an alteration in the electrophysiological properties of this system. Although both this system and the Olds approach system involve neurons in the septal area, an experiment by Ball & Gray (1971), coupled with the experiments reported by Gray (1970*a*), shows that this anatomical overlap between the two systems is not accompanied by functional interaction at this locus: the role of the septal area in the control of behavioural inhibition is exercised in virtue of its control over the theta rhythm in the hippocampus, whereas the self-stimulation phenomenon in the septal area is independent of the effects of septal stimulation on hippocampal electrical activity.

The distinction between active and passive avoidance made earlier also receives important support, and physiological underpinning, from a consideration of experiments involving these two systems. Those *lesions* to the behavioural inhibition system which impair passive avoidance also enhance active avoidance in the shuttlebox (McCleary 1966; Douglas 1967; Olton & Isaacson 1968; Albert & Bignami 1968), as does sodium amylobarbitone (Kamano *et al.* 1966). Conversely, electrical *stimulation* of Olds' reward system also impairs passive avoidance (more precisely, the Estes-Skinner conditioned emotional response: Brady & Conrad 1960) and improves active avoidance (Stein 1965). In support of the hypothesis, suggested earlier in this paper (and see Gray 1971*a*, 1972*a*), that active avoidance is learnt on the same basis as approach to rewards, Olds & Olds (1965) report that treatments (administration of chlorpromazine and cortical spreading depression [see Leão 1947]) which disrupted self-stimulation also disrupted learnt escape behaviour. Furthermore, the disruption in learnt escape behaviour caused by spreading cortical depression was accompanied by reduced firing in neurons of Olds' reward system. Thus we may reasonably conclude that Olds' reward system mediates approach behaviour in response to signals of either reward or relieving non-punishment—that is, it is isomorphic to the approach system delineated earlier on behavioural grounds; and that the behavioural inhibition system just described mediates passive avoidance in response to signals of either punishment or frustrative non-reward—that is, it is isomorphic to the stop system delineated on behavioural grounds.

The third system located in the forebrain has been described partly through a series of lesioning experiments (see Deutsch & Deutsch 1966 for review) and partly as a result of de Molina & Hunsperger's (1962) stimulation experiments in the cat. It is concerned in fight/flight behaviour and involves structures (Fig. 3) in the amygdala, the medial hypothalamus (to which the amygdala is connected by the stria terminalis)* and the central grey of the midbrain (to

---

* See, however, p. 156.

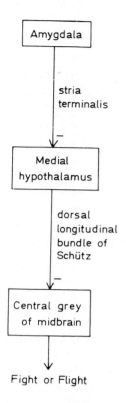

FIG. 3. The fight/flight system as mapped by de Molina & Hunsperger's (1962) stimulation experiments in the cat. — indicates inhibition.

which the medial hypothalamus is connected by way of the dorsal longitudinal bundle of Schütz). Stimulation of this system produces a cat with arched back and raised hair, which hisses and growls and will attempt to escape if escape is possible, will learn to turn such stimulation off if such a response is available, or will attack anything suitable in its environment (the optimum stimulus for attack being another cat) if the former two courses of action are not open to it. As in experiments on the intact animal (Ulrich 1967), whether fight or flight occurs depends not on the eliciting stimulus but on the environment in which the eliciting stimulus is presented. Thus we may regard this system as isomorphic with the fight/flight system already delineated on behavioural grounds, and our Table 2 is complete.

An important distinction which emerges from the physiological work on the fight/flight system is the distinction between defensive and predatory aggression. In the cat these two forms of aggression are very distinct behaviourally in any

case. Defensive aggression has already been described above, for it is this that
is elicited by the electrical stimulation of de Molina & Hunsperger's (1962)
system. Predatory aggression is typically seen when a cat is stalking a rat or a
bird: the back is not arched, the hair is smooth and no vocalization occurs.
This kind of aggression is never elicited from electrodes in the fight/flight
system; rather, it can be elicited from electrodes located in the lateral hypothalamus, where eating behaviour is also controlled (Adams & Flynn 1966).
Furthermore, whereas stimulation which elicits defensive attack is negatively
reinforcing (Adams & Flynn 1966), stimulation which elicits predatory attack
is rewarding by Olds' self-stimulation test (Roberts & Kiess 1964; Hutchinson
& Renfrew 1966). Thus the fight/flight system is concerned only with defensive
attack: that is, with the kind of aggression usually elicited by a conspecific
or by a threatening animal from a different species (cat-cat or cat-dog, rather
than cat-rat). Predatory aggression, in contrast, appears to be mediated by
the approach system.

INTERRELATIONS BETWEEN THREE EMOTIONAL SYSTEMS

Having delineated these three major emotional systems, I shall say a few
words about their interrelations. These are set out schematically in Fig. 4.

As already mentioned, the experiments reviewed by Olds & Olds (1965), as
well as de Molina & Hunsperger's (1962) experiments, strongly suggest that
the medial hypothalamus is a nodal point in the interrelations between the
approach, stop and fight/flight systems. Hunsperger's experiments on the
fight/flight system in the cat have produced the clearest evidence to indicate
what may be the main principle on which these interrelations are based. The
results of combined lesion and stimulation experiments showed that the medial
hypothalamus exerts a tonic inhibition over the final common pathway for
fight/flight behaviour, the components of which are organized in the central
grey of the midbrain. The amygdala (which projects to the medial hypothalamus by way of the stria terminalis) in turn, upon the receipt of appropriate
environmental signals, inhibits the medial hypothalamus, thus *dis*inhibiting
the midbrain fight/flight output mechanism. The interrelations between this
amygdalo–hypothalamo–midbrain fight/flight system and the septo-hippocampal stop system are indicated by a series of experiments by Kling and his
collaborators and by King & Meyer (see reviews by Deutsch & Deutsch 1966;
Gray 1971a) in which rats were subjected to both septal and amygdaloid
lesions and the resulting 'septal rage' syndrome, or its absence, was noted.
These experiments suggest that the medial hypothalamic tonic inhibition of the

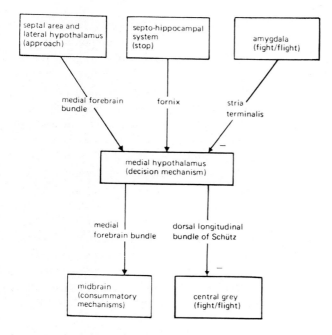

FIG. 4. Interrelations between three emotional systems. The medial hypothalamus appears to act as a nodal point in the resolution of influences proceeding downstream from limbic structures. These promote approach behaviour (from the septal area via the medial forebrain bundle) or fight/flight behaviour (from the amygdala via the stria terminalis). The medial hypothalamus may inhibit both these outcomes via its control of the final common pathways in the midbrain, and this inhibition is intensified by influences proceeding from the septo-hippocampal stop system via the fornix and mammillary bodies. (From Gray 1971a.)

midbrain final common pathway for fight/flight behaviour is enhanced by influences proceeding from the septal area. Thus, the outcome (fight/flight or inhibition of fight/flight) on any particular occasion depends on the balance of influences playing upon the medial hypothalamus from the amygdala and the septal area respectively. The most likely route whereby influences from the septal area reach the medial hypothalamus is via septal control of the electrical activity of the hippocampus, as suggested by Gray (1970a); the major outflow of the hippocampus, in turn, goes by way of the fornix to the mammillary bodies, situated medially at the base of the hypothalamus.

Similar principles of organization appear to be at work in approach behaviour. Behavioural fragments of particular consummatory acts appear to be organized in the midbrain in a rather specific manner (Glickman & Schiff 1967). 'Drive centres', in which information concerning the current state of the internal milieu is integrated, and appetitive and subsequent consummatory behaviour is initiated, are located at hypothalamic level. For example, in eating behaviour, the execution of food-seeking and ingestive behaviour is known to be mediated by the lateral hypothalamus, while the integration of information about the internal milieu appears to be mediated by the medial hypothalamus (specifically the ventro-medial nucleus: Grossman 1967). The medial hypothalamus exerts inhibitory control over the lateral hypothalamus (Grossman 1967; Sclafani & Grossman 1969), this inhibition presumably being released when appropriate messages about the state of the internal milieu are received by the medial hypothalamus. Little is known about the structures which mediate the effects of environmental signals concerning the availability or rewarding value of food (i.e. those which mediate Hull's 'incentive motivation' or Mowrer's 'hope'); but the available evidence suggests loci in the forebrain, perhaps in the septal area (e.g. Donovick et al. 1968) or more likely in the amygdala (Klüver & Bucy 1937; Grossman 1967). The role of the septo-hippocampal stop system in inhibiting appetitive behaviour in the face of signals of punishment or frustrative non-reward is well known (Gray 1970a). Presumably, this inhibition too is exercised along the pathway (fornix to mammillary bodies) described at the end of the previous paragraph.

Papez's (1937) and MacLean's (1949) original intuitions that emotion is a function of the limbic structures of the forebrain, then, appear to have been good ones. The distinction which we have in our ordinary language—and which is presumably based on some kind of demarcation in our common subjective experience—between emotions and those other kinds of internal state called by psychologists 'drives' appears to correspond rather well to a distinction which, in learning theory terms, is one between internal states which arise in consequence of exposure to certain kinds of environmental influences and those that are autonomous; and which, in anatomical terms, is one between internal states mediated by structures in the limbic system—septal area, hippocampus, amygdala—and internal states mediated by structures at the level of the hypothalamus or below. In this connection, it is worth noting that the septo-hippocampal stop system, unlike the approach and fight/flight systems, appears to have no continuation below the hypothalamus: passive avoidance behaviour does not seem to be elicited by midbrain stimulation (Glickman & Schiff 1967).

EMOTION AND PERSONALITY

Let us turn briefly to the link between these postulated emotional systems, on the one hand, and the major dimensions of human temperament, on the other. Here, I take as my starting-point the work of H. J. Eysenck (1967; Eysenck & Eysenck 1969).

Eysenck has claimed that, in the temperamental sphere, there are three major axes of variation in behavioural abnormalities, laboratory test performance, and responses to questionnaires: Extraversion (E), Neuroticism (N) and Psychoticism (P), each being independent of the others (e.g. Eysenck & Eysenck 1968, 1969). Extreme positions on these dimensions predispose the individual concerned to the development of 'dysthymic' neuroses (phobias, anxiety states, obsessive-compulsive neurosis and reactive depression, all associated with high N and low E scores), of antisocial behaviour (associated with high N together with high E scores), or of psychotic symptoms (associated with high P scores). Other workers (e.g. Pawlik 1973) in the multivariate field are in broad agreement with Eysenck on the nature of his E and N factors, though Cattell (e.g. Cattell & Scheier 1961) claims that there are also other factors which differentiate between diagnosed neurotic and normal individuals. Research on the P dimension is, however, much less far advanced.

I have suggested (Gray 1970b, 1972b, 1973) that, corresponding to these three orthogonal factors of personality, there are underlying differences in the reactivity of the three major emotional systems indicated in Table 2. In order to see how this postulated correspondence works, we must first rotate Eysenck's two factors E and N through 45°, thus constituting two new factors: 'Anxiety', running from Eysenck's stable extravert quadrant to his neurotic introvert quadrant, and measured fairly directly by such instruments as the Manifest Anxiety Scale (Spence & Spence 1966); and 'Impulsivity', running from Eysenck's stable introvert quadrant to his neurotic extravert quadrant, and measured fairly directly by the 'behavioural extraversion' or 'impulsivity' sub-factor of Eysenck's existing E scales (Eysenck & Eysenck 1969). The reasons for this rotation* have been advanced in previous papers (Gray 1970b, 1972b, 1973).

The relation between my proposed rotation and Eysenck's original two factors, as well as the hypothesis which relates the rotated factors to individual differences in the reactivity of two of the postulated emotional systems, are

---

* It is well known that factor analysis, the statistical technique on which the multivariate description of personality is based, can tell you how many independent dimensions of variation there are in a given domain of data, such as questionnaire and rating scale scores, but not where the resulting factors should be located so that they correspond to underlying causal factors, assuming that these exist. The correct location can only be decided on in the light of the same kind of theoretical and empirical considerations which determine the fate of any scientific theory.

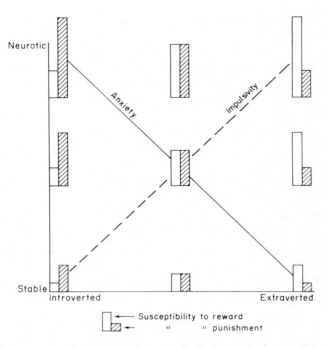

Fɪɢ. 5. Proposed relationships of (*a*) susceptibility to signals of reward and susceptibility to signals of punishment to (*b*) the dimensions of introversion–extraversion and neuroticism. The dimensions of anxiety and impulsivity (diagonals) represent the steepest rates of increase in susceptibility to signals of punishment and reward, respectively. (From Gray 1970*b*.)

outlined in Fig. 5. This shows how a person with high scores on the Anxiety dimension is conceived as having high sensitivity to signals of impending punishment or of impending frustrative non-reward; while a person with high scores on the Impulsivity dimension is conceived as having high sensitivity to signals of impending reward or relieving non-punishment. Thus, the dimensions of Anxiety and Impulsivity correspond, respectively, to the 'behavioural inhibition' and 'approach' systems listed in Table 2. Scores on Eysenck's Neuroticism dimension reflect sensitivity to both classes of signals of reinforcement—that is, an average of the individual's sensitivity to signals of aversive and appetitive reinforcement taken separately. Similarly, Extraversion scores reflect the relative balance of sensitivity to signals of punishment and reward, respectively: an individual relatively more sensitive to signals of punishment (or non-reward) than to signals of reward (or non-punishment) is introverted; one relatively more sensitive to signals of reward than to signals of punishment is extraverted. Our first experiments directed to the testing of these hypotheses (in children) have produced promising results (Nicholson & Gray 1971, 1972).

With regard to Eysenck's Psychoticism dimension, I have suggested (Gray 1973)—but much more tentatively, as befits the paucity of knowledge in this area—that P scores may in some way reflect activity in the third of the emotional systems listed in Table 2, the 'fight/flight' system.

THE BEHAVIOURAL INHIBITION SYSTEM

Let us now turn to a more detailed consideration of the psychophysiological nature of the behavioural inhibition system, individual differences in the reactivity of which are conceived as underlying the personality dimension of Anxiety (i.e. neurotic introversion) and the formation of such symptoms as phobias, anxiety states, obsessive-compulsive rituals, reactive depression and (perhaps more germane to the theme of this symposium) ulcers. I shall dwell only on those features of the behavioural inhibition system about which I have something new to say.

Amylobarbitone and behaviour

One of the major clues as to the unity of the behavioural inhibition system, as well as to its differentiation from other emotional systems, has been the highly specific pattern of behavioural effects produced by the drug sodium amylobarbitone. These effects on behaviour may best be summarized by reference back to Table 1 (p. 91), setting out the classification of logically possible reinforcing events. Sodium amylobarbitone has been found to attenuate, or sometimes block completely, the behavioural effects of signals of punishment and signals of frustrative non-reward, but not to reduce the behavioural effects of signals of reward or signals of relieving non-punishment, nor any of the behavioural effects of unconditioned reinforcing events (Miller 1964; Wagner 1966; Gray 1967, 1971a; and many studies by Ison and his colleagues, e.g. Ison & Rosen 1967). Thus this drug seems to have a highly selective affinity for the behavioural inhibition system. Two recent experiments from my laboratory throw further light on the nature of the psychological effects of amylobarbitone.

One possible explanation of the selective effects of amylobarbitone would not call upon differences in classes of reinforcing event at all. It would postulate, instead, that this drug makes it harder for the animal to detect any departure from established expectations of reinforcement. The plausibility of this ex-

planation is dependent on the fact that, in virtually all experiments involving
the delivery of punishment (to produce in the simplest case passive avoidance)
or the non-delivery of anticipated reward (producing extinction), the subject
has first to be trained on the response which is to be punished or extinguished.
Thus the fact that amylobarbitone attenuates both passive avoidance and
extinction (see Gray 1971a, for review) could be explained by saying that this
drug attenuates the effects of a second reinforcing event experienced by the
animal in the experimental situation, but not the effect of the first reinforcing
event so experienced. According to the view that amylobarbitone affects the
behavioural inhibition system, in contrast, it would be only the behavioural
consequences of *negative* departures from expectation of reinforcement which
this drug would affect.

We have been attempting for some years to test these alternatives by looking
at the influence of amylobarbitone on the 'elation effect'. This is an enhance-
ment in the performance of a response when it is followed by a higher reward
than has usually followed it. The phenomenon was originally reported by
Crespi (1942), using varying amounts of food reward for rats running in a
straight alley. The analogous 'depression effect', in which performance is
depressed when a response is followed by a lower reward than usual, was also
reported by Crespi in the same paper. The depression effect has been shown
by Rosen *et al.* (1967) to be blocked by amylobarbitone; but this would be
expected on either view of the effects of the drug. It is the influence of amylobarbitone on the *elation* effect which offers a critical test of the two views: if
any departure from expectation is attenuated by the drug, the elation effect
should be reduced; if only *negative* departures from expectation are so affected,
it should be unaltered.

This experiment sounds straightforward enough. Unfortunately, it is extremely difficult to obtain reliable elation effects in the runway using Crespi's
technique when the proper control group—one given the high reward throughout
—is used (Spence 1956). However, we (A. Ridgers & J. A. Gray, in preparation)
have now re-examined the problem using a technique pioneered by Baltzer &
Weiskrantz (1970). The animal (a rat) presses a lever for a reward in a Skinner
box. It is given, on alternate days, high reward (four pellets of food) and low
reward (one pellet) on a variable interval (VI) schedule (Ferster & Skinner 1957).
Distinctive stimuli are associated with high and low reward respectively. Both
on high- and low-reward days there is an 'intrusion' period: during this period
(which in our own experiment lasted four minutes and occurred twice during
the daily 48-minute experimental session) the reward condition and the stimulus
signalling level of reward change to the opposite to the ones (the 'baseline')
operating during the rest of the session. That is to say, there are low-reward

intrusion periods during high-reward days and high-reward intrusions during low-reward days. The depression effect can then be estimated as the difference between response rates when low reward is the intrusion and when it is the baseline condition; and similarly the elation effect can be estimated as the difference between response rates when high reward is the intrusion and when it is the baseline condition. A lower response rate during low-reward intrusion than during low-reward baseline is a depression effect; and a higher response rate during high-reward intrusion than during high-reward baseline is an elation effect. Thus the animal serves as its own control, and the depression and elation effects can be studied simultaneously.

Using this technique, we have investigated the effects of 15 mg/kg amylobarbitone sodium (given intraperitoneally just before the daily session) on the depression and elation effects in three rats which showed both these phenomena clearly. The size of the two effects was first measured over a period of 15 days; saline injections, given on the final eight days of this period, proved to have no effect.

We then injected the drug for a further 15 days of experimentation. Finally, the animals were tested for four days in the undrugged condition. As is clear from Fig. 6, amylobarbitone greatly reduced the depression effect while leaving the elation effect untouched. Analysis of variance of the data from the pre-drug and drug phases of the experiment established the reliability of the depression and elation effects beyond doubt ($P < 0.001$ in both cases); and also showed that the reduction of the depression effect by amylobarbitone was highly significant ($F = 7.03$, $df = 1/12$, $P < 0.025$), and the absence of an influence of the drug on the elation effect equally clearcut ($F < 1$). Ison & Northman (1968) have previously reported a failure of amylobarbitone to influence the elation effect in the runway; but in their experiment it was by no means clear that an elation effect occurred in the placebo controls.

These results, then, strengthen our confidence in the belief that amylobarbitone has a specifically antagonistic effect on the behavioural consequences of *negative* departures from expectation (punishment, omission or reduction of reward). Such an effect could well be the basis of the tranquillizing effects of the barbiturate drugs in their clinical applications in man.

A second experiment which we (H. J.Dudderidge, J. A. Gray & H. de Wit, in preparation) have recently completed on the behavioural effects of amylobarbitone suggests, along with earlier evidence, that this drug affects the behavioural consequences only of conditioned signals of non-reward and punishment, not those of the unconditioned events of non-reward and punishment themselves (Barry & Miller 1965; Gray & Dudderidge 1971). The starting-point for this experiment was the finding, now reported several times (Ison &

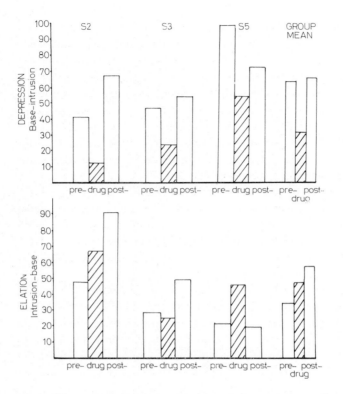

FIG. 6. Effect of 15 mg/kg amylobarbitone sodium on operant depression and elation effects in a group of three rats, separately and collectively. The depression and elation effects are measured as the difference between numbers of responses during intrusion periods and corresponding baseline periods. (A. Ridgers & J. A. Gray, in preparation.)

Pennes 1969; Gray 1969; Gray & Dudderidge 1971; Capaldi & Sparling 1971), that the partial reinforcement extinction effect (PREE: Lewis 1960) can be attenuated or even blocke dcompletely if rats are trained under amylobarbitone and extinguished without the drug. The basic experimental situation in which this finding is made uses the straight alley and two conditions of reward, one (continuous reinforcement, CRF) in which reward is delivered on every trial, the other (partial reinforcement, PR) in which reward is delivered on a random 50% of trials. It is well known that, during subsequent extinction when no further rewards are delivered to either group, the group given PR is much more resistant to extinction than the one given CRF.

Analysis of the mechanisms (e.g. Sutherland & Mackintosh 1971) at work in this phenomenon strongly suggests that the PREE can be produced in two different ways. In one (the 'inter-trial' route) the animal subjected to a PR schedule comes to use the immediate 'after-effects' of frustrative non-reward as cues for the performance of the partially reinforced response (Capaldi 1967). In the other (the 'intra-trial' route) there are two processes: first, stimuli emanating from the experimental environment, as a result of repeated pairing with the unconditioned event of frustrative non-reward, become conditioned 'frustrating' stimuli and evoke a conditioned state of 'anticipatory frustration'; then internal stimuli from this state become cues for the performance of the partially reinforced response (Amsel 1962). (In the language I have been using, the 'after-effects' of non-reward would be activity in the fight/flight system and 'anticipatory frustration' would be activity in the behavioural inhibition system: the terms in quotation marks are those used by Capaldi and Amsel.)

Now, in most experimental situations, the PREE is undoubtedly produced by both routes. However, it is possible to maximize the degree to which either is involved by manipulating various parameters of the experimental situation. It appears that the inter-trial route is favoured by short inter-trial intervals, few trials and large rewards, and the intra-trial route by the converse of these conditions (Black & Spence 1965). If amylobarbitone attenuates the behavioural effects of *signals* of frustrative non-reward, but not those of non-reward itself, this drug would block the PREE optimally under those conditions which favour the intra-trial route at the expense of the inter-trial route.

The first experiments to report the attenuation of the PREE by amylobarbitone (Ison & Pennes 1969; Gray 1969) already contained clues that this analysis might be correct: the blocking of the PREE was much more complete in Gray's experiment than in that of Ison and Pennes, and the most likely reason for this discrepancy is that Ison and Pennes used fewer training trials than Gray (40 as against 64), a condition which would favour the inter-trial route at the expense of the intra-trial route. A recent experiment by Ziff & Capaldi (1971) adds to this impression. They used conditions which undoubtedly favour the inter-trial route: only six trials, a short inter-trial interval (1.5 minutes) and a large reward (18 pellets). In these conditions they report that the PREE is unaffected by amylobarbitone injections during training. In our own experiment (H. J. Dudderidge, J. A. Gray & H. de Wit, in preparation) we did the opposite to Ziff & Capaldi (1971): we maximized the chances of the intra-trial route at the expense of the inter-trial route. We did this by using an inter-trial interval which was so long (24 hours) that it is highly unlikely that the inter-trial route could be used at all.

We used four groups of rats (eight per group), each given 19 training trials in the straight alley, one trial per day. Two groups were given CRF and two

PR, and of these one in each case was given daily intraperitoneal injections of 20 mg/kg sodium amylobarbitone 15 minutes before the daily trial and the other an injection of saline. Extinction, also at one trial a day, was carried out with all animals receiving saline. Our results are shown in Fig. 7. In the placebo groups a clearcut PREE was obtained, replicating Weinstock's (1958) results. There is absolutely no sign, however, of a PREE in the groups which received amylobarbitone during training. Indeed, this is the most complete blockage of the PREE by amylobarbitone yet reported, and it is unlikely to be a coincidence that it was obtained under conditions which virtually guarantee that only the intra-trial route was open. Taken in conjunction with the previous results, especially Ziff & Capaldi's (1971) failure to affect the PREE with amylobarbitone under conditions which maximally favour the inter-trial route, these results support the view that amylobarbitone specifically antagonizes the behavioural effects of *signals* of non-reward (or of punishment).

Effects of drugs on septal control of hippocampal electrical activity

The highly specific effects of amylobarbitone on behavioural inhibition (blockage of effects of only signals of punishment and signals of non-reward) made me think (Gray 1970*a*) that a profitable way of investigating the neural basis of behavioural inhibition might be to investigate the route by which this drug produces its effects on behaviour. On the basis of the similarity of the behavioural picture produced by, on the one hand, injections of amylobarbitone and, on the other, lesions to the hippocampus and the septal area, it seemed that this part of the limbic system might be a good place to begin such an investigation. Furthermore, since the septal area and the hippocampus were themselves known to be interrelated in such a way that the medial septal nucleus acts as the pacemaker for the hippocampal theta rhythm (Stumpf 1965), a more specific hypothesis could be formed: that amylobarbitone alters septal control of the theta rhythm. This would account for the fact that all three treatments (septal lesions, hippocampal lesions and amylobarbitone administration) affect behaviour in similar ways.

This hypothesis was still further refined after experiments in which we recorded from the hippocampus through electrodes implanted in the brains of free-moving rats taking part in learning experiments. We (Gray & Ball 1970) observed a correlation between the particular *frequency* of the theta rhythm and what the rat was doing or having done to him. Typical records are presented in Fig. 8.

In the rat the hippocampal theta rhythm covers the range of frequencies

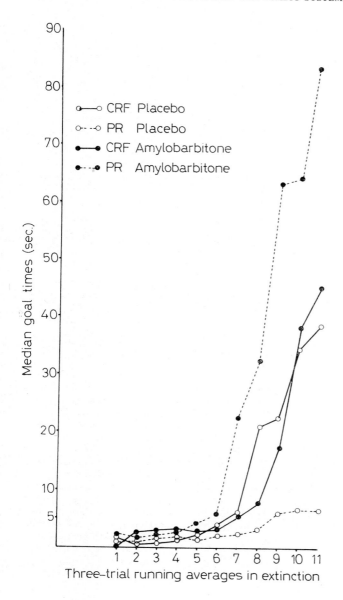

FIG. 7. Abolition of partial reinforcement (PR) extinction effect in runway at 24-hour inter-trial interval by 20 mg/kg sodium amylobarbitone during acquisition. Points plotted are running averages of three consecutive daily trials during 13 days of extinction. CRF, continuous reinforcement (H. J. Dudderidge, J. A. Gray & H. de Wit, in preparation.)

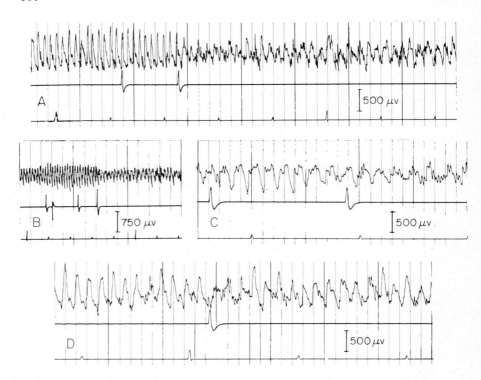

FIG. 8. Hippocampal activity in free-moving rats under various conditions. Top channel: hippocampus. Middle channel: breaking of photobeam. Bottom channel: time in seconds. (A) Rat no. 15: eighth rewarded trial. Water delivered at second mark on middle channel. Note 10-Hz theta rhythm changing to lower-amplitude 5-Hz theta overlaid with faster waves when goal is reached. (B) Rat no. 287: complete rewarded trial on slower paper speed. Note 8-Hz theta in startbox (up to first mark on middle channel) followed by burst of high-amplitude 9-Hz theta as rat traverses runway and reaches goal (final mark), when this pattern is replaced by low-amplitude 6-Hz theta. (C) Rat no. 443: third trial of extinction, paper speed 50 mm/second. Note anticipatory slowing of theta rhythm and reduction in amplitude between penultimate photobeam (first mark) and reaching goal (second mark), and preservation of low-frequency theta in goalbox in spite of non-reward. (D) Rat no. 15: eighth trial of extinction. Compare with A, noting reduction in theta frequency and amplitude before goal is attained (mark on middle channel) and increase in theta frequency and amplitude after it is attained. There is a transient appearance of reward-type theta for about 0.3 second after the goal is reached, followed by theta at about 8.5 Hz. (From Gray & Ball 1970.)

from about 6 to about 10 Hz. Within this range, three bands can be distinguished. A low-amplitude, somewhat irregular theta rhythm of 6-7.5 Hz accompanies the receipt of a reward and the performance of fixed action patterns such as eating, drinking and grooming; a regular theta rhythm of

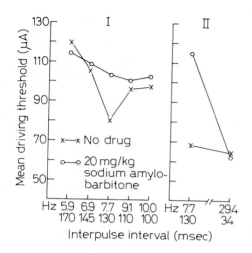

FIG. 9. Effect of 20 mg/kg amylobarbitone sodium on threshold for septal driving of hippocampal theta rhythm as a function of driving frequency in two groups (I and II) of five rats. (From Gray & Ball 1970.)

intermediate amplitude in the 7.5-8.5 Hz band is seen when the animal is exploring or is frustratively non-rewarded; a regular high-amplitude and high-frequency (8.5-10 Hz) theta rhythm is seen when the animal is initiating approach to a known reward, including avoidance of punishment (Bremner 1964). Thus, since amylobarbitone blocks the effects of non-reward, with which the middle theta band is associated, it is only hippocampal theta rhythms *in this band* that the drug should affect.

We (Gray & Ball 1970) investigated this hypothesis by looking at the effects of amylobarbitone, in doses known to attenuate the behavioural effects of frustrative non-reward, on the threshold for septal driving of the hippocampal theta rhythm as a function of driving frequency. The preparation used was the free-moving rat, with bipolar electrodes implanted in the medial septal nucleus and in the dorsal hippocampus. Driving was judged as synchrony between the stimulating pulses, 0.5 millisecond in duration, applied to the septal area and the theta waves recorded from the hippocampus. Fig. 9 shows the effect of 20 mg/kg amylobarbitone on the resulting 'theta-driving curve'. It can be seen that the drug increases the threshold for theta driving quite specifically in the middle frequency band.

These results (Gray & Ball 1970) thus support the view that the behavioural effects of small doses of amylobarbitone are produced by way of a selective antagonism to the hippocampal theta rhythm in the frequency band 7.5-8.5

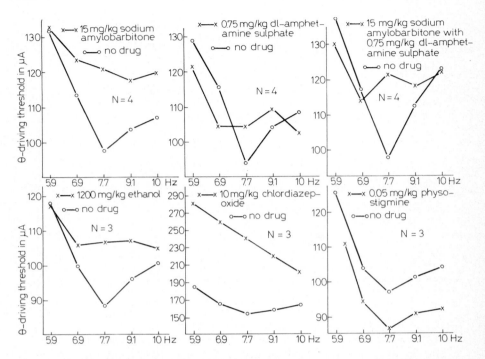

FIG. 10. Effects of a number of drugs on thresholds of driving of hippocampal theta rhythm as a function of septal stimulation frequency in free-moving male rats. *N* indicates number of rats from which determinations were taken, each contributing both to baseline and drug curves. (J. A. Gray, D. T. D. James & H. J. Dudderidge, in preparation.)

Hz. The same view also receives support from experiments in which we investigated the effects on behaviour of artificially eliciting a theta rhythm in this frequency band (by stimulating the medial septal nucleus at 7.7 Hz) or of artificially blocking the theta rhythm in this band (by high-frequency stimulation of the medial septal nucleus) at times when it would be likely to occur spontaneously. The former treatment would be expected to have *opposite* effects on behaviour to those produced by amylobarbitone (i.e. to potentiate or mimic the effects of signals of punishment or non-reward), the latter to have the same effects as amylobarbitone. Both predictions have been upheld by experiments on resistance to extinction in the runway (Gray 1972c; Gray et al. 1972).

A further way of testing the hypothesis that a theta rhythm in the frequency band 7.5–8.5 Hz is critical to the functioning of the behavioural inhibition system is to look at the effects of other drugs on the theta-driving curve of Fig. 9. Drugs which, like amylobarbitone, reduce behavioural inhibition should give

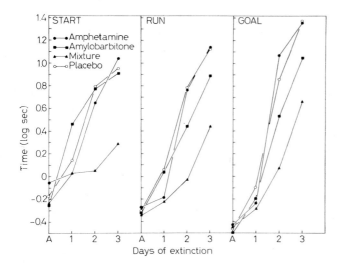

FIG. 11. Effects of 0.75 mg/kg amphetamine sulphate, 17.5 mg/kg amylobarbitone sodium, and a mixture of the two drugs injected during extinction on the resistance to extinction of a food-rewarded running response in the rat. (H. J. Dudderidge & J. A. Gray, in preparation.)

rise to a similar selective increase in the threshold for septal driving of the hippocampal theta rhythm in the 7.5–8.5 Hz frequency band; drugs with different behavioural effects should not produce this effect. We (J. A. Gray, D. T. D. James & H. J. Dudderidge, in preparation) have begun to look at a range of drugs in this way, and the results so far are quite promising. Without doubt the drug whose effects on behaviour are most similar to those of amylobarbitone is alcohol (Miller 1959; Gray 1971a). It is also the drug which, in our hands, affects the theta-driving curve in the most amylobarbitone-like way (Fig. 10). Other drugs so far investigated, which produce rather different effects on the theta-driving curve, are chlordiazepoxide, physostigmine, amphetamine and a number of hormones of both gonadal (see below) and pituitary–adrenal origin. Some of the relevant results are shown in Fig. 10.

The results for a combination of amylobarbitone with amphetamine shown in Fig. 10 are of particular interest. Whereas amylobarbitone on its own abolishes the dip in the theta-driving curve normally seen at 7.7 Hz, the combination of this drug with amphetamine actually *raises* the threshold at 7.7 Hz in comparison with either of the two adjoining frequencies. It may be that this effect is related to the summative behavioural effects often reported when the two drugs are injected together (e.g. Rushton & Steinberg 1963). These interactions between the two drugs have been observed in a variety of behavioural

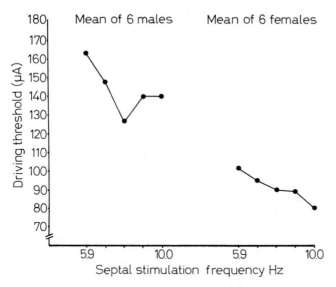

FIG. 12. Mean thresholds for septal driving of hippocampal theta rhythm as a function of driving frequency in male and female rats. (R. F. Drewett & J. A. Gray, in preparation.)

situations. We (H. J. Dudderidge & J. A. Gray, in preparation) have recently shown such an interaction in a paradigmatic situation for the operation of the behavioural inhibition system: simple extinction after reward for running in a straight alley. As shown in Fig. 11, injections of 0.75 mg/kg amphetamine sulphate plus 17.5 mg/kg amylobarbitone sodium, given daily throughout extinction, had a considerably greater effect in retarding extinction than either drug injected alone.

Sex differences in behavioural inhibition

As I have reviewed elsewhere (Gray 1971*b*) there is much evidence that, in rodents, the female is less fearful than the male. However, the experiments on which this claim is based have been rather different from those on which the notion of a behavioural inhibition system is based. The latter idea, as we have seen, depends on experiments in which the behavioural effects of signals of punishment or of non-reward are observed (e.g. passive avoidance or extinction). The experiments which have disclosed the sex difference in fearfulness, in contrast, have generally investigated responses to novelty, such as defecation or ambulation in the open field test, or time to emerge into a novel en-

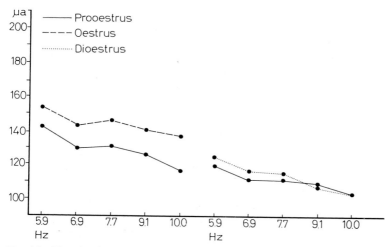

Fig. 13. Thresholds of driving of hippocampal theta rhythm as a function of septal stimulation frequency at different stages of the oestrous cycle. N = 4, of which three rats are common to left and right-hand graphs. (R. F. Drewett & J. A. Gray, in preparation.)

vironment. However, there is good reason to suppose that the behavioural inhibition system is set into operation by novel stimuli (Gray 1971a, pp. 117–119, 203–208), as well as by signals of punishment and non-reward; and a further rapprochement between the two areas of data has recently been accomplished by the report (Jonason & Enloe 1971) that lesions to the septal area (which are well known to impair both passive avoidance and extinction: McCleary 1966) reduce open field defecation, the key measure on which male rodents have been shown to differ from female rodents. The last of our own data that I wish to mention provide a more direct indication of sex differences at the heart of the behavioural inhibition system.

As part of our experiments on the effects of various drugs and hormones on the theta-driving curve, we (R. F. Drewett & J. A. Gray, in preparation) implanted female fats with septal stimulating and hippocampal recording electrodes. To our surprise we found that the basic theta-driving curve was quite different in these females from what we had observed in all our previous work with male rats. The females show no sign of the dip in the theta-driving curve at 7.7 Hz which is such a conspicuous feature of the male curve (Fig. 12). The male curve in this figure is the average of six rats, different from the five whose average curve is shown in Fig. 9: the complete identity of the two curves shows the great replicability of the results obtained from male animals. By contrast, no female has yet given us a typical male curve. We have investigated the effects in the female of the oestrous cycle, of ovariectomy and of injections of oestradiol. None of these treatments has in any way affected the female theta-driving curve; the results from the study of the oestrous cycle are presented in Fig. 13. Thus this sex difference is apparently independent of sex hormones circulating in the bloodstream of the adult female. We have also investigated the effects of castration in four adult males; there is no effect of this treatment on the characteristic shape of the male theta-driving curve up to six weeks after operation; however, all four curves changed to that characteristic of the female between 7 and 11 weeks after castration.

It seems probable, therefore, that there is a fundamental difference between the sexes in the response of the hippocampus to stimulation of the septal area. In the light of the sex differences in fearfulness (Gray 1971b), it is perhaps no coincidence that this difference takes the form that the female theta-driving curve in the undrugged state (Fig. 12) is closely similar to the curve obtained from a male which has received an injection of amylobarbitone or alcohol (Figs. 9 and 10): electrophysiologically, as well as behaviourally, a female rat resembles a tranquillized male one. These results thus hold out the hope that we may soon be in a position to synthesize two large, and so far rather separate, bodies of data on emotional behaviour and its physiological basis: the data on 'behavioural inhibition' (McCleary 1966; Gray 1970a) and the data on 'fear' or 'emotionality' (Broadhurst 1960; Gray 1971a).

ACKNOWLEDGEMENTS

My thanks are due to all my colleagues who have allowed me to anticipate the publication of their results. Part of this paper was presented at the Third Banff Conference on Theoretical Psychology, September 1971 (see Gray 1973).

Most of the new experimental work reported is supported by the Medical Research Council; additional funds were provided by the Smith, Kline and French Foundation.

References

ADAMS, D. & FLYNN, J. P. (1966) Transfer of an escape response from tail shock to brain-stimulated attack behaviour. *J. Exp. Anal. Behav.* **9**, 401-408

ADELMAN, H. M. & MAATSCH, J. L. (1956) Learning and extinction based upon frustration, food reward, and exploratory tendency. *J. Exp. Psychol.* **52**, 311-315

ALBERT, M. & BIGNAMI, G. (1968) Effects of frontal median cortical and caudate lesions on two-way avoidance learning by rats. *Physiol. Behav.* **3**, 141-147

AMSEL, A. (1958) The role of frustrative nonreward in non-continuous reward situations. *Psychol. Bull.* **55**, 102-119

AMSEL, A. (1962) Frustrative nonreward in partial reinforcement and discrimination learning: some recent history and a theoretical extension. *Psychol. Rev.* **69**, 306-328

AMSEL, A. & ROUSSEL, J. (1952) Motivational properties of frustration: I. Effect on a running response of the addition of frustration to the motivational complex. *J. Exp. Psychol.* **43**, 363-368

BALL, G. G. & GRAY, J. A. (1971) Septal self-stimulation and hippocampal activity. *Physiol. Behav.* **6**, 547-549

BALTZER, V. & WEISKRANTZ, L. (1970) Negative and positive behavioural contrast in the same animals. *Nature (Lond.)* **228**, 581-582

BARRY, H. & MILLER, N. E. (1965) Comparison of drug effects on approach, avoidance, and escape motivation. *J. Comp. Physiol. Psychol.* **59**, 18-24

BLACK, R. W. & SPENCE, K. W. (1965) Effect of intertrial reinforcement on resistance to extinction following extended training. *J. Exp. Psychol.* **70**, 559-563

BRADY, J. V. & CONRAD, D. G. (1960) Some effects of limbic system self-stimulation upon conditioned emotional behaviour. *J. Comp. Physiol. Psychol.* **53**, 128-137

BREMNER, F. J. (1964) Hippocampal activity during avoidance behaviour in the rat. *J. Comp. Physiol. Psychol.* **58**, 16-22

BROADHURST, P. L. (1960) Applications of biometrical genetics to the inheritance of behaviour. In *Experiments in Personality*, vol. 1 (Eysenck, H. J., ed.), pp. 3-102, Routledge & Kegan Paul, London

BROWN, J. S., KALISH, H. I. & FARBER, I. E. (1951) Conditioned fear as revealed by magnitude of startle response to an auditory stimulus. *J. Exp. Psychol.* **41**, 317-328

BULL, J. A. III (1970) An interaction between appetitive Pavlovian CSs and instrumental avoidance responding. *Learn. & Motiv.* **1**, 18-26

BUTTERS, N. & ROSVOLD, H. E. (1968) Effect of caudate and septal nuclei lesions on resistance to extinction and delayed alternation . *J. Comp. Physiol. Psychol.* **65**, 397-403

CAPALDI, E. J. (1967) A sequential hypothesis of instrumental learning. In *The Psychology of Learning and Motivation: Advances in Research and Theory*, vol. 1 (Spence, K. W. & Spence, J. T., eds.), pp. 67-156, Academic Press, London

CAPALDI, E. J. & SPARLING, D. L. (1971) Amobarbital and the partial reinforcement effect in rats: isolating frustrative control over instrumental responding. *J. Comp. Physiol. Psychol.* **74**, 467-477

CATTELL, R. B. & SCHEIER, I. H. (1961) *The Meaning and Measurement of Neuroticism and Anxiety*, Ronald Press, New York

CRESPI, L. P. (1942) Quantitative variation of incentive and performance in the white rat. *Am. J. Psychol.* **55**, 467-517

DE MOLINA, A. F. & HUNSPERGER, R. W. (1962) Organization of the subcortical system governing defence and flight reactions in the cat. *J. Physiol. (Lond.)* **160**, 200-213

DEUTSCH, J. A. & DEUTSCH, D. (1966) *Physiological Psychology*, Dorsey Press, Homewood, Ill.

DONOVICK, P. J., BURRIGHT, R. G. & GITTELSON, P. L. (1968) The effects of septal lesions on saccharine choice as a function of water deprivation. *Physiol. Behav.* **3**, 677-681

DOUGLAS, R. J. (1967) The hippocampus and behaviour. *Psychol. Bull.* **67**, 416-442

ESTES, W. K. & SKINNER, B. F. (1941) Some quantitative properties of anxiety. *J. Exp. Psychol.* **29**, 390-400

EYSENCK, H. J. (1967) *Crime and Personality*, 2nd edn, Granada Press, London

EYSENCK, H. J. & EYSENCK, S. B. G. (1969) *Personality Structure and Measurement*, Routledge & Kegan Paul, London

EYSENCK, S. G. B. & EYSENCK, H. J. (1968) The measurement of psychoticism: a study of factor stability and reliability. *Br. J. Soc. Clin. Psychol.* **7**, 286-294

FERSTER, G. B. & SKINNER, B. F. (1957) *Schedules of Reinforcement*, Appleton-Century-Crofts, New York

GALLUP, G. G. JR. (1965) Aggression in rats as a function of frustrative nonreward in a straight alley. *Psychonomic Sci.* **3**, 99-100

GLICKMAN, S. E. & SCHIFF, B. B. (1967) A biological theory of reinforcement. *Psychol. Rev.* **74**, 81-109

GRAY, J. A. (1967) Disappointment and drugs in the rat. *Adv. Sci.* **23**, 595-605
GRAY, J. A. (1969) Sodium amobarbital and effects of frustrative nonreward. *J. Comp. Physiol. Psychol.* **69**, 55-64
GRAY, J. A. (1970a) Sodium amobarbital, the hippocampal theta rhythm and the partial reinforcement extinction effect. *Psychol. Rev.* **77**, 465-480
GRAY, J. A. (1970b) The psychophysiological basis of introversion-extraversion. *Behav. Res. Ther.* **8**, 249-266
GRAY, J. A. (1971a) *The Psychology of Fear and Stress*, Weidenfeld & Nicolson, London; McGraw-Hill, New York
GRAY, J. A. (1971b) Sex differences in emotional behaviour in mammals including man: endocrine bases. *Acta Psychol.* **35**, 29-46
GRAY, J. A. (1972a) Learning theory, the conceptual nervous system and personality. In *The Biological Bases of Individual Behavior* (Nebylitsyn, V. D. & Gray, J. A., eds.), pp. 372-399, Academic Press, New York
GRAY, J. A. (1972b) The psychophysiological nature of introversion-extraversion: a modification of Eysenck's theory. In *The Biological Bases of Individual Behavior* (Nebylitsyn, V. D. & Gray, J. A., eds.), pp. 182-205, Academic Press, New York
GRAY, J. A. (1972c) Effects of septal driving of the hippocampal theta rhythm on resistance to extinction of an instrumental running response in the rat. *Physiol. Behav.* **8**, 481-490
GRAY, J. A. (1973) Causal theories of personality and how to test them. In *Contributions of Multivariate Analysis to Psychological Theory: Third Banff Conference on Theoretical Psychology*, 1971 (Royce, J. R., ed.), Academic Press, New York, in press
GRAY, J. A. & BALL, G. G. (1970) Frequency-specific relation between hippocampal theta rhythm, behavior and amobarbital action. *Science (Wash. D.C.)* **168**, 1246-1248
GRAY, J. A. & DUDDERIDGE, H. (1971) Sodium amylobarbitone, the partial reinforcement extinction effect, and the frustration effect in the double runway. *Neuropharmacology* **10**, 217-222
GRAY, J. A., ARAUJO-SILVA, M. T. & QUINTÃO, L. C. R. (1972) Resistance to extinction after partial reinforcement training with blocking of the hippocampal theta rhythm by septal stimulation. *Physiol. Behav.* **8**, 497-502
GROSSEN, N. E., KOSTANSEK, D. J. & BOLLES, R. C. (1969) Effects of appetitive discriminative stimuli on avoidance behaviour. *J. Exp. Psychol.* **81**, 340-343
GROSSMAN, S. P. (1967) *A Textbook of Physiological Psychology*, Wiley, New York
HEBB, D. O. (1955) Drives and the C.N.S. (conceptual nervous system). *Psychol. Rev.* **62**, 243-254
HULL, C. L. (1952) *A Behavior System*, Yale University Press, New Haven
HUTCHINSON, R. R. & RENFREW, J. W. (1966) Stalking attack and eating behaviour elicited from the same sites in the hypothalamus. *J. Comp. Physiol. Psychol.* **61**, 360-367
ISON, J. R. & NORTHMAN, J. (1968) Amobarbital sodium and instrumental performance changes following an increase in reward magnitude. *Psychon. Sci.* **12**, 185-186
ISON, J. R. & PENNES, E. S. (1969) Interaction of amobarbital sodium and reinforcement schedule in determining resistance to extinction of an instrumental running response. *J. Comp. Physiol. Psychol.* **68**, 215-219
ISON, J. R. & ROSEN, A. J. (1967) The effects of amobarbital sodium on differential instrumental conditioning and subsequent extinction. *Psychopharmacologia* **10**, 417-425
JONASON, K. R. & ENLOE, L. J. (1971) Alteration in social behaviour following septal and amygdaloid lesions in the rat. *J. Comp. Physiol. Psychol.* **75**, 286-301
KAMANO, D. K., MARTIN, L. K. & POWELL, B. J. (1966) Avoidance response acquisition and amobarbital dosage levels. *Psychopharmacologia* **8**, 319-323
KIMBLE, D. P. (1969) Possible inhibitory functions of the hippocampus. *Neuropsychologia* **7**, 235-244
KLÜVER, H. & BUCY, P. C. (1937) 'Psychic blindness' and other symptoms following

bilateral temporal lobectomy in rhesus monkeys. *Am. J. Physiol.* **119**, 352-353

LEÃO, A. A. P. (1947) Further observations on the spreading depression of activity in the cerebral cortex. *J. Neurophysiol.* **10**, 409-414

LEWIS, D. J. (1960) Partial reinforcement: a selective review of the literature since 1950. *Psychol. Bull.* **57**, 1-28

MCCLEARY, R. A. (1966) Response-modulating functions of the limbic system: Initiation and suppression. In *Progress in Physiological Psychology*, vol. 1 (Stellar, E. & Sprague, J. M., eds.), pp. 209-272, Academic Press, New York

MACLEAN, P. D. (1949) Psychosomatic disease and the 'visceral brain': recent developments bearing on the Papez theory of emotion. *Psychosom. Med.* **11**, 338-353

MILLER, N. E. (1951) Learnable drives and rewards. In *Handbook of Experimental Psychology* (Stevens, S. S., ed.), Wiley, New York

MILLER, N. E. (1959) Liberalization of basic S-R concepts: extensions to conflict behaviour, motivation and social learning. In *Psychology: A Study of a Science, Study 1*, vol. 2 (Koch, S., ed.), pp. 196-292, McGraw-Hill, New York

MILLER, N. E. (1964) The analysis of motivational effects illustrated by experiments on amylobarbitone. In *Animal Behaviour and Drug Action (Ciba Found. Symp.)*, pp. 1-18, Churchill, London

MISCHEL, T. (1969) *Human Action*, Academic Press, New York

MOWRER, O. H. (1947) On the dual nature of learning: a re-interpretation of 'conditioning' and 'problem solving'. *Harvard Educ. Rev.* **17**, 102-148

MOWRER, O. H. (1960) *Learning Theory and Behavior*, Wiley, New York

NICHOLSON, J. N. & GRAY, J. A. (1971) Behavioural contrast and peak shift in children. *Br. J. Psychol.* **62**, 367-373

NICHOLSON, J. N. & GRAY, J. A. (1972) Peak shift, behavioural contrast and stimulus generalization as related to personality and development in children. *Br. J. Psychol.* **63**, 47-62

NOTTERMAN, J. M., SCHOENFELD, W. N. & BERSH, D. J. (1952) Conditioned heart rate response in human beings during experimental anxiety. *J. Comp. Physiol. Psychol.* **45**, 1-8

OBRIST, P. A., WOOD, D. M. & PEREZ-REYES, M. (1965) Heart rate during conditioning in humans: effects of UCS intensity, vagal blockade and adrenergic block of vasomotor activity. *J. Exp. Psychol.* **70**, 32-42

OLDS, J. & OLDS, M. (1965) Drives, rewards and the brain. In *New Directions in Psychology*, vol. 2 (Barron, F. *et al.*, ed.), pp. 329-410, Holt, Rinehart and Winston, New York

OLTON, D. S. & ISAACSON, R. L. (1968) Hippocampal lesions and active avoidance. *Physiol. Behav.* 3, 719-724

PAPEZ, J. W. (1937) A proposed mechanism of emotion. *Arch. Neurol. Psychiatr.* **88**, 725-743

PAWLIK, K. (1973) Right answers to the wrong questions? A re-examination of factor-analytic personality research and its contribution to personality theory. In *Contributions of Multivariate Analysis to Psychological Theory: Third Banff Conference on Theoretical Psychology* (Royce, J. R., ed.), Academic Press, New York, in press

RESCORLA, R. A. & SOLOMON, R. L. (1967) Two-process learning theory: relationships between Pavlovian conditioning and instrumental learning. *Psychol. Rev.* **74**, 151-182

ROBERTS, W. W. & KIESS, H. O. (1964) Motivational properties of hypothalamic aggression in cats. *J. Comp. Physiol. Psychol.* **58**, 187-193

ROSEN, A. J., GLASS, D. H. & ISON, J. R. (1967) Amobarbital sodium and instrumental performance following reward reduction. *Psychon. Sci.* **9**, 129-130

RUSHTON, R. & STEINBERG, H. (1963) Mutual potentiation of amphetamine and amylobarbitone measured by activity in rats. *Br. J. Pharmacol.* **21**, 295-305

SCHACHTER, S. (1967) Cognitive effects on bodily functioning: studies of obesity and eating. In *Neurophysiology and Emotion* (Glass, D. C., ed.), pp. 117-144, Rockefeller University Press and Russell Sage Foundation, New York

SCLAFANI, A. & GROSSMAN, S. P. (1969) Hyperphagia produced by knife cuts between the medial and lateral hypothalamus in the rat. *Physiol. Behav.* 4, 533-537

SPENCE, J. T. & SPENCE, K. W. (1966) The motivational components of manifest anxiety: drive and drive stimuli. In *Anxiety and Behaviour* (Spielberger, C. D., ed.), pp. 291-326, Academic Press, New York and London
SPENCE, K. W. (1956) *Behaviour Theory and Conditioning*, Yale University Press, New Haven
STEIN, L. (1965) Facilitation of avoidance behaviour by positive brain stimulation. *J. Comp. Physiol. Psychol.* **60**, 9-19
STUMPF, CH. (1965) Drug action on the electrical activity of the hippocampus. *Int. Rev. Neurobiol.* **8**, 77-138
SUTHERLAND, N. S. & MACKINTOSH, N. J. (1971) *Mechanisms of Animal Discrimination Learning*, Academic Press, London
ULRICH, R. E. (1967) Pain - aggression. In *Foundations of Conditioning and Learning* (Kimble, G. A., ed.), pp. 600-622, Appleton-Century-Crofts, New York
WAGNER, A. R. (1963) Conditioned frustration as a learned drive. *J. Exp. Psychol.* **66**, 142-148
WAGNER, A. R. (1966) Frustration and punishment. In *Current Research on Motivation* (Haber, R. M., ed.), pp. 229-239, Holt, Rinehart and Winston, New York
WEINSTOCK, S. (1958) Acquisition and extinction of a partially reinforced running response at a 24-hour inter-trial interval. *J. Exp. Psychol.* **56**, 151-158
ZIFF, P. R. & CAPALDI, E. J. (1971) Amytal and the small trial partial reinforcement effect: stimulus properties of early trial nonrewards. *J. Exp. Psychol.* **87**, 263-269

Discussion

Hinde: (1) As I made clear in my own contribution (pp. 1-13), I am not so confident that there is a 'reasonably clear distinction between states which are or are not emotional', as Dr Gray suggests. His distinction between drives and emotions according to whether they are caused by factors internal or external to the organism will not hold water:

(*i*) The dichotomy between states caused by internal factors and those caused by external factors is superficial: in most of the cases he cites both are usually involved. Thirst may be caused by eating dry food, for instance.

(*ii*) On his view externally elicited curiosity is an emotion; 'rational' fear is an emotion and 'irrational' fear a drive; and the hope that springs eternal in the human breast is a drive.

(*iii*) The argument from pathology is a *non sequitur*. To say that a number of states normally caused by internal factors are more likely to be abnormal or pathological when external factors predominate, and that states normally caused by external factors are more likely to be abnormal or pathological when internal factors predominate, is little more than stating the obvious, and bears not at all on whether one group is properly called drives and the other emotions.

(2) To suggest that the work of the various learning theorists cited can be distilled to give a 'moderately simple definition of the emotions' is not strictly accurate. Though most of them used intervening variables such as 'fear',

except for Mowrer (1960) they discussed the problem of emotion in a fairly cursory way, if at all. Furthermore:

(*i*) Dr Gray implies that 'emotion' or 'drive' words were used to refer to hypothetical internal states of the organism, when in fact most of the theorists used them as intervening variables without physiological reference.

(*ii*) He uses the terms 'reinforcement' and 'punishment' loosely. Operant theorists, at least, would limit the term reinforcement to operations which *increase* the strength of responses, so that increasing the frequency of a response via shock avoidance would be an example of negative reinforcement. Response contingent stimuli which *decrease* response strength would be described as 'punishment'. Dr Gray uses the term 'punishment' loosely as an equivalent for shock, which may be acting as an unconditioned stimulus in a Pavlovian situation, as a negative reinforcer (see above), or as punishment (see above).

(*iii*) The conditioned emotional response to which he refers is now more generally called conditioned suppression, and is measured by the decrease in ongoing instrumental behaviour. This decrease is attributed to the elicitation of incompatible (emotional) *responses*.

(3) Dr Gray argues that the study of learning suggests that we should recognize the existence of only three major emotional systems. He reaches this conclusion by first specifying the maximum possible number on so-called 'logical' grounds, and then amalgamating some of them. But in generating the 'maximum possible number' he considers only three characteristics—whether the state is appetitive or aversive, whether the eliciting factor is presented or withheld, and whether their relationship is or is not conditioned. His conclusion concerning the maximum possible number is a product solely of the number of variables he considers. Why does he restrict himself in this way? He recognizes that common parlance differentiates more than three emotions, but somehow implies that his argument, with the aid of neuroanatomical data, is in some sense more correct, failing to recognize that his analysis depends on his own limited assumptions. And his final reduction to three runs contrary to the wealth of objective evidence now available for the emotional expressive movements (e.g. Ekman & Friesen 1969).

In collapsing his 'maximum possible' number of categories, he comes up against difficulties at a number of points:

(*i*) The evidence that the effects of signals of punishment (of all sorts?) and of frustrative non-reward (of all sorts?) are 'functionally identical' is based on few dependent variables; furthermore, evidence that the same neuroendocrine systems are involved is not evidence of identity.

(*ii*) The view that the effects of reward and 'non-punishment' are 'physiologically identical' runs into a similar difficulty.

(*iii*) He treats all forms of approach behaviour as similar, which is at most only partly true even if one neglects the differential responsiveness to stimuli with which they are associated.

(*iv*) Unconditional punishment and frustrative non-reward are grouped together because both may elicit agonistic behaviour. A common consequence does not prove identity.

(*v*) His distinction between active escape induced by unconditioned stimuli and passive avoidance elicited by conditioned stimuli is valid only for certain selected cases. In many species a predator may elicit crouching even in the absence of previous experience of that predator, and the effect of a conditioned aversive stimulus depends on the previous history of reinforcement.

(4) Others present at this meeting are better qualified than I to comment on Dr Gray's neurophysiological material, but I suspect him of oversimplifying. For instance, the view that the main controlling centres for drives (note—an intervening variable somehow enmeshed in the real nervous system) are predominantly in the hypothalamus is surely a dated conclusion from earlier work in which more anterior structures were not studied.

Gray: Professor Hinde has made a number of points and I shall take them in the same order.

(1*i*) Of course I agree that in any real case both internal and external factors jointly control behaviour, but that does not mean that the distinction between (*a*) internal states (usually) mainly controlled by internal factors and (*b*) those (usually) mainly controlled by external factors is superficial; any more than the distinction between town and country is superficial because the country contains houses and the town contains parks. Furthermore, the nervous system appears to recognize this distinction; and I am not alone in concluding that the hypothalamus is largely responsible for the drive aspects of behaviour (i.e. is responsive to internal factors) and the limbic system for the emotional aspects of behaviour (i.e. is responsive to external factors) (see, for example, Gloor 1972).

(*ii*) Professor Hinde is correct in stating that, according to my view, curiosity is an emotion. Fear, too, is an emotion, whether 'rational' or 'irrational', since the latter term means only that the external stimulus for the fear is one not normally found fearful by other members of the group (e.g. fear of cats in a case of cat phobia). Hope, too, is an emotion: its eternal springing in the human breast is an obstacle more poetic than real, since hope is very much a state that depends on external factors. (I regard inputs to the emotions from verbal sources, whether proceeding from others or from the subject himself, as *external* factors. I also distinguish between an instance of an emotion and a constitutional disposition towards certain emotions: one may be a person in whom hope is a very easily aroused emotion, and this is to do with permanent, and therefore internal, features of one's personality; but the hope, when it comes, is—usually and mainly—a response to external factors.)

(*iii*) The argument from pathology is not quite as Professor Hinde puts it. Our very recognition that fear independent of external factors (or eating largely controlled by external factors) is abnormal indicates our awareness that *normally* the emotions are in the main responses to external events and drives are not. And this is not a *non sequitur*.

(2) The distinction within learning theory between motivational states which are largely due to internal factors and those due to external factors is at least as old as Hull and Spence's distinction between drive and incentive (e.g. Hull 1943). The linkage between states which are responses to external events and the traditional names of the emotions is well represented in Neal Miller's work on fear in the 1940's and 1950's (e.g. Miller 1951, 1964), Amsel's work on frustration (e.g. Amsel & Roussel 1952), and Estes & Skinner's (1941) work on the 'conditioned emotional response'. It is true that Mowrer's (1960) treatment of emotion in the context of learning theory is the only extended one; but the features I distilled are common to these other workers as well.

(*i*) I make no important distinction between intervening variables and hypothetical internal states of the organism. The aim of psychological theory of any kind is to give a true description of how the brain and the endocrine system control behaviour. In producing such a theory, there is no need to refer to any physiological events; it is possible, and perhaps even desirable, to treat the organism as a black box about which theories are made and tested by the usual experimental and deductive methods of science. But any theory which eventually survives such testing is nonetheless an attempt to describe the physiological systems which control behaviour; and it is open to disproof if and when our physiological knowledge is sufficiently advanced to offer such disproof. Thus an 'intervening variable' is a crypto-internal state, to the extent that it is anything more than a computational aid; and, if it is no more than that, it is not very interesting. Both Hull and Pavlov explicitly regarded themselves as theorizing about the brain, and the tenor of the work of Miller, Amsel and Mowrer is of the same kind. But, even if these authors did not have this intention, my only way of taking them seriously (and I believe they merit serious attention) would be to treat them as though they were theorizing about the brain.

(*ii*) The criticism that I use the words 'reinforcement' and 'punishment' loosely would be valid if there were instances in which a stimulus which could be used as a punishment (i.e. one which decreases the probability of behaviour upon which its delivery is contingent) could not also be used as a negative reinforcer (i.e. one which increases the probability of behaviour upon which its termination or omission is contingent); or *vice versa*. I know of no such instances. Thus it seems, at the moment, reasonable to treat 'punishment' and 'negative reinforcer' as equivalent insofar as they refer to classes of stimuli. They are different as experimental procedures; and in fact the empirical dissimilarities between active and passive avoidance (the former involving negative reinforcement, the latter punishment) figure prominently among the considerations which led to my three-emotion model. The only reason I use 'shock' as synonymous with both 'punishment' and 'negative reinforcement' is that most experiments in this field have used electric shock as the punishing or reinforcing stimulus. Again, however, I know of no evidence to suggest that, at the level of abstraction of my argument, different conclusions would emerge from consideration of the results of experiments using other aversive stimuli.

(*iii*) On the conditioned emotional response, since the alleged 'incompatible emotional responses' appear to be capable of suppressing *any* ongoing positively reinforced instrumental behaviour, no matter what its actual motor topography, it is more parsimonious to postulate that the organism is equipped with a single system for doing precisely that—suppressing ongoing behaviour—upon receipt of appropriate signals. On very different grounds, Razran (1971) has recently come to the same conclusion.

(3) The short answer to Professor Hinde's third point is that the history of how I arrived at my hypotheses is not as important as whether the hypotheses pass the test of experiment. I hope I have shown in my paper that these hypotheses are worth putting to that test. The fact that we are able to recognize and name more than three emotions is no more fundamental an obstacle to my model than our ability to name many more than three colours is to a trichromatic theory of colour vision. Different names may be given according to different intensities of activation of any one of my three emotional systems; according to different interactions between them; or according to simultaneous activation of more than one of them; and, no doubt, there are other possibilities. One very important way in which our highly differentiated vocabulary of emotion words arises has been shown by Schachter's work (Schachter & Singer 1962). He has demonstrated that the verbal labelling of emotions depends in part only on the internal state in which we find ourselves and to a great extent on what we know about the circumstances which led to that internal state.

With regard to the specific points (*i*) to (*v*), we must agree to differ in our assessment of the evidence. I would regard the evidence on (*i*) as very good, and on (*iii*), (*iv*) and (*v*) as fairly good, while (*ii*) is at this time only a very tentative hypothesis. In a short discussion it would not be profitable to attempt to add to what I said in my paper and in the references given there.

(4) See my answer to (1*i*) and (2*i*).

Hinde: As a general point, you are discussing two separate issues. One is your three behavioural systems, each of which may have a certain unity and may respond in predictable ways to barbiturates and so on; the other is the link that you want to make between those systems and emotional words and emotional states. I suggest that it is a mistake to make this link to emotional states. Discuss your behavioural systems and link them to physiological systems if you can, but don't confuse this with the material about emotional expression.

Gray: I think there is a dilemma about the use of emotion words. The emotional systems that I am trying to explain are very close to what people in everyday speech call 'emotions'. I could call them systems A, B and C and avoid using any words which could lead to misunderstanding, but I don't want to divorce myself from all discussion of human experience and behaviour, especially since I believe that my work is related, for example, to clinical observations of obsessive-compulsive neuroses, anxiety states and so on. It would be unfortunate if I then had to use completely new words for what clinicians are describing when they talk about anxiety, for example. There are dangers in both directions.

Sandler: Dr C. Dare and I took a random sample of the emotion words in the *Oxford English Dictionary*. In a group of general psychiatrists who used a repertoire of words to describe the affective aspects of mental status we found a small number (four) of common factors (using factor analysis), and many idiosyncratic usages of well-known 'affect' terms. It seems there is a much smaller number of basic common elements than the number of words used. When we took an emotion word like 'anxiety' and correlated it with several hundred other emotion words, we found four main distinct meanings attributed to the word 'anxiety' by the psychiatrists. There was a difference in their use of the term in regard to whether a person feared that something awful might happen; or whether he was reacting to something awful which he felt *had* happened; or whether he had no feeling of anxiety but showed bodily changes which were identified as anxiety; or whether the psychiatrist interpreted a state of underlying anxiety. This study emphasizes how much we need to distinguish between feelings and the words used to relate to feelings and to the bodily changes which also come under the heading of 'emotion'. We cannot assume a one-to-one correlation between them. We talk about emotion in diverse ways, to refer to feeling-experiences as well as to physiological changes.

Fonberg: I cannot agree with Dr Gray that active avoidance and approach can be put in the same category, because different brain areas control these two kinds of behaviour. Experiments on avoidance and approach have mostly been done by different people with different schedules. In order to see how differently brain lesions affect these two types of reactions they should both be studied in the same animals (Fonberg 1968). When I lesioned the part of the amygdala which controls feeding behaviour, I found that instrumental alimentary reactions were impaired but instrumental avoidance reactions in the same dog were not.

It is true that experiments on spreading depression have shown similar results for active avoidance and approach behaviour; this was because they were both instrumental reactions. If we impair the motor system the performance of both reactions is impaired, but this does not prove that the approach and avoidance systems are similar.

Gray: I am not committed to saying that *any* lesion which impairs food motivation will also impair active avoidance. My hypothesis is that there is a single approach system which is at the service of all positively reinforced behaviour and of active avoidance behaviour. But the effect of different rewards must *also* depend on different drive states. This is one consequence of the distinction I have drawn between drives and emotions. Your suggestion that cases where a physiological treatment (such as spreading depression) impairs both positively reinforced behaviour and active avoidance behaviour can be accounted for by saying that both of these are 'instrumental' reactions is not necessarily different from what I am claiming. I would regard 'instrumental' behaviour precisely as positively reinforced goal-directed behaviour, and active avoidance as involving (after an initial phase of learning) the positive reinforcement of attainment of safety signals. Impairment of the animal's ability to direct its motor behaviour towards such goals is the same (in my terms) as impairment of the approach system.

Levine: How do you account for the marked differences in the extinction of active avoidance behaviour and normal approach?

Gray: The model that we have put forward at the behavioural level, with a moderately simple mathematical apparatus attached to it (Gray & Smith 1969; Gray 1971), treats active avoidance, after an initial phase of conditioning of fear to conditioned stimuli paired with unconditioned punishing stimuli, as being motivated by the search for, and reinforced by the attainment of, safety signals, where a 'safety signal' is any stimulus which is paired (by classical conditioning) with relieving non-punishment, and 'relieving non-punishment', in turn, is the non-occurrence of punishment in the presence of stimuli which have previously been paired with punishment. This is a brief account of a complicated theory, of which I hope soon to give a more detailed treatment. With regard to the specific point on the extinction of active avoidance, our model treats extinction of approach behaviour as due to frustrative non-reward, as in Amsel's theory. Thus, you now have to ask what could constitute the equivalent of frustrative non-reward for an animal working for safety signals in an active avoidance situation. What can disappoint the animal's expectation? Well, he expects, when he reaches safety, that nothing, i.e. non-punishment, will occur. So the only way to produce extinction will be either by preventing the avoidance response from attaining the safety signals, or by punishing the avoidance response. This, by and large, fits the facts. In simple one-way avoidance situations extinction does not easily occur unless either the avoidance response is punished or it is blocked so that the erstwhile safety signals are no longer attained (Gray 1971).

Hill: There seems to be a shift in your terms here and some hiatus in my understanding of your concept. When you begin to talk in terms of a search for safety signals, it sounds as if it were Dr Sandler talking!

Engel: Dr Gray, what is the basis for the use of the terms 'depression' and 'elation'? What do the rats look like when they show 'depression' and 'elation'?

Gray: These are technical terms used in experimental psychology for this kind of response. Behaviourally speaking, a rat that is exposed to frustrative non-reward looks excited; it bites things, and you can see that it is emotionally upset. The elated animal looks no different from a normal animal but it presses the lever faster.

Hill: I thought that the distinction was based on the rate of response: an elated animal simply responds at a higher rate and a depressed animal at a lower rate.

Gray: Not necessarily. One has to define it in a more complex way than that. If you observe a decrease in response vigour as a result of exposure to frustrative non-reward, then this would be a depression effect. Conversely, an elation effect is an increase in response vigour as a result of exposure to an unexpected increase in reward. In other words, it depends both on the response and on the technique used to obtain the response.

Hofer: Dr Gray, would you speculate on the observations that clinicians have made on patients with hysterical amnesia, like the patient described by Dr Nemiah? Under the influence of sodium amylobarbitone very frequently they can recall, in great detail and often with emotional concomitants, events which they could not remember before, or even after amylobarbitone. Does that suggest anything about the physiological mechanisms underlying psychological defences?

Gray: I have thought about this and I wish I could draw a beautiful sketch-map in answer to your question. The problem of the relationship between behavioural inhibition in the sense that I was using it on the one hand, and memory functions on the other, is a very real issue in the study of animal behaviour after brain lesions. The classic result of hippocampectomy in man is an apparently profound difficulty in converting short-term memory into long-term memory. No animal experiment in any species that I am aware of, from rats up to monkeys, has yet produced that sort of result of hippocampectomy. On the contrary, the results (Douglas 1967; Kimble 1969) have always fitted the picture of a disturbance of behavioural inhibition. So from rat to monkey, the hippocampus is involved with behavioural inhibition, and in man it is involved in the laying-down of long-term memories. Various ways have been suggested for getting out of this difficulty, short of the obvious one of saying that man is different from every other mammal. The approach that looks most promising is that being tried by Warrington & Weiskrantz (1970; Weiskrantz 1971). They reinvestigated patients who were amnesic either as a result of Korsakoff psychosis or, in one case, after right unilateral temporal lobectomy. They found that if they used special training procedures the patients were not amnesic; they could learn and retain just as well as normal people. The training procedure used is one which prevents interference from items similar to the material to be learned. Now, one of the classic symptoms of damage to the hippocampus in animals is a failure of 'reversal' learning (Douglas 1967; Kimble 1969), where the animal has to learn to do the opposite of what it has done before, or a new response in place of the old. Thus, the bridge between the behaviour of man and animals offered by Warrington and Weiskrantz's work is this: it may be that, to learn something new in an old context, you need a system which can (a) inhibit old responses and (b) clearly label the situations in which new and old responses should be given; and the hippocampus may provide such a system in man and in other mammals. How this might apply to a patient with hysterical amnesia, where the amnesia is apparently due to a negative affect attached to the forgotten (or 'suppressed') material, I don't know. Perhaps that part of the system which is concerned with suppressing material so that new material may be learned is in some way disturbed or over-active.

Storey: The hippocampal lesion in Korsakoff's syndrome affects verbal memory more than other forms, and in animals this cannot be detected.

Gray: That may be the case; but, if so, it is perhaps a consequence of the more general distinction that I have drawn, because verbal learning in man is learning of a kind where there is a particularly large amount of interference from other activities using the same materials. If we learn a particular set of words for a particular set of circumstances, we may use the same words in many different contexts between one day and the next. Warrington and Weiskrantz used both verbal and non-verbal material and, provided they chose their material in a way which is relatively 'interference-free', they obtained just as good learning in amnesic patients as in normal subjects. In the test of non-verbal memory they gave their patients a series of line-drawings of familiar objects, such as aeroplanes, which started as a set of unconnected lines and became increasingly close to the final drawing of the aeroplane. The subject had to anticipate the aeroplane from seeing the first few unconnected lines, which are almost incapable of reminding him of anything other than the aeroplane. In a typical verbal learning experiment with nonsense syllables, we use the same syllables in so many contexts that one syllable can be the beginning of a large number of words. However, Warrington & Weiskrantz (1970) also designed their verbal material to be interference-free, and, with either verbal or non-verbal material of this kind, their amnesic patients were capable of good retention.

Incidentally, Korsakoff patients do not have lesions in the hippocampus. The chief site of neuropathology is the mammillary bodies (Brierley 1966), to which, however, the hippocampus sends a massive projection via the fornix.

Sandler: Dr Hofer mentioned the effect of amylobarbitone on hysterical patients with amnesia. Part of the function of the psychological apparatus I referred to earlier is to sample trial actions and trial experiences and, if these threaten to give rise to too much pain, to inhibit them. Amylobarbitone might slow down this inhibition, so that impulses and forms of behaviour which might otherwise be inhibited break through. If one adds methamphetamine (Methedrine) to the amylobarbitone, a lot of this normally repressed material breaks through, and we may assume that there is a *disinhibition*. One other point: learning experiments by Betlheim & Hartmann (1924) on Korsakoff patients showed that the material they produce—the slips of the tongue, the ramblings, the associations—was dealt with in exactly the same way as dream material is dealt with in ordinary subjects. It wasn't chaotic; the same mechanisms were actually working in the productions of the patients with Korsakoff's syndrome.

References

AMSEL, A. & ROUSSEL, J. (1952) Motivational properties of frustration: I. Effect on a running response of the addition of frustration to the motivational complex. *J. Exp. Psychol.* **43**, 363-368

BETLHEIM, S. & HARTMANN, H. (1924) Ueber Fehlreaktionen bei der Korsakowschen Psychose. *Arch. Psychiatr. Nervenk.* **72**, 275-286

BRIERLEY, J. B. (1966) in *Amnesia* (Whitty, C. W. M. & Zangwill, O. L., eds.), pp. 150-180, Butterworths, London

DOUGLAS, R. J. (1967) The hippocampus and behaviour. *Psychol. Bull.* **67**, 416-442

EKMAN, P. & FRIESEN, W. V. (1969) The repertoire of nonverbal behaviour: categories, origins, usage and coding. *Semiotica* **1** (1), 49-98

ESTES, W. K. & SKINNER, B. F. (1941) Some quantitative properties of anxiety. *J. Exp. Psychol.* **29**, 390-400

FONBERG, E. (1968) The instrumental alimentary avoidance differentiation in dogs. *Acta Biol. Exp.* **28**, 303-373

GLOOR, P. (1972) in *The Neurobiology of the Amygdala* (Eleftheriou, B. E., ed.), pp. 423-458, Plenum Press, New York

GRAY, J. A. (1971) *The Psychology of Fear and Stress*, Weidenfeld & Nicolson, London

GRAY, J. A. & SMITH, P. T. (1969) in *Animal Discrimination Learning* (Gilbert, R. & Sutherland, N. S., eds.), pp. 243-272, Academic Press, London

HULL, C. L. (1943) *Principles of Behavior*, Appleton-Century, New York

KIMBLE, D. P. (1969) Possible inhibitory functions of the hippocampus. *Neuropsychologia* **7**, 235-244

MILLER, N. E. (1951) Learnable drives and rewards. In *Handbook of Experimental Psychology* (Stevens, S. S., ed.), Wiley, New York

MILLER, N. E. (1964) The analysis of motivational effects illustrated by experiments on amylobarbitone sodium. In *Animal Behaviour and Drug Action (Ciba Found. Symp.)*, pp. 1-18, Churchill, London

MOWRER, O. H. (1960) *Learning Theory and Behavior*, Wiley, New York

RAZRAN, G. (1971) *Mind in Evolution*, Houghton Mifflin, Boston

SCHACHTER, S. & SINGER, J. E. (1962) Cognitive, social and physiological determinants of emotional state. *Psychol. Rev.* **69**, 379-399

WARRINGTON, E. K. & WEISKRANTZ, L. (1970) Amnesic syndrome: consolidation or retrieval? *Nature (Lond.)* **228**, 628-630

WEISKRANTZ, L. (1971) in *Cognitive Processes of Nonhuman Primates* (Jarrard, L. E., ed.), pp. 25-46, Academic Press, New York

Control of emotional behaviour through the hypothalamus and amygdaloid complex

E. FONBERG

Limbic Laboratory, Department of Neurophysiology, Nencki Institute of Experimental Biology, Warsaw

Abstract One way to investigate the mechanisms underlying neurotic symptoms and pathological emotions is to look for the neuronal substratum responsible for these disturbances. The limbic system seems to be the most important brain system in this respect. Our experiments on dogs showed that lesions of the dorso-medial amygdala as well as lesions localized in the lateral hypothalamus produced, besides alimentary disturbances, profound changes in motivational and emotional behaviour. The dogs became apathetic, indifferent, sad and uncooperative. They lost their friendly relations with people and showed negativism and catatonic-like postures. Subsequent bilateral destruction of the lateral part of amygdala abolished all these symptoms. The dogs again became lively, interested in their surroundings, gay and friendly. They returned to their previous habits which they had lost after the first operation. Several mechanisms may be involved in this recovery. The restoration of a disturbed balance between excitation and inhibition, by the removal of the source of excess inhibition, seems to be the most important mechanism.

The mechanisms underlying neurotic states and pathological emotions have been investigated by various workers. Although most of them agree that conflict is the main cause of neurotic disturbance and that the basic mechanisms are similar in man and animals, we still do not know what these mechanisms are. We are not certain whether the most important factors are disturbances in the electrical activity of the neurons, biochemical changes (in metabolic or storage processes) or other unknown mechanisms. We also do not know whether neurotic disturbances involve the whole brain or are limited to particular specific structures, and, if this last is true, whether various overt manifestations of illness may depend on the different localization of neurotic disturbances within the central nervous system.

We may assume that the process underlying the neurosis occurs primarily in three different systems. First, it may take place in the afferent part of the nervous system, in perceptive cortical areas. This was the original idea of Pavlov, who stated that neurotic 'clash' takes place in cortical analysers concerned with the segregation of afferent impulses and their synthesis (Pavlov 1952). Second, the neurotic process may originate in the limbic system and subcortical areas, which are generally believed to control emotional states. In every conflict the emotions play a very important role, and it is doubtful whether neurosogenic conflict can be created without the engagement of the emotions. The third possibility is that neurotic processes mainly invade the particular effector system (which may be different in various types of neurosis).

From the very beginning of my scientific research I was interested in the pathophysiological mechanisms underlying neurotic symptoms. In my earlier studies I tried to find out the causes of different types of neurotic syndromes. I showed that it is possible to evoke neurotic disturbances in dogs limited to a specific motor reaction if this very reaction is involved in the conflictual task. In this way it is possible to produce pathological reactions in the form of 'tics' or 'contractions' of the chosen extremity (Fonberg 1953, 1968b, 1971b). In such 'neuroses', after the first period of conflict in which emotional reactions dominate, later the pathological symptoms are limited to the particular motor reactions and the emotional state and performance of the dog apart from these reactions does not differ from normal. We can call this the 'efferent' type of neurosis. Maier's fixations (1949) are another example of this type. Further experiments on the manifestation of defensive reactions in neurotic states evoked in the absence of any nociceptive stimuli (Fonberg 1958, 1968b) led me to the assumption that generalized and chaotic emotional excitation (in which excitation of the fear system plays a dominant role) is the main basis of the development of neuroses. It was therefore not accidental that I moved from studies on the experimental neuroses *sui generis* to the investigation of the limbic structures, including the hypothalamus, since these structures are considered to be the centres for the regulation of emotional behaviour and biologically motivated needs.

The relationship of emotional reactions to the limbic system has been well known since the work of Papez (1937) and MacLean (1958). Beginning with Hess (1928, 1947), various investigators have been able to produce emotional behaviour by stimulating the hypothalamus and amygdaloid complex, and it therefore became clear that these particular structures are important in the emotions. Experiments by Flynn (1967), Fonberg (1967), Fonberg & Flynn (1963), Wasman & Flynn (1962), Egger & Flynn (1963), de Molina & Hunsperger (1962) and others proved that reactions evoked by brain stimulation are evidently not 'sham emotions', or motor automatisms. They are states equivalent to true emotions, which are able to motivate purposeful, adequate, goal-directed behaviour.

Before describing our experiments concerned with the brain areas controlling emotional behaviour we must define what we understand by 'emotions', since the use of this word is controversial. The term 'emotional', primarily derived from psychology, is also widely used by physiologists. It cannot be denied that the emotional states exist in reality, and that they must therefore depend upon physiological mechanisms, and it follows that we should be able to investigate them by physiological methods. However, the psychological ballast weighs heavily on the definition of the word 'emotional' and various authors use it in different senses.

The word 'emotion' comprises (1) subjective feelings; (2) external emotional symptoms such as motor reactions (including facial expressions), vocalization and various autonomic changes, specific for different emotional states. All these changes may or may not be accompanied by subjective feelings; and (3) complex forms of behaviour, which enable motivated actions to be performed.

The appearance of various emotional reactions depends upon the excitation of corresponding brain structures. They are known as the 'centres of emotional reactions'. The terms 'emotional centres' and 'motivational centres' or 'drive centres' overlap widely and are even used as synonymous by some authors. It seems to me that motivation might be defined as the excitation of certain structures of the nervous system, which evokes definite emotional states and leads to directed behaviour—that is, to the performance of instrumental acts. As follows from this definition, at the base of motivated activity lie the emotional states, which are the 'fuel for drive'. On the other hand, the emotional state itself may not lead to a motivated instrumental reaction. To motivate behaviour certain conditions are indispensable: (1) a certain level of excitation of the so-called emotional centres (such as centres of 'fear', 'rage', sexual drive, hunger and so on); (2) the presence of the objects (such as an enemy, aggressor, prey, sexual object, food) that are adequate goals for a particular emotional state. The quality of these reactions in each situation is determined by the corresponding perceptions and efficacy of the ongoing action, which may be called the conditioned feedback; and (3) excitation of the particular centres patterning both innate and acquired forms of activity, corresponding to specific emotional states.

Both the external signs of emotions and the behaviour motivated by emotions are accessible to experiment. Subjective emotional feelings in animals can be judged only by extrapolation, although it seems probable that identical motor and autonomic reactions and facial expressions, and also goal-directed, adequate, complex forms of behaviour in animals and man in experimental and normal life situations, correspond to identical emotional feelings. Studies on the electrical stimulation of the human brain also indicate that stimulation of similar structures to those from which emotional reactions can be evoked in animals produces emotional feelings in people (Chapman 1960; Heath & Mickle 1960; King 1961; Sem-Jacobsen & Torkildsen 1960).

Emotional reactions have been classified in several ways. From the psychological point of view emotions may be divided into pleasant and unpleasant ones. In terms of the direction of the reactions, we can distinguish negative emotions, which are avoided, and positive ones, which are sought out. Olds *et al.* (1960) proposed a map of the brain divided into positive (rewarding) and negative (punishing) areas on the basis of self-stimulation experiments and avoidance performance. Lilly (1958), Levtova & Slyozin (1968) and others showed in monkeys, dogs and other animals that prolonged stimulation of the negative points may produce a state similar to a neurotic one. By contrast, stimulation of positive, rewarding areas may reduce neurotic tension and produce recovery of the normal nervous balance (Lilly 1958). Stimulation of the negative areas may serve as reinforcement for the avoidance reactions in a similar way to external negative reinforcement, as shown by many authors. Similarly, stimulation of positive areas is the reward for instrumental reactions (Fonberg 1967, 1969*b*; Hoebel & Teitelbaum 1962; Margules & Olds 1962).

The direction of the reaction, however, does not always show the character of the emotion within these two categories. In our experiments (Fonberg 1963*c*, 1967) on dogs we showed that by stimulating the hypothalamus it is possible to evoke three different patterns of aversive behaviour—rage–attack, fear–flight and fear–defence. Only stimulation of fear–flight points served as a good reinforcement for avoidance training. Most of the dogs did not learn to avoid stimulation of rage–attack points. Stimulation of fear–defence points, although obviously aversive, was also much weaker as negative reinforcement than stimulation of the fear–flight area.

In the amygdala of dogs we also found some points in the cortico-medial division, as well as in the piriform cortex, where stimulation produces fear–flight reactions. The dogs learned to avoid this stimulation by definite instrumental reactions in a similar way as seen after stimulation of hypothalamic fear–flight points (Fonberg 1963*b*). However, we found no points in the amygdala of dogs where stimulation produced rage reactions with directed attack, so we are unable to compare this particular form of behaviour evoked from two different brain structures. Although avoidance training to stimulation of rage–attack points failed, we cannot conclude that this stimulation is completely non-aversive. Avoidance reactions are not the only detector of the intensity of aversive emotion. The facility of learning a particular reaction is, among other factors, dependent on both the intensity of the motivation and the adequacy of the reaction itself. Rage leads to attack, which is incompatible with avoidance. This might be the reason for our failure in avoidance training.

In our recent studies we have been more interested in the role of the hypothalamus and amygdala in controlling positive emotions. The existence of both positive and negative emotions seems to be without doubt. However, there is some tendency to consider only the negative emotions as true emotions. Fear, anger, rage, sorrow—that is, the states produced by anticipation of pain, danger, fight or discomfort—produce no doubts that they are emotional, whereas the appetites—anticipation of pleasant events like a good meal or a sexual object, or pleasures in any sense—produce among some scientists a strong hesitation whether their character is emotional. Most learning theories are based on reward by drive reduction, and in particular they stress reward by stopping or avoiding unpleasant events. This philosophy of 'lack' might be due, I would suggest, to introspective experience resulting from some aspects of civilization. I cannot agree with the theories which imply that the most pleasant or even the only pleasant state is when imminent danger or an uncomfortable situation is avoided or stops. It is true that in the civilized world, very few people preserve the ability to enjoy the signals of positive biological rewards like food, because we are not very often hungry, or signals from sexual objects, because we are saturated by sexual signals in advertising. Children and dogs (if they are not spoiled by too much comfort!) on the other hand demonstrate positive emotional states produced by the anticipation of, say, a tasty cake. The positive emotions accompany both the expectation of pleasures and their consumption. Our behaviour is in the same extent motivated by the anticipation of pleasures which we like to obtain and by the anticipation of unpleasant events which should be avoided. The brain contains areas where stimulation is punishing and others where it is rewarding. The same reciprocity occurs in subjective feelings. The positive emotions are connected with biological needs, as are the negative ones. For example, stimulation of the lateral hypothalamic 'feeding centre' is rewarding. It cannot, however, be rewarding because it evokes hunger, but, I suggest, because it produces the anticipation of a good meal or even some kind of sensation of its taste, together with a positive emotional state connected with these sensations. This conclusion is based on the results of my experiments in which dogs easily learned to perform an instrumental reaction to a conditioned stimulus which was rewarded only by brain stimulation of the feeding centre in the lateral hypothalamus (Fonberg 1967, 1969b). I hope that the experiments I shall describe below provide further evidence for the existence of positive emotions and their relation to feeding mechanisms.

Food is one of the best known external positive reinforcements, and is widely used in experiments on animals. Since the well-known work of Anand & Brobeck (1951) it has been known that the hypothalamus deals with feeding reactions. Stimulation of the lateral hypothalamus both produces voracious eating in satiated animals and serves as positive reinforcement (Olds 1962; Margules & Olds 1962; Hoebel & Teitelbaum 1962; Fonberg 1967, 1969b). It also evokes instrumental alimentary reactions learned before the stimulation as well as other types of alimentary behaviour (Wyrwicka et al. 1959, 1960; Miller 1957; Fonberg 1967). Lesions of this area produce the well-known syndrome of aphagia and loss of instrumental reactions (see Teitelbaum 1967). The ventro-medial nucleus of the hypothalamus has an opposite role: stimulation produces cessation of eating and lesions result in hyperphagia.

The alimentary functions of the amygdala have not been investigated so thoroughly. In our previous studies (Fonberg & Delgado 1961; Fonberg 1963a, 1966, 1967; Fonberg & Sychowa 1968; Fonberg 1968a, 1969a, 1969b, 1971a) we showed that the dorso-medial part of the amygdala has similar functions to the lateral hypothalamus in that it acts as a positive alimentary centre, whereas the lateral amygdala has an inhibitory role.

More recently we have been comparing the effect of lesions situated in the amygdala and hypothalamus on the alimentary motivation and emotional reactions of dogs. We use dogs for these experiments because their social behaviour and emotional expression are multiform and also easy to recognize, as the dog has over the centuries grown up as the companion of man. Dogs are also used to man, and easy to train in different procedures, both classical and instrumental.

Our dogs were observed for 3–4 months before the operation and were trained in different procedures (instrumental and classical salivary reactions). Food intake and body weight were measured. Some dogs were trained postoperatively. The operations were performed stereotaxically under Nembutal anaesthesia. Details of the experimental procedures and surgery are described elsewhere (Fonberg 1969a, b, 1971a; Rożkowska & Fonberg 1970, 1971, 1972).

Lesions were placed in the dorso-medial amygdala, lateral amygdala, lateral hypothalamus and ventro-medial hypothalamus (Fig. 1; Fig. 8, p. 147).

Lesions in the dorso-medial amygdala severely affected the behaviour of the dogs. Damage in this area produced aphagia with adipsia (refusal to eat and drink) and vomiting. Aphagia lasted from a few days to three weeks and was followed by a long period of hypophagia and food preference. However, the most striking changes were in the general behaviour and motivational state of the dogs. For the first few postoperative days they spent most of the time lying down, half asleep. Then they sometimes started to walk around aimlessly,

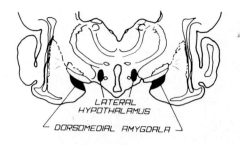

Aphagia and adipsia

Vomiting

Decrease of body weight

Impairment of positive instrumental and classical reactions

Apathy

Negativism

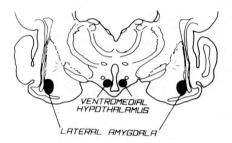

Hyperphagia

Obesity

Disinhibition of instrumental and classical reactions

FIG. 1. Schematic drawing of two types of hypothalamic and amygdala lesions producing two opposite syndromes.

but most of the time they stood or sat motionless, not varying their position. They held a position in which they were put, even an uncomfortable one. This reminded us of the catatonic reactions observed in neurotic dogs in Pavlov's laboratory and in schizophrenic patients. Sometimes the dogs spontaneously spent hours in bizarre positions or showed bizarre habits. When presented with food they showed no interest at all in it (Fig. 2) and when fed forcibly they resisted actively, pushing away the bowl and spitting out food put into their mouths (Fig. 3).

The only active behaviour of these dogs is to resist. They resist not only feeding but also all other manipulations, and do not respond to orders. Normal dogs go willingly to the experimental room, come when called, jump on the stand and help the harnessing by lifting their legs. Operated dogs resist entering the experimental building, withdraw or hold back on all four legs, and when put on the stand they extend their extremities and shake out the recording equipment. This 'negativism' may be part of a loss of the social relations toward people which had made the dogs so cooperative before the operation. The dogs with dorso-medial amygdala lesions seem not to recognize the experimenter,

FIG. 2. Dogs A79 *(upper)* and A135 *(lower)* after bilateral dorso-medial amygdala damage. Notice the lack of interest in the various kinds of food presented, and the sad appearance of the animals. (From experiments by J. Lagowska & E. Fonberg.)

whom they had previously greeted cheerfully. They are also completely indifferent to environmental stimuli. Normal dogs put into new surroundings explore them or if they are shy, look for a hiding-place. Operated dogs stay in one position, indifferently, and in the place where they are left. They do not strive or work for anything, nor do they perform the trained instrumental alimentary reactions. This apathy persists during the period when voluntary food intake is restored, even if a preferred kind of food is used for the rein- forcement. It is not caused by the fact that the dogs have 'forgotten' how to

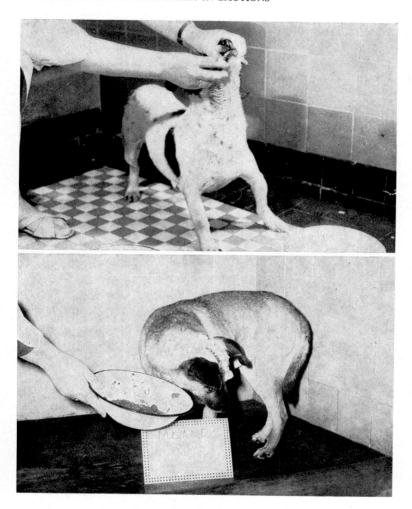

FIG. 3. Dogs A85 *(upper)* and A36 *(lower)* after bilateral dorso-medial amygdala lesions, showing refusal to feed. (From experiments by J. Lagowska & E. Fonberg.)

react to the conditioned stimulus. In some dogs the instrumental reaction reappears soon after the operation but it is abortive, irregular and easy to extinguish. They 'know' what to do but they are not motivated to do it.

Postoperative training of the instrumental reactions was also unsuccessful in most of the dogs although it was not started before the period when they began to eat voluntarily (Fonberg 1969a). Some dogs were able to learn to make the correct instrumental reaction to the conditioned stimulus, but their performance was labile and never reached 100%, as occurs as a rule in normal dogs. Salivary reactions were also greatly diminished after dorso-medial amygdala lesions, which might be the result of the profound changes in basic alimentary mechanisms; on the other hand it might be caused by a decrease in the rewarding properties of food or changed taste values.

It is interesting to note that lesions of the dorso-medial amygdala produced similar effects to lateral hypothalamic lesions. The lateral hypothalamic syndrome has been investigated by many workers but most of the observations concerned alimentary mechanisms and did not take into account the emotional symptoms. In dogs we were able to compare the effects of the two kinds of lesions on emotional reactions. Damage to the lateral hypothalamus produced similar effects to lesions in the dorso-medial amygdala: aphagia with adipsia, vomiting, and changes in instrumental performance and salivary reactions (Fonberg 1969b; Fonberg & Rożkowska 1968; Rożkowska & Fonberg 1970, 1972). Moreover, the dogs were also depressed and indifferent, showed negativism, and took up bizarre, catatonic-like positions. Like dogs with dorso-medial amygdala lesions they lost their friendly attitude to people, stopped jumping and playing, and showed no other signs of joy or affection (Fig. 4).

Apart from obvious individual differences, we have not been able to find dissimilarities between the groups of dogs with dorso-medial amygdala and lateral hypothalamic lesions. Some dogs in each group never recovered their instrumental reactions; in others, the performance improved greatly after a few weeks. In some dogs of both groups aphagia lasted 2–3 days only; in others, it lasted 2–3 weeks and was followed by more or less pronounced hypophagia.

There is a striking similarity in the emotional behaviour of dogs with these two types of brain lesion (lateral hypothalamic and dorso-medial amygdala). If these animals do show feelings, they are always negative ones. They do not act spontaneously, but they can actively resist, as is shown in their negative response to all manipulations. They do not show any positive emotions, but are sometimes irritable and aggressive. Their general appearance is sad and depressed, with the head held low and the ears and tail hanging down. The behaviour of these animals reminds one very much of the behaviour of neurotic dogs in a state of depression (Fonberg 1958, 1968b, 1971b). If we like to extrapolate to human psychoses, we may say that these dogs remind us of psychiatric patients with endogenous depression, and some of them, because of their negativism, mannerisms and catatonic-like positions, show some similarity to schizophrenic patients. It seems not accidental that in man, tumours of the third ventricle involving the hypothalamus, and tumours of the temporal lobe

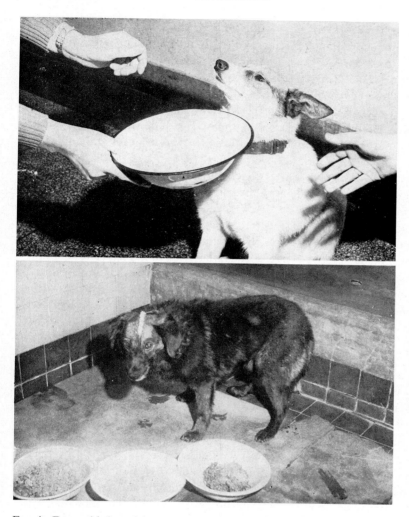

FIG. 4. Dogs with lateral hypothalamic lesions. Note the indifference and lack of interest in presented food. (Unpublished experiments by E. Rożkowska & E. Fonberg.)

involving the amygdaloid complex, produced symptoms which were diagnosed as schizophrenic because of the resemblance of the symptoms in both cases (Malamud 1967). The suggestion can be made, but needs further proof, that the cause of deep emotional changes in neuroses and psychoses may lie in the disturbed functioning of the hypothalamus and amygdala.

In spite of using various experimental procedures we were unable to find any detectable difference between the functions of the lateral hypothalamus and dorso-medial amygdala. Therefore we have no evidence that rather basic alimentary functions like food intake and salivation are destroyed by lateral hypothalamic lesions and rather emotional mechanisms by damage to the dorso-medial amygdala. In both cases lesions impaired not only alimentary functions as such, but also the general drive state and emotions, and in a similar way. It therefore seems that there is a duplication of the positive alimentary and emotional functions within the hypothalamus and amygdaloid complex.

Another parallel duplication of functions is found in the lateral amygdala and ventro-medial hypothalamus. Lesions of the lateral amygdala produce effects which are very similar to the effects of lesions of the ventro-medial hypothalamus, in respect of alimentary functions; both lesions produce hyperphagia and an increase in body weight (Fonberg 1971a; Rożkowska & Fonberg 1971). We did, however, observe some differences in the behaviour of these last two groups of dogs. Dogs with ventro-medial hypothalamic lesions are very voracious and seem to be unable to stop eating. They eat two to four times as much as before the operation, if fed *ad libitum*, and some of them must be interrupted during feeding because of the danger of rupturing the stomach (Rożkowska & Fonberg 1971). Dogs with lateral amygdala lesions strive for food and approach it eagerly but they usually do not eat more than 50–100% of the preoperative intake and they stop eating before becoming oversatiated. This may be due to the presence of regulatory mechanisms in which the gluco-receptors of the ventro-medial nucleus of the hypothalamus are involved, whereas in the group of dogs with ventro-medial hypothalamic lesions, these mechanisms are destroyed.

The instrumental reactions of dogs with either lateral amygdala or ventro-medial hypothalamic lesions were unchanged or slightly disinhibited, mostly during inter-trial intervals. Lesions of the lateral amygdala seem to influence emotional behaviour much more than do lesions of the ventro-medial hypo-thalamus, as this last may be more primarily involved with feeding mechanisms. After lateral amygdala lesions the dogs became very lively, friendly and playful, like puppies. If they had been aggressive toward other dogs before operation they no longer display aggression postoperatively. Hyperphagia produced by lateral amygdala lesions is transient but changes in emotional behaviour seem to be long-lasting.

The most striking effect of a lateral amygdala lesion is noticed when this operation is performed as the second one on dogs previously damaged in the dorso-medial amygdala. The day after electrocoagulation of the lateral amyg-dala the dogs showed an increased interest in food. Some of them were able

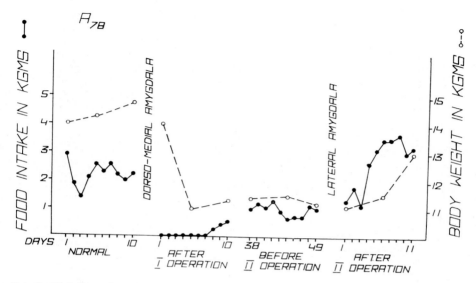

FIG. 5. The effect of dorso-medial amygdala damage and subsequent damage to the lateral amygdala on food intake in a representative dog. Notice the period of aphagia after the first operation, then the partial recovery before the second operation and the sudden increase in food intake after the second operation.

to eat 3–4 kg of food immediately after being awakened from the anaesthetic. They not only ate food that was presented but they looked for food, followed the technician preparing food, jumped up to the food bowl and when food was easy to reach they ran toward it and ate it quickly and voraciously. Their daily food intake increased; the peak of this hyperphagia occurred about 5–10 days postoperatively in most of the dogs (Fig. 5). Then the food intake started to fall and in most dogs reached the normal level of intake, as before the two operations.

The most striking changes occurred in the emotional behaviour of the dogs. In a few days, and in some even in a few hours, they seemed to return to their former state before the two operations. They became lively and gay again and interested in everything, like normal dogs. They returned to their old habits, which had seemed to be definitely abolished after the operation on the dorso-medial amygdala. They were again friendly toward the experimenters and technicians, jumping up on greeting and licking their faces, and rolling on their backs, asking for play. Negative emotions like fearfulness or aggression disappeared or were greatly diminished. The instrumental performance of the dogs was restored or greatly improved. They went willingly to the experimental

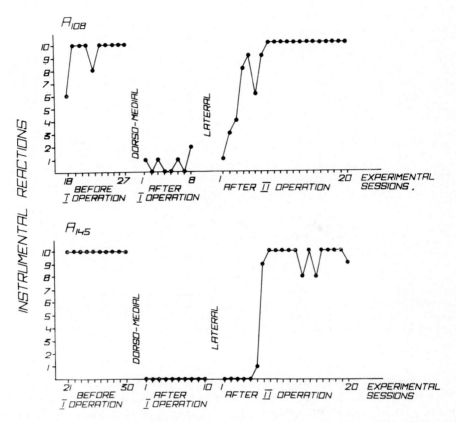

FIG. 6. The effect of dorso-medial amygdala damage and subsequent damage to the lateral amygdala on instrumental performance in representative dogs, A108 and A145. Notice the recovery of the instrumental performance after the second operation.

room, jumped on the stand and were cooperative, as they had been in their normal state.

Fig. 6 shows the instrumental performance of dogs A145 and A108 in their normal unoperated state and after the dorso-medial amygdaloid operation, when the instrumental reactions were greatly impaired or completely abolished, and after the subsequent operation on the lateral amygdala, when they were restored. Fig. 7 shows dog A79 in his apathetic state after the first, dorso-medial amygdala operation, and after the second operation, on the lateral amygdala, when his feeding and emotional reactions were restored.

From our preliminary observations it appears that damage to the lateral amygdala similarly normalizes the food intake and emotional reactions impaired

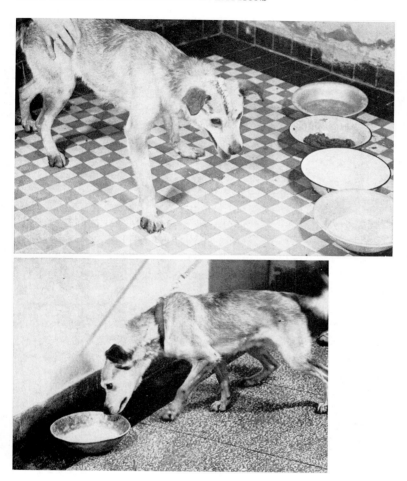

Fig. 7. Dog A79, after dorso-medial amygdala damage *(upper)* and after subsequent damage to the lateral amygdala *(lower)*. Notice the recovery of interest in food after the second operation.

after the lateral hypothalamic lesions. These results may mean that positive emotions and general arousal are closely connected with alimentary functions, since lesions in different parts of the brain abolish all these functions altogether. It seems improbable that in two different areas, i.e. hypothalamus and amygdala these two systems (positive emotional and alimentary) run in the vicinity of each other only by coincidence. It is more probable that, at least in the dog, alimentary functions are one of the main sources of positive emotions. It is interesting to recall that gourmands are often the most gay and emotional kind of people. Our lesion experiments provide some evidence that positive emotions exist and that certain brain lesions abolish them and other lesions may enable them to be restored. Our data also seem to indicate that 'positive centres' in both the dorso-medial amygdala and the lateral hypothalamus cannot be considered as the loci of neurons patterning the alimentary and emotional reactions or pathways where important connections cross. In this case these reactions would be irreversibly impaired by the lesions. It rather seems that these centres are excitatory in function, which classifies them as real 'drive centres'. Their excitatory influences may therefore concern both alimentary and emotional reactions in parallel. On the other hand the lateral amygdala, as shown by various experiments, plays a wide inhibitory role (Fonberg & Delgado 1961; Morgane & Kosman 1957; Fonberg 1963a, 1971a; Egger & Flynn 1963). Its inhibitory influence on the lateral hypothalamus has also been proved by electrophysiological experiments (Oniani & Neneishvili 1968; Oomura et al. 1970). Moreover, stimulation of the lateral amygdala acts on the cerebral cortex to produce slow sleep-like waves (Kreindler & Steriade 1963). This overflow of inhibitory influences in the absence of excitatory ones after damage to either the lateral hypothalamus or the dorso-medial amygdala may produce all the symptoms of apathy and depression. Further removal of the source of inhibition, by a lesion in the lateral amygdala, restores the normal balance between inhibition and excitation and behaviour becomes normalized. This cancelling of the effect of the first amygdala operation by the second explains why various authors, including ourselves, found no prominent changes after large lesions of the amygdaloid complex. When the two antagonistic systems were simultaneously excluded in one operation the effects balanced each other out. Damage restricted to the crucial points is therefore the most effective.

Interesting observations supporting the same line of thinking were made by Mempel on patients (1971, 1972). Using a cooling method he made small stereotaxic lesions within the amygdaloid complex in patients with emotional disturbances as the results of epileptic seizures. He found an impressive amelioration of all symptoms. In his work, the pathological disturbances were produced by an epileptic brain focus which we should consider as a brain injury. His most interesting observations, however, come from those cases having the mildest epileptic symptoms. For example, in his unpublished dissertation for docent degree in 1970 Mempel described a boy who before the operation was extremely aggressive and uncooperative. He beat his mother and sister, came into conflict with the police, and for several years neither worked nor studied. This patient did not have overt epileptic seizures, although

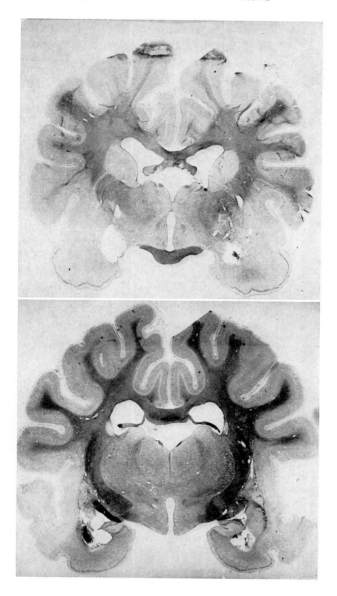

FIG. 8. Frontal brain sections in a representative dog, A145, showing damage to the dorso-medial amygdala *(upper)* and subsequent damage to the lateral amygdala *(lower)* (see Fig. 1).

the epileptic brain activity could be provoked pharmacologically. After the operation, which consisted of a small lesion in the amygdala made by the cooling method, the boy became pleasant, quiet and cooperative, and started to work and to study in evening school.

These observations show once more that it is possible to abolish pathological symptoms and to produce an improvement in behaviour by definite, circumscribed brain lesions. The problem remains whether it would be possible to abolish by the same means neurotic symptoms produced functionally.

It is an interesting question for further investigations whether the mechanisms of depression and emotional disturbances produced by lesions of the brain and by external conflict are similar and what their biochemical and electrophysiological basis is.

ACKNOWLEDGEMENTS

Thanks are due to Dr W. Budohowska and Miss J. Knight for reading the manuscript and making valuable suggestions and to Mrs H. Kurzaj and Miss U. Miaczynska for their technical assistance.

References

ANAND, B. K. & BROBECK, J. R. (1951) Hypothalamic control of food intake in rats and cats. *Yale J. Biol. Med.* **24**, 123-140

CHAPMAN, W. P. (1960) Depth electrode studies in patients with temporal lobe epilepsy. In *Electrical Studies on the Unanesthetized Brain* (Ramey, E. R. & O'Doherty, D. S., eds.), pp. 334-351, 351-368, Hoeber, New York

DE MOLINA, A. F. & HUNSPERGER, R. W. (1962) Organization of the subcortical system governing defence and flight reactions in the cat. *J. Physiol. (Lond.)* **160**, 200-213

EGGER, M. D. & FLYNN, J. P. (1963) Effects of electrical stimulation of the amygdala on hypothalamically elicited attack behaviour in cats. *J. Neurophysiol.* **26**, 705-720

FLYNN, J. P. (1967) The neural basis of aggression in cats. In *Neurophysiology and Emotion* (Glass, D. C., ed.), chapt. 40, Rockefeller University Press, New York

FONBERG, E. (1953) Chronic experimental neurosis with dominating motor symptoms in dog. *Soc. Sci. Lodz.* **27**, 1-41 (in Polish)

FONBERG, E. (1958) The manifestations of the defensive reactions in neurotic states. *Acta Biol. Exp.* **18**, 89-116

FONBERG, E. (1963a) The inhibitory role of amygdala stimulation. *Acta Biol. Exp.* **23**, 171-180

FONBERG, E. (1963b) Conditioned avoidance responses established to hypothalamic and amygdalar stimulation. In *Proc. IX Congr. Polish Physiological Association*, p. 72 (in Polish)

FONBERG, E. (1963c) Emotional reactions evoked by cerebral stimulation in dogs. *Bull. Pol. Acad. Sci.* **11**, 47-49

FONBERG, E. (1966) Aphagia produced by destruction of dorso-medial amygdala in dogs. *Bull. Pol. Acad. Sci.* **14**, 719-722

FONBERG, E. (1967) The motivational role of the hypothalamus in animal behavior. *Acta Biol. Exp.* **27**, 303-318

FONBERG, E. (1968a) The role of the amygdaloid nucleus in animal behaviour. In *Progress in Brain Research*, vol. 22, *Brain Reflexes* (Asratyan, E. A., ed.), pp. 273-281, Elsevier, Amsterdam

FONBERG, E. (1968b) The defensive reactions in neurotic states. *Lodz. Assoc. Sci.* **93**, 7-62 (in Polish)

FONBERG, E. (1969a) Effects of small dorsomedial amygdala lesions on food intake and acquisition of instrumental alimentary reactions in dogs. *Physiol. Behav.* **4**, 739-743

FONBERG, E. (1969b) The role of the hypothalamus and amygdala in food intake, alimentary motivation and emotional reaction. *Acta Biol. Exp.* **29**, 335-358

FONBERG, E. (1971a) Hyperphagia produced by lateral amygdalar lesions. *Acta Neurobiol. Exp.* **31**, 19-32

FONBERG, E. (1971b) *Neuroses*, Wiedza Powszechna, Warsaw (in Polish), 1-189 pp.

FONBERG, E. & DELGADO, J. M. R. (1961) Avoidance and alimentary reactions during amygdala stimulation. *J. Neurophysiol.* **24**, 651-664

FONBERG, E. & FLYNN, J. P. (1963) Conflict evoked by double cerebral stimulation. In *Proc. IX Congr. Polish Physiological Association*, p. 79 (in Polish)

FONBERG, E. & ROŻKOWSKA, E. (1968) The effect of hypothalamic and amygdalar lesions in dogs. In *Proc. III Int. Conf. on the Regulation of Food and Water Intake*, Haverford

FONBERG, E. & SYCHOWA, B. (1968) Effect of partial lesions of the amygdala in dogs. *Acta Biol. Exp.* **28**, 35-46

HEATH, R. G. & MICKLE, W. A. (1960) Evaluation of seven years experience with depth electrode studies in human patients. In *Electrical Studies on the Unanesthetized Brain* (Ramey, E. R. & O'Doherty, D. S., eds.), pp. 214-242, Hoeber, New York

HESS, W. R. (1928) Stammganglien Reizversuche. *Ber. Gesamte Physiol. Exp. Pharmakol.* **42**, 554

HESS, W. R. (1947) Vegetative Funktionen and Zwischenhirn. *Helv. Physiol. Pharmacol. Acta* suppl. 4, 1-65

HOEBEL, B. H. & TEITELBAUM, P. (1962) Hypothalamic control of feeding and self-stimulation. *Science (Wash. D.C.)* **135**, 375-377

KING, H. E. (1961) Psychological effects of excitation in the limbic system. In *Electrical Stimulation of the Brain* (Sheer, D. E., ed.), pp. 477-497, Hogg Foundation, University of Texas Press, Houston

KREINDLER, A. & STERIADE, M. (1963) Functional differentiation within the amygdaloid complex inferred from peculiarities of epileptic afterdischarges. *Electroenceph. Clin. Neurophysiol.* **15**, 811

LEVTOVA, F. A. & SLYOZIN, W. B. (1968) Neurotic state evoked by stimulation of definite brain structures. *J. Higher Nerv. Activ.* **18**, 984 (in Russian)

LILLY, J. C. (1958) Learning motivated by subcortical stimulation. In *Reticular Formation of the Brain* (Jasper, H. H. *et al.*, eds.), pp. 705-722, Little, Brown, Boston

MACLEAN, P. D. (1958) The limbic system with respect to self-preservation and the preservation of the species. *J. Nerv. Ment. Dis.* **127**, 1

MAIER, N. R. F. (1949) *Frustration: the Study of Behavior without a Goal*, McGraw-Hill, New York

MALAMUD, N. (1967) Psychiatric disorder with intracranial tumors of limbic system. *Arch. Neurol.* **17**, 113-124

MARGULES, D. L. & OLDS, J. (1962) Identical 'feeding' and 'rewarding' system in the lateral hypothalamus of rats. *Science (Wash. D.C.)* **135**, 374-375

MEMPEL, E. (1971) The influence of partial amygdalectomy on the emotional disturbances and epileptic seizures. *Neurol. Neurochir. Pol.* **1**, 81-86

MEMPEL, E. (1972) The influence of partial (dorso-medial) amygdala lesions on emotional disturbances and epileptic fits in humans. In *Proc. IV European Congr. Neurosurgery, Prague Conf. Neurology*, in press

MILLER, N. E. (1957) Experiments on motivation. *Science (Wash. D.C.)* **126**, 1271-1278

OLDS, J. (1962) Hypothalamic substrates of reward. *Physiol. Rev.* **42**, 554-604

OLDS, J., TRAVIS, R. P. & SCHWING, R. C. (1960) Topographic organization of hypothalamic self-stimulation functions. *J. Comp. Physiol. Psychol.* **53**, 23-32

OOMURA, Y., ONO, T. & OOYAMA, H. (1970) Inhibitory action of the amygdala on the lateral hypothalamic area in rats. *Nature (Lond.)* **228**, 1108-1110

ONIANI, T. N. & NENEISHVILI, T. L. (1968) *The Role of Amygdaloid Complex and Piriform Cortex in Regulation of Alimentary Behaviour*, vol. 2, pp. 89-99, Kiev University Press (in Russian)

PAPEZ, J. W. (1937) A proposed mechanism of emotion. *Arch. Neurol. Psychiatr.* **38**, 725-743

PAVLOV, I. P. (1952) *Twenty Years of Studies on the Higher Nervous Activity* (Polish edition), Polish House of Medical Publications, Warsaw

ROŻKOWSKA, E. & FONBERG, E. (1970) The effects of lateral hypothalamic lesions on the food intake and instrumental alimentary reflexes in dogs. *Acta Neurobiol. Exp.* **30**, 59-68

ROŻKOWSKA, E. & FONBERG, E. (1971) The effects of ventro-medial hypothalamic lesions on food intake and alimentary instrumental conditioned reflexes in dogs. *Acta Neurobiol. Exp.* **31**, 354-364

ROZKOWSKA, E. & FONBERG, E. (1972) Impairment of salivary reflexes after lateral hypothalamic lesions in dogs. *Acta Neurobiol. Exp.* **32**, 711-720

SEM-JACOBSEN, C. W. & TORKILDSEN, A. (1960) Depth recording and electrical stimulation in the human brain. In *Electrical Studies on the Unanesthetized Brain* (Ramey, E. R. & O'Doherty, D. S., eds.), pp. 275-287, Hoeber, New York

TEITELBAUM, P. (1967) Motivation and control of food intake. In *Handbook of Physiology, Alimentary Canal*, section 1, chapt. 24, American Physiological Society, Washington, D.C.

WASMAN, M. & FLYNN, J. P. (1962) Directed attack elicited from hypothalamus. *Arch. Neurol.* **6**, 220-227

WYRWICKA, W., DOBRZECKA, C. & TARNECKI, R. (1959) On the instrumental reaction evoked by electrical stimulation of the hypothalamus. *Science (Wash. D.C.)* **130**, 336-337

WYRWICKA, W., DOBRZECKA, C. & TARNECKI, R. (1960) The effect of electrical stimulation of the hypothalamic feeding centre in satiated goats on alimentary conditioned reflexes type II. *Acta Biol. Exp.* **20**, 121-136

Discussion

Hill: Professor Fonberg used emotion words like 'sadness', 'apathy' and so forth. These are really inferences, or descriptions of behaviour.

Engel: I feel we should avoid words like 'depression' and 'sadness' when working with animals where we have no psychological data but only behavioural and biological data. We don't know what the dog is feeling. We have defined conservation–withdrawal in biological terms and I am struck that Dr Fonberg's dogs with dorso-medial amygdala and lateral hypothalamic lesions seem to fulfil virtually all our criteria for conservation–withdrawal. They became immobile, apathetic, unresponsive to familiar humans, and ceased to eat. After removal of the lateral amygdala as well the dogs regained their interest in the external environment, became lively, friendly and active again and began to eat normally. It was as if the first lesions induced the same kind of reaction as the stranger provoked in Monica whereas lateral amygdala lesions terminated the reaction, just as the return of the familiar person did for Monica. I would be fascinated to know what the gastric secretion of these dogs was under the two conditions. I would predict that it was absent in the dogs with lesions of the lateral hypothalamus and dorso-medial amygdala, and that it would return after the lateral amygdala lesion. Dr Fonberg mentioned the finding by Kreindler & Steriade (1963) that stimulation of the lateral amygdala produces slow, sleep-like waves in the cortex. This, combined with the general and profound inhibitory effect, encourages me to think that the lateral amygdala as a mediator of excess inhibition may be a place to start investigating the neural mechanisms underlying conservation–withdrawal.

Sachar: Dr Fonberg, what are the neurochemical characteristics of the pathways you have interrupted, for example, in the dorso-medial amygdala and lateral hypothalamic system? Is this a primarily noradrenergic system, or serotonergic or dopaminergic?

Fonberg: There is some evidence that the dorso-medial amygdala and stria terminalis are adrenergic while the lateral amygdala is cholinergic. Recently Dr Dabrowska from our department studied the effects of lesions of the amygdala on the neurochemistry of other parts of the limbic system in rats (Dabrowska *et al.* 1971). But there are differences in the biochemistry of rodents and carnivores, as shown recently by Hall & Geneser-Jensen (1971). They also found considerable differences among the amygdaloid nuclei in the extent to which they could be stained for acetylcholinesterase (AChE) and for monoamine oxidase (MAO). The dorso-medial part of the amygdala and stria terminalis stained with methods for MAO and hardly at all by methods for AChE, while staining of the baso-lateral area was the other way round. These are important findings, because depression is probably due to overactivity of MAO and the therapeutic action of some antidepressant drugs is to block this enzyme. Grossman (1960) and many investigators since have become interested in the neurochemistry of the hypothalamus and amygdala in relation to behaviour. Recently Leibovitz (1971) reported further differentiation into α- and β-adrenergic systems within the hypothalamus and their relation to the cholinergic system. But the problem is complicated and the relationships of biochemical changes to behaviour are not direct.

Other evidence that profound metabolic changes occur in our dogs after amygdala and hypothalamic lesions is that not only is their behaviour altered but also the appearance of the skin and hair is changed. After the dorso-medial amygdala lesion the skin is thin and the hairs are weak and fall out.

After the lateral amygdala operation the fur becomes shiny and thick again. We have not studied gastric secretion but we have studied the stomach contractions immediately after lateral hypothalamic lesions; in the depressed and aphagic state the 'hunger' contractions were completely abolished and the stomach was atonic and showed automatic activity due to the local reflex. Before the operation the dogs had elaborated conditioned reflexes in the form of stomach relaxation. These reflexes were also abolished by lateral hypothalamic lesions. After several weeks we sometimes observed large, irregular gastric contractions. At autopsy (2–4 months postoperatively) we found no gastric ulcers but hypertrophy of the mucosa was found in some dogs (Glavcheva *et al.* 1970).

Nemiah: Some of your dogs went for as long as two months without eating. How did you maintain the nutrition in such cases, and wasn't a whole new set of variables introduced thereby into your relationship with the dogs? Furthermore, I wonder whether the loss of hair might not have been a nutritional problem rather than the result of the neurological lesions.

Fonberg: If the operation involves only either the dorso-medial amygdala or the lateral hypothalamus, the dogs are aphagic for only 1–3 weeks. During this period we intubate them at first because they won't swallow and they spit the food out; after some time they start to swallow if we put food deep into their mouths. We also tried having different people feed the animals, and the results were the same. The dog which did not eat for more than two months had combined lesions of the dorso-medial amygdala and lateral hypothalamus. He was force-fed all the time.

Sandler: Have you tried giving antidepressant drugs after the first operation?

Fonberg: Yes, I am just starting to do this with Dr Golebiowska, but it requires training a separate group of dogs. We have found some interesting excitatory effects but it is too early to talk about them.

Sachar: Is sexual behaviour affected, when the dogs are exposed to a female on heat?

Fonberg: We didn't try this systematically. However, we observed homosexual behaviour in one dog with lateral hypothalamic lesions.

Sifneos: Have you any information about the aggressive behaviour of these dogs? Mark & Ervin (1970) have investigated patients with episodic aggressive behaviour which they call 'periodic discontrol'. They claim that an operative procedure in the area of the limbic system may alter such behaviour in a similar way as the operation on the lateral amygdala that you described alters the behaviour of your dogs. Have you made any observations on patients?

Fonberg: Some of our dogs with lesions in the dorso-medial amygdala show signs of aggression. They show their teeth and growl, but the attack is not well directed. These reactions were abolished after the lesion of the lateral amygdala. The most aggressive dogs are produced if the lesion invades the upper dorsal part of the amygdala at the region of the nucleus centralis. If the lesion is circumscribed enough, the dogs are aggressive after the operation and not apathetic and aphagic (Fonberg 1965).

Most of Mempel's patients had epileptic seizures and at the same time they were very aggressive. The boy I described was extremely aggressive, but after small lesions of the amygdala he became quiet and started to work and study. His report of his subjective feelings before and after operation is interesting. During his interview he said that before the operation he was at the same time indifferent and nervous. After the operation he feels quiet and cheerful and has become motivated to work for his future. He is interested in many things, desires them and can enjoy small rewards.

Hill: Klüver & Bucy (1938) removed the anterior part of the temporal lobe bilaterally in the monkey, which must have included the amygdala on both sides, and produced a picture of altered behaviour, which included a so-called psychic blindness; the animals couldn't recognize objects and were unable to distinguish between food and inedible objects, and would put everything in their mouths. Professor Fonberg, on the other hand, suggested that the dogs who first had the dorso-medial amygdala nuclei removed and then the lateral amygdala were 'normal' again. This seems remarkable after the removal of both amygdala nuclei. Do you really mean that the animal was normal?

Fonberg: I mean that they look normal. After the first operation, there is probably too much inhibition and this is the cause of the altered behaviour. After the second one this inhibition decreased because its source in the lateral amygdala is removed. I don't think that the dogs can be completely normal after having two lesions within the amygdaloid complex. The amygdala must have some function and probably we would find differences between these dogs and normal dogs by more subtle tests. Also, if the hypothalamus is intact, it may take on some of the functions of the amygdala. But I was amazed how after the second operation the dogs regained their normal behaviour.

Levine: I would add a cautionary point about the normality or otherwise of the amygdalectomized dogs. Probably of all the known limbic structures, the amygdala has been most studied by most people. There is a huge literature on the amygdala in many species. The effects of total amygdalectomy are multiple and also subtle. Rats have shown many behavioural deficits after amygdalectomy (Goddard 1964). Even if eating behaviour returns to normal, other more subtle functions may not.

Hill: I have seen one patient who had a unilateral temporal lobectomy for epilepsy, which removed the amygdala on his dominant side, followed by a further partial operation removing most of the amygdala complex on the other side. After this operation the patient was relieved of his epilepsy but he couldn't recognize his doctor, and couldn't learn to recognize anybody or to find his way about the hospital. This patient was permanently crippled by a very serious learning difficulty; he had no memory for any new information.

Storey: This recalls the eight cases described by Scoville & Milner (1957) with permanent memory disturbances after bilateral removal of the anterior hippocampus.

Sachar: In the early amygdalectomy experiments in monkeys which Sir Denis mentioned, much more was involved than amygdalectomy. Klüver and Bucy removed whole sections of the temporal lobes as well, and that also interrupted short association pathways to the visual cortex, so the effects noted were only partly due to amygdalectomy *per se*. We don't therefore need to be too puzzled by Dr Fonberg's results, which were produced by a more discrete lesion.

Donald: Were behavioural tests done on the dogs that had had two operations? Did they acquire new conditioned reflexes, for example? How did their behaviour compare with that of normal dogs?

Hill: This is part of the larger question of exactly what has been done in these experimental situations set up by Dr Fonberg.

Fonberg: The dogs that had both operations seem to have a normal ability to learn. But our experiments concern basically the retention of reactions trained before both operations and lost or impaired after the first one. The dogs were exposed to the conditioned stimuli for the first five postoperative experimental sessions. If the instrumental reactions did not appear at all, retraining started. Most dogs began to perform the instrumental reaction before retraining. Between the operations, retraining was unsuccessful (Fig. 6, p. 144). The behaviour of the dogs in other situations appears the same as that of normal, unoperated dogs.

Weiss: The learned responses took some time to recover completely, often longer than they took to be acquired initially; this makes one wonder whether the dogs were learning a new response, although it looks similar, rather than recovering a previously inhibited response.

Fonberg: The instrumental reactions did not usually recover at once, although in some dogs retraining was not necessary after the second operation. If it was used, the time for retraining was usually shorter than the initial training time before the two operations. The dogs do not seem to be learning a new response. We have not tried to establish new conditioned responses. Most of the dogs remember which kind of reaction was trained originally.

Weiss: Your data are most exciting. Can you say whether the motivational system in any particular area—that is, in the lateral or dorso-medial amygdala as opposed to the hypothalamic areas—is dominant? Is either of those systems able to supersede the other, and obliterate its effects? Perhaps you don't have enough data to speculate on that.

Fonberg: I thought that there must be some basic differences between the functions of the hypothalamus and amygdala, and our experiments were designed to find these differences. But so far we have only observed individual differences within groups but not differences between the two groups. The differences between individual dogs are caused by the dimensions of the lesions in each of these two brain areas.

Hill: Have you tried to induce experimental neurosis in a dog that has had both operations?

Fonberg: No. I have only some preliminary results on one dog, which was very nervous and difficult to manage, both in his normal state and after the first operation on the dorso-medial amygdala. After the lesion in the lateral amygdala he was quieter and more cooperative.

Zanchetti: Have you tried lesioning the lateral amygdala before the dorso-medial? Going back to the problem of aggression, Egger & Flynn (1963) showed that electrical stimulation of two different sites in the amygdala, though not exactly the same sites you refer to, could affect hypothalamically induced aggressive behaviour in the cat in opposite directions. This fits rather well with your work, so one should look at fighting and defence behaviour more carefully. The experimenter may not be a good object for a previously friendly dog to attack. Before doing the operations one should find some object which the dog will attack, for instance a rat, and see whether he still attacks it after the operation.

Fonberg: We have not yet done the two operations in the reverse order. We have produced the single lateral amygdala lesion, which made the dogs hyperphagic. They also become more lively and playful, like puppies (Fonberg 1971). They do not attack other dogs, as they did before the operation, but seem to be only interested in them, approaching, sniffing and so on.

Egger & Flynn (1963) showed that the medial ventral part of the lateral amygdala inhibits aggression, and the dorsal part increases aggression evoked by stimulation of the hypothalamus. The most effective of our lesions was in the ventral part of the lateral amygdala, confirming Egger & Flynn's finding. In a previous paper (Fonberg 1963) we showed that stimulation of this part of the amygdala also inhibits fear reactions—the panic fears, not the well-trained avoidance reaction.

Gray: I am alarmed by references to the therapeutic use of amygdala lesions.

Jacobsen's (1935) report of the results of his work on lesions to the frontal cortex in monkeys was followed by a spate of leucotomies in patients with a variety of different diagnoses, with ill effects for most of them and advantageous effects almost never (Willett 1960; Mayer-Gross *et al.* 1969). I hope that we are not inadvertently the cause of a similar spate of amygdalectomies.

Hill: These operations have been done in the United States for a number of years; however, my impression is that they are not being used as frequently as in the past.

Levine: Unfortunately, in Californian prisons at least, psychosurgery is quite common. I would agree with Dr Gray that this is a frightening development.

Gray: I should like to comment on a possible connection between Professor Fonberg's experiments and the general model I proposed in my paper. Fig. 3 (p. 97) showed a simple scheme for one of the three postulated systems for emotional behaviour—the 'fight/flight system'. According to this scheme, the amygdala is capable of inhibiting the ventro-medial hypothalamus from exercising its own tonic inhibition on the final common pathway for fight/flight in the central grey of the midbrain, thus releasing or facilitating fight/flight behaviour. This scheme is, of course, too simple. The amygdala contains areas which inhibit aggression, as well as some which facilitate it (Kaada 1972); and de Molina & Hunsperger's (1962) contention that the key pathway from the amygdala to the ventro-medial hypothalamus lies in the stria terminalis— which has been assumed in my Fig. 3—is questionable (Zbrożyna 1972) (though Zbrożyna's alternative suggestion that the true route lies in the ventral amygdalo-fugal pathway suffers from the defect that so far there is no certainty that *any* fibres arising in the amygdala travel this route: Lammers 1972). However, if this simplicity can be accepted for the moment, I should like to ask Dr Fonberg how she thinks this scheme—which is largely based on de Molina & Hunsperger's work—relates to her own results.

I am struck by a number of observations which suggest that the amygdala may have something to do with psychotic behaviour. This suggestion is not new. My own reasons for making it—which are of a rather general and insubstantial kind—are set out in a recent paper (Gray 1973). In considering Dr Fonberg's results with this in mind, I notice that her dogs with lesions in the dorso-medial portion of the amygdala displayed two classical psychotic symptoms—behavioural depression and negativism. She attributes this syndrome to the unbalanced inhibitory activity of the intact lateral amygdala. Another symptom found commonly in the psychotic disorders is aggressiveness (e.g. Lorr *et al.* 1963), and that is one reason why I have suggested a link between psychotic behaviour and activity in the fight/flight system (Gray 1973). In the light of both de Molina & Hunsperger's work and some of Dr Fonberg's previous reports (Fonberg 1968; Kaada 1972), it seems that the dorso-medial amygdala is facilitatory for the expression of fight/flight behaviour (perhaps by inhibiting neurons in the ventro-medial hypothalamus, as shown by Dreifuss 1972), and the lateral amygdala inhibitory for this behaviour (perhaps by exciting these same ventro-medial hypothalamic neurons: Dreifuss 1972). That is to say, the relations between these two amygdaloid areas and fight/flight behaviour appear to be essentially the same as their relations to eating, as studied by Dr Fonberg. Might one, therefore, speculate that the psychotic disorders represent functional disturbances in the balance of interacting amygdaloid influences on the hypothalamus? In the particular cases we have been considering, unbalanced activity in the dorso-medial amygdala might lead to aggressive outbursts, and unbalanced activity in the lateral amygdala to depression and negativism.

Hill: Psychiatrists have reservations, specific and general, about the use of the word 'psychotic', and we would not all agree with Eysenck's use of the term. I know that you rely for your human data on Eysenck's results. Interesting though these are, I do not agree with his use of the term 'psychotic'.

Zanchetti: One problem is to what extent lesions of the medial part of the amygdala can cut fibres coming from more lateral regions—perhaps from the ventro-lateral or medio-lateral portions that Egger & Flynn (1963) described—with inhibitory properties.

Fonberg: I have some ideas on how these systems interact, and how they are anatomically connected. I agree that the lateral amygdala plays an inhibitory role in aggressive, defensive behaviour, and also in alimentary responses.

The amygdaloid complex consists of several nuclei and its function is not a simple one. Unfortunately many of the results described in the huge literature on the amygdala are conflicting. This conflict forced me into the investigation of the amygdaloid complex and I am now, after 13 years' work, convinced that many of our difficulties are due to the fact that large lesions invade different nuclei and neurons belonging to different or even opposing systems (alimentary and defensive, positive and inhibitory, as well as sexual, and perhaps others) and their connections with the hypothalamus and midbrain. Thus opposite results may be found, depending on which systems are most affected. De Molina & Hunsperger (1959, 1962) proposed the scheme for the system governing flight-fight reactions in cats which Dr Gray mentions. The dorso-medial amygdala constitutes the upper part of this system and is connected by the stria terminalis to the hypothalamus; then the fibres travel through the periventricular system down to the midbrain centres controlling defensive behaviour. On the other hand, we found that the dorso-medial amygdaloid region deals also with alimentary responses (Fonberg 1966, 1969*a, b;*

Fonberg & Sychowa 1968). Fibres pass from the dorso-medial amygdala region in the stria terminalis but lesions of this part of the amygdala may involve fibres from other amygdaloid regions which also pass through this area. Fortunately in the dog (though less so in the cat) most of these fibres avoid the dorso-medial region, passing rostrally to it. We can therefore say with probability that the effects of dorso-medial lesions in the dog are due solely to damage to this part of the amygdala.

The stria contains different components, in dogs as well as cats, as was recently shown by one of my co-workers (Kosmal 1972), who also showed that in the dog two kinds of fibres (thick and thin) are found. These findings may indicate that fibres of the stria belong to both excitatory and inhibitory systems and also may be concerned with both alimentary and defensive responses. Besides the stria terminalis, other pathways connect the amygdala with the hypothalamus, described in cats by Nauta (1961) and Valverde (1965). As Dr Gray mentioned, Hilton & Zbrożyna (1963) suggest that not the stria terminalis but the diffuse ventral system of Nauta (1961) is the amygdalo-fugal pathway for defensive reactions.

The midbrain also contains both alimentary and defensive centres (Skultety 1968). Positive alimentary and defensive systems are therefore represented at three levels (amygdala, hypothalamus and midbrain), whereas the lateral amygdaloid nucleus (mostly its medial and ventral part), and probably the adjacent part of the baso-lateral nucleus, inhibit alimentary (Fonberg & Delgado 1961; Fonberg 1968, 1971), aggressive (Egger & Flynn 1967) and fear responses (Fonberg 1963). The existence of an inhibitory function of the lateral amygdala is further supported by biochemical, histological and electrophysiological findings. Tombol & Kosmal (1972) have found in this region in the cat specific glia-like cells with short axons which are likely to have an inhibitory role. The inhibitory system for both defensive and alimentary functions proceeds to the hypothalamus and then further down to the midbrain.

Oomura et al. (1970) have shown that stimulation of the lateral amygdala produces both an increase in activity of single cells in the ventro-medial hypothalamus and a decrease in the lateral hypothalamus. They think that the two different characteristics of lateral amygdala stimulation are probably mediated through separate pathways. They suggest that postsynaptic inhibition of the lateral hypothalamus may account for suppression of feeding behaviour. Stimulation of the dorso-medial amygdala may have the opposite effect. We (R. Tarnecki, E. Fonberg, E. Mempel & J. Lagowska) are now studying the electrophysiological effects of both dorso-medial and lateral amygdaloid areas on the hypothalamus. The preliminary results provide some evidence supporting the antagonistic effects of dorso-medial and lateral

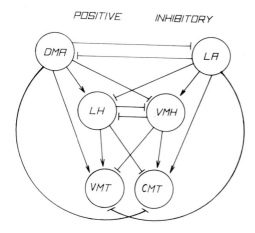

F IG . 1 (Fonberg). Scheme of the three levels of the alimentary system divided into positive and inhibitory channels and their reciprocal relations. Arrows indicate positive effects and lines with bars, inhibitory effects. For simplicity only the downward (from the amygdala through hypothalamus to mesencephalon) connections are drawn and feedback or other reciprocal connections are omitted. DMA: dorso-medial amygdala; LA: lateral amygdala; LH: lateral hypothalamus; VMH: ventro-medial hypothalamus; VMT: ventral midbrain tegmentum; CMT: central part of midbrain tegmentum.

amygdaloid areas on the hypothalamus, but the problem is more complicated. One of the components of the stria terminalis ends near the ventro-medial hypothalamic nucleus; therefore a positive role of the dorso-medial amygdala might be to inhibit the 'satiation' centre of the ventro-medial hypothalamus and in this way to assure excitation of the lateral hypothalamus. The excitatory effect of the dorso-medial amygdaloid area on the feeding mechanism may act through a pathway described by Valverde which goes to the lateral hypothalamus. Inhibitory effects on feeding behaviour may be mediated indirectly by excitation of the ventro-medial hypothalamic satiation centre (Fig. 1).

I do not now see any conflict between results claiming the existence of de- fensive or alimentary or inhibitory roles for the amygdala and the amygdalo- hypothalamus-midbrain systems. All these systems may run in parallel along the same anatomical pathways and may even be reciprocally linked by inter- neurons which enable interactions to occur between the systems, thus securing the essential functions of the animal. If the positive emotional system is disturbed in at least one of two levels of this chain (amygdala or hypothalamus), depressive and negativistic symptoms appear. I therefore agree with Dr Gray and have even suggested (Fonberg 1969, 1971, 1972) that my dogs remind one of psychotic patients, although I realize that this is a very wide extrapolation.

References

DABROWSKA, J., KLODOS, J., ODERFELD-NOWAK, B. & WEISS, K. (1971) An effect of lesions of amygdala on acetylcholinesterase activity in the limbic system of rats. *Proc. III Int. Meeting of the International Society for Neurochemistry, Budapest*, p. 225

DE MOLINA, A. F. & HUNSPERGER, R. W. (1959) Central representation of affective reactions in forebrain and brain stem. *J. Physiol. (Lond.)* **145**, 251-265

DE MOLINA, A. F. & HUNSPERGER, R. W. (1962) Organization of the subcortical system governing defence and flight reactions in the cat. *J. Physiol. (Lond.)* **160**, 200-213

DREIFUSS, J. J. (1972) in *The Neurobiology of the Amygdala* (Eleftheriou, B. E., ed.), pp. 295-318, Plenum Press, New York

EGGER, M. D. & FLYNN, J. P. (1963) Effects of electrical stimulation of the amygdala on hypothalamically elicited attack behavior in cats. *J. Neurophysiol.* **26**, 705-720

EGGER, M. D. & FLYNN, J. P. (1967) Further studies on the effects of amygdaloid stimulation and ablation on hypothalamically elicited attack behaviour in cats. In *Progress in Brain Research*, vol. 27, *Structure and Function of the Limbic System* (Adey, W. R. & Tokizane, T., eds.), pp. 165-182, Elsevier, Amsterdam

FONBERG, E. (1963) The inhibitory role of amygdala stimulation. *Acta Biol. Exp.* **23**, 171-180

FONBERG, E. (1965) The effects of partial destruction of amygdaloid complex on the emotional-defensive behaviour of dogs. *Bull. Pol. Acad. Sci.* **13** (7), 429-432

FONBERG, E. (1966) Aphagia produced by destruction of dorso-medial amygdala in dogs. *Bull. Pol. Acad. Sci.* **14**, 719-722

FONBERG, E. (1968) The role of the amygdaloid nucleus in animal behaviour. In *Progress in Brain Research*, vol. 22, *Brain Reflexes* (Asratyan, E. A., ed.), pp. 273-281, Elsevier, Amsterdam

FONBERG, E. (1969a) Effects of small dorso-medial amygdala lesions on food intake and acquisition of instrumental alimentary reactions in dogs. *Physiol. Behav.* **4**, 739-743

FONBERG, E. (1969b) The role of the hypothalamus and amygdala in food intake, alimentary motivation and emotional reaction. *Acta Biol. Exp.* **29**, 335-358

FONBERG, E. (1971) Hyperphagia produced by lateral amygdalar lesions. *Acta Neurobiol. Exp.* **31**, 19-32

FONBERG, E. (1972) The motivational role of hypothalamus and amygdala. *Congress of Int. Assoc. for theScientific Study of Mental Deficiency*, Warsaw (Primrose, D. A. A., ed.), pp. 578-580, Polish Medical Publications

FONBERG, E. & DELGADO, J. M. R. (1961) Avoidance and alimentary reactions during amygdala stimulation. *J. Neurophysiol.* **24**, 651-664

FONBERG, E. & SYCHOWA, B. (1968) Effect of partial lesions of the amygdala in dogs. *Acta Biol. Exp.* **28**, 35-46

GLAVCHEVA, L., ROŻKOWSKA, E. & FONBERG, E. (1970) The effects of the lateral hypothalamic lesions on the gastric motility in dogs. *Acta Neurobiol.* **30**, 279-294

GODDARD, G. V. (1964) Functions of the amygdala. *Psychol. Bull.* **62**, 89-109

GRAY, J. A. (1973) in *Contributions of Multivariate Analysis to Psychological Theory: Third Banff Conference on Theoretical Psychology* (Royce, J. R., ed.), Academic Press, London, in press

GROSSMAN, S. P. (1960) Eating or drinking elicited by direct adrenergic or cholinergic stimulation of hypothalamus. *Science (Wash. D.C.)* **132**, 301-302

HALL, E. & GENESER-JENSEN, F. A. (1971) Distribution of acetylcholinesterase and monoamine oxidase in the amygdala of the guinea pig. *Z. Zellforsch. Mikrosk. Anat.* **120**, 204-221

HILTON, S. M. & ZBROŻYNA, A. W. (1963) Amygdaloid region for defence reactions and its efferent pathway to the brain stem. *J. Physiol. (Lond.)* **165**, 160-173

JACOBSEN, C. F. (1935) Functions of the frontal association areas in primates. *Arch. Neurol. Psychiatr.* **33**, 558-569

KAADA, B. R. (1972) in *The Neurobiology of the Amygdala* (Eleftheriou, B. E., ed.), pp. 205-281, Plenum Press, New York

KLÜVER, H. & BUCY, P. C. (1938) An analysis of certain effects of bilateral temporal lobectomy in the rhesus monkey, with special reference to 'psychic blindness'. *J. Psychol.* **5**, 33-54

KOSMAL, A. (1972) The role of the stria terminalis for functional connections of the amygdaloid complex with hypothalamus in dogs. *Proc. XX Congr. of the Polish Physiological Association*, Olsztyn, Poland

KREINDLER, A. & STERIADE, M. (1963) Functional differentiation within the amygdaloid complex inferred from peculiarities of epileptic afterdischarges. *Electroenceph. Clin. Neurophysiol.* **15**, 811

LAMMERS, H. J. (1972) in *The Neurobiology of the Amygdala* (Eleftheriou, B. E., ed.), pp. 123-145, Plenum Press, New York

LEIBOVITZ, S. F. (1971) Pharmacological studies of hypothalamic systems mediating hunger and thirst. *Proc. IV Int. Conf. on the Regulation of Food and Water Intake*, Cambridge (British Nutrition Foundation)

LORR, M., KLETT, C. J. & McNAIR, D. M. (1963) *Syndromes of Psychosis*, Pergamon Press, Oxford

MARK, V. H. & ERVIN, F. R. (1970) *Violence and the Brain*, Harper & Row, New York

MAYER-GROSS, W., SLATER, E. T. O. & ROTH, M. (1969) *Clinical Psychiatry*, Bailliere, Tindall & Cassell, London

NAUTA, W. J. H. (1961) Fibre degeneration following lesions of the amygdaloid complex in the monkey. *J. Anat. (Lond.)* **95**, 515-531

OOMURA, Y., ONO, T. & OOYAMA, H. (1970) Inhibitory action of the amygdala on the lateral hypothalamic area in rats. *Nature (Lond.)* **228**, 1108-1110

SCOVILLE, W. B. & MILNER, B. (1957) *J. Neurol. Neurosurg. Psychiatr.* **20**, 11-21

SKULTETY, F. M. (1968) Mesencephalic influence on diencephalic mechanisms regulating food intake. *Proc. III Int. Conf. on the Regulation of Food and Water Intake*, Haverford

TOMBOL, T. & KOSMAL, A. (1972) Golgi study of the amygdaloid complex. *Acta Neurobiol. Exp.* **32**, in press

VALVERDE, S. (1965) *Studies on the Piriform Lobe*, Harvard University Press, Cambridge, Mass.

WILLETT, R. (1960) in *Handbook of Abnormal Psychology* (Eysenck, H. J., ed.), pp. 566-610, Pitman, London

ZBROŻYNA, A. W. (1972) in *The Neurobiology of the Amygdala* (Eleftheriou, B. E., ed.), pp. 597-606, Plenum Press, New York

Anxiety: a behavioural legacy

BENSON E. GINSBURG

Department of Biobehavioral Sciences, The University of Connecticut, Storrs

Abstract It is characteristic of wild forms to react sensitively and extremely to environmental novelty. This genetic wariness extends to strangers of the same species and of other species that do not constitute normal prey. The taming of a wild animal constitutes an exercise in social bond formation which involves overcoming the fear and alleviating the anxiety of the subject. Taming of a very young animal does not produce a social bond capable of withstanding a fear-induced crisis, whereas the taming of an older animal, already fearful, does. The sustained use of a variety of tranquillizing drugs thought to have differing mechanisms of action results in a pseudosocial state that reverts to baseline when the pharmacological prop is removed, however slowly and on a variety of handling paradigms. The transition from a highly anxious state, as judged by overt behaviour and autonomic signs, to a drug-induced pseudosocial state occurs in a temporal sequence that closely resembles that which occurs in the permanent socialization of adult wild animals tamed without drugs, but on a dramatically compressed time-scale.

The implications of the biologically invariant pattern of social bond formation in a given species, with and without drugs, are considered in an evolutionary context, including possible homologies with human anxieties.

The relevance of an animal model for human behaviour is no longer controversial. Darwin, particularly in his *Expression of the Emotions in Man and Animals*, laid the essential groundwork for evolutionary continuities and developmental homologies extending to the behavioural as well as the morphological realm. Modern ethology and behavioural genetics have filled in many of the gaps and provided hard data where anecdotes and analogies previously existed. The consideration of how much is inborn and how much is environmentally induced has, as a matter of quantification and description, been reduced to the heritability statistic, and, as a matter of causal analysis, become amenable to scientific investigation by means of the use of replicable genotypes in specifiable developmental situations. Heritability measures provide an approximation to the variance contributed by the genes to a quantifiable parameter, but only across a given range of genotypes interacting across a range of environmental conditions. Another species, race or genealogy might provide a significantly different heritability statistic when tested in the same way under the same conditions from one previously obtained from a related population (Ginsburg 1966). Two populations representing somewhat different gene pools within a species might show identical heritabilities across one spectrum of developmental situations and differing heritabilities across another. At the level of common experience, parents having more than one child are usually aware that even if it were possible to treat each child exactly alike, the behavioural outcomes would be different. At the clinical level, the psychiatrist knows that identical symptomatologies may have differing underlying aetiologies in different patients. From the point of view of possible hereditary components, we have referred to this concept as 'geneticity', or the 'genomic repertoire' of each genotype across the range of environmental conditions it is likely to encounter (Ginsburg & Laughlin 1971). With respect to any given syndrome presumably brought on by environmental stress, individuals would be expected to differ in their thresholds as well as in their modes of response, on a hereditary basis.

Despite the reasonable possibility of diverse aetiologies for indistinguishable syndromes, it is both parsimonious and consonant with observations to consider as a hypothesis that they share common mechanisms. This is the organizing assumption behind any taxonomy. Analogous symptoms in animals and humans might, on this view, well involve identical mechanisms by means of a common evolutionary legacy, and the evidence for this would rest on establishing that the mechanisms are homologous.

In the present paper I shall consider the possible behavioural homologies between the extreme shyness of the wild Canid and some aspects of the behaviour of the clinically anxious human.

The wild Canidae differ from their domestic counterparts in many behavioural attributes. Indeed, as between wolf, coyote and dingo, they also differ from each other in important behavioural respects. At the same time, they are interfertile, have the same chromosome complement, and are perfectly capable of exchanging genes through natural mating. Geographic and behavioural isolation have been the principal barriers to such exchange, although there is evidence of some interbreeding between all three of these forms with domestic dogs, and it has been suggested that the vanishing red wolf, now principally confined to the gulf region of Texas and Louisiana in the southern United States, has hybridized with the coyote. The large, coyote-like Canid that is becoming common in the northeastern United States, ecologically replacing the wolf, has been variously considered to be an oversize coyote, a feral dog or the result of hybridization between coyote and dog.

So far blood antigen and protein fractionation studies have not settled the matter. Neither have morphological studies. However, our observations show that distinct behavioural differences exist, and do not typically blend on hybridization but, instead, form mosaics which are composites of the behavioural features of the two parent species. With respect to emotionality and temperament, however, our F_1's exhibit a far greater shyness than the wild parent. We have, for example, crossed highly inbred beagles developed at the Jackson Laboratory with coyote stock that we have maintained and inbred. The F_1 progeny (coy-dogs) were uniformly hyper-wary, exhibiting a low threshold of response to environmental novelty and an exaggerated reaction to it characterized by shrinking, freezing, avoidance, muscle tremors, defecation and urination, salivation, pupillary dilatation and tachycardia. This is in spite of various handling paradigms in which paired littermates were regularly handled from two weeks of age, another pair from six weeks, and the remaining pair not at all. Of handled animals, one of the pair on each schedule was handled by only one investigator, and the other by several (at least five). Unlike our results with the coyotes, where previous early experience determined the degree of fearfulness of strangers and the response to a familiar handler, the coy-dogs remained extremely shy to strangers, and the observable variation was not correlated with the previous handling history of the individual.

It is usual to consider hyper-additive behavioural manifestations resulting from crosses of inbred stocks as examples of 'hybrid vigour'. This is, perhaps, a simplistic interpretation. It appears to be the rule in the wild form that deviation from the normative phenotype is maladaptive, and most species have developed various buffering mechanisms that permit the assimilation of a high degree of genotypic variation to a far narrower range of phenotypic expression (Ginsburg 1968). By contrast, many domesticated forms have been selected precisely because they are exotic in appearance or behaviour, and the phenotypic expression of the genetic variation in such a form as the domestic dog is maximal rather than minimal in part because genetic variation is sought and preserved, and in part because a larger proportion of the genotypic variation is directly exhibited in the phenotype. With crosses between inbred stocks, a super-additive effect might be nothing more than a compensation for possible deleterious effects of particular homozygotes, or, in some instances, a restoration of co-adapted gene complexes that were broken up during inbreeding. In the present case, assuming that the level of shyness or wariness that is typical of the wild Canid is adaptive, the exaggerated response of the hybrid, which, moreover, is far less responsive to early experience variables that influence the behaviour of both the coyote and the dog, would not seem to be a manifestation of 'vigour'. I strongly suspect that those who use the criterion of quantitative augmentation after a cross as their indicator of hybrid vigour, would, if they encountered hyper-shyness as a consequence of inbreeding, consider it to be a case of inbreeding deterioration, since there is an assumption of fitness implied in the concept of vigour. It is more reasonable to hypothesize that the genetic determinants of shyness achieve hyper-expression on the less buffered background of the genome of the domestic dog, rather than on the more highly buffered background of the coyote.

The shyness or wariness of the wild animal is in many ways analogous, if not homologous, to extreme anxiety in the human. It may be free floating, or it may attach to particular circumstances. It has strong components of avoidance and escape. It is persistent. It involves autonomic components with parasympathetic elements predominating. There is an adrenal picture reminiscent of stress. Various tranquillizing agents are capable of altering the behaviour during the period over which they are administered, but none permanently. It can occur later in life in an animal 'that was previously thought to be thoroughly tame. It can be overcome by conditioning (Ginsburg 1965, 1967).

Whether the wild animal is a good neurological model for human emotional distress cannot be entirely settled by resemblances in behaviour, responses to psychopharmacological agents and involvement of common mechanisms. These suggest common components and the validity of carryover from one form to the other at these levels. From an evolutionary point of view, there is an important difference. Extreme wariness and a highly emotional response to a perceived alteration in the environment was and is undoubtedly adaptive to the coyote, and even to an animal such as the wolf that is essentially a predator and, except by man, is not preyed upon. Like man, the wolf is highly social and must form close associations with certain of his conspecifics—the members of his own pack—but not with others, towards whom he displays hostile behaviour. The same may be said for many primates and, most likely, for man's immediate ancestors. If primitive man was 'wild' and xenophobic in this sense, he may later have lost these exaggerated response mechanisms or he may have developed others that suppress and control them. When the balance between these evolutionarily older mechanisms and those that control them is disrupted, an emotional reaction characterized by fear, anxiety, dissolution of social bonds and distorted perceptions occurs. On this view, there may be an additional evolutionary and neurological component in man that is lacking in the wild animal model, but that may occur in domestic forms. Given the number of times that domestication has occurred, with an attendant loss of shyness, it is simpler to imagine a genetic loss or the disassociation of a complex necessary to maintain 'wildness', than it is to hypothesize that a new controlling mechanism was developed each time.

It is entirely possible that the animal model may be even closer to man than this speculation suggests. The behaviour characterizing wildness is, after all, not so extreme in a familiar surrounding, and the wild animal can be adapted to new situations even as an adult and despite its initial extreme reactions. It may, therefore, be that the control mechanisms also exist in the animal model and that it is a matter of where the homeostat is set, rather than whether or not there is one. This concept provides an easy way out for explaining the behaviour of domestic animals. It is not only a matter of how they are reared, but involves significant biological differences as well.

Our experience, in addition to the coyote and its hybrids, has been with the North American grey wolf. We have observed this species in free-living captive groups and compared the behaviour in these conditions with that observed in the wild. In particular, we have focused our attention on behavioural ontogeny in controlled situations, where the groups were constituted by placing cubs from several litters together so that there were no tutors from the wild, then describing the development of the social structure of the group, including its mating behaviour, denning and rearing of young (Rabb *et al.* 1967; Woolpy & Ginsburg 1967; Woolpy 1968). We have also reared wolves individually in kennel conditions, usually with other wolves, but also in visual isolation from other animals and humans from nine weeks until ten months of age. We have placed tame wolves that we ourselves had handled daily until eight months of age with wild wolves, isolated from familiar handlers and from further handling for periods of 18–22 months, and then brought them back into the kennel. We have done the same with a wolf socialized through the adult period and intensively handled, beginning with sexual maturity (after whelping). Finally, we have attempted to socialize wild wolves to human handlers with and without tranquillizers and at varying ages (Ginsburg 1965, 1967).

While the latter studies are of the greatest relevance for the purposes of this symposium, it is worth noting that groups constituted of young wolves that had never been in the wild develop the social organization and individuate the social roles characteristic of their species if they are permitted free social interaction with each other from infancy to adulthood. Those social bonds that endure in the pack are formed when the wolves are in their second season (Woolpy 1968). This may be most easily seen in the case of females who come to prefer the male who was dominant at that time to other males. Less enduring social bonds form earlier, and this is also seen in the handling experiments, where those animals that have been thoroughly socialized as cubs and extensively handled to eight months, regress if they are placed with wild, fearful animals and are given no further handling or contact with previous handlers for prolonged periods (18–22 months). By contrast, an adult two years of age or older, thoroughly tamed, remains tame after a comparable experience. The difference between the two situations as inferred from the behaviour is that in the first, the fear of human beings has never developed, and when it does, as a consequence of isolation from human handling and living with animals that are fearful, it must then be overcome. One has a wild, anxious animal. In the case of the adult, the fear had developed and been overcome, and the behavioural change is much more stable.

In the one instance where we have reared a wolf in isolation, it was taken from the mother at birth and bottle-fed along with a littermate. From the beginning of the ninth week, it was kept in complete visual isolation until it was ten months old. At that time, it was introduced to people and to other wolves, first through an open mesh fence barrier, then under leash restraint and finally without restraint. The isolate's behaviour was open and friendly. It was possible to handle her at once. She did not, however, distinguish the social signals of other wolves and made only random responses to threats and other social gestures. By the fourth day she was both interpreting and communicating well, and from that time forward showed no behavioural deficits. At sexual maturity she interacted normally with males. It was as though the isolation had heightened her interest in social contact to the point where whatever fear she may have initially experienced was easily overcome. There was no additional conditioning necessary to make her amenable to human handling. Her first contacts with people after her prolonged isolation were reinforcing, and this seemed to be all that was necessary. On controlled exposure to other wolves, she very quickly learned to interpret their signals and to react in an organized and appropriate manner. Until we have repeated this procedure with animals isolated from birth, we shall not know how much difference the exposure to a human handler and a littermate during the first nine weeks contributed. Judging from the fear reactions of previously tamed and handled animals that develop after prolonged periods of not being handled, the isolation from nine weeks to ten months produced an unexpected result. The instant taming following isolation suggests two possible alternatives: (1) That isolation prolongs or displaces the sensitive period for socialization described by Scott (1962). (2) That initial experiences during a period of extreme disruption can be used to reprogramme behaviour.

Social behaviour is highly characteristic of the wolf and appears to be inherent in its genetic makeup. As mentioned, groups of very young individuals left to interact with each other will develop the social organization and individuate the social roles characteristic of the species. This organization maintains the pack structure and determines mating preferences within it. This, in turn, leads to a behavioural population control and ensures that mating is non-random within the species. It also leads to a certain degree of inbreeding, to the maximizing of genetic drift, and to rapid phenotypic differentiation that is favourable for evolution.

Even though the biological impetus to social interaction is great, the isolated wolf who forms social bonds with people easily is not typical of what happens when an adult wild wolf is brought into the kennel situation for taming. Such an animal adopts a slinking posture, urinates, defecates, salivates, trembles and shows pupillary dilatation. It may jump for hours, or bite at the fencing, breaking its teeth and bloodying its gums and tongue. This behaviour eventually becomes episodic, particularly if the pen is fairly large and is never entered while the wolf is in it. For that purpose, the animal has access to an outside connecting run that can, however, be controlled by the investigator. Perhaps the appropriate logistics could bring about rapid socialization at this time. If so, we have been unable to produce these, and must attribute our lack of success to the extensive fear displayed by the animals.

The formation of a social bond with the handler is induced by gradually familiarizing the wolf to his presence. Once the wolf has accepted its new quarters and appears more normal, the handler sits just outside the pen for regular periods, separated only by the chain link mesh barrier. The handler mixes the animal's food with his hands and works in old clothes well permeated with his own body odour. At first, the wolf typically reacts by retreating, slinking and other activities characteristic of his original fearful responses. Standing or moving during the early phases of socialization heightens these responses; sitting quietly reduces their severity and duration.

After the wolf is thoroughly familiar with the presence of the investigator just outside the pen, and no longer responds fearfully to his natural movements, he can be induced to approach, to sniff at the investigator, accept food from him and even to rub against him and permit physical contact through the barrier. This phase can be accelerated if perfumed hand cream or other similar odour-bearing substances are used. Even at this stage, a sudden unfamiliar move can startle and frighten the animal, causing its behaviour to regress.

When the behaviour has stabilized, the investigator enters the pen and sits down as before. The anxious behaviour is again elicited and eventually subsides. The investigator then begins to move his body, reach his hand out, stretch his leg, etc., all from the same fixed sitting position. Eventually he stands, but does not walk within the pen. Instead, he confines himself to a position just inside the barrier.

At each successive stage, the fear responses are re-instituted, and eventually subside. At times, the wolf will approach the investigator, pulling at his clothing, particularly if he is wearing a loose garment such as an unbuttoned laboratory coat, or biting at his boot if his leg is extended away from his body. He will rub in the area where the investigator recently sat, and may mark it with urine. Occasionally he will do this to the person of the investigator (coyotes do it much more often). At this stage he is still shy, but aggressive. To frighten him is to cause him to regress. To do nothing more is to remain on a plateau and to strengthen the wolf's aggressive responses.

At some point, it is necessary to begin to make physical contact with the animal in a manner that will not frighten him and will minimize the aggressive responses. These are usually limited to those mentioned, but may also include grabbing the person. It has been our experience that if one remains perfectly still, no serious biting occurs. Our method for coping with this situation is to have another investigator approach or enter the pen. This distracts the animal and the first investigator is able to exit. A ha ty retreat or a rout produces further aggression, and may lead to a situation where a particular handler is no longer able to cope with a given animal.

We have found no way around this aggressive phase. To intimidate or punish the animal leads either to regression (i.e., fear responses) or to a serious attack. Our judgment of when to interact and how far to go is based on the behaviour of each wolf. Schenkel (1948) has described the various threat postures of the wolf, and these, with minor individual variations, constitute a reliable lexicon for predicting the wolf's behaviour. On the basis of our inter-actions with untamed wolves, it is what the investigator does that matters. Each of us has been in situations where our own subjective fear was great, but the wolf reacted to us on the basis of our overt movements. Thus, the notion that there is an odour of fear, or that the wolves are able to interpret our autonomic reactions, seems untenable. On the other hand, they do monitor each other very closely, and respond to their own body language, which in-cludes autonomic manifestations, quite reliably. They do not, therefore, react to us in this respect as though we were wolves.

Interactions involving body contact initiated by the investigator, come to be tolerated, with intercurrent aggressive episodes. At this stage, the investigator absents himself for several days and, if he has interpreted his subject correctly, may receive a wolf greeting, initiating contact, on his return. From then on, a social bond has been established, and the wolf is soon relatively tame. Once this stage has been reached, the wolf, unlike most other Canids, tends to generalize and can be handled by unfamiliar persons.

Whether this is the only or best method for inducing social bond formation with a handler is under investigation. Thus far we can only say that it works.

Subsequent to these studies, we attempted to socialize wolves with the aid of tranquillizers. Chlorpromazine, reserpine and chlordiazepoxide (Librium) were used, as each has a different mode of action and our expectation was that we would see quite different effects. The drugs were given orally. In each instance dogs of equal body weight were tested until an ataxic response occurred. The dose was then adjusted downward empirically to a maximal sub-ataxic level. This was the dosage used on the wolves.

The results were unexpected. In a period of six to eight hours after the administration of each of these agents, the animals went through all the stages encountered in natural taming and then returned to baseline. The major variation from normal behaviour occurred during the aggressive phase. It consisted of a diminution—sometimes to the vanishing point—of threat responses, so that it was difficult to tell what the animal was going to do. Assuming that an effect of the drug is to reduce subjective fear, a connection between fear or anxiety and a threat response may be hypothesized. The picture with each of these three psychoactive agents was substantially the same—a temporally compressed recapitulation of the events occurring over a period of months during natural taming to a period of hours, with the two exceptions noted: (1) an absence of reliable threat before aggression, and (2) a return to the previous level of highly anxious and fearful behaviour once the effects of the drug have worn off.

Further studies were made, using Librium over a period of months in an attempt to produce permanent socialization. No such effect was obtainable despite efforts to reduce the dose gradually while continuing the handling.

It is our interpretation, therefore, that the subjective concomitants of fear must be experienced and overcome in order to produce a permanent change in behaviour. In the case of wolves tamed as cubs who never developed these fear responses, placing them in an environment where fear responses were eventually induced necessitated having to tame them all over again. Only then was the effect lasting. In the case of the ataractic drugs, it is postulated that these responses were sufficiently dulled, so that when they occurred later, after the drug effects were gone, the animals returned to a highly anxious state. With the sole exception of the isolated wolf, where 'instant socialization' occurred, all of our experience is consistent with the interpretation that a highly anxious, fearful state cannot be permanently modified unless the affect is present during the process of behavioural interaction. Only then can the affect and the behaviour be changed, and new social bonds formed.

ACKNOWLEDGEMENT

The research reported in this paper was aided by grant MH-17088 from the National Institute of Mental Health.

References

GINSBURG, B. E. (1965) in *Sex and Behavior* (Beach, F., ed.), pp. 53-75, Wiley, New York & London
GINSBURG, B. E. (1966) All mice are not created equal — recent findings on genes and behavior. *Soc. Serv. Rev.* **40**, 121-134
GINSBURG, B. E. (1967) in *Comparative Psychopathology: Animal and Human* (Zubin, J. & Hunt, H. F., eds.), pp. 95-114, Grune & Stratton, New York
GINSBURG, B. E. (1968) in *Genetics* (Glass, D. C., ed.), pp. 117-128, The Rockefeller University Press and Russell Sage Foundation, New York
GINSBURG, B. E. & LAUGHLIN, W. S. (1971) in *Intelligence: Genetic and Environmental Influences* (Cancro, R., ed.), pp. 72-87, Grune & Stratton, New York & London
RABB, G. B., WOOLPY, J. H. & GINSBURG, B. E. (1967) Social relationships in a group of captive wolves. *Am. Zool.* **7**, 305-311
SCHENKEL, R. (1948) Ausdrucks-Studien an Wolfen. *Behaviour* **1**, 81-130
SCOTT, J. P. (1962) Critical periods in behavioral development. *Science (Wash. D.C.)* **138**, 949-958
WOOLPY, J. H. (1968) The social organization of wolves. *Nat. Hist.* **77**, 46-55
WOOLPY, J. H. & GINSBURG, B. E. (1967) Wolf socialization: a study of temperament in a wild social species. *Am. Zool.* **7**, 357-363

Discussion

Sachar: Your hypothesis is that socialization in wolves only endures if it has taken place in association with fear. But there may be a snag in your reasoning. When the animal returns from the period in the wild it is once again dealing with fear, and it sounds as if socialization lasts not just because it has been conducted in an atmosphere where the animal has had to overcome fear, but because when, from the wild state, he re-encounters man, he has to cope with fear again. Whereas the wolf that was previously tranquillized may have to learn not only how to cope with strangers but also how to handle his associated emotional reactions when he meets the experimenter again.

Ginsburg: This is really the point I was making. I would not say that it is the training ritual that is learned; this simply is one way in which we could be successful. What seems to be the common ingredient is that the animal has to be able to 'cope' with the subjective experience of fear, to use your language. If he has never coped with it, then when it arises, he has to 'learn' to cope with it.

Sachar: One interpretation would be that fear acts like an aversive stimulus that drives the learning. That doesn't appear to be the case here. The problem seems to be whether, when anxiety is re-evoked, the animal's learnt behaviour includes coping with that response.

Sandler: The effect of the drugs suggests that it is the feeling of anxiety that the animal is learning to cope with rather than the situation, because presumably the drugs don't affect the situation.

Gray: There are many empirical observations of a similar kind to those that Dr Ginsburg has described, in which an animal's behaviour is changed by the action of a drug but when the drug is removed the original behaviour recurs. This is sufficiently common to have been given a technical term, 'drug dissociation' or 'state-dependent learning' (Overton 1966). Many of the forms of behaviour described in these sorts of experiment are 'emotional', but many others are not. Usually one thinks of such situations in terms of different mechanisms in the brain coming into play when the animal is under the influence of the drug and when it is not. What bothers me is this talk about the animal 'coping with its emotions' as though there are two separate animals inside the wolf's skin, one experiencing emotions and the other coping with them.

What is this 'other animal', apart from the wolf? I don't understand what coping with fear is, other than coping with the situation that the animal is put into. This shows up a terrible confusion of language. The language of coping with emotions is subjective language derived from our own intuitive experience. Although I can conceive of an animal subjectively *experiencing* emotions, I don't find it useful to try to analyse behaviour by thinking of it 'learning to cope' with them. What the animal is doing is learning to behave in a particular situation. I am not complaining about the observations—I think these are fascinating—but that you are using dualist language to describe them.

Ginsburg: I accept that I am using two languages; I agree with you.

Hill: We are using the phrase 'learning to cope' very loosely, not with its strict, psychology of learning meaning. We are not necessarily implying a cognitive appraisal of the alternatives. We know that a great deal of learning in this loose sense is unconscious. Surely the acquisition of a 'coping behaviour', or how it's done, is not within our awareness.

Sleight: People don't necessarily cope by thinking or learning about it.

Delius *et al.* (1972), using tungsten electrode recordings from the sympathetic nervous system in man, observed an increase in sympathetic discharge whenever someone came into the laboratory; if this happened two or three times, the discharge decreased. In the same sort of way as an animal 'learns', the sympathetic nervous system 'learned', or accommodated, in subjects who were apparently not disturbed or thinking about how they were doing this. This sort of learning must occur at an unconscious level.

Nemiah: A clinical situation analogous to that of the wolves, but with a different result, occurs in the phobic patient who learns to master his phobia with the help of tranquillizers. When the dose is reduced, he maintains his ability to manage the phobic situation without the extreme anxiety he experienced before taking tranquillizers. In other words, he has retained what he has learned. Although the initial situation is similar to what you have described in your wolves, Dr Ginsburg, the end result is exactly the opposite.

Ginsburg: The domestic dog retains behaviours acquired under drugs, but we have not been able to demonstrate this in the wolf.

Sachar: Do you taper your drugs off?

Ginsburg: We have tried this and it makes no difference to the results, even after 18 months.

Hinde: Strong evidence is accumulating that the human smile is phylogenetically derived from a fear face. A phylogenetic sequence can be traced that in this respect resembles the ontogenetic sequence from fear to greeting that you describe in wolves (van Hooff 1972).

References

DELIUS, W., HAGBARTH, K. E., HONGELL, A. & WALLIN, B. G. (1972) Manoeuvres affecting sympathetic outflow in human skin nerves. *Acta Physiol. Scand.* **84**, 177-186

HOOFF, J. A. R. A. M. VAN (1972) A comparative approach to the phylogeny of laughter and smiling. In *Non-verbal Communication* (Hinde, R. A., ed.), pp. 209-242, Cambridge University Press, London

OVERTON, D. A. (1966) State-dependent learning produced by depressant and atropine-like drugs. *Psychopharmacologia* **10**, 6-31

Physiological and behavioural processes in early maternal deprivation

MYRON A. HOFER

Department of Psychiatry, Montefiore Hospital and
Albert Einstein College of Medicine, Bronx

Abstract These studies describe changes in behavioural and cardiorespiratory physiology following abrupt, early maternal separation of the infant rat. Experiments will be described which begin to analyse the behavioural and biological mechanisms responsible for the impact of this early experience.

A 40% decrease in cardiac rate occurs within the first 12 hours of separating two-week-old rats from their mothers. The possible roles of factors such as body temperature, the environment during separation, starvation-dehydration, the presence of a non-lactating foster mother and the level and frequency of feeding are tested experimentally. Evidence is presented for adrenergic cardiac regulation by nutrition over a neural (rather than metabolic) pathway at this stage of development.

The behaviour of two-week-old rats after similar periods of separation was found to be significantly different from that of mothered littermates. Experiments on mechanism indicate that, for the behavioural effects, level of nutrition is not as important as body temperature and the behavioural interaction with the mother.

These results suggest how the experience of early maternal separation may become translated into physiological and behavioural changes by separate and different mechanisms.

We have known for some time that people often become disturbed both emotionally and physically (Parkes *et al.* 1969) in the aftermath of losing someone close to them. Many illnesses that we call psychosomatic are made worse by separation or may even arise for the first time in the setting of an important loss (Engel 1967). Yet we know very little about the biological state of the bereaved, although we have reason to think that this state has special properties which account for the associated susceptibility to psychological and physical disease. This association between separation and disturbed functioning is most dramatically and regularly observed during infancy, when separation from a mother figure can literally be lethal. Since Spitz, in 1945, reported profound behavioural changes and substantially increased susceptibility to illness among institutionalized children despite excellent medical care, studies of maternal deprivation in humans have become unconscionable.

This situation calls out for the development of animal models which can be studied experimentally so as to arrive at some understanding of this puzzling and important 'psychosomatic' phenomenon. There has been, I think, a certain reluctance on our part to accept the idea that relationships between animals would have sufficient importance to generate any appreciable biological or behavioural effects when such relationships were broken. Enough evidence has now accumulated to overcome that prejudice (Bronfenbrenner 1968). Infant monkeys of two species have shown depression of activity, social withdrawal and postural and facial appearance strongly reminiscent of human depression after removal of their mothers at approximately 5 to 6 months of age (Kaufman & Rosenblum 1969; Hinde & Spencer-Booth 1971). Other species of monkeys fail to show this phenomenon (Kaplan 1970; Kaufman & Rosenblum 1969). When they reached adulthood, rats which had been prematurely separated from their mothers showed increased susceptibility to gastric ulcer (Ader et al. 1960) and to a transplanted tumour (Ader & Friedman 1965).

I have found that young rats are affected both behaviourally and physiologically by separation from their mothers when they are two weeks old. What has seemed most important is to try to find out how the experience of separation becomes translated into changes in the infants' behaviour and physiology. This focus on *process* forces one to ask several questions which are relevant to an understanding of psychosomatic aetiology in general. Is the young rat responding to all the aspects of the experience taken together as a form of Gestalt or complex patterned stimulus? If this were the case, omission of one or two components would alter the pattern so that it would cease to elicit the response. Alternatively, the individual components of the experience (e.g. altered temperature, nutrition, unfamiliar sensory environment, etc.) could be additive in their effect on behaviour and physiology. Thirdly, the response to separation might depend primarily upon one aspect of the total experience, the other components being simply incidental. The next major step is to find out which neural and humoral pathways mediate the response, both on the afferent and efferent sides. We may be able to answer these questions in a model system such as the one I will describe, and thus arrive at a better understanding of how this early experience exerts its biological and behavioural effects.

CARDIAC RATE REGULATION

We developed methods for recording heart rate, electromyogram and respiration from young rats of all ages while they were moving about freely in their home cage, nursing from their mother and interacting with their littermates (Hofer & Reiser 1969; Hofer & Grabie 1971). A sample polygraph tracing is illustrated in Fig. 1. By using the electromyogram and impedance pneumograph channels, the duration of periods of activity could be measured and heart rates expressed separately for both the active and the inactive states, as will appear below.

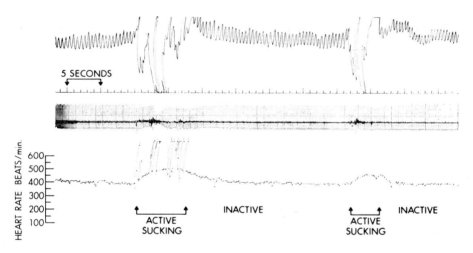

FIG. 1. Sample polygraph page showing, on the top channel, the impedance pneumograph tracing with both regular quiet respiration and activity artifact during suckling. The second is a time channel; the third channel is electrocardiogram and electromyogram, the latter showing characteristic electromyogram bursts during activity. The bottom channel is the cardiotachometer write-out, with its scale given at the left. Two characteristic rises of the heart rate during suckling bursts are shown, the first containing a number of movement artifacts. Paper speed is 5 mm/s. (Reproduced with permission of *Developmental Psychobiology*.)

If immature rats are removed abruptly from their mothers at the end of the first, second and third postnatal weeks, it is the two-week-old rats which show the most pronounced differences in cardiac rates from their mothered littermates (see Fig. 2). The younger two groups had their temperature maintained in an incubator, but the same effect took place if they were left in their home cages and heat was supplied through the cage floor. (Separated

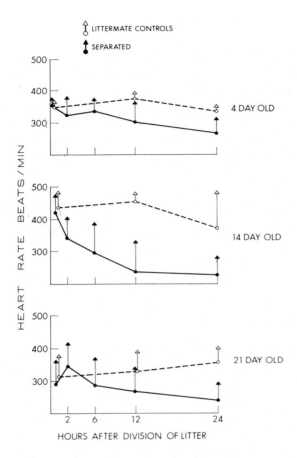

FIG. 2. Cardiac rates during inactivity (circles) and activity (triangles) over 24 hours after separation from mother, compared to those of littermate controls left with mother. Responses of 4-, 14- and 21-day-old pups are compared (N = 6 animals at each point, total 36). (Reproduced with permission of *Psychosomatic Medicine*.)

two-week-old rats left in room temperature lose about 3°C in axillary temperature but do not show a significantly different cardiac response to separation from those kept at nest temperature.) Thus, loss of body heat and absence of the familiar home cage environment were not the factors responsible for the separation effect.

The low heart rates of the separated rats were not fixed at this low level, for any form of stimulation caused increases in rate, and vigorous tail pinching resulted in the heart rates returning to pre-separation levels for several minutes, an effect which could be prevented by β-adrenergic blockade. The results of giving β-adrenergic and cholinergic blocking agents (propranolol and atropine) indicated that the low heart rates of separated rats were not primarily the result of increased vagal tone but were due mainly to a decrease in sympathetic cardiac tone over the period of separation (Hofer & Weiner 1971).

By what means did this autonomic readjustment take place? Since we already knew that the mother as a source of thermal input was relatively unimportant, was it the withdrawal of the mother as a source of nutrient or a source of olfactory, tactile and behavioural interaction to which the pup was responding? Several litters of two-week-old rats were provided with non-lactating mothers by the technique of mammary ligation, and their heart rates decreased exactly as if they had no mothers at all. Although these results could have been due to qualitative alteration in the behavioural interaction with non-lactating mothers, the results turned our attention to the area of nutrition.

The first experiments we did involved intubation feeding of a milk formula every four hours over the 24-hour separation period and although these infants gained one gramme while the unfed ones lost two grammes, the heart rate changes took place as before and were identical in both groups (Hofer 1970). This indicated that starvation and dehydration were not responsible for the low heart rates but left open the possibility that a more delicate regulation of cardiac rate occurs, within the normal range of nutrient intake, when more frequent feedings are given by the nursing mother. Therefore, rat pups separated for 18 hours were fed graded amounts of milk by tube and their heart rates followed at frequent intervals. Littermates received a non-nutrient liquid to control for the effects of gastric distension. A dose–response relationship was discovered (see Fig. 3) which demonstrated that milk was capable of reversing the autonomic cardiac effects of separation within five minutes and lasting for 1–2 hours, but that the effects of all but massive doses were over by four hours, which explained the negative results in the previous study. Sympathetic blockade with propranolol totally prevented this effect of intragastrically fed milk, indicating the participation of adrenergic receptors in the mechanism by which milk acted (Hofer 1971). We did not know, however, which constituent of the milk was responsible for the effect.

By giving some of the major constituents of milk individually in chemically pure form we were able to demonstrate that the capacity to raise heart rate was not limited to any single one of these constituents. Although the response to casein had the most rapid onset, lactose, and even vegetable oil caused increases in heart rate at 30 minutes which were statistically no different from that caused by milk.

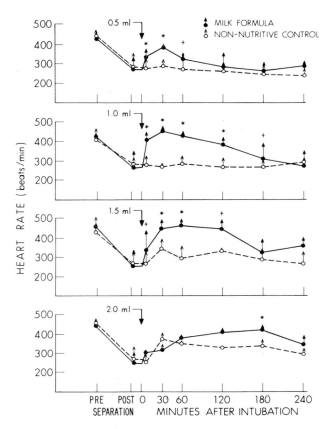

Fig. 3. Cardiac rates of two-week-old rats separated from their mothers for 18 hours and given feedings of milk or control fluid in four different volumes. The first points after intubation values are at five minutes. Each point represents six pups. Circles indicate median inactive heart rates (solid circles, milk formula; open circles, non-nutritive control); arrow points are median active rates. Statistically significant differences between inactive heart rates of milk-fed and control pups are indicated by asterisk ($P < 0.01$) or cross ($P < 0.05$; Wilcoxon-White two-sample ranks test). (Reproduced from Hofer 1971 with permission of *Science*.)

If the cardiac response was due to absorption from the gastrointestinal tract, and transport of these nutrients to the heart, then the same or even more consistent effects would be expected from intravenous injection. Using a dissecting microscope, I was able to implant very fine cannulas in the jugular veins of young rats several days before testing. Intravenous solutions could then be infused by micrometer barrelled syringe without disturbing the animal. The results of these experiments were clearcut and surprising. Neither lactose nor casein nor even 50% glucose solutions had any effects on the heart rates of separated pups, even though 20% or more of the entire intragastric load was given intravenously over a two-minute period. These results seemed to rule out a mechanism involving transport of absorbed nutrient, and suggested that the afferent pathway of the response depends in some way upon the local effect of food in the gastrointestinal tract.

The last major question that we have been able to answer so far concerns the participation of the central nervous system and the efferent pathway. We knew that intact β-adrenergic receptors were necessary for the response (see above), but these may be activated either neurally or humorally. Using microsurgical techniques, spinal cord sections were made on two-week-old rats and they were allowed to recover for 20 hours after surgery and separation from the mother. Milk was then given by intragastric tube. Those with spinal cord sections at the level of the first thoracic vertebra (T1) showed no cardiac acceleration to milk while those with cord sections at T8 showed normal rapid accelerations. Since a spinal cord section at T1 severs sympathetic neural connections between heart and brain while T8 section does not, we reasoned that the milk response depends on this central neural pathway being intact, although the interruption of afferent spinal pathways could also be involved.

These findings suggest that the efferent limb of the response mechanism consists of a direct neural connection between brainstem and heart via classical sympathetic cardio-accelerator pathways. Current studies are exploring possible afferent pathways by which the brain is informed of the presence of nutrient in the gastrointestinal tract. So far we have evidence that it is unlikely to be the splanchnic sympathetic or the vagus nerves. The response may depend on a shift in blood volume into the splanchnic regional vascular bed in response to the local digestive processes, with a resulting fall in systemic blood pressure. The cardiac rate changes, then, would be mediated by compensatory baroreceptor mechanisms involving the carotid sinus and its brainstem connections.

Thus, the heart rate of the normally mothered rat pups of this age may be maintained at high levels by the provision of milk by the mother. The longer she is absent, the lower the heart rate, until a plateau is reached after 12 to 18 hours of separation. The infant rat's heart rate responds to the mother's absence by pathways apparently involving the gastrointestinal tract locally on the afferent side, and the central nervous system and the sympathetic neural pathways on the efferent side. This was an unexpected role for nutrition to play in the early development of central neural regulation of cardiac rate and we were led to enquire whether behaviour was similarly regulated.

BEHAVIOURAL RESPONSES

An increase in vocalization and agitated motor behaviour have been reported to occur as an immediate response to maternal separation of human and primate infants. In some primates, this is followed after a period of hours by decreases in a variety of normal activities and, in one species of monkey, by abnormal postures and facial expressions reminiscent of human depression. In other species of primate the phase of decreased or inhibited activity is not present (Kaufman & Rosenblum 1969; Kaplan 1970). Little is known about the factors responsible for these species differences, and not enough studies have been done to know whether separation responses of this sort are present in less highly evolved mammalian species such as the rat.

Furthermore, we do not know which aspects of the separation experience are critical for the appearance of the behavioural response. If we knew, we might get some leads as to how such a transformation from experience to behaviour takes place.

During our studies of cardiac regulation in separated infant rats we had measured the amount of time spent active during three minutes' observation in the home cage and had found no significant differences between separated and mothered infants. This method was sufficient for specifying whether the animal was active or not during physiological recording but did not contain enough qualitative detail nor long enough periods of observation to draw firm conclusions about behaviour.

We observed the behavioural responses of two-week-old rats to being placed alone for six minutes in an unfamiliar transparent plastic box. Those which had been separated from their mothers for 18 hours showed significantly more locomotor-exploratory behaviour than their mothered littermates. Self-grooming and elimination were not different in the two groups. Using an automated activity platform sensitive to displacement, we found that the overall activity count of both groups was identical in the first two minutes, but the separated infants' activity continued at high levels while the mothered ones became progressively less active over the six minutes' observation. It appeared as if the separated infants had a much reduced capacity for habituation in this setting. Similar results occurred when the rat pups were observed in small groups of four for ten minutes. The separated ones were generally more active, and in addition showed significantly more self-grooming and defecation and/or urination. The mothered infants became rapidly less active and most of them had entered paradoxical or REM sleep (as judged behaviourally) before the end of the test period. The separated ones remained active and appeared to have a relatively delayed onset of sleep.

The body temperatures of the two groups were nearly identical, since thermoregulated heat was supplied through the home cage floor of the separated groups. What would happen if infants of this age were allowed to set their own body temperatures during separation in an environment at room temperature?

The separated infants lost a mean of 3°C in axillary temperature and in this case were *less* active than their mothered littermates. All observed behaviours were inhibited in cooled separated infants, and the number of squares crossed showed a high degree of correlation with body temperature ($r = 0.70$)—the cooler the infant, the less locomotor behaviour.

Thus we could conclude that one of the ways by which maternal separation affects the behaviour of the infants is through withdrawal of a source of heat. However, some other aspect of the experience must also be of considerable importance to account for the clearcut differences in behaviour observed even when heat was artificially supplied.

Since cardiac rate had been returned to pre-separation levels by a single large intubation feeding after 18 hours' separation, we set out to see if refeeding would have a similar effect on behaviour. It seemed reasonable to suppose that the increased activity of separated pups was a concomitant of hunger, a familiar association in adult animals. The experimental results did not support this plausible hypothesis. Milk and a non-nutrient control solution (Maalox) were indistinguishable in their effects. There was an initial inhibition of all behaviour five minutes after gastric distension with either milk or Maalox, but one hour later there was little difference between the fed and the intubated control animals. The one exception was for self-grooming behaviour which paradoxically seemed to be stimulated by milk feeding.

These results were quite unlike those obtained for cardiac rate and suggested that there might be quite different underlying mechanisms. Further support for this idea was provided by the results of an experiment with non-lactating foster mothers.

Rat pups were housed under three different conditions for the 18 hours prior to behavioural testing. One group was normally mothered, one was separated, with heat supplied as before, and the third group was given a non-lactating foster mother. They were tested in small groups of four pups and the results (see Fig. 4) showed that the presence of a foster mother, even if she supplied no nutrient, was sufficient to prevent most, but not all, of the behavioural effects of separation. This was again at variance with the results obtained with cardiac rate responses. The only category in which normally mothered (and nourished) pups were clearly different from both other groups was in the onset of paradoxical sleep (as judged by behavioural criteria).

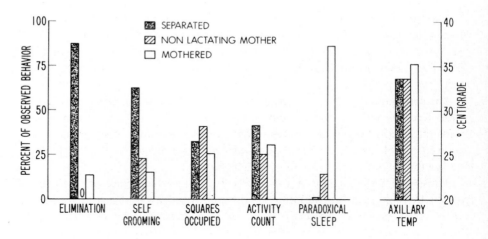

Fig. 4. Behaviour of 2-week-old rats after being housed for 20 hours under three different conditions: with no mother, with a non-lactating foster mother and normally mothered. All rats were observed in groups of four, for ten minutes, on an unfamiliar plastic tray. The percentage figures are based on the total for the three conditions in each behavioural category. Rats which had been separated (N = 24) were significantly different from both mothered groups in elimination, self-grooming and the total activity count ($P < 0.05$; Wilcoxon-White two-sample ranks test).

Thus it would appear that most of the behavioural effects of maternal separation, when body temperature is maintained, are not mediated by a nutritional mechanism as are the cardiac rate changes, but depend rather on some aspect of the behavioural interaction between mother and pup. This could be a simple factor such as olfactory stimulation or a complex one involving reciprocal patterns of interaction; we have no data on this as yet.

CONCLUSIONS

We are used to thinking of the emotional and the somatic components of a person's 'psychosomatic' response as proceeding from the same cognitive processing of sensory information and from some common element in the event. The many examples of dissociations between psychological and somatic reactions to apparently stressful situations have made it necessary to re-examine our assumptions.

In the model system I have been studying, the young animal does not respond to a pattern made by all the various aspects of the experience of separation, nor does one aspect determine both the behavioural and the physiological responses. Rather, one aspect of the experience becomes translated into changes in cardiac regulation while another determines the behavioural response. Responses may thus be concomitantly elicited by the experience but not reflect a common reactive process. In fact, by manipulating individual aspects of the experience, one response can be made to occur without the other (see above).

This finding may mean that a person responds to different aspects of a stressful situation with different neural processes which may in turn have different response properties (i.e. latency, duration etc.), different learning characteristics and different sensitivities to early experience. If this is generally true, dissociations between affect, behaviour and physiological change are not surprising. Response patterns to stress such as 'fight–flight' may be patterns only because the individual components frequently occur together rather than because of a unitary organizational structure. This independence of individual components may be most easily demonstrated early in development.

The implications for studies on the longterm effects of early experience are that the impact of the early experience cannot be understood simply in terms of its affecting the development of integrated stress response patterns in adult life. Rather, we must be prepared to deal with the co-existence of several discrete behavioural and physiological processes set in motion by the early experience, each of which interacts with subsequent developmental processes. The resulting response patterns may be different at one age from those at another because of the different developmental schedules followed by the individual behavioural and physiological subsystems.

The task, then, seems to be to define the functional units or individual processes involved in the interaction between the organism and the event. Only by experimentally testing the degree to which the workings of these processes are independent and different can we understand the psychosomatic patterns displayed by the organism in natural life.

ACKNOWLEDGEMENTS

This work was supported by a Research Scientist Development Award from the National Institute of Mental Health and project grant MH 16929. I thank Dr Herbert Weiner of this department and Dr Ethel Tobach of the American Museum of Natural History for their advice and Mr Harry Shair and Miss Hedda Orkin for assistance in the laboratory.

References

ADER, R. & FRIEDMAN, S. B. (1965) Social factors affecting emotionality and resistance to disease in animals. V. Early separation from the mother and response to a transplanted tumor in the rat. *Psychosom. Med.* **27**, 119-122

ADER, R., TATUM, R. & BEELS, C. C. (1960) Social factors affecting emotionality and resistance to disease in animals: I. Age of separation from mother and susceptibility to gastric ulcers in rats. *J. Comp. Physiol. Psychol.* **53**, 446-454

BRONFENBRENNER, U. (1968) Early deprivation in mammals: A cross-species analysis. In *Early Experience and Behavior* (Newton, G. & Levine, S., ed.), pp. 627-764, Thomas, Springfield, Ill.

ENGEL, G. (1967) The concept of psychosomatic disorder. *J. Psychosom. Res.* **11**, 39

HINDE, R. A. & SPENCER-BOOTH, Y. (1971) Effects of brief separation from mother on rhesus monkeys. *Science (Wash. D.C.)* **173**, 111-118

HOFER, M. A. (1970) Physiological responses of infant rats to separation from their mothers. *Science (Wash. D.C.)* **168**, 871-873

HOFER, M. A. (1971) Cardiac rate regulated by nutritional factor in young rats. *Science (Wash. D.C.)* **172**, 1039-1041

HOFER, M. A. & GRABIE, M. (1971) Cardiorespiratory regulation and activity patterns of rat pups studied with their mothers during the nursing cycle. *Dev. Psychobiol.* **4**, 169-180

HOFER, M. A. & REISER, M. F. (1969) The development of cardiac rate regulation in pre-weanling rats. *Psychosom. Med.* **31**, 372-388

HOFER, M. A. & WEINER, H. (1971) The development and mechanisms of cardiorespiratory responses to maternal deprivation in rat pups. *Psychosom. Med.* **33**, 353-362

KAPLAN, J. (1970) The effects of separation and reunion on the behavior of mother and infant squirrel monkeys. *Dev. Psychobiol.* **3**, 43-52

KAUFMAN, I. C. & ROSENBLUM, L. (1969) Effects of separation from mother on the emotional behavior of infant monkeys. *Ann. N.Y. Acad. Sci.* **159**, 681-696

PARKES, C. M., BENJAMIN, B. & FITZGERALD, R. G. (1969) A statistical study of increased mortality among widowers. *Br. Med. J.* **1**, 740-743

SPITZ, R. A. (1945) Hospitalism. An inquiry into psychiatric conditions in early childhood. *Psychoanal. Study Child* **1**, 53-80

Discussion

Hill: In this work we have an entirely different stimulus situation from those which evoke any of the three forms of behaviour suggested by Dr Gray. Here the animal is *deprived* of a situation upon which it is dependent.

Sandler: I gather that each of the constituents of milk is capable of raising the heart rate in the rat pups but water is not. Does the taste of the constituents of milk affect the heart rate? Taste is a subjective experience. If milk-tasting but non-nutritive substances were available, you could control for this.

Hofer: The dose–response relationship should argue against it being a question of taste. If it was simply a matter of a small amount of a substance that was reacted to as a chemical stimulus alone, one would not find a dose–

response relationship. Also, the food is given by intragastric tube and very little enters the mouth. I have not used saccharin or anything like that in the mouth; but if you let the pups suck on the end of the tube and slowly squeeze out drops of milk there is no increase in heart rate; you have to give a lot of it into the stomach to produce a tachycardia.

Denenberg: Have you looked at the adult behaviour of rats separated from their mothers as pups?

Hofer: No. In one experiment we weaned the rats early and looked at cardiac rate in adulthood, and found no differences from those weaned at the normal age. Then we looked more closely at what happens to an early-weaned rat, and although the heart rate is low for a couple of days after permanent separation from the mother at 14–15 days of age, it rapidly recovers and by 21 days the preliminary results indicate that the heart rate is considerably higher than normal. From their weight gains these rats eat very little for the first few days after separation and then eat an enormous amount for three or four days. It is at the end of this period of supernormal food intake that their heart rates are so high. There seem to be compensatory mechanisms by which the animal 'neutralizes' the early experience in this way. The other possibility is that we looked at the adults at the wrong age, and, even more likely, that we weren't looking at cardiovascular regulation in a sophisticated enough manner; we just looked for changes in heart rate in response to handling and habituation to a new environment. The cardiac habituation curve, we thought, would be subtle enough, but it showed no differences.

Sleight: Can I be more simple-minded still and suggest that the effect is entirely physiological? The newborn baby feeds a good deal and feeding is the equivalent of exercise and demands an increased cardiac output. The mechanism might be through the mediation of glucagon, say, which has powerful cardio-vascular effects in the same direction as you have shown. Could that be the explanation? It could certainly explain the behaviour of the rats that you just described, in that when they are weaned early they have less food in the stomach, less production of glucagon, and therefore less tachycardia to cope with the increased gastrointestinal flow. When they have access to food and eat more, when their weight increases rapidly, this would be paralleled by an increased cardiac output and tachycardia. Again, on the neural mechanism, your T1 transection denervated the sympathetic nervous system, which would be expected to cause the changes you saw. This is not to say that mother isn't good for you, but it's an alternative explanation of some of the cardiovascular findings!

Hofer: This is the distinction that I am trying to make. We have investigated the effects of glucagon, insulin and histamine and have found no change in heart rate by injecting them by several routes and in various dosages (M. A. Hofer, unpublished findings 1972). But there must be some way by which the nutrient in the gut communicates with the heart and this seems to be through the CNS rather than through the circulation. If the changes were simply due to glucagon reaching the heart via the bloodstream one would expect some effect to remain after spinal cord section. These findings intrigued us, because this may be a new pathway by which nutrient can affect the developing CNS. In that sense it becomes more than physiological; it becomes neuro-physiological and may be capable of influencing other behaviours controlled by the CNS.

Sleight: The rat may feel more contented inside if it's getting nutrient in its stomach instead of getting Maalox!

Hill: I take it that the rats who are given non-lactating mothers attempt to suckle them, and are allowed to do so?

Hofer: Yes, and this entirely failed to prevent the decrease in heart rate. Separated rat pups put with a non-lactating foster mother become very active, and go after the nipples and suck them. Their heart rate goes up temporarily, but that was also true if we pinched their tails. If the foster mother is removed, the heart rate immediately goes down again. So there are two kinds of control systems, a short-acting one which is behaviourally mediated or stimulus-mediated, and a longer-acting one which is mediated through a nutritional mechanism.

Sifneos: I would think that the time at which these separations occur would play a crucial role. Do your rats develop any special compensatory mechanism later on? For example, there is evidence that temporary absence of the mother affects behavioural development in infant monkeys and that brief separation may produce longterm effects in both monkeys and man (Hinde & Spencer-Booth 1971). Do you have any similar observations on your rats at various ages?

Hofer: I looked at cardiac responses to separation at three developmental ages, at 4, 14 and 20 days. The heart rate decline is much more striking at 14 days, but then the baseline is different at that age. One can explain the differences as part of the overall integration of the animal's autonomic and behavioural systems, which differs at different ages. The 21-day-old rat shows a very slight decline in heart rate with 24 hours of separation, but by 21 days vagal restraint at rest has developed so that the resting heart rate is considerably lower than it was at 14 days (Hofer & Reiser 1969). What environmental events contribute to the development of this vagal restraint needs to be worked out.

Sleight: Shinebourne is studying the baroreflex response to rises in arterial pressure in the foetus in the pregnant ewe, as an index of cardiovascular control at different ages *in utero* and after birth. He finds that this reflex increases steadily, as you might expect, and could account for the increase in vagal restraint you have found (Shinebourne *et al.* 1972).

Zanchetti: The effect of food on the heart rate is surely a reflex effect, so there is no reason to be surprised that it can be dissociated from the behavioural effect. One might even find it in the anaesthetized animal. This reflex effect might be induced through stimulation of sympathetic afferent fibres from the stomach. This can only be demonstrated by comparing the heart rate response in animals with a transection at T8 (i.e. receiving sympathetic afferents from the stomach) and in animals with a T4 transection (i.e. with sympathetic afferents from the stomach disconnected). Of course, a section at T1 would disconnect all sympathetic afferents and efferents.

On the nature of the stimulus, Dr Hofer's evidence suggests that only nutrient substances are stimulating while non-nutrient substances are not. However, we cannot yet rule out stomach distension itself, because if you compare a nutrient solution with distilled water, the distilled water will be absorbed by the stomach very quickly so that the filling stimulus, although equal in size, is shorter in duration. Distending the stomach with a balloon might be a good test for the duration of stomach distension.

Wolff: Have you tried giving food by stomach tube continuously?

Hofer: We have done continuous feeding, using a chronic gastric cannula. The heart rate can be maintained at high levels by giving an adequate flow rate; as flow is reduced, heart rate is maintained less successfully. We have been looking at the behaviour of rats fed in this way. The preliminary results support the earlier observations, that differences in nutrition do not have important *acute* effects on behaviour. I agree that distension of the stomach cannot yet be entirely ruled out as a possible physical factor accounting for the cardiac changes; we used Maalox because it presents some of the solute load and osmotic characteristics of milk and it had none of the cardiac effects of milk.

Zanchetti: How long does the dilute Maalox stay in the stomach? Is it absorbed quickly?

Hofer: We can't be completely sure until we have measured the amount of distension through the osmotic effects of Maalox. However, we found heart rate acceleration only with as much as 2 ml of Maalox and the time course of cardiac acceleration was quite different from the milk effect. If one distends the stomach progressively with increasing amounts of Maalox, or distilled water, it is bradycardia, not tachycardia, which occurs early, and it is not until an hour afterwards that any tachycardia becomes evident. In fact the whole procedure of intubation is associated with bursts of bradycardia which occur through a vagal mechanism.

Donald: Did you measure blood pH? And is there any acid in the stomach of the rat pups?

Hofer: I haven't measured blood or stomach pH. We considered a number of possible afferent pathways. Sharma & Nasset (1962) have shown that perfusion of the gut in adult cats with amino acids and sugars results in increased firing rates along the mesenteric afferent nerves. That seemed an intriguing possibility. Our spinal cord sections at T1 interrupted both afferent and efferent routes so that the blocking effect of this lesion on the cardiac acceleration after milk could be due to interruption of either or both of these pathways. We have sectioned the greater splanchnic nerves and removed the coeliac ganglion and two paravertebral ganglia on both sides in rat pups of this age and this does not obliterate the effect of milk on the heart rate, nor does diaphragmatic vagotomy. Drugs or constriction of blood vessels which affect blood pressure do affect the heart rate as one would expect, according to our knowledge of classical baroreceptor pathways. These are certainly intact at this age (14 days).

Our present thoughts on the mechanism are that there is a local increase in splanchnic blood flow due to local vasodilatation in the gut, causing a change in the central circulatory blood volume. This is sensed by vascular volume and/or pressure receptors and fed back to the CNS through fairly well-known pathways. The changes in cardiac rate may be part of the young organism's adaptation to relatively large shifts in blood volume into the splanchnic area during the digestive process.

Fonberg: I would like to make some bridges between your experiments and mine, Dr Hofer! The separation of mother and rat pup may produce depressive changes, perhaps through the lateral amygdala, but separation also causes an increase in fear. In unpublished experiments on the effect of ablating the dorso-medial amygdala (so that inhibition from the lateral amygdala predominates) we found that in some dogs the heart rate is markedly decreased, to about half its normal value. This may be an instance of general inhibitory effects being reflected in the heart rate. Changes in heart rate may also be regulated through the fear mechanism. Fear might increase in response to stimuli which became more frightening after separation of the infant from the mother. With Dr I. Weinstein from Moscow we recorded the ECG after stimulating the fear area in the hypothalamus in adult dogs. Stimulation of the anterior hypothalamus and the most caudal part of the posterior hypothalamus produced passive fear and a decrease in the heart rate accompanied by pronounced ECG changes: the T-potentials were changed and sometimes extrasystoles appeared. Stimulation of the area for active fear in the posterior and medial hypothalamus produced active fear with acceleration of the heart rate (I. Weinstein & E. Fonberg, in preparation). In our neurotic dogs given difficult tasks there were marked changes in heart rate, but it increased in some dogs and decreased in others; in other words, heart rate was more variable than before the neurosis. These changes may reflect both the passive and active aspects of fear (J. Lagowska & E. Fonberg, in preparation).

Hofer: It is these individual differences in response to a standard environmental situation which have led people to look for early developmental experience as the variable which explains the individual differences in adults. It could be genetic, but it's intriguing to think that early experience could account for it. We often know very little about the early experience of our laboratory animals; this is a completely open area. Some work has been done; Professor Levine has shown that you can systematically predict differences in response pattern from early experiences. However, the question of fear responses in separated animals is complicated because at least three phases can be distinguished in primates, including man: an initial stage with hyperactivity, vocalization, searching and so on; then a phase of apparent inhibition of activity; and finally a return to normal behaviour (Kaufman & Rosenblum 1967). Other species show only the initial stage. I haven't seen three stages in my rats, but only the first stage, with increased searching and hyperactivity. It's not clear how this is mediated or whether there is a second stage. Separations begun when the pups are older might show the biphasic response pattern.

Denenberg: We have been studying the interaction between genetic endowment and postnatal experience by fostering newborn mice to a lactating rat mother. The rat mother accepts the mouse babies without hesitation, nurses them and takes care of them in a beautifully adequate fashion. Our control group consists of mice fostered to mouse mothers. By this procedure we are able to separate postnatal experiences from genetic factors and from prenatal experiences. However, there is a difficulty with this technique: any differences we find between mice raised by a rat mother and mice raised by a mouse mother either may be a function of the behaviour of the rat mother towards the pups or may be due to biochemical differences in the milk of these different species. Therefore, not only do we have a rat mother preparation; we also have a rat 'aunt' preparation, where we place a virgin female rat in with a pregnant mouse. The pregnant mouse gives birth to the young, nurses them and engages in the usual maternal care patterns, but within a few days the rat aunt takes over the caretaking duties. For example, she will retrieve the pups, clean them, build a nest for them, and hover over them. However, she has no milk, and the pups are fed quite competently by the mouse mother. The rat aunt preparation, therefore, avoids the problem of differences in the nature of the milk between the two species, yet the rat aunt's behavioural pattern toward the mice is similar to that of the rat mother.

We then look at the subsequent behaviour of the pups and we can relate these behaviours to their maternal experiences. We have studied two strains of mice, the C57BL/10 inbred strain and the outbred Swiss Albino. We looked at four measures: the open field test; passive avoidance learning, which requires the animal to inhibit his behaviour; aggression (this is intra-species fighting); and plasma corticosterone concentrations as a response to a novel stimulus. We find that the mother, by her behaviour, has a massive impact on the animal's subsequent adult performance, and that the rat aunt and rat mother have equivalent effects; therefore this is not an effect of any differences in the milk. Both strains of mice, when reared by a rat mother or in the presence of a rat aunt, are less active in the open field. They are poorer at passive avoidance learning; that is, they are less able to inhibit their behaviour than animals raised by mouse mothers.

We find an interesting genetic interaction with aggression. In the C57BL/10 strain, the rat aunt or mother decreases fighting; with the Swiss Albino strain there is no effect.

The decrease in aggression is particularly impressive, since aggression is a genetically determined characteristic and appears to have major adaptive value to the organism, in that those animals who are competent fighters are more likely to survive. Yet we are able almost to turn off this behaviour. In several of our experiments we have obtained less than 10% of the usual amount of fighting if C57BL/10 mice are raised by a rat mother or in the presence of a rat aunt. Since we have been unsuccessful so far in reducing the aggression of the Swiss Albino mouse, this is clear evidence of an interaction between the animal's genetic constitution and the nature of its postnatal maternal environment.

The final set of results, on plasma corticosterone concentrations, are with the Swiss Albino strain only. When exposed to a new stimulus, they are less responsive when mothered by a rat or reared with a rat aunt. The hypothalamic–pituitary–adrenal system is less reactive. We have not yet done this experiment with our C57BL/10 mouse.

In summary, in this symposium we have been discussing the effects of lack of the mother but we have not yet discussed her positive contribution. Our data show that the mother's behaviour between birth and weaning will modify, affect and influence genetically determined characteristics, fundamental phenomena which are of adaptive significance to the animal throughout adult life. In our future research we hope to find out just what the mother is doing in her physical interaction with the young that causes these differences. (For further details of this work see Denenberg 1970, Denenberg *et al.* 1972, and Paschke *et al.* 1971).

Hinde: A comparable study by Caroline Hall (1971), using hybrids between different strains of mice, has shown a similar effect of maternal behaviour on the offspring and *vice versa.*

Nemiah: Dr Denenberg, could you hazard a guess as to what the significant behavioural variable is in the interaction between the mice and their rat mothers?

Denenberg: Yes. If you'll let me use the expression, I think they are 'over-mothered'. Typically a rat or mouse mother starts to reduce her attention to her own pups after about ten days and by 21 days she has little contact with them. But this is not so when a rat mother or aunt attends to mouse pups. She is still quite attentive at 20 days of age. I think this is because as far as the rat mother or aunt is concerned, even a 20-day-old mouse looks like a very small rat. So we think that they are over-handled and given more attention and stimulation. We hope to study this further.

Ginsburg: Our studies (Ginsburg 1966, 1968) have indicated that if different strains of mice are handled in the same way during the period before weaning and aggression is later measured, some strains become more aggressive, some are not affected, and some become less aggressive. We also found that the time at which handling produces the maximum effect can be strain-specific. Some respond throughout the suckling period, some respond very early, and some respond only after the first two weeks.

Denenberg: Thoman & Arnold (1968*a,b*) hand-raised rats from birth without a mother and demonstrated deficiencies caused in their subsequent adult behaviour by the lack of mothering. Clearly the psychiatric emphasis on the lack of early maternal experience is consistent with the observations from animal studies.

Grinker: What are the longterm effects of separation, not only on the pup, but also on the mother? (See for example, Young 1965.)

Hinde: We have been concerned with teasing apart the interaction between mother and infant rhesus monkey. The mother affects the behaviour of the infant, and that of the infant affects the mother. Furthermore, the interaction may be affected by other animals—for instance mothers are likely to be more restrictive of the infants if aunts are present (e.g. Hinde 1969; Hinde & Spencer-Booth 1970). To what extent are your rat mothers influenced by the young, Dr Denenberg?

Denenberg: It's a dynamic feedback system. What the mother does affects the baby; what the baby does affects the mother. We can demonstrate this with rats and with mice quite nicely and are able to study and analyse this dyadic system.

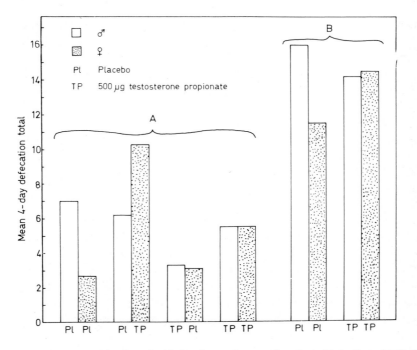

FIG. 1 (Gray). Mean four-day defecation scores as a function of injection of infant rats with testosterone (TP) and of the treatment of siblings. A: results obtained by Gray *et al.* (1969). B: results obtained by Gray *et al.* (1965). (From Gray *et al.* 1969.)

Ginsburg: Alan Fisher (1955) has worked with inbred terriers with a very aggressive pedigree. These dogs are difficult to rear in groups because severe fighting sets in and the puppies may kill each other. One pup can stand off two but usually not three others! Fisher took them away from the mother at birth and raised them by hand on bottles. After weaning, when he put them together, they did not develop the aggressive behaviour characteristic of the pedigree. Dr J. P. Scott raised some of these terriers on beagle mothers, and the effect on them was extremely disruptive. We have tried raising dingos, which are quite aggressive, in the way in which Alan Fisher raised the terriers. The aggression of the dingo is sufficiently invariant that the same kinds of manipulation do not reduce the later aggression.

Gray: With regard to the possible interactions that can take place in the rodent family, we have shown what looks like a behavioural interaction between sibling and sibling (Gray *et al.* 1965, 1969). We injected infant rats either with 500 μg testosterone propionate or with an oil placebo at four days of age.

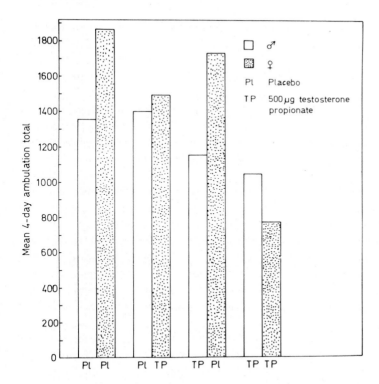

FIG. 2 (Gray). Mean four-day ambulation scores as a function of injection of infant rats with testosterone (TP) and of the treatment of siblings. (From Gray *et al.* 1969.)

Males and females within each litter were allotted to hormone or placebo according to a 2 × 2 orthogonal design, so that in some litters both sexes received oil, in some litters both sexes received the hormone, and in some litters the males received the hormone and the females oil or *vice versa*. In adulthood all animals were tested in the open field and defecation and ambulation were recorded. As shown in Figs. 1 and 2, the effects of the testosterone injection to either sex depended on the treatment (hormone or placebo) given to the other sex in the litter.

Denenberg: Do you know whether the siblings' behaviour fed back to the mother and changed her behaviour, which changed theirs, or whether siblings acted directly upon the other siblings?

Gray: I don't know. An indirect mechanism is certainly possible.

Hill: Professor Hinde, would you like to comment on your work on effects of separation of monkeys?

Hinde: We are studying the effects of separation on infant monkeys. Recently we have investigated what it is about the separation experience that produces both the immediate and the longterm effects on behaviour. We think now that at least three aspects of a separation experience are important in producing these effects.

First, the trauma of the separation itself. In most of our early experiments we removed the mother from the infant monkey, which was left in the group situation in which it had grown up: the only change, therefore, was the removal of the mother. During the 6- or 13-day separation period the infants showed depressed locomotor activity and distress calling, and often sat in a hunched posture.

Second, a number of lines of evidence indicate that disturbance to the mother–infant relationship is an important aspect of a separation experience. Our earlier work showed that, on reunion, the mothers played an important part in determining the nature of the mother–infant relationship (Hinde 1969). We also found that the infants that were most affected by the separation during the post-separation period were those that had been rejected most by their mothers and had had to play the greatest role in staying near them. In other words, the distress shown by the infants was related to these two aspects of what one can call colloquially 'tension' in the mother–infant relationship, and not to the amount of time that mother and infant actually spent together. Furthermore, the degree of distress shown immediately on reunion was related more closely to the tension in the relationship before separation than to the contemporaneous tension in the mother–infant relationship: as time went on it became more closely related to the contemporaneous relationship and less to the pre-separation one (Hinde & Spencer-Booth 1971).

Recently we have done experiments in which the mother was left in the home pen and the infant was removed for 13 days. We expected these separations to produce much more dramatic symptoms, because the infant was being exposed to a strange environment as well as being separated from its mother. In so far as our measures allowed comparisons to be made, it was true that during the separation period such infants were more strongly affected, but on reunion they were much less affected than the infants whose mothers had been removed. We can trace this primarily to one factor: the mother–infant relationships were re-established much more rapidly in those infants whose mothers had been left in the home situation and were themselves therefore much less disturbed. So we believe that another important factor, in addition to the trauma of separation, is the degree of disturbance to the mother–infant relationship that is consequent upon the separation experience. If the mother–infant relationship is very little disturbed, the effects of separation are much reduced (Hinde & Davies 1972).

At present my colleague Miss L. M. Davies is doing the other two possible experiments, namely mother and infant are removed from the home pen together and not separated, and mother and infant are removed and separated, so that each spends the separation period in a separate strange place. These experiments are beginning to suggest that an additional factor is involved, namely that when the infant spends the separation period in a strange place it does not suffer any adverse experience in the home environment, whereas when mother goes to hospital and the infant is left in the home pen, the infant is subject to the stress of separation while in the home environment and becomes to some extent conditioned to the home environment as an adverse one. It looks as though this is an additional aspect of the separation which has to be taken into account.

Hill: Would Dr Rutter like to make any comments on *human* emotional development at this point?

Rutter: There are, I think, parallels between Professor Hinde's findings with rhesus monkeys and the human situation. Although there are fewer systematic data on individual differences in children's responses to brief separation experiences, the same principles seem to apply (Rutter 1972*a*). The sequence of protest, despair and detachment seen in some children admitted to hospitals or to residential nurseries is probably due in part to deprivation of some aspect of bonding or attachment behaviour. The trauma of the separation itself is one factor but probably not the most important one. Separation is likely to be most upsetting to the child when it is associated with disturbance of the parent–child relationship, and to have minimal effects when it is not. This means that the effects will be dependent on the type of care provided during the separation, the child's previous separation experiences, and the nature of the parent–child relationship before and after the separation. Traditionally, separation has usually been thought of in terms of the *mother*–infant relationship but the findings in humans suggest that this is too narrow a view. Although the evidence is still meagre, it appears that similar effects are seen with other close relationships. The child's relationship with his mother is often the strongest he has, but this is not always the case and with some children bonds with the father or with older sibs may take precedence.

In man, as in monkey, there are marked individual differences in children's responses to separation or to other stress experiences. For example, we found that children's temperamental characteristics were important determinants of their reaction to the stresses associated with living with a mentally ill parent (Graham & George 1972; Rutter 1971). Non-fastidious children who were markedly irregular in their eating and sleeping patterns, who were unconcerned by mess and disorder, and whose behaviour was very difficult to change in any direction, were the ones most likely to show emotional and behavioural disturbance in this situation.

There are also important sex differences in children's responses to stress (Rutter 1970a). We showed that boys were more susceptible than were girls to the ill-effects of family discord. It is, of course, well known that the male is generally more vulnerable to biological stresses. The limited available evidence suggests that this applies to many forms of psychological stress as well, but not to all types. Whereas boys are more disturbed by unhappy quarrelsome homes and by the family disturbance associated with brief admissions into foster care or Children's Homes (Wolkind & Rutter 1972), girls seem at least as likely as boys to become 'maladjusted' after an institutional up-bringing (Yule & Raynes 1972). This finding also highlights the need to differentiate between different varieties of 'maternal deprivation' (Rutter 1972a). The term covers a quite diverse range of experiences with varying effects mediated by a heterogeneous mixture of psychological mechanisms.

The finding that, apparently, boys are more vulnerable to many types of psychological stress seems dissonant with the universal finding that most types of psychiatric disorders in adults are very much commoner in women than in men. In this connection, it is relevant to note that this is not the case in childhood and that there is surprisingly little continuity between neurotic disorders in childhood and adult neurosis (Rutter 1972b). Most neurotic children do *not* become neurotic adults and only a minority of neuroses in childhood persist into adult life. Quite what this means in terms of our concepts of neurosis remains uncertain. However, it may mean that the psychological mechanisms underlying emotional disorders in childhood differ from those leading to adult neurosis. Certainly, it means that any discussion of emotional disturbance must take into account developmental considerations.

There are both continuities and discontinuities in emotional development. Although there are well-demonstrated consistencies in children's behaviour over time, it is also true that the correlations over periods of several years (especially in early childhood) are quite low (Rutter 1970b). There are many reasons why this could be the case, but one of them is that psychological development continues to be modifiable until quite late in the maturational process. The expression of both normal and abnormal emotions differs according to the age of the child (Freedman *et al.* 1967). Thus, agoraphobia begins at any time from late childhood to middle life, social anxieties usually start after puberty, specific situational phobias have no characteristic age of onset, and specific animal phobias always begin in childhood (Marks 1969; Rutter 1972b). We do not know whether this means that these age-specific phobias differ in kind or whether it is merely that the mode of expression is influenced by the child's age.

I should add that children's responses to stress also vary to some extent according to developmental level. The most striking example of this concerns children's distress after admission to hospital or other forms of unpleasant separation experience. Distress rarely occurs before the child is six months old, reaches a peak in the next year or so and becomes progressively less frequent after the age of four years or thereabouts (Rutter 1972*a*).

References

DENENBERG, V. H. (1970) The mother as a motivator. In *Nebraska Symposium on Motivation, 1970* (Arnold, W. J. & Page, M. M., eds.), pp. 69-93, University of Nebraska Press, Lincoln, Nebraska

DENENBERG, V. H., PASCHKE, R. E. & ZARROW, M. X. (1972) Mice reared with rats: effects of prenatal and postnatal maternal environments upon hybrid offspring of C57BL/10J and Swiss Albino mice. *Dev. Psychobiol.* **16**, 251-255

FISHER, A. (1955) Ph.D. Thesis, Pennsylvania State University

FREEDMAN, D. G., LORING, C. B. & MARTIN, R. M. (1967) Emotional behaviour and personality development. In *Infancy and Early Childhood* (Brackbill, Y., ed.), Collier-Macmillan, London and Free Press, New York

GINSBURG, B. E. (1966) All mice are not created equal—recent findings on genes and behavior. *Soc. Serv. Rev.* **40**, 121-134

GINSBURG, B. E. (1968) Genotypic factors in the ontogeny of behavior. *Sci. Psychoanal.* **12**, 12-17

GRAHAM, P. & GEORGE, S. (1972) Children's response to parental illness: individual differences. *J. Psychosom. Res.* in press

GRAY, J. A., LEAN, J. & KEYNES, A. (1969) Infant androgen treatment and adult open-field behavior: direct effects and effects of injections to siblings. *Physiol. Behav.* **4**, 177-181

GRAY, J. A., LEVINE, S. & BROADHURST, P. L. (1965) Gonadal hormone injections in infancy and adult emotional behaviour. *Anim. Behav.* **13**, 33-43

HALL, C. L. M. (1971) *The Role of Genetics in the Study of Behaviour*. Ph.D. Thesis, Cambridge University

HINDE, R. A. (1969) Analyzing the roles of the partners in a behavioral interaction—mother-infant relations in rhesus macaques. *Ann. N.Y. Acad. Sci.* **159**, 651-667

HINDE, R. A. & DAVIES, L. M. (1972) Comparison between removing infant rhesus from mother for 13 days with removing mother from infant. *J. Child Psychol. Psychiatr.* in press

HINDE, R. A. & SPENCER-BOOTH, Y. (1970) Individual differences in the responses of rhesus monkeys to a period of separation from their mothers. *J. Child Psychol. Psychiatr.* **11**, 159-176

HINDE, R. A. & SPENCER-BOOTH, Y. (1971) Effects of brief separations from mother on rhesus monkeys. *Science (Wash. D.C.)* **173**, 111-118

HOFER, M. A. & REISER, M. F. (1969) The development of cardiac rate regulation in preweanling rats. *Psychosom. Med.* **31**, 372-388

KAUFMAN, I. C. & ROSENBLUM, L. A. (1967) The reaction to separation in infant monkeys: anaclitic depression and conservation-withdrawal. *Psychosom. Med.* **29**, 648-675

MARKS, I. (1969) *Fears and Phobias*, Heinemann, London

PASCHKE, R. E., DENENBERG, V. H. & ZARROW, M. X. (1971) Mice reared with rats: an inter-strain comparison of mother and 'aunt' effects. *Behaviour* **38** (3-4), 315-351

RUTTER, M. (1970a) Sex differences in children's response to family stress. In *The Child and his Family* (Anthony, E. J. & Koupernik, C., eds.), Wiley, New York

RUTTER, M. (1970b) Psychological development: predictions from infancy. *J. Child Psychol. Psychiatr.* **11**, 49-62

RUTTER, M. (1971) Parent-child separation: psychological effects on the children. *J. Child Psychol. Psychiatr.* **12**, 233-260

RUTTER, M. (1972a) *Maternal Deprivation Reassessed*, Penguin Books, Harmondsworth, Middlesex

RUTTER, M. (1972b) Relationships between child and adult psychiatric disorders: some research considerations. *Acta Psychiatr. Scand.* **48**, 3-21

SHARMA, U. N. & NASSET, E. S. (1962) Electrical activity in mesenteric nerves after perfusion of gut lumen. *Am. J. Physiol.* **202**, 725-730

SHINEBOURNE, E. A., VAPAAVOURI, E. K., WILLIAMS, R. L., HEYMANN, M. & RUDOLF, A. M. (1972) The development of baroreflex activity in unanesthetized fetal and neonatal lambs. *Circ. Res.* in press

THOMAN, E.B. & ARNOLD, W. J. (1968a) Incubator rearing in infant rats without the mother: effects on adult emotionality and learning. *Dev. Psychobiol.* **1**, 219-222

THOMAN, E. B. & ARNOLD, W. J. (1968b) Effects of incubator rearing with social deprivation on maternal behavior in rats. *J. Comp. Physiol. Psychol.* **65**, 441-446

WOLKIND, S. & RUTTER, M. (1972) Children who have been in care: an epidemiological study. *J. Child Psychol. Psychiatr.* in press

YOUNG, R. D. (1965) Influence of neonatal treatment on maternal behavior: a confounding variable. *Psychon. Sci.* **3**, 295-296

YULE, W. & RAYNES, N. V. (1972) Behavioural characteristics of children in residential care. *J. Child Psychol. Psychiatr.* in press

Emotion and the cardiovascular system in the cat

ALBERTO ZANCHETTI, GIORGIO BACCELLI, GIUSEPPE MANCIA
and GAYLORD D. ELLISON

*Istituto di Ricerche Cardiovascolari, Università di Milano,
and Centro di Ricerche Cardiovascolari, CNR, Milan*

Abstract Cardiovascular changes have been measured in cats in response to various emotional stimuli, such as presentation of an attacking cat, a threatening dog, or a mouse, and during motor conditioning. Particular attention has been paid to blood flow to skeletal muscles, as several authors have assumed that emotion is accompanied by activation of a specialized sympathetic system, cholinergic in nature, originating from the hypothalamus, and inducing dilatation of muscle blood vessels.

Our observations have shown that muscle circulation can be influenced in opposite directions during the immobile confrontation behaviour in the presence of an attacking cat and during the ensuing defence-fighting behaviour: indeed there is muscle vasoconstriction in the anticipatory warning phase, and cholinergic (as well as metabolic) vasodilatation during the fighting phase. This cholinergic vasodilatation is specific and motor-related, in so far as it is observed at the same time as fighting movements and is limited to moving limbs only. A similar pattern of muscle vasoconstriction followed by highly specific motor-related cholinergic vasodilatation has been observed during motor conditioning. It should be noticed, however, that some emotional stimuli, either of an aversive or rewarding significance, such as presentation of a threatening dog or of an appealing mouse, can occasionally induce a diffuse bilateral cholinergic dilatation of muscle blood vessels during the immobile watching behaviour preceding the fighting or grasping reactions.

An attempt is made to correlate these observations on cardiovascular regulation with current psychological knowledge on the major emotions and the neural systems underlying them; and to suggest experiments likely to clarify some of the disputed issues.

Until a few years ago information on bodily changes and emotion was largely limited to the somatic side. This kind of interest is well exemplified by Charles Darwin's (1872) classical treatise *The Expression of the Emotions in Man and Animals*. His approach was a descriptive one, of the appearances of both animals and man under the influence of emotions. While his descriptive techniques may seem rather naive today, nonetheless his work places him among the founding fathers of the behaviourist approach to the study of emotions. In fact, even several decades after Darwin's work, information on visceral manifestations of behaviour was substantially limited to anecdotal reports of tachycardia, pupillary dilatation, sweating, and the like.

Physiological study of behavioural influences on visceral functions had to await the thoughtful investigations made by Walter Cannon (1929) and his group at Harvard about fifty years ago, mainly in the decorticate or thalamic preparation displaying rhythmic outbursts of what Cannon defined as sham rage behaviour. This behaviour was shown to be accompanied by a diffuse discharge of the sympathetic system involving the heart, blood vessels, pupils, digestive system, adrenals and so on. Of course, the limitation of these observations lay in the peculiar, stereotyped behaviour of the thalamic cat, and any extrapolation to natural emotional behaviour and to other kinds of behaviour, as attempted by Cannon, was not without risk.

An experimental approach widely used in the thirties and in later years was that of electrically stimulating various parts of the central nervous system, particularly the hypothalamus, which are known to be involved in one or the other type of behaviour. After the pioneer experiments of Karplus & Kreidl (1927) early in this century, Ranson & Magoun (1939) carefully mapped most of the diencephalon in anaesthetized animals and listed all the areas where electrical stimulation yielded sympathetically mediated responses. In the same years Hess (1949) was mapping the same subcortical areas in unanaesthetized animals and describing the behavioural reactions which could be elicited by central neural stimulation. It seemed reasonable that the cardiovascular changes induced by electrical stimulation of a given region of the brain in the anaesthetized state might represent the cardiovascular manifestations of the behavioural reaction that could be elicited by stimulation of the same region in the absence of anaesthesia.

This assumption seemed even more reasonable when it began to become clear, particularly through the ingenious studies of Uvnäs' and Folkow's groups in Sweden, that stimulation of definite areas in the hypothalamus and midbrain—the perifornical region in the lateral hypothalamus and parts of the tegmentum and central grey matter in the midbrain—elicited a peculiar association of sympathetically mediated visceral changes. This pattern consists of an increase in arterial pressure; cardiac stimulation with increase in cardiac output, heart rate and stroke volume; and adrenergic vasoconstriction in visceral beds, such as the renal and the intestinal beds, and in the skin. These signs of diffuse adrenergic activation, involving also the adrenal medulla and intestinal motility, are associated with dilatation of muscle blood vessels, a response brought about through special sympathetic fibres, cholinergic in nature (see Uvnäs 1960, 1971; Folkow et al. 1965).

It remained for Hilton (Abrahams et al. 1960) to show that the hypothalamic and mesencephalic areas whose stimulation elicited this peculiar pattern of cardiovascular changes coincided with the areas from which, in the absence of anaesthesia, electrical stimulation induced a definite behavioural reaction, consisting of alerting, turning of the head, pupillary dilatation, pilo-erection, hissing, snarling, unsheathing of the claws, flattening of the ears and, finally, a sudden attack: this is what Hess & Brügger (1943) had described as the *Abwehr-reaktion*, the defence reaction. Hilton therefore suggested that the pattern of cardiovascular response described by Uvnäs and Folkow might simply represent the cardiovascular manifestations of defence behaviour, or more broadly of emotional behaviour. Extending Cannon's concept that the manifestations of behavioural reactions are always adapted to the individual's welfare and preservation, Hilton insisted that cholinergic sympathetic dilatation in the muscle vessels would represent an example of centrally induced anticipatory reaction, sympathetic vasodilatation being a useful preparation for the subsequent metabolic vasodilatation precipitated by movements (Abrahams et al. 1964).

I have discussed the defence reaction at length because these fine investigations clearly show how fruitfully our knowledge of cardiovascular manifestations of emotional behaviour has grown. However, there are obvious limitations in interpreting stimulation experiments in anaesthetized animals in terms of natural behaviour. These difficulties can only be overcome by studies on unanaesthetized animals during naturally induced behavioural reactions. Recent technical developments have made it increasingly feasible to monitor several cardiovascular variables in free-moving animals. The combination of these new methods with denervation techniques, systemic or local administration of blocking drugs, and experimental manipulation of behaviour can provide much more than a mere description of bodily changes. This approach may help us to understand how behaviour and the conceptual nervous system act on the autonomic nervous system, and how far the ensuing changes in visceral functions are diversified and adapted to the animal's welfare. In turn, our knowledge of the brain structures controlling the visceral functions engaged by different behaviours may help to clarify the neural mechanisms involved in behavioural regulation.

CONFRONTATION AND FIGHTING BETWEEN CATS

During the last few years we have approached these problems by measuring several cardiovascular variables in unanaesthetized cats during natural defence or fighting behaviour (see Zanchetti *et al.* 1971). We started with fighting behaviour mainly because the well-known cardiovascular pattern described by Uvnäs and Folkow (see Uvnäs 1960, 1971) following hypothalamic stimulation is commonly related to the defence reaction and its anticipation (Abrahams *et al.* 1960, 1964). Our experimental design to produce natural defence behaviour (Adams *et al.* 1969) consisted of a cage subdivided into two compartments by a movable opaque screen. In one compartment a cat was placed with an electrode chronically implanted in the mesencephalic grey matter. Electrical stimulation through this electrode invariably elicited attacking behaviour. This cat was used solely as a stimulus for evoking natural defence and fighting behaviour in another cat (the subject of the cardiovascular study) which was placed in the other compartment of the cage. Blood pressure was monitored through an indwelling catheter, and heart rate was recorded by a cardiotachometer. Chronically implanted electromagnetic flow probes and the use of suitable integrating amplifiers gave continuous, simultaneous recording of cardiac output, mesenteric or renal blood flow, and blood flow through a hind limb.

In most experiments particular attention was concentrated on the iliac circulation, and on the possible role of cholinergic sympathetic fibres dilating muscle blood vessels, as suggested by experiments with hypothalamic stimulation.

Three types of confrontation were tested. When electrical stimulation was delivered through the midbrain electrode, attacking behaviour was elicited in the stimulated cat and—as a response to this attack—defence behaviour with fighting movements occurred in the subject cat (Fig. 1, lower part). These fighting movements could involve (*supportive fighting*) or not involve (*nonsupportive fighting*) the hind limbs whose blood flow was recorded (Adams *et al.* 1969). 'Anticipatory' reactions were studied in a third type of trial, called confrontation without fighting, in which the potential aggressor was simply moved toward the subject cat, but no electrical stimulation was given, no attack took place, and the subject cat simply flinched, retracted its ears, dilated its pupils, and watched the first cat closely, remaining otherwise immobile (Fig. 1, upper part) (Adams *et al.* 1968, 1971; Mancia *et al.* 1972).

Fig. 2 compares cardiovascular changes observed in one of several cats studied during numerous randomly alternated trials of confrontation without fighting and of supportive fighting. Immobile confrontation, both in the shorter anticipatory periods which preceded the actual fighting, and in the longer trials in which no fighting was elicited, was associated with bradycardia, decreased cardiac output, decreased total peripheral conductance, mesenteric

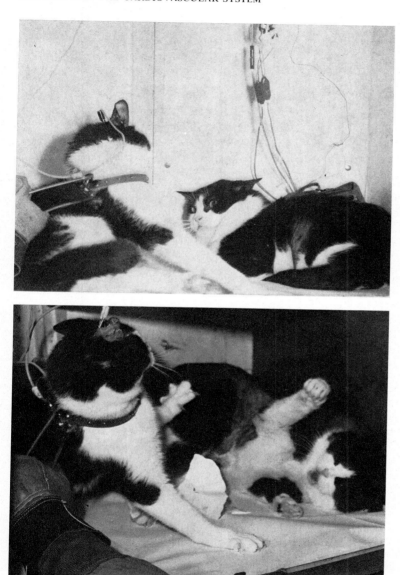

Fig. 1. Photographs of trials of confrontation without fighting *(upper)* and of fighting between cats *(lower)*. In both trials the subject cat is on the right. (Modified from Zanchetti *et al.* 1971.)

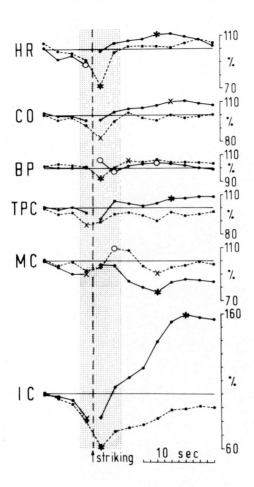

FIG. 2. Comparison of cardiovascular changes occurring during confrontation without fighting (dashed lines) and during fighting (continuous lines) with a threatening cat. Each dot is the mean of measurements taken during six episodes of either type of behaviour in one cat. The shaded area represents the time during which the partition was opened, and the vertical line (relating to fighting episodes only) indicates the first strike of the attacked cat, that is, the beginning of fighting. All values are expressed as percentage changes with reference to baseline measurements when the cat was quiet before the trials. HR: heart rate; CO: cardiac output; BP: mean blood pressure; TPC: total peripheral conductance; MC: mesenteric conductance; IC: iliac conductance. Conductances are ratios of flows to mean blood pressure. Statistical significance indicated by asterisks ($P < 0.01$), crosses ($P < 0.05$), and open circles ($P > 0.05$). (Adams *et al.* 1968.)

vasoconstriction, and a stronger constriction of muscle blood vessels in the hind limbs. On the other hand, the beginning of fighting, signalled by the first forelimb strike and marked in Fig. 2 by the vertical dashed line, was accompanied by cardiovascular changes, many of which were in the reverse direction to those noticed during immobile confrontation. Heart rate, cardiac output and total peripheral conductance all increased, and the blood vessels in active skeletal muscles underwent an extremely strong dilatation. Only the mesenteric bed (as well as the renal one when it was recorded) showed vasoconstriction in both kinds of trial, though to a larger degree during fighting. Blood pressure was slightly affected in either type of behaviour. In all cats which were tested both during immobile confrontation and during supportive fighting cardiac output and muscle blood flow were the two cardiovascular variables which were consistently affected in opposite directions. The difference in the heart rate response was somewhat more variable, however, as bradycardia was the most common though not the only kind of response observed during immobile confrontation between cats (Adams et al. 1968, 1971).

It can be concluded that (1) cardiovascular changes during the immobile confrontation behaviour in the presence of a threatening cat and during supportive fighting are different and even opposite in several respects, and (2) in the immobile period cholinergic muscle vasodilatation does not seem to anticipate the vasodilatation occurring during fighting movements, as the anticipatory response is rather a muscle vasoconstriction. Muscle vasodilatation observed during supportive fighting could be interpreted as being largely dependent upon muscle activity itself. As a matter of fact, in non-supportive fighting—that is, when the cat struck only with the forelimbs and did not use the hind limbs during fighting—there was iliac vasoconstriction instead (Adams et al. 1969).

However, more refined investigations had to be made before one could conclude that the cholinergic sympathetic system, though it so powerfully dilates muscle blood vessels when the hypothalamic defence area is electrically stimulated, is not engaged during natural defence behaviour. These investigations (Ellison & Zanchetti 1972) have indeed shown that the cholinergic sympathetic system is mobilized during natural defence behaviour, though in a way quite different from the one previously supposed. Four cats were studied with two electromagnetic flow probes, one on each external iliac artery: vasomotor reactions in both hind limbs could therefore be compared after the cholinergic sympathetic innervation of one hind limb had been blocked by unilateral intra-arterial perfusion with methylatropine, while innervation of the opposite hind limb remained intact. Fig. 3 shows that during a prolonged period of immobile confrontation between the two cats there is equal vaso-

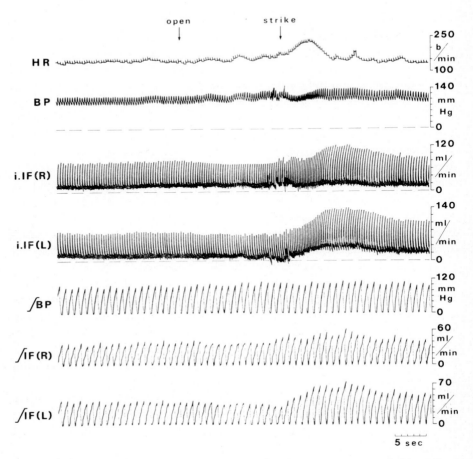

FIG. 3. Unilateral blockade of cholinergic vasodilating fibres and cardiovascular changes during fighting with another cat. First arrow marks the moment when the cage partition was opened and the immobile confrontation period started. The second arrow (strike) indicates the beginning of a brief outburst of fighting, shortly after perfusion of the right hind leg with 0.125 mg methylatropine in saline. iIF(R) and iIF(L): instantaneous blood flow through the right and left external iliac arteries; ∫IF(R) and ∫IF(L): 1-s integrals of those flows. BP: pulsatile blood pressure; and ∫BP: its 1-s integral (mean flow pressure). HR: heart rate. (Ellison & Zanchetti, unpublished figure.)

constriction in both hind limbs, but as soon as fighting movements start and the hind limbs become active, there is a much larger vasodilatation in the intact limb than in that under cholinergic blockade. This indicates that muscle vasodilatation during fighting movements is due not only to obvious metabolic factors (the importance of which will be greater, the more vigorous and prolonged is muscle activity), but also to activation of cholinergic sympathetic fibres. It is interesting that cholinergic vasodilatation seems specifically limited to the time when fighting movements occur. Furthermore, if this observation is combined with data from non-supportive fighting indicating that, even when the cat fights, muscles not engaged in movement are vasoconstricted rather than vasodilated, then we can conclude that cholinergic sympathetic vasodilatation occurs during natural defence behaviour only *when* and *where* movement occurs, according to a motor-related pattern which is specific both in time and space. The functional significance of this specificity is commented on below.

CONDITIONED MOVEMENTS

Another emotional condition in which Ellison & Zanchetti (1971, 1972) have observed a similar pattern of specific motor-related cholinergic vasodilatation, associated with vasoconstriction in immobile limbs, is conditioned movement. Cats were pretrained, using classical Pavlovian conditioning, with a 500 Hz tone of moderate intensity which signalled the coming, 5–6 seconds later, of a 1–3 mA shock of very brief duration (400 ms) to one of the two hind limbs. Each cat always received the shock to the same limb. Those animals which learned to give a relatively specific unilateral leg flexion response during the tone were implanted with Statham electromagnetic flow probes on both iliac arteries and an arterial pressure cannula. As can be seen from Fig. 4 (each curve representing a total of 40 similar trials from four cats), during trials in which the tone evoked a leg flexion response unilaterally in the trained limb only, flow increased only in the trained (that is, flexed) limb, while the contralateral limb, which had remained immobile, had a net decrease in flow. During trials when no conditioned flexion occurred in either limb, there was equal vasoconstriction to both limbs. The lowest part of Fig. 4 shows that the selective vasodilatation occurring in the conditioned limb during conditioned movement is cholinergic in nature, as it was wiped out and substituted by vasoconstriction after cholinergic blockade by methylatropine. It is also remarkable that even in the trained limb cholinergic vasodilatation was usually preceded by a vasoconstrictive wave in the few seconds preceding conditioned movement.

This shortlasting vasoconstriction is not clearly apparent in the upper left quarter of Fig. 4 because that curve results from averaging second by second across 40 trials, while conditionedmovements occurred at different times in different trials. The time course of the initial vasoconstriction and of the following vasodilatation could be assessed correctly by examining individual

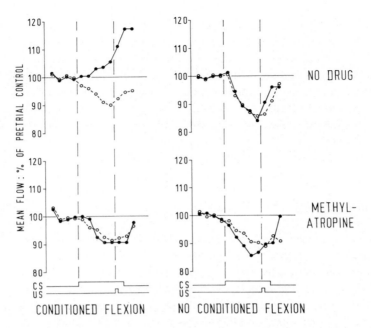

FIG. 4. Changes in external iliac blood flow to the trained (filled circles, continuous lines) and untrained limb (open circles, interrupted lines), during conditioning trials in which the trained limb gave conditioned flexion (left column), and during trials in which there was no conditioned flexion (right column). Two upper sections (no drug): trials before; and two lower sections (methylatropine): trials after injection of the cholinergic blocking agent. In all the curves each point represents the mean of 1-s measurements performed during 40 similar trials (ten trials in each of four cats), expressed as percentage changes with reference to baseline values measured while the animals were quiet before each trial. Timing of conditioned (CS) and unconditioned stimuli (US) indicated at the bottom of the figure. (Ellison & Zanchetti 1971.)

trials, and especially those in which the animal made a single vigorous conditioned flexion movement just before the normal time of shock presentation, but no shock was then presented (Fig. 5).

DIFFUSE CHOLINERGIC VASODILATATION DURING IMMOBILE EMOTIONAL BEHAVIOUR

The emotional behaviours discussed so far, namely confrontation and fighting between cats and conditioned movement, seem to lead to uniform patterns of vasomotor control in the skeletal muscles: adrenergic vasoconstriction in the immobile warning or anticipation period, followed by

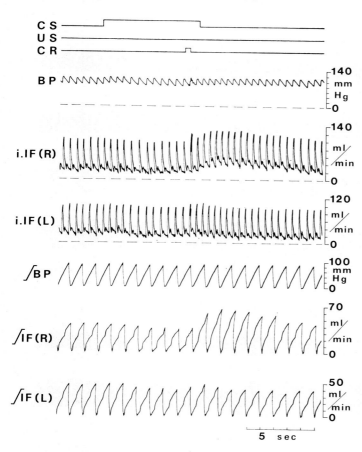

FIG. 5. Time-course of conditioned vasodilatation. Tracings from a conditioning trial in which a single vigorous conditioned flexion movement was made by the right hind limb but no electric shock was presented. Tracings from the top are: duration of conditioning stimulus (CS), mark for unconditioned stimulus (US), mark signalling conditioned flexion responses of the trained (right) hind limb (CR). Abbreviations for other tracings as in Fig. 3. (Ellison & Zanchetti, unpublished figure.)

cholinergic vasodilatation at the time when emotional movements are made and only in those muscles participating in movement, inactive muscles remaining vasoconstricted throughout. It has to be mentioned, however, that there are other emotional stimuli which can occasionally induce a different vasomotor response, namely cholinergic vasodilatation during immobile confrontation behaviour (Baccelli *et al.* 1971; Zanchetti *et al.* 1971; Mancia *et al.* 1972; Ellison & Zanchetti 1972).

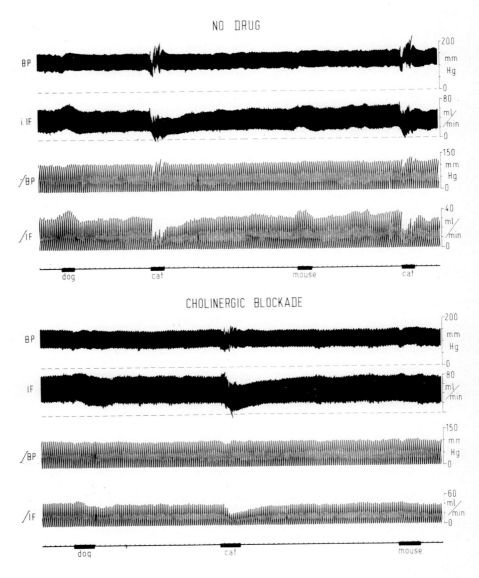

FIG. 6. Cardiovascular reaction of a cat to presentation of a dog, of another cat, or of a mouse (stimulus signals at the bottom of each panel) before (upper panel: no drug) and after the intravenous administration of 1 mg/kg methylatropine (lower panel: cholinergic blockade). Abbreviations for tracings as in Fig. 3. (Baccelli *et al.* 1971.)

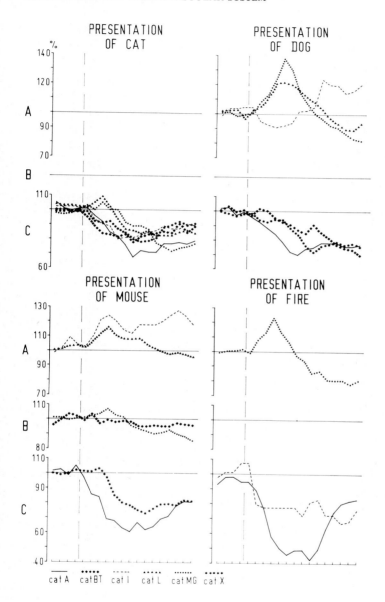

Fig. 7. Percentage changes in left external iliac conductance during presentation of another cat, of a dog, of a mouse, and of fire (presentation begun at broken vertical line). Each cat identified by symbols at bottom. For each stimulus curves have been drawn on three separate rows. A: for significant increases over baseline, B: for no significant changes, C: for significant decreases. (Zanchetti *et al.* 1971.)

Fig. 6 shows records from a cat that had the usual iliac vasoconstriction whenever it was presented with an attacking cat; but when the cat was approached by a barking dog, or a mouse was put in the cat's cage, there was a moderate but definite iliac vasodilatation. The difference in vasomotor reaction to the different stimuli occurred in spite of the fact that the cat reacted with no limb movement to all stimuli. Furthermore, the cholinergic nature of this muscle vasodilatation is proved in the lower part of Fig. 6 by its disappearance after intravenous injection of suitable doses of methylatropine.

A curious aspect of the response of muscle circulation to stimuli such as presentation of a dog, of a mouse, or of fire, was its variability from animal to animal: Fig. 7 shows that, while the presentation of an attacking cat invariably caused vasoconstriction in all the six animals tested, the other stimuli elicited vasodilatation only in some of the cats, the remaining cats (for instance A and X) responding with iliac vasoconstriction to all stimuli tested. It is also interesting that, when confrontation with a dog was continued to the point when the cat ceased its immobile watching behaviour and reacted with striking movements, then motor-related cholinergic vasodilatation was observed, whether the previous immobile behaviour had been accompanied by vasoconstriction or by vasodilatation. In summary, some of the cats reacted to the dog in much the same way as they reacted to another cat, while other cats differed in their response to cat and dog in the immobile confrontation period, though responding in a similar way during subsequent fighting behaviour.

We have also tried to assess whether confrontation with cat, dog, mouse or fire could also induce different heart rate and arterial pressure responses. On the whole, however, if there were differences in these parameters, they were small and obscured by some degree of variability between individuals. Confrontation with a threatening cat more often induced a slight bradycardia, while presentation of a barking dog generally gave a mild tachycardia, but there was no correlation between the responses of muscle circulation and heart rate to the various emotional stimuli. Mean blood pressure responded in an even more variable way than heart rate, and in all behaviours studied it could increase or decrease slightly.

PSYCHOPHYSIOLOGICAL CORRELATIONS

As this meeting is devoted to filling gaps and building bridges between different approaches, it might be useful at this point to attempt some psychophysiological correlations. Using Gray's (1971, 1972) scheme as a simplifying (and probably oversimplified) frame of reference, we shall tentatively consider that different emotional behaviours can be separated into three major types: the approach–active avoidance behaviour, the stop–passive avoidance behaviour, and defensive, aggressive behaviour; and that underlying these emotions there are three separate, though interacting, neural systems.

In confrontation between cats, the flinching, flattening of the ears and otherwise immobile behaviour occurring when the threatening cat is first seen is likely to correspond to the stop kind of behaviour, in which the septo-hippocampal system is thought to inhibit the mechanisms responsible for defensive aggression (Gray 1971). Our observation that in this warning phase many cardiovascular signs, and particularly muscle circulation, change in a direction opposite to that found during the subsequent active behaviour (Adams *et al.* 1968, 1971), fits in with and extends Gray's scheme of opposite responses to conditioned and unconditioned aversive events. Our observations on motor conditioning (Ellison & Zanchetti 1971, 1972) have a similar meaning: a conditioned warning signal elicits muscle vasoconstriction as long as the animal is immobile, but cholinergic vasodilatation occurs as soon as the conditioned movement is made. Anticipation of an aversive event, therefore, is not accompanied by circulatory changes which are in the same direction as those occurring during the unconditioned aversive event itself, but rather by opposite changes, much as is known to occur with somatic behaviour (crouching or freezing versus jumping or running).

This conclusion, however, has to be qualified by other observations. Firstly, there are cardiovascular variables, other than muscle blood flow, heart rate and cardiac output, which change in the same direction in the anticipatory and in the ensuing motor reaction: for instance, visceral blood vessels are constricted, though to a different degree, in both kinds of emotional behaviour (Adams *et al.* 1968, 1971). Secondly, and most importantly, during confrontation with a threatening dog, an overt behaviour apparently identical to that occurring in the presence of an attacking cat is sometimes associated with cholinergic muscle vasodilatation, rather than vasoconstriction; that is, the anticipatory cardiovascular changes are similar rather than opposite to those later occurring during fighting movements (Baccelli *et al.* 1971; Mancia *et al.* 1972; Ellison & Zanchetti 1972). Thirdly, the occurrence of either vasodilatation or vasoconstriction in skeletal muscles upon presentation of a mouse (Baccelli *et al.* 1971; Mancia *et al.* 1972; Ellison & Zanchetti 1972) poses other difficult questions. The behavioural response to this stimulus is obviously quite different from that to a threatening cat or dog, and represents the third major emotion in Gray's (1972) scheme, that depending on the approach–reward system. Does muscle vasoconstriction in the immobile sniffing behaviour in response to a mouse mean that the septo-hippocampal 'stop' system is not limited to conditioned aversive behaviour, and also plays a role in some phases of approaching behaviour? And what is the meaning of the diffuse cholinergic muscle vasodilatation sometimes, though not regularly, occurring at the very beginning of such different emotional stimuli as a threatening dog or an appealing mouse? Does the septo-hippocampal system inhibit the cholinergic vasodilating mechanisms less effectively than somatic behavioural components? Or is this initial cholinergic vasodilatation indicative of a different hypothetical state of the conceptual nervous system, be it emotional or not, like alerting, exploration, surprise? Finally, should the cholinergic dilator system be conceived as a part of the fight–flight system, or as a sort of visceromotor system, involved whenever movement, or at least any emotional movement, occurs (see Bolme & Novotny 1969 and Ellison & Zanchetti 1972)? The motor-related specificity of this system, as described by Ellison & Zanchetti (1972), fits in well with the properties of a motor system. Some of the cardio-vascular differences between warning and fighting might indeed simply derive from the superposition, during fighting movements, of the cholinergic (Ellison & Zanchetti 1972) as well as metabolic (Adams *et al.* 1971) mechanisms brought about by movement.

In summary, our data suggest some tentative conclusions and at the same time a number of difficult questions. It seems reasonable to conclude from our findings that the septo-hippocampal 'stop' system can mobilize adrenergic sympathetic neurons constricting blood vessels, and perhaps vagal cardio-inhibitory neurons as well. In its turn, the amygdalo-hypothalamo-midbrain system, responsible for responses to unconditioned aversive events, mobilizes in a very specific and motor-related fashion the cholinergic sympathetic neurons dilating muscle blood vessels, and also inhibits (see Bruno *et al.* 1961 and Hilton 1963) vagal cardio-inhibitory neurons.

Many other questions remain unanswered, but some understanding is likely to come from behavioural experiments combining cardiovascular recording with lesion of, or recording from, selected neural structures. Can lesions in the septo-hippocampal system abolish, together with 'stop' behaviour, the initial muscle vasoconstriction and turn it into a cholinergic vasodilatation? The observation that the sham rage of the acute thalamic cat is associated with a prompt and diffuse cholinergic vasodilatation (Abrahams *et al.* 1960) makes this hypothesis a very promising one. Can the appearance of either dilatation or constriction in muscle blood vessels upon presentation of a dog be correlated with absence or presence of the hippocampal theta rhythm, which is supposed to mediate the behavioural inhibition of the septo-hippocampal system (Gray 1970; Ball & Gray 1970)? On the other hand, can amygdaloid lesions hinder cholinergic vasodilatation and favour muscle vasoconstriction?

PHYSIOLOGICAL CONSIDERATIONS

From the physiological viewpoint, we should now comment on the observation that the main cardiovascular differences between the various emotions are found in the circulation of the skeletal muscles. In an optimistic mood, one could be content with the comment that this supports the wisdom of ordinary language, which in the most obvious way has related emotion to motion. Deeper insight is gained if we concentrate on the patterns of muscle blood flow change in confrontation and fighting between cats, namely diffuse vasoconstriction in the warning stage followed by a motor-related specific cholinergic vasodilatation in moving limbs during fighting. It is the current opinion, however, that a diffuse cholinergic vasodilatation occurs in preparation for defence movements, and that it has adaptive functions in preparing the muscles for the forthcoming movements (Abrahams *et al.* 1964; Folkow *et al.* 1965).

Although we have occasionally observed a 'preparatory' vasodilatation upon presentation of a dog or mouse (see above), we would like to emphasize here that a diffuse muscle vasodilatation in the absence of movement is clearly non-adaptive (see Hyman *et al.* 1959; Folkow *et al.* 1961). If movement does not occur, diffuse muscle vasodilatation would simply result in a fall in blood pressure, and if localized movement supervenes, unspecific vasodilatation in inactive muscles would make less blood available to the active ones. A motor-related muscle vasodilatation, if it is an adaptive response, has to be specific in so far as it has to occur when and where movement occurs in order to shunt blood to active muscles only, and will be most conveniently effected if preceded by vasoconstriction and accompanied by vasoconstriction in inactive muscles. That is exactly the pattern we have usually observed and have tentatively attributed to the successive play of the septo–hippocampal 'stop' system and of the fight–flight system. Cholinergic vasodilatation can therefore be defined as preparatory for movement, not in so far as it actually precedes muscle contraction but as it quickly occurs at its very beginning before metabolic vasodilators can exert their full effect (Ellison & Zanchetti 1972).

The fine specificity of the cholinergic portion of the sympathetic system has another implication. If this component of the defence behaviour can act in a highly specific motor-related fashion, then the brain systems underlying this kind of emotional behaviour can operate in a highly organized way, which is not usually attributed to regions such as the hypothalamus and the mesencephalic periaqueductal grey.

References

ABRAHAMS, V. C., HILTON, S. M. & ZBROŻYNA, A. (1960) Active muscle vasodilatation produced by stimulation of the brain stem: its significance in the defence reaction. *J. Physiol. (Lond.)* **154**, 491-513

ABRAHAMS, V. C., HILTON, S. M. & ZBROŻYNA, A. (1964) The role of active muscle vasodilatation in the alerting stage of the defence reaction. *J. Physiol. (Lond.)* **171**, 189-202

ADAMS, D. B., BACCELLI, G., MANCIA, G. & ZANCHETTI, A. (1968) Cardiovascular changes during preparation for fighting behaviour in the cat. *Nature (Lond.)* **220**, 1239-1240

ADAMS, D. B., BACCELLI, G., MANCIA, G. & ZANCHETTI, A. (1969) Cardiovascular changes during naturally elicited fighting behavior in the cat. *Am. J. Physiol.* **216**, 1226-1235

ADAMS, D. B., BACCELLI, G., MANCIA, G. & ZANCHETTI, A. (1971) Relation of cardiovascular changes in fighting to emotion and exercise. *J. Physiol. (Lond.)* **212**, 321-335

BACCELLI, G., ELLISON, G. D., MANCIA, G. & ZANCHETTI, A. (1971) Opposite responses of muscle circulation to different emotional stimuli. *Experientia* **27**, 1183-1184

BALL, G. G. & GRAY, J. A. (1971) Septal self-stimulation and hippocampal activity: separate processes. *Physiol. Behav.* **6**, 547-549

BOLME, P. & NOVOTNY, J. (1969) Conditioned reflex activation of the sympathetic cholinergic vasodilator nerves in the dog. *Acta Physiol. Scand.* **77**, 58-67

BRUNO, F., GUAZZI, M. & PINOTTI, O. (1961) On the mechanism of the tachycardia produced by electrical stimulation of the posterior hypothalamus. *Arch. Ital. Biol.* **99**, 68-87

CANNON, W. C. (1929) *Bodily Changes in Pain, Hunger, Fear and Rage*, 2nd edn, Charles T. Brandford Company, Boston

DARWIN, C. (1872) *The Expression of the Emotions in Man and Animals*, John Murray, London

ELLISON, G. D. & ZANCHETTI, A. (1971) Specific appearance of sympathetic cholinergic vasodilatation in muscles during conditioned movements. *Nature (Lond.)* **232**, 124-125

ELLISON, G. D. & ZANCHETTI, A. (1972) Diffuse and specific activation of the sympathetic cholinergic fibers of the cat. Submitted

FOLKOW, B., HEYMANS, C. & NEIL, E. (1965) Integrated aspects of cardiovascular regulation. In *The Handbook of Physiology, Circulation* (Hamilton, W. F. & Dow, P., eds.), section 2, vol. III, chapt. 49, pp. 1787-1823, American Physiological Society, Washington, D.C.

FOLKOW, B., MELLANDER, S. & ÖBERG, B. (1961) The range of effect of the sympathetic vasodilator fibres with regard to consecutive sections of the muscle vessels. *Acta Physiol. Scand.* **53**, 7-22

GRAY, J. A. (1970) Sodium amobarbital, the hippocampal theta rhythm and the partial reinforcement extinction effect. *Psychol. Rev.* **77**, 465-480

GRAY, J. A. (1971) *The Psychology of Fear and Stress*, McGraw-Hill, New York

GRAY, J. A. (1972) The structure of the emotions and the limbic system. This volume, pp. 87-120

HESS, W. R. (1949) *Das Zwischenhirn. Syndrome, Lokalizationen, Funktionen*, Benno Schwabe & Co., Basel

HESS, W. R. & BRUGGER, M. (1943) Das subkorticale Zentrum der affektiven Abwehrreaktion. *Helv. Physiol. Pharmacol. Acta* **1**, 33-52

HILTON, S. M. (1963) Inhibition of baroceptor reflexes on hypothalamic stimulation. *J. Physiol. (Lond.)* **165**, 56P-57P

HYMAN, C., ROSELL, S., ROSEN, A., SONNENSCHEIN, R. R. & UVNÄS, B. (1959) Effects of alterations of total muscular blood flow on local tissue clearance of radio-iodide in the cat. *Acta Physiol. Scand.* **46**, 358-374

KARPLUS, J. P. & KREIDL, A. (1927) Gehirn und Sympathicus. VII: Über Beziehungen der Hypothalamus Zentren zu Blutdruck und innerer Sekretion. *Pflügers Arch. Ges. Physiol.* **215**, 667-670

MANCIA, G., BACCELLI, G. & ZANCHETTI, A. (1972) Hemodynamic responses to different emotional stimuli in the cat: patterns and mechanisms. *Am. J. Physiol.* In press

RANSON, S. W. & MAGOUN, H. W. (1939) The hypothalamus. *Erg. Physiol.* **41**, 56-163
UVNÄS, B. (1960) Central cardiovascular control. In *The Handbook of Physiology* (Magoun, H. W., ed.) section 1, vol. II, chapt. 40, pp. 1131-1162, American Physiological Society, Washington, D.C.
UVNÄS, B. (1971) Cholinergic muscle vasodilatation. In *Cardiovascular Regulation in Health and Disease* (Bartorelli C. & Zanchetti, A., eds.), pp. 7-16, Cardiovascular Research Institute, Milan
ZANCHETTI, A., BACCELLI, G. & MANCIA, G. (1971) Cardiovascular effects of emotional behaviour. In *Cardiovascular Regulation in Health and Disease* (Bartorelli, C. & Zanchetti, A., eds.), pp. 17-32, Cardiovascular Research Institute, Milan

Discussion

Lader: We have some results in man that support your point that the vasodilatation taking place in the muscles is due to sympathetic stimulation and not merely to local accumulation of metabolites. Forearm blood flow has been widely used in psychiatric patients to assess levels of anxiety. It seemed possible that this parameter was merely reflecting the raised muscle activity found in anxiety. We recorded forearm blood flow using venous occlusion plethysmography, and simultaneously measured the electromyogram from two sites on the same forearm within the plethysmograph. We used normal subjects and alerted them by asking them to do mental arithmetic. No correlations were found between changes in forearm blood flow and changes in muscle activity but there were good correlations between blood flow and heart rate. We therefore concluded that the change in blood flow was not an indirect effect of muscle activity (Mathews & Lader 1971).

Similar experiments indicated that the physiological changes seen in intense emotions are only moderate. For example, we have recorded forearm blood flow from two or three anxious patients who happened to have spontaneous panic attacks while they were connected to the polygraph. Blood flow increased from about 4 ml/min per 100 ml of arm volume to 27 or 30 ml/min per 100 ml. But when patients are asked to exercise the forearm by clenching the fist, the blood flow rises to over 50 ml/min per 100 ml. So even in intense panic the changes are only about half those following exercise (Lader & Mathews 1970).

Reichsman: Professor Zanchetti's results are at variance with the results of studies in man by Brod (1971) and by Barcroft *et al.* (1960) who found that under the stress of mental arithmetic, the subjects being 'harassed' during the task, vasodilatation occurred almost uniformly, but this vasodilatation differed from that of muscular exercise in several respects. For example, the difference in arteriovenous oxygen saturation did not increase during mental arithmetic (Barcroft *et al.* 1960) nor was there a rise in the capillary filtration coefficient (Brod *et al.* 1966). These findings were interpreted to mean that the 'emotional' vasodilatation in muscles is out of proportion to their metabolic demand and that during 'emotional' hyperaemia additional capillaries do not open in muscles. Barcroft *et al.* (1960) could block only 20–30% of this 'emotional' vasodilatation in the forearm (which was accompanied by vasoconstriction in skin and splanchnic vessels) by injecting atropine intra-arterially. Brod (1971) cites the work of other investigators (Holmberg *et al.* 1965; Konzett *et al.* 1968) who succeeded in abolishing the major part of 'emotional vasodilatation' by β-adrenergic blocking agents.

Zanchetti: I am familiar with this series of papers by Brod. His group showed forearm vasodilatation when their subjects were excited by a difficult mental arithmetic task (Brod *et al.* 1959; Fencl *et al.* 1959), but when they studied the mechanisms of this vasodilatation (Barcroft *et al.* 1960), the response was only slightly decreased by atropine. Blair *et al.* reported that muscle vasodilatation in response to a frightening stimulus in man was largely abolished by atropine (1960*a*), but the same group (1960*b*) couldn't later confirm these findings. As you say, Konzett *et al.* (1968) have reported that emotional muscle vasodilatation can be blocked in man by blockers of the sympathetic β-receptors. One should keep in mind that many species differences in the organization and sensitivity of sympathetic vasodilating fibres are still incompletely understood. Uvnäs' group (Bolme *et al.* 1970) showed that atropine-sensitive vasodilatation could be elicited in the muscles of various carnivores, but no neurogenic vasodilatation could be obtained in monkeys, and they suggested that the cholinergic sympathetic system is absent in primates, including man. More recently, however, Schramm *et al.* (1971) have shown that neurogenic dilatation of muscle blood vessels can also be obtained in monkeys, but the response is insensitive to atropine while it is abolished by β-blocking drugs.

In comparing cardiovascular emotional responses in man to those in other species, one should also consider that it is very difficult to produce emotional responses reliably and repeatedly in man. Difficult mental arithmetic is the only test which has been extensively studied in man, but this has no relation with most of the emotional behaviours that are commonly studied in animals, and particularly with those employed in our experiments. Mental arithmetic is probably nearer to active avoidance behaviour.

Sleight: I agree with you about mental arithmetic. I tested a patient who was a bookmaker's clerk with mental arithmetic. His blood pressure and heart rate went up rapidly. I thought that this might be an unusual activity for him so I asked him to calculate the odds, something he does all the time. But his blood pressure went up just as much!

A more important point is about the effect of the situation on the response. Hunt (1970) was concerned because the response of the heart rate of car drivers reacting to a sudden incident, a panic effect, was different according to whether the incident was expected or unexpected. He devised experiments in which the subject blew up a balloon, and he could bypass their blowing efforts and burst the balloon. When the subject was expecting this burst his heart rate went up. In the same set of experiments Hunt sounded a loud horn (unexpected) underneath the seat at the same time as the balloon burst, and then there was an immediate bradycardia. That sort of experiment shows that when one is studying the cardiovascular effects of a stimulus one must take expectation into account.

Zanchetti: I have been aware of this problem, and so we have always presented different stimuli to the cat with random alternation of the stimuli, so the cat was not able to learn whether he was going to be attacked or simply approached by the other cat, or whether it was a cat that was going to be presented, or a dog or mouse or some other stimulus. So we can rule out that either vasoconstriction or vasodilatation was induced according to whether the stimulus was expected or unexpected. However, we didn't know the previous life history of our cats—that is, how often they had been confronted with an aggressive cat or a threatening dog, or had hunted a mouse in natural conditions. This might have influenced the type of vasomotor response to the stimulus administered in the laboratory.

Engel: These are interesting observations and relevant to vasodepressor fainting—the vasovagal attack—in man, which we studied before these more elegant techniques were available (Engel & Romano 1947). We formulated a hypothesis, on clinical grounds, that vasodepressor fainting was a reaction occurring typically in a situation of threat, particularly threat of injury, in individuals who, for psychological or circumstantial reasons or both, were unable either to acknowledge that they were afraid or to do anything about it. This recalls Dr Zanchetti's experiment where the one thing the cat can't do is escape. I think Dr Zanchetti demonstrated the same physiological changes that we encountered in humans in situations, such as in the dental chair, or before a venepuncture or a minor surgical procedure, where they feel they must submit but in fact want to flee or protest. Usually there is an initial increase in heart rate and in blood pressure: then there is an abrupt change, the blood pressure beginning to fall, usually with tachycardia at first, but then commonly bradycardia, sometimes with sinus arrest or heart block. Barcroft *et al.* (1944) showed that the point at which the blood pressure began to fall was a point of abrupt decrease in peripheral vascular resistance, occurring mainly in muscle. Can you develop your results with the cat and relate them to the vasovagal attack in man?

Zanchetti: As a matter of fact, Barcroft & Edholm (1945) claimed that fainting might involve activation of sympathetic vasodilator mechanisms, though their hypothesis has never been substantiated. Physiologically, it wouldn't seem unreasonable to postulate that muscle vasodilatation participates in fainting, because (as I argued in my paper) diffuse activation of the cholinergic system in the absence of widespread movement is a non-adaptive response. However, one should also consider that the sympatho-inhibitory system described by Folkow *et al.* (1959), which I mentioned earlier in relation to your conservation–withdrawal behaviour (p. 81), might well be involved in fainting.

References

BARCROFT, H. & EDHOLM, O. G. (1945) On the vasodilatation in human skeletal muscle during post-haemorrhagic fainting. *J. Physiol. (Lond.)* **104**, 161

BARCROFT, H., BROD, J., HEJL, Z., HIRZJÄRVI, E. A. & KITCHIN, A. H. (1960) The mechanism of the vasodilatation in the forearm muscle during stress (mental arithmetic). *Clin. Sci.* **19**, 577-586

BARCROFT, H., EDHOLM, O. G., McMICHAEL, J. & SHARPEY-SCHAFER, E. (1944) Posthaemorrhagic fainting. Study of cardiac output and forearm flow. *Lancet* **1**, 489-491

BLAIR, D. A., GLOVER, W. E., GREENFIELD, A. D. M. & RODDIE, I. C. (1960*a*) Excitation of cholinergic vasodilator nerves to human skeletal muscles during emotional stress. *J. Physiol. (Lond.)* **148**, 633-647

BLAIR, D. A., GOLENHOFEN, K. & SEIDEL, H. (1960*b*) Muscle blood flow during emotional stress. *J. Physiol. (Lond.)* **149**, 61-62P

BOLME, P., NOVOTNY, J., UVNÄS, B. & WRIGHT, P. G. (1970) Species distribution of sympathetic cholinergic vasodilator nerves in skeletal muscle. *Acta Physiol. Scand.* **78**, 60-64

BROD, J. (1971) Psychological influences on the cardiovascular system. In *Modern Trends in Psychosomatic Medicine* (Hill, O. W., ed.), pp. 53-70, Appleton-Century-Crofts, New York

BROD, J., FENCL, V., HEJL, Z. & JIRKA, J. (1959) Circulatory changes underlying blood pressure elevation during acute emotional stress (mental arithmetic) in normotensive and hypertensive subjects. *Clin. Sci.* **18**, 269-279

BROD, J., PŘEROVSKÝ, I., ULRYCH, M., LINHART, J. & HEINE, H. (1966) Changes in the capillary filtration in muscles during muscular hyperaemia accompanying emotion, exercise and adrenaline, acetylcholine and isopropyladrenaline intra-arterial infusion. In *L'Hypertension Arterielle* (International Club on Arterial Hypertension, Paris 1965), p. 433, L'Expansion scientifique française, Paris

ENGEL, G. L. & ROMANO, J. (1947) Studies of syncope. IV. Biological interpretation of vasodepressor syncope. *Psychosom. Med.* **9**, 288-294

FENCL, V., HEJL, Z., JIRKA, J., MADLAFOUSEK, J. & BROD, J. (1959) Changes of blood flow in forearm muscle and skin during an acute emotional stress (mental arithmetic). *Clin. Sci.* **18**, 491-498

FOLKOW, B., JOHANSSON, B. & ÖBERG, B. (1959) A hypothalamic structure with a marked inhibitory effect on tonic sympathetic activity. *Acta Physiol. Scand.* **47**, 262-270

HOLMBERG, G., LEVI, L., MATHE, A., ROSEN, A. & SCOTT, H. M. (1965) Comparison of the plasma catecholamine levels and the influence of propranolol on peripheral hemodynamic manifestations of emotional stress in labile hypertensive and normal subjects. *Circulation* **32**, suppl. 2, 11

HUNT, T. J. (1970) Tachycardia and bradycardia associated with particular forms of stimuli. *J. Physiol. (Lond.)* **210**, 64P

KONZETT, H., STRIEDER, N. & ZIEGLER, E. (1968) Die Wirkung eines beta-Receptoren-blockers auf emotionell bedingte Kreislaufreaktionen, insbesondere auf die Durchblutung des Unterarms. *Wien. Klin. Wochenschr.* **80**, 953-959

LADER, M. H. & MATHEWS, A. M. (1970) Physiological changes during spontaneous panic attacks. *J. Psychosom. Res.* **14**, 377-382

MATHEWS, A. M. & LADER, M. H. (1971) An evaluation of forearm blood flow as a psycho-physiological measure. *Psychophysiology* **8**, 509-524

SCHRAMM, L. P., HONIG, C. R. & BIGNALL, K. E. (1971) Active muscle vasodilatation in primates homologous with sympathetic vasodilatation in carnivores. *Am. J. Physiol.* **221**, 768-777

Changes in catecholamine-controlling enzymes in response to psychosocial activation of the defence and alarm reactions

J. P. HENRY, D. L. ELY and P. M. STEPHENS

Department of Physiology, University of Southern California, Los Angeles

Abstract The confrontations that occur between the various members of a social grouping of mammals as they seek desiderata, such as food, nesting areas and mates, are accompanied by behavioural evidence of emotional arousal. The physiological concomitants of the ensuing behaviour include the activation of two separate neuroendocrine response patterns, the pituitary–adrenal cortical 'alarm reaction' of Selye and the sympathetic–adrenal medullary 'defence reaction' of Folkow. Repeated confrontations leading to prolonged psycho-social stimulation of colonies of mice have been shown to be associated with high blood pressure and arteriosclerotic deterioration. Others have demonstrated increased adrenal cortical activity. We are currently engaged in a collaborative study of the role of the sympathetic–adrenal medullary pathway by measurement of the catecholamine-synthesizing enzymes tyrosine hydroxylase and phenyl-ethanolamine *N*-methyltransferase. Isolation during maturation induces behavioural deficiencies that preclude the development of a stable social order in the adult community. Behaviour is followed by magnets implanted in the mice and Hall Effect detection units placed at the entrances of the boxes composing the population cages. The blood pressure of the dominant animals appears to be higher, yet their adrenal weights are lower than those of the subordinates. The responses of the A/J, a timid strain; of the very reactive NZB; and of the exploratory, well-socialized CBA mice have been contrasted using blood pressure and open field tests as well as the enzyme assays. The three measures are all low in the A/J and high in the NZB strain, but A/J mice that have developed high blood pressure show increases in catecholamine–synthesizing enzymes and open field exploration. Unilateral adrenal denervation is accompanied by a fall in the enzyme content of the gland, supporting the concept that the sympathetic nerves help to determine rates of enzyme synthesis in mice.

There appear to be three major subdivisions of the human brain from the viewpoint of its control function. There is the huge 'sociocultural' neocortex which physically overshadows the entire human organ (Washburn & Hamburg 1968). It is necessary for memory, foresight, planning, inhibition of inappropriate action, for speech and for the complex technical activity that characterizes man. A second region is the brainstem including the hypothalamus, a mechanism which harbours the physical basis of consummatory acts like sex, eating and drinking, and of behaviour typical of anger and pleasure. It is also involved in the integration and coordination of endocrine and autonomic nervous activity as well as of the cardiovascular and other systems (Folkow & Neil 1971; Ganong 1970, 1971).

Set apart from these subdivisions and serving as a counterpoise as well as a loose junction between them is a third zone—the limbic brain. This appears to be responsible for emotionally toned behavioural responses to the external environment. It is critical for the environmentally stable patterns of behaviour exhibited by the species in connection with the self-preservative activities of feeding and drinking, and the species-preservative activities of courtship, mating and care of the young (MacLean 1970; Ganong 1971).

THE LIMBIC SYSTEM AND EMOTIONS IN INDIVIDUALS AND GROUPS

In his general review of medical physiology the neuroendocrinologist Ganong (1971) entitles one chapter 'The neurophysiologic basis of instinctual behavior and the emotions'. In his introductory paragraph defining emotion he points to the elusive combination it presents, of awareness of sensation, of the feeling itself, and of the urge to action combined with certain physiological changes, for example, high blood pressure, tachycardia or sweating. Indeed the hypothalamus and limbic systems are concerned not only with emotional expression, but with the genesis of emotions as well. One implication of this viewpoint is that since these systems are the same in all mammals, there is no reason to suppose that a mouse does not have the same basic emotions as a man. A further corollary is that both men and mice may well suffer from the same physiological disturbances and pathological effects if the defence and alarm responses based in the hypothalamus are activated long enough and with sufficient intensity.

This paper describes a method for studying the behaviour and physiological responses of individual mice while they are living in social groupings. These groupings result in psychosocial stimulation as the various members of the hierarchy interact with each other. Crook (1970) has expressed the need for more social ethological studies viewing man as a member of the animal kingdom and raises the question how far the problems of stress physiology in rodents may not also apply to man. The high ranking animals in rodent as well as human societies feel free to initiate interactions, thereby suppressing the competing activity of a subordinate. The subordinates learn to avoid, restraining their behaviour and leaving the high ranker with easy access to commodities and social desiderata. The repeated constraints imposed on each other can lead to chronic physiological disturbance in the members of a murine community as well as in a group of men.

THE PITUITARY ADRENOCORTICAL SYSTEM AND THE ALARM RESPONSE

In all mammals the complex reaction to 'stress' known as the alarm response of Selye (1936) is initiated by a corticotropic releasing factor which passes down the portal vessel system from the median eminence to the anterior pituitary. There corticotropin (ACTH) enters the bloodstream to effect the production of corticosteroid hormones from the adrenal cortex itself (Ganong 1971). Of interest in the present context is the fact that efferent nerve pathways from those parts of the brain involved in emotion and motivation converge on the median eminence of the hypothalamus. Thus Ganong (1971) comments that the fibres from the amygdaloid nuclei which travel to the hypothalamus can mediate responses to emotional reactions. Indeed, in his important review of psychoendocrine research into the pituitary–adrenal cortical system, Mason (1968a) points to the massive evidence from many sources that psychological influences are among the most potent natural stimuli known to affect this system. This sensitivity is so great as to suggest a constant tonic influence from the higher centres. The state of anticipation—that is, of having to cope with novel and unpredictable situations—is particularly potent in eliciting an increased output of 17-hydroxycorticosteroids from the adrenal and the organization of psychological defences is critical in determining their level in the circulation. In this connection, threats to the integrity of the territorial sense and perceptions of place in the social organization are overriding considerations.

The relationship of increased population density to increased adrenal cortical activity was studied in detail by Christian et al. (1965). In general, the higher the social rank of the animal, the less the effect of higher population density on the adrenal output. The threat induced by infringement of social status and territory by crowding emerges clearly, as it does from Calhoun's (1962) studies of colonies of rats.

In his review of the regulation and adaptive functions of the pituitary–adrenocortical system, Bajusz (1969) concludes that the terminal pathways in the laboratory animal and in man are probably the same. He emphasizes the need for the living organism to be studied from the viewpoint of its particular history and its particular environmental setting in order for effective understanding of the operation of the hypothalamus and related limbic system to be achieved.

Bourne (1970), speaking of animals as well as man, comments that in addition to individual differences, social factors will significantly affect an individual's perception of stress and hence the resulting level of adrenocortical secretion. In small groups with free communication among members of equal standing there is a tendency for a consensus to develop as to how a stress should be perceived; this, in turn, minimizes individual differences. He notes that group support prevents the prolongation of feelings of uncertainty, but that animals high in the hierarchy present different endocrine responses from their subordinates.

In summary, in order to assess a threat, it is necessary to consider the psychological style of the individual in coping with the environment and the social context of the stimulus.

THE SYMPATHETIC–ADRENAL MEDULLARY SYSTEM AND THE DEFENCE REACTION

It has been customary to restrict analysis of the reactions involved in adaptation to psychosocial stimuli to the hypothalamo–hypophyseal adrenocortical system—that is, to the alarm response first described by Selye (1936). However, the susceptibility of the adrenal gland to emotional stimuli, first demonstrated by Cannon in 1911, cannot be overlooked or dismissed as a transient phenomenon (Cannon & de La Paz 1911). Mason accords this sympathetic–adrenal medullary response equal status with the adrenocortical response as an independent neuroendocrine system (Mason 1968b). There is evidence of this separation of the responses. Thus injections of adrenaline do not increase the secretion of ACTH, and Goldfien & Ganong (1962) have shown that when the hypothalamus is electrically stimulated, the points triggering catecholamine release differ from those leading to release of ACTH. The output of 17-hydroxycorticosteroid can be increased without changing that of catecholamines and *vice versa*. In fact, a recent report by Ganong (1970) suggests that adrenergic systems in the ventral hypothalamus may actually participate in the inhibition of ACTH secretion.

It is in the forward extension of the brainstem reticular formation in the anterior part of the hypothalamus that stimulation induces response patterns which are behaviourally and physiologically characteristic of the defence reaction. Folkow & Neil (1971) point out that it induces a state which is highly suited for either attack or flight. It is activated by situations inducing tenseness and alertness in anticipation of dramatic events. The somatomotor behaviour characteristic of this arousal in the cat includes hissing, spitting, arching the back, and raising of the hair on the back and tail. At the same time, sympathetic cholinergic vasodilator fibres to the arterioles of the skeletal muscles are activated. There is also violent excitation of the adrenergic fibres to all other parts of the vascular bed and to the heart while the release of catecholamines from the adrenal medulla is much enhanced.

Using human subjects, Brod *et al.* (1959) have elicited this response in the course of elegant experiments in which the emotional stimulus was that of harassing insistence by the investigators that the subject do accurate mental arithmetic in time with the beat of a metronome. Haemodynamically the ensuing sympathetic–adrenal medullary arousal results in an increase in arterial pressure, cardiac output and heart rate. The increase in cardiac output is taken up in skeletal muscle blood flow, while the flow through the kidneys is radically reduced.

Charvat *et al.* (1964) defined mental stress as 'a set of events in the social milieu which modify steady state conditions so as to activate adaptive mechanisms' and suggest that appropriate symbolic stimuli resulting from psychosocial interaction can activate the defence reaction. Folkow and Rubinstein have shown that the changes noted by Brod *et al.* (1959) following mental arithmetic can be induced in rodents by direct stimulation of the anterior hypothalamus (Folkow & Rubinstein 1966). Using an implanted electrode they induced chronic elevation of systolic pressure in otherwise normal unanaesthetized rats by exposing them to several months of mildly alerting daily stimulation of the hypothalamic defence area. The fact that the typical blood flow changes could be induced by stimulation of unanaesthetized animals in the same location suggests that their electrodes were eliciting the same cardiovascular response as mental stimuli. This response is a central anticipatory adjustment of the cardiovascular system, and it will become fully established before the alerting of the somatomotor system explodes into an all-out fight or flight response. It is therefore highly suited for providing the skeletal muscles with the maximum of nutrition at the start of a situation which demands a swift and effective coping response. Its appropriateness in situations that do not permit massive muscular response has been questioned (Charvat *et al.* 1964).

MURINE SOCIAL BEHAVIOUR IN INTERCOMMUNICATING POPULATION CAGES

We have used communities of mice to study the affiliative network that glues

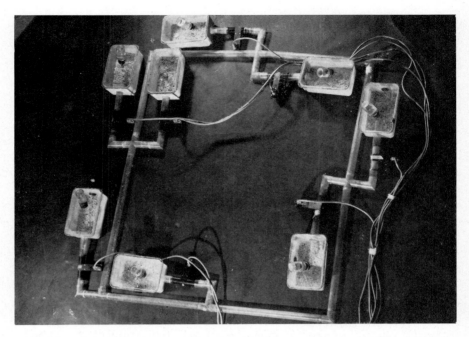

FIG. 1. A population cage based on the Reimer-Petras design. Food and water are available in every box. All boxes have a right-angle to be negotiated in the tubular runway leading to the single entrance. The Hall Effect magnetic detection modules are seen at the portal of each box. (Reimer & Petras 1967.)

even rodent groups together. Social ties determine the behaviour of rodents to a much greater extent than is commonly believed (Barnett 1963), and when these ties are disrupted with consequent repeated and persistent arousal of the defence and the alarm responses, pathophysiological changes typical of human psychosomatic disease ensue.

There are many advantages of using mice in the laboratory situation, not the least, after economy, being their genetic homogeneity, their brief lifespan (3 weeks of gestation; 12 weeks to puberty; 16 weeks to full sexual maturity; and 30 months to senility), and their small size which makes them safe and easy to handle. Our study uses complex cage systems in which six to a dozen standard boxes are connected by Lucite tubing just sufficiently large to permit them to squeeze past each other (Fig. 1). Each 23 × 11 × 11 cm box is to an average 30 gramme mouse of four inches body length about the size that the average 20 × 10 × 10 foot room in a house is to a man. In human architecture the function of various living regions is differentiated. In socially adjusted murine colonies, separate regions develop for nursing, as a latrine area, as a

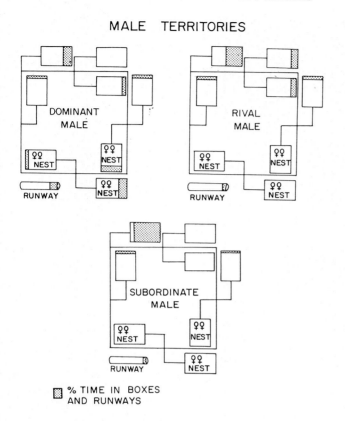

FIG. 2. Illustrating the different territorial distribution of dominants, rivals and subordinate male mice.

nesting area for sleeping activities, and for feeding and drinking. The complex population cages are provided with a two-inch layer of fluffy shavings to help the mice make these differentiations. Those boxes that are chosen for nesting are kept scrupulously clean by the females. On the other hand, in the latrine boxes the mice allow large accumulations of feces and urine. Standard laboratory chow and water are made available in various areas according to the design (Henry *et al.* 1967).

A MAGNETIC DETECTION SYSTEM

We study social behaviour by using an automatic counting device triggered by

FIG. 3. Individual mice are socially deprived by raising in glass jars with wire mesh tops. The process starts at weaning at 14 days and continues up to maturity at four months.

a tiny magnet implanted either in the back or in the belly of the mouse. Such a magnet is placed in each member of a standard colony of five males and ten females that we wish to monitor. The animals can then be tagged two at a time by magnetizing and demagnetizing them with a simple solenoid. Detectors at the portal of each box together with a central data processing unit and a write-out will permit recognition of box entry-exits, time spent in boxes, and events such as the isolation of an intruder or parturient female, nest building, and patrols in which a number of boxes are visited by the dominant and other high status animals in rapid succession. Thus from the activity records we can identify various patterns of behaviour (Fig. 2) (Ely *et al.* 1972). The animal playing the alpha role enjoys a very general freedom of movement throughout the whole system. Rivals have less mobility, while confinement to the latrine area is the typical fate of the subordinate or of an intruder male (Fig. 2). Females are found in nesting boxes, and, depending on population density and stability,

FIG. 4. Intercommunicating box system used to induce social interaction. It is designed to hold up to 50 mice of both sexes. Lucite boxes are of standard size (23 × 11 × 11 cm) and are connected into a circle by plastic tubes (internal diameter 3.4 cm). The central hexagon holds food and water and is connected with each box by radial tubes (internal diameter 2.5 cm). The stoppers close off holes used to add extra wooden nesting boxes for conversion of the system from six to twelve or more boxes.

many or few will be pregnant or lactating. The social situation determines the vigour of the defensive activity displayed to intruders by the males. Mutual recognition by the various members of the group is learned and some aspects may depend on the olfactory cortex in the mouse.

EFFECTS OF SOCIAL DEPRIVATION ON MURINE BEHAVIOUR

In order to disturb the social order, we have employed the isolation technique used by Harlow (Harlow *et al.* 1971) and by Fuller & Clark (1966) with monkeys and dogs, respectively.

Our method is to raise the mice in one-pint glass jars from an early weaning at 12 to 14 days until they are fully mature at four months (Fig. 3) (Henry *et al.* 1967). Unlike normally socialized groups, complex population cages stocked with such socially inexperienced animals show no division into dominants and

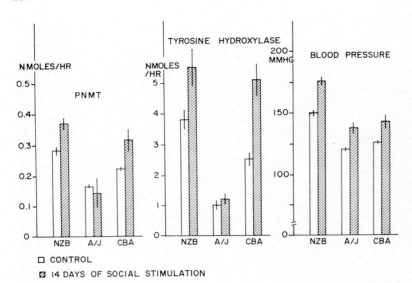

□ CONTROL
▨ 14 DAYS OF SOCIAL STIMULATION

FIG. 5. Comparison of the responses of previously isolated (Fig. 3) NZB, A/J and CBA mice to their first 14 days in a population cage (Fig. 4). From left to right: phenylethanolamine *N*-methyltransferase (PNMT), tyrosine hydroxylase and blood pressure. The enzymes of the A/J strain mice have not yet responded but their blood pressure has risen. Enzyme activity expressed in nmoles per hour (10^{-9} moles per hour).

subordinates. There are fewer pregnancies, and after delivery, the young die from neglect and as a result of constant disturbance by the other females. This failure of role differentiation has recently been confirmed by the use of magnetic tagging.

BLOOD PRESSURE AND CATECHOLAMINE-SYNTHESIZING ENZYMES AFTER SOCIAL STIMULATION

Fig. 4 shows a type of complex population cage that differs from that used in the behavioural work. It is used in conjunction with social deprivation during maturation in order to induce maximum psychosocial stimulation. There is only one source of food, in a central hexagon whose wire roof holds the water bottles and the food. The arrangement with six boxes in a ring around the hexagon fosters social interaction. The multiple entrances to each box make defence of territory far more difficult than with the single entry, right-angle bend of the cage system used to study social structure (see Fig. 1). The central feeding and water station forces close association between rivals, serving as a 'behavioural sink' as described by Calhoun (1962).

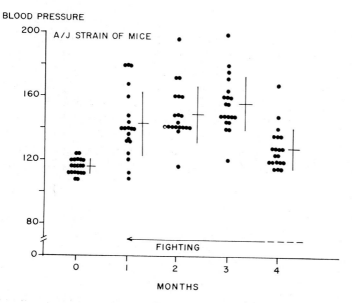

FIG. 6. Blood pressure (mmHg) of 20 adult male A/J strain mice which had been isolated from ten weeks until four months and then placed with ten females in an intercommunicating box system. Abscissa: 0, pressure while still isolated; 1, 2, 3 and 4, monthly measurements of systolic blood pressure when in the system. Horizontal arrow: evidence of fighting from observation and fresh scarring.

In previous papers we have presented the results of a series of studies using the CBA strain of mice, each lasting for the better part of a year (Henry *et al.* 1967; Henry & Cassel 1969). The CBA mouse is a very active, exploratory animal with a resting systolic blood pressure of 126 ± 10 mmHg (see Fig. 5). Previously isolated CBA males will eventually develop and sustain a pressure of approximately 160 mmHg in a socially disturbed colony, and the females about 145 mmHg. There is a good deal of fighting and scarring of the rump as a result of the bites. Fig. 6 presents data we are collecting from a strain of a very different temperament. The A/J albino mouse is a quiescent and inactive animal that likes to hide under the shavings. It has a blood pressure of only 115 ± 5 mmHg, and when placed in the colony, A/J mice take several hours to explore their confines. Monthly blood pressure readings were made on the male members of a group of 20 males and 10 females that were isolated at ten weeks of age and placed in the colony when four months old. The mean systolic pressure of the group gradually rose to 155 mmHg before subsiding (due perhaps to social structuring) at the last monthly measurement. The standard deviation for these data is significant. At the beginning, while the A/J mice were still in their isolation cells, it was $\pm$ 5 mmHg and the systolic pressure of 115 mmHg was 10 mmHg lower than that of CBA mice. With exposure to a socially interacting situation with access to females, sex-related behaviour patterns were activated and fighting developed among the males. The $\pm$ 20 mmHg standard deviation shows that a great range of blood pressure variation had developed. Had these animals' behaviour been followed by magnetic detection, we suspect that individual behaviour patterns could have been determined and perhaps related to the blood pressure score. Observation and counts of nicks and scars indicate that fighting reached a peak at the third month and had died down at the time of the final pressure reading.

OPEN FIELD TESTS OF THREE STRAINS OF MICE

Open field tests of exploratory behaviour were made using a standard method, namely a disc marked off in squares. The results show significant differences in behaviour between the strains (Fig. 7). In addition to the timid A/J and the active, curious CBA, we used the New Zealand Black strain. NZB mice are known for their development of autoimmune disease and incidence of gastric erosions (Wynn Williams *et al.* 1967). They are also suspected of having high blood pressure. In the A/J mice the open field test shows an interesting change on progressing from isolation, through the fraternal groups in a box, to the complex population cage. There is a dramatic rise in exploratory activity under social stimulation in the population cage, though it is not to the level of the CBA group and falls far short of that of the very reactive NZB strain. The isolated A/J mice scarcely moved off the square on which they were placed, nor did the isolated CBA. For both strains, this first exposure to open space after maturing in the restricted world of a bottle inhibits any exploratory behaviour. On the other hand, the reactive NZB has no such inhibition (Fig. 7).

When siblings are boxed together instead of being isolated, each to his own glass jar, the CBA mouse changes into an active, exploratory animal, but not so the A/J. Finally, prolonged social interaction significantly changes the behaviour of the previously quiescent and shy A/J but does not grossly affect the other two strains. The rise in exploratory activity is compatible with an increased level of arousal of the sympathetic–adrenal system in association with a defence reaction. From this point of view, it is relevant to contrast the blood pressures and catecholamine-synthesizing enzyme activities of the A/J mice with those of the other two strains.

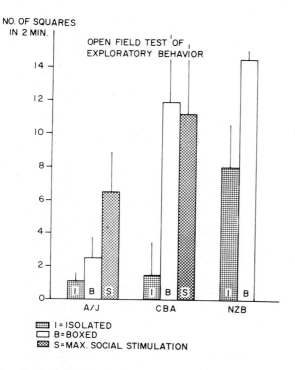

Fig. 7. Comparison of the open field activity of adult males of three strains of mice. The animals were exposed to one of the three following conditions: (1) isolation in glass jars from 14 days until adult at four months, (2) normal maturation as siblings in 23 × 11 × 11 cm boxes, and (3) exposure for several months to maximum social stimulation in an intercommunicating box system (see Fig. 4).

BLOOD PRESSURE RESPONSES OF THREE STRAINS OF MICE

The right-hand section of Fig. 5 (p. 234) contrasts the blood pressures of control groups of the three strains with those taken after two weeks of exposure to social interaction. The A/J mice start somewhat lower than the CBA but both respond with a significant elevation. The control observations of both strains were made on boxed siblings. Contrast these with the NZB: although the latter control mice were kept in isolation, their blood pressures were still 150 mmHg rather than the 115 mmHg and 126 mmHg control values for the other two groups. However, the NZB mice were still capable of response to stimulation and the blood pressure of 175 mmHg they attained after being placed in a box boded ill for the longterm well-being of their cardiovascular system.

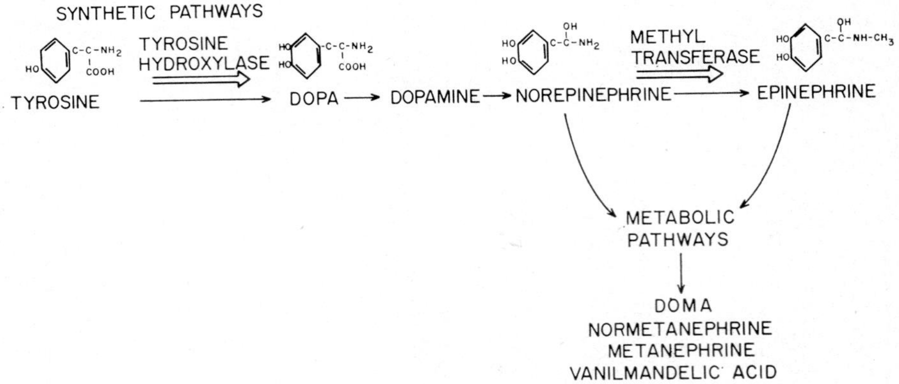

SYNTHETIC PATHWAYS

FIG. 8. Enzymes studied in biosynthesis and metabolism of catecholamines. DOPA, dihydroxyphenylalanine; DOMA: dihydroxy mandelic acid.

CATECHOLAMINE-SYNTHESIZING ENZYMES IN THREE STRAINS OF MICE

Having completed earlier collaborative work (Henry *et al.* 1971*b*) in which changes in catecholamine-synthesizing enzymes during social stimulation were established, we are now pursuing the question whether differences of behaviour are associated with physiological and/or biochemical changes. The left-hand and centre sections of Fig. 5 show the differences in levels of the catecholamine-synthesizing enzymes, tyrosine hydroxylase and phenylethanolamine *N*-methyltransferase (PNMT). Their roles in the chain of synthesis of noradrenaline and adrenaline, respectively, are shown in Fig. 8. There is no alteration in enzyme levels in the A/J mice in spite of 14 days of social interaction (Fig. 5). Further, their resting activity levels are less than half of those of the control CBA mice. On the other hand, even without social stimulation the NZB mice have higher enzyme levels than the CBA. With social stimulation these levels increase, but not so much, proportionately, as they do in the CBA mice.

This difference is more clearly seen in Fig. 9 which is a normalized composite of data from two different experiments. For this reason the 14-day values do not correspond precisely with the absolute data given in Fig. 5. However, the diagram effectively combines data for the A/J and CBA strains after a 14-day and a six-month exposure to social strain in a population cage with mixed sexes, and gives an idea of trends. In line with the increases in blood pressure and open field exploration in A/J mice after social stimulation, by six months their catecholamine-synthesizing enzymes have moved up to levels that at least approach those of the other strains. On the other hand, by six months the

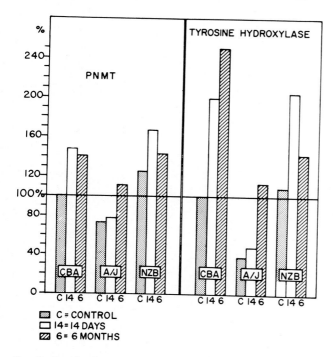

FIG. 9. Results from two sets of experiments showing the response of the adrenal catechol-amine-synthesizing enzymes, phenylethanolamine *N*-methyltransferase (PNMT) and tyrosine hydroxylase, of male mice to 14 days and to six months of social stimulation. Three strains were tested (CBA, A/J and NZB). The data were normalized taking the control values in the CBA group in the 14-day experiment as 100%.

NZB mice show, if anything, a fall from the enzyme activities after 14 days of social stimulation. This is in keeping with preliminary behavioural observations which indicate that, given time, the NZB mice may settle down to living peaceably together. Furthermore, these results were derived from boxed sibling NZB mice only, for they could not be placed in the population cage because their pattern of intense conflict among the males would have led to unacceptable mortality. Under these conditions the fall in enzyme activity from the high level at 14 days is not surprising.

EFFECT OF ADRENAL DENERVATION AND SOCIAL STIMULATION ON CATECHOLAMINE-SYNTHESIZING ENZYMES

Fig. 10 presents observations on the effects of denervating the left adrenal of

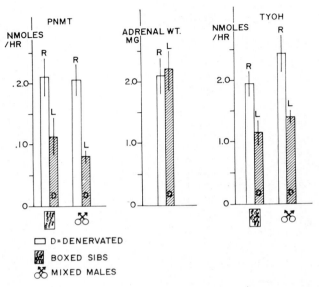

FIG. 10. Effects of unilateral denervation of the adrenal gland on the adrenal content of the catecholamine-synthesizing enzymes, phenylethanolamine *N*-methyltransferase (PNMT) and tyrosine hydroxylase (TYOH). Mean adrenal weight is given in mg. The symbols beneath the abscissa denote normal boxed siblings and strange males mixed in a box for 96 hours, respectively.

grouped CBA mice. The sharp falling off of production of PNMT and tyrosine hydroxylase in the denervated gland, although it has not lost weight, suggests that the vascular supply remains intact and that nervous stimuli play a part in determining the levels of these enzymes. After exposure to 96 hours of moderate social stimulation there is a suggestion of a greater increase in the activity of tyrosine hydroxylase on the innervated side. The activity of PNMT remains unchanged, but, as Fig. 9 shows, the level of this enzyme seems to show less response to the effects of social stimulation. Work is underway with more severe social stimulation to see if this effect will become more clearly defined.

BEHAVIOURAL PATTERNS AND PHYSIOLOGICAL CHANGES

Our data throw light on the sympathetic–adrenal medullary 'defence' reaction; so far we have not studied the pituitary–adrenal cortical 'alarm' response. The question arises whether there is any evidence of biochemical or physiological differences between these two responses. Fig. 11 is presented as very preliminary evidence which suggests that observations directed at this

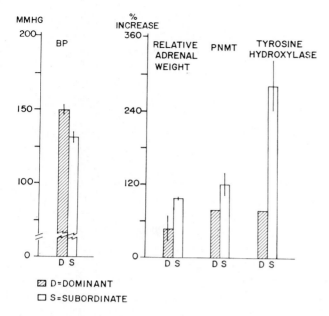

Fig. 11. Preliminary data contrasting the blood pressure, relative adrenal weight, and phenylethanolamine N-methyltransferase (PNMT) and tyrosine hydroxylase levels of dominant CBA male mice with those of subordinates in three colonies housed in population cages, as shown in Fig. 1. Note that the dominant's blood pressure exceeds that of the subordinate, but that the situation appears to be reversed for the other parameters (N = 6 and 13 for dominants and subordinates, respectively, with the exception of the preliminary observations on PNMT and tyrosine hydroxylase, when N was 2 and 5 respectively.)

question may be profitable. It is derived from our studies of the differentiation of behaviour in colonies of CBA mice by the use of magnetic detection. We have sent the adrenals of two dominant and five subordinate male mice to Dr Julius Axelrod's laboratory at the National Institute of Mental Health, Bethesda, Maryland. The preliminary data point to a higher blood pressure but lower adrenal weight in the alpha male. The data on the enzyme levels need to be extended to more animals before a definite trend can be established.

It may be that an embattled dominant unable, because of the closed system, to chase away the rival and subordinate males, feels he can 'cope' but is frustrated. This may set the scene for a predominantly noradrenaline and 'defence' reaction type of response. The subordinate, and worst of all, the male or female who is introduced into an established colony as an intruder may, on the other hand, experience a response which is primarily of the pituitary–adrenal cortical 'alarm' type. Of course, genetically differing strains may well give different exaggerations of this dichotomy. Thus the A/J mice might be expected to tend to an 'alarm' response and the CBA and NZB mice more to a 'defence' type of reaction, although a mixed response remains the most likely possibility.

DISEASE, THE ALARM RESPONSE AND THE DEFENCE REACTION

The most familiar reaction to psychosocial stimuli which are perceived as threatening is the so-called alarm response. Mason (1968*a*) suggests that this pituitary–adrenal cortical mechanism is triggered by emotional arousal in anticipation of activity or coping. He finds that the elements of novelty, uncertainty and unpredictability are particularly potent in eliciting the release of 17-hydroxycorticosteroids. Both Bourne (1970) and Katz *et al.* (1970) note that in environmentally threatening situations for which the human subject has adequate coping processes, the level of 17-hydroxycorticosteroids may be effectively reduced. Even if this process involves an unrealistic denial of the threat or an assumption of invulnerability, it may well be effective. On the other hand, as Sachar *et al.* (1970) point out, in acute schizophrenic crises when the individual is flooded with anxiety and feels that his ego will be 'annihilated', blood levels of 17-hydroxycorticosteroids and adrenaline reach great heights. Cushing's disease is very frequently associated with increased secretion of ACTH. According to Gifford & Gunderson (1970), many of these patients have developed a need for intense personal relationships during maturation and at the onset of the clinical symptoms had suffered from a significant emotional loss with ensuing depression. These various observations support the hypothesis that the subject who lacks an adequate coping process will be liable to a sustained alarm response. This condition, incidentally, may be associated with raised blood levels of not only adrenal corticoids, but also of adrenaline, for the chief effect of this hormone is upon the heart. Noradrenaline, on the other hand, affects the resistance of the arteries and is more responsible for increases of blood pressure.

The defence reaction with its sympathetic drive and increase in noradrenaline and adrenaline synthesis stands in partial contrast with the above picture. For the generalization that has resulted from work by Frankenhaeuser and others (Frankenhaeuser & Rissler 1970) with animals and men is that the blood pressure-raising hormone, noradrenaline, is increased by psychosocial stimuli with which the individual is familiar and feels that he can cope.

The recent description by Harris & Singer (1968) of the personality of the patient with essential hypertension as hostile, tense, vigilant and defensive fits with the picture of an individual who is prepared to try to cope with a threat he perceives as familiar. They write of abrasive interactions with other people leading to emotional arousal. This may be a basic response due to sympathetic and reticular formation arousal, for it fits with our observations in mice. When a colony of even so peaceable a strain as the A/J are mixed together, eventually fighting breaks out, and with it, hypertension develops with an accompanying rise in the catecholamine-synthesizing enzymes and in exploratory behaviour. With better differentiation of the various role players in biochemical and physiological terms, it may be found that those strains and those individuals who are unable to develop effective coping responses will show more of the classical adrenal cortical 'alarm' response. Those who are successfully defending territory, maintaining their position in the social hierarchy, and meeting their own self-preservative and the species' preservative requirements may show a level of sympathetic–adrenal medullary activity proportional to the difficulties they are experiencing in achieving this goal. Differing emotions may be responsible for the observation of Anderson & Brady (1972) that the blood pressure of dogs faced with a shock-avoidance task increases, while the pulse rate decreases. By contrast, if the task is maintained by giving food, there is a rise in both pressure and pulse rate.

PSYCHOSOCIAL STIMULATION AND ACUTE AND CHRONIC DISEASE

The fact that sustained social interaction can be lethal, even without the intervention of infection, tumour formation or malnutrition, is demonstrated by the fate of intruder mice placed in our systems and of the rats introduced by Barnett into established groups (Barnett 1963). In both cases, many of the animals die within a few days. The elegant work of D. von Holst with tree shrews has thrown some light on the cause of these sudden deaths. He allowed one male to achieve dominance over the other by brief periods of fighting and found that when placed in a closely adjacent mesh-walled cage, the subordinate would then betray his sympathetic arousal by a sustained and conspicuous fluffing of the tail. This piloerection served as a convenient indicator of activation of the sympathetic nervous system—that is, of the defence reaction (von Holst 1972). By determining the percentage of a 12-hour observational day spent in a state of arousal, as indicated by a bushy tail, he showed that a whole series of disturbances ensued. When the animal was aroused 20% to 40% of the time, there was a failure to raise the young. At 40% to 60%, reproductive function was disturbed, with retraction of the testicles from the scrotum, and the oestrous cycle ceased. In the most intensive states when there was sympathetic arousal for more than 80% of the time, the threatened and alarmed but unwounded animal gradually lost strength and died in about a week. The cause of death appears to have been renal failure, for the blood urea concentration rose steadily throughout the period between confrontation and *exitus*.

With regard to chronic disease, we have recently published evidence that sustained arousal of the defence and/or the alarm reactions with gross elevation of blood pressure over long periods will lead to serious arteriosclerotic disease in mice (Henry *et al.* 1971a). Over 300 male and female mice and 200 controls were studied; the former had been exposed to six months of maximal social stimulation in intercommunicating population cages of the type shown in Fig. 4. Histological sections were scored for severity of the ensuing acute and chronic interstitial nephritis, of glomerular mesangial changes, of myocardial fibrosis, and of arteriosclerotic degeneration of the intramural coronary vessels and the aorta. In all the conditions studied, significantly higher scores were obtained in the group exposed to maximal social stimulation.

SUMMARY

This work has presented a methodology by which the social psychophysiology of mice can be studied in individuals throughout their lifespan. Using the same principles that apply to man, sustained emotional arousal has been generated in murine societies and shown to be associated with measurable physiological and biochemical disturbances. By breaking down the 'coping' processes, chronic disease has been induced, supporting the thesis long sustained by students of animal behaviour (Crook 1970) that man as the object of study of the social sciences is not a being apart. Rather, it is necessary to think of him from this viewpoint as just another animal. Both mice and men can be exposed to powerful emotions of attachment and competitive behaviour and can suffer from anxiety and the defeat that in primates goes with depression. These emotions agitate the same neurophysiological mechanisms in the limbic system and hypothalamus, and the defence and alarm reactions that are activated have the same neuroendocrine base and the same pathophysiological consequences.

These facts suggest that the growing suspicion that social stimuli play a part in the genesis of much human disease need not depend solely on human studies supported by work with expensive primate colonies. Useful observations on chronic cardiovascular disease and tumorigenesis can be effectively made using groups of these tiny mammals as models. The advantages include maturation in four months, death from old age before they are three years old, and their availability in genetically homogeneous strains of widely disparate temperament.

ACKNOWLEDGEMENTS

This work has been supported by Grant No. NGL-05-018-003 of the National Aeronautics and Space Administration and by Grant No. MH 19441-01 of the National Institute of Mental Health. The latter involves a continuing collaboration with the Section on Pharmacology of the Laboratory of Clinical Science at the NIMH with Dr Julius Axelrod and Dr Roland Ciaranello. It is a pleasure to acknowledge Dr Axelrod's initiative in proposing the studies of catecholamine-controlling enzymes and his group's continuing advice and support. We also wish to thank Dr Flora Watson for making the observations of the comparative behaviour in the open field.

References

ANDERSON, D. E. & BRADY, J. V. (1972) Prolonged pre-avoidance effects upon blood pressure and heart rate in the dog. *Psychosom. Med.* in press

BAJUSZ, E. (1969) *Physiology and Pathology of Adaptation Mechanisms: neural–neuroendocrine–humoral*, Pergamon Press, Oxford

BARNETT, S. A. (1963) *The Rat: A Study in Behavior*, pp. 202-203, Aldine, Chicago

BOURNE, P. G. (1970) *Men, Stress and Vietnam*, p. 22, Little, Brown, Boston

BROD, J., FENCL, V., HEJL, A. & JIRKA, J. (1959) Circulatory changes underlying blood pressure elevation during acute emotional stress (mental arithmetic) in normotensive and hypertensive subjects. *Clin. Sci.* **18**, 269-279

CALHOUN, J. B. (1962) A behavioral sink. In *Roots of Behavior: Genetics, Instinct and Socialization in Animal Behavior* (Bliss, E. L., ed.), pp. 295-315, Hoeber-Harper, New York

CANNON, W. B. & LA PAZ, D. DE (1911) Emotional stimulation of adrenal secretion. *Am. J. Physiol.* **27**, 64-70

CHARVAT, J., DELL, P. & FOLKOW, B. (1964) Mental factors and cardiovascular diseases. *Cardiologia* **44**, 124-141

CHRISTIAN, J. J., LLOYD, J. A. & DAVIS, D. E. (1965) The role of endocrines in the self-regulation of mammalian populations. *Recent Prog. Horm. Res.* **21**, 501-578

CROOK, J. H. (1970) Social organization and the environment: aspects of contemporary social ethology. *Anim. Behav.* **18**, 197-209

ELY, D. L., HENRY, J. A., HENRY, J. P. & RADER, R. D. (1972) A monitoring technique providing quantitative rodent behavior analysis. *Physiol. Behav.* 9 in press

FOLKOW, B. & NEIL, E. (1971) *Circulation*, pp. 344-349, Oxford University Press, London

FOLKOW, B. & RUBINSTEIN, E. H. (1966) Cardiovascular effect of acute and chronic stimulations of the hypothalamic defense area in the rat. *Acta Physiol. Scand.* **28**, 48-57

FRANKENHAEUSER, M. & RISSLER, A. (1970) Effects of punishment on catecholamine release and efficiency of performance. *Psychopharmacologia* **17**, 378-390

FULLER, J. L. & CLARK, L. D. (1966) Genetic and treatment factors modifying the post-isolation syndrome in dogs. *J. Comp. Physiol. Psychol.* **61**, 251-257

GANONG, W. F. (1970) Control of adrenocorticotrophin and melanocyte-stimulating hormone secretion. In *The Hypothalamus* (Martini, L., Motta, M. & Fraschini, F., eds.), pp. 313-331, Academic Press, New York

GANONG, W. F. (1971) Neurophysiologic basis of instinctual behavior and emotions. In *Review of Medical Physiology* (Ganong, W. F., ed.), pp. 173-185, Lange Medical Publications, Los Altos, Calif.

GIFFORD, S. & GUNDERSON, J. G. (1970) Cushing's disease as a psychosomatic disorder: a selective review of the clinical and experimental literature and a report of ten cases. *Perspect. Biol. Med.* **13**, 169-221

GOLDFIEN, A. & GANONG, W. F. (1962) Adrenal medullary and adrenal cortical response to stimulation of diencephalon. *Am. J. Physiol.* **202** (2), 205-211

HARLOW, H., McGOUGH, J. L. & THOMPSON, R. F. (1971) *Psychology*, Albion Publishing Co., San Francisco

HARRIS, R. E. & SINGER, M. T. (1968) Interaction of personality and stress in the pathogenesis of essential hypertension. In *Hypertension: Neural Control of Arterial Pressure*, vol. 16, pp. 104-113 (Proc. Council for High Blood Pressure Research), American Heart Association, New York

HENRY, J. P. & CASSEL, J. C. (1969) Psychosocial factors in essential hypertension: recent epidemiologic and animal experimental evidence. *Am. J. Epidemiol.* **90** (3), 171-200

HENRY, J. P., ELY, D. L., STEPHENS, P. M., RATCLIFFE, H. L., SANTISTEBAN, G. A. & SHAPIRO, A. P. (1971*a*) The role of psychosocial factors in the development of arteriosclerosis in CBA mice: observations on the heart, kidney, and aorta. *Atherosclerosis* **14** (2), 203-218

HENRY, J. P., MEEHAN, J. P. & STEPHENS, P. M. (1967) The use of psychosocial stimuli to induce prolonged systolic hypertension in mice. *Psychosom. Med.* **29** (5), 408-432

HENRY, J. P., STEPHENS, P. M., AXELROD, J. & MUELLER, R. A. (1971*b*) Effect of psychosocial stimulation on the enzymes involved in the biosynthesis and metabolism of noradrenaline and adrenaline. *Psychosom. Med.* **33** (3), 227-237

KATZ, J. L., WEINER, H., GALLAGHER, T. S. & HELLMAN, L. (1970) Stress distress and ego defenses: psychoendocrine response to impending tumor biopsy. *Arch. Gen. Psychiatr.* **23**, 131-142

MACLEAN, P. D. (1970) The limbic brain in relation to the psychoses. In *Physiological Correlates of Emotion* (Black, P., ed.), pp. 130-144, Academic Press, New York

MASON, J. W. (1968*a*) A review of psychoendocrine research on the pituitary–adrenal cortical system. *Psychosom. Med.* **30**, 576-607

MASON, J. W. (1968*b*) A review of psychoendocrine research on the sympathetic–adrenal medullary system. *Psychosom. Med.* **30**, 631-653

REIMER, J. D. & PETRAS, M. L. (1967) Breeding structure of the house mouse, *Mus musculus*, in a population cage. *J. Mammal.* **48**, 88-99

SACHAR, E. J., KANTER, S. S., BUIE, D., ENGLE, R. & MEHLMAN, R. (1970) Psychoendocrinology of ego disintegration. *Am. J. Psychiatr.* **126** (8), 1067-1078

SELYE, H. (1936) A syndrome produced by diverse nocuous agents. *Nature (Lond.)* **138**, 32

VON HOLST, D. (1972) Renal failure as the cause of death in *Tupaia belangeri* exposed to persistent social stress. *J. Comp. Physiol.* **78**, 236-273

WASHBURN, S. L. & HAMBURG, D. A. (1968) Aggressive behavior in old world monkeys and apes. In *Primates: Studies in Adaptation and Variability* (Jay, P., ed.), pp. 458-468, Holt, Rinehart & Winston, New York

WYNN WILLIAMS, A., HOWIE, J. B., HELYER, B. J. & SIMPSON, L. O. (1967) Spontaneous peptic ulcers in mice. *Aust. J. Exp. Biol. Med. Sci.* **45**, 105-108

Discussion

Sandler: You have shown that there are physiological differences between the dominant and submissive mice in your experiments. What do you feel is the cause of the differences and how are they linked with the concept of dominance and submission? Do you link emotional states with dominance and submission?

Henry: Yes; I would view dominance that meets with resistance on the part of those dominated as associated with the sense of coping and frustration on the part of the would-be dominant animal, and submission with fear and withdrawal. A study of the personality of subjects with essential hypertension confirms the earlier impression of an angry person with a 'chip on the shoulder' (Harris & Singer 1968). I am assuming that the anger goes with the attempt to cope and with the defence reaction—that is, with the type of defence response of the sympathetic–adrenal medullary system that Folkow has described (Folkow & Neil 1971). Repeated activation of this response is connected with increased levels of catecholamine-synthesizing enzymes in the adrenal (Henry *et al.* 1971). It may be that this state will be proved to differ physiologically from the state of fear which, I suspect, is more closely associated with the release of ACTH. I am thinking of a situation where the animal is helpless as, for example, when he is strapped down on a laboratory bench. In this circumstance he cannot meet the problem by escape. The emotional state characterized as fear and that characterized as frustration may differ in that, in one, the pituitary–adrenocortical and, in the other, the sympathetic–adrenal medullary system is being activated preferentially (Mason 1968*a,b*). However, I suspect that there will usually be a mixture of the two responses and the physiological consequence will depend in part on the proportion.

Sandler: Would one consequence be that the roles of dominance and submission have physiological correlates which may result in changed physiological functioning which may be temporary or long-standing?

Henry: Yes; we would speculate that this is so in the mouse and that different long-standing changes in physiological functioning may follow different long-standing states of emotional arousal. We do not, however, have solid data to support this idea.

In man there is the further problem that his social behaviour is so complex that he may be submissive in one role but dominant in another. Indeed as Professor Hinde has pointed out (personal communication), you often can't speak of the one dominant cat or monkey in a group. One animal may take precedence in one form of activity, such as eating, but not in another, such as sexual activity. However, in general, dominant animals have better access to all desiderata than subordinates and exhibit fewer fear-withdrawal and more frustration-coping responses.

Gray: To ask a very simple question, is essential hypertension in man more common in social class 1 than in social class 5?

Tibblin: It depends upon the culture you are studying, since blood pressure is linked to obesity and in some cultures there is a relationship between obesity and social class. But, in general, blood pressure is not linked to social class (Tibblin 1967).

Henry: Essential hypertension is more common in people who are not meeting their life expectations. Their life has programmed them to expect certain patterns and these demands are not being effectively met in later life. Suppose a man has been in a position of precedence in his society and in later life can no longer maintain that position. It doesn't profit him to be openly enraged at this but his covert anger is associated with an elevation of blood pressure (Henry & Cassel 1969).

Sleight: One should be very careful when talking about the personality associated with particular diseases and never more so than in the case of hypertension. Many of the studies of hypertensive subjects are open to serious criticism, mostly related to the methods of selecting the subjects, but also to the scientific validity and objectivity of the personality tests employed. The subject has recently been critically reviewed by Davies (1971). Cochrane (1969) and Robinson (1969) have attempted to avoid many of the pitfalls and contrary to earlier studies they found that when random samples of the population were examined subjects with high blood pressure had fewer complaints and less neuroticism than others. Robinson found that only a very small proportion of this hypertensive population was referred to hospitals and that this highly selected group differed markedly from the others on personality testing. Similar findings have been reported by Dr Tibblin and will be enlarged upon later in this symposium (see pp. 321-331).

Levine: Do you consider the dominant mice as essentially hypertensive, Dr Henry?

Henry: I can answer your question in part. Initially when the blood pressure of a mouse rises in response to prolonged social stimulation it appears to follow the sequence, first of labile, then of essential or sustained hypertension. However if the condition persists, then at some point renal function will alter and finally lesions will develop. We suspect that at this point the pressure elevation will have components of renal origin.

You asked specifically whether I consider dominant mice as essentially hypertensive. It is not possible to predict the pressure of a dominant animal without defining the social conditions. If the dominant animal that emerges is little challenged, then his blood pressure will remain normal. But if the maintenance of his status involves him in frequent confrontations, and the spatial arrangements make it difficult for him to monitor the activity of the other animals, he will develop a labile increase in blood pressure. I say labile because if such an animal is isolated, his blood pressure reverts to normal. In general, the intensity and persistence of the pressure elevation of a socially stimulated CBA mouse and the incidence of renal pathological changes are related to the intensity and duration of the stimuli. In our experience, this intensity and duration has been greatest in colonies of formerly socially deprived animals placed for six months in circular box systems with a central feeding station. These are the only animals in which we have observed fixed hypertension. So far, we have observed the blood pressure of only a few dominants that we have identified as such. This is because our initial project was to study colonies with prolonged, intense and generalized social disorder to see if they developed disease. Only recently have we been watching individual behaviour in the Reimer-Petras box systems equipped with food and water in each cage and with single entrances with magnetic detection at the entrance to each cage. Our preliminary observations of the relative pressure of dominant and submissive animals, shown in Fig. 11 (p. 241), were made in this system.

Hofer: Is the incidence of renal lesions, shown histologically, different in dominant and subordinate mice and if so does it follow the direction of the blood pressure?

Henry: I regret that we have not made any such histological evaluation of the kidneys of dominants and subordinates. We studied the heart, aorta and kidneys of socially deprived, formerly isolated animals, but we did not determine the social roles of the various members of these disordered colonies. We found that the severity of the lesions varies enormously. Only about 8% had severe interstitial nephritis. The rest showed varying degrees of lymphoid infiltration. We suspect that only some are severely stimulated. The rest escape, perhaps by avoiding confrontation. In a situation where such escape is not possible death may occur, as Barnett (1963) showed with formerly dominant rats put in colonies to which they do not belong. Von Holst (1972) has shown that in tree shrews which have been forced to intrude on the dominant's territory, death occurs due to acute renal failure.

Gray: In Fig. 11 you showed that a higher blood pressure occurred with lower amounts of catecholamine-synthesizing enzymes in the dominant mouse. One interpretation of this result is that the blood pressure is higher in the dominant animal as a result of influences other than adrenergic or noradrenergic stimulation, the adrenergic component being marked in the subordinate animal.

Henry: The results shown in Fig. 11, and the enzyme assay results in particular, are preliminary. One would have expected the dominant animal to produce more noradrenaline because his role is associated with vigorous coping efforts. However, the enzyme assays do not suggest this so far. In the particular cage situation described, in which the Reimer-Petras system (1967) was used, the dominant mouse has a higher blood pressure than the subordinate. Nevertheless, the adrenal gland is heavier in the subordinate. This suggests that adrenal cortical responses are also involved and this is the lead that we are following in trying to differentiate between the physiology of dominant and subordinate animals.

Zanchetti: Axelrod (1971) showed that if one destroys the sympathetic nervous system of an animal a compensatory mechanism operates and the activity of tyrosine hydroxylase in the adrenal medulla increases. If one assumes that the lower blood pressure of the subordinate mouse is due to a decreased sympathetic activity as compared to its dominant partner, its more active adrenal medulla might have developed in compensation for the reduced sympathetic activity.

Gray: Adrenal weight is a measure which fluctuates with all sorts of things, but Dr Henry is measuring the activity of tyrosine hydroxylase and phenylethanolamine *N*-methyltransferase as indicators of the likely effective levels of adrenaline and noradrenaline. If these data are confirmed, the difference in blood pressure between dominant and subordinate animals is presumably not produced by an adrenergic mechanism.

Zanchetti: The enzyme concentration is a measure of adrenal function.

Levine: These levels are a measure of the amount of enzyme in the adrenal; there is no way of knowing how much enzyme gets into the circulation. One way of testing the relationship between blood pressure and catechol enzymes would be to remove the adrenal medulla. This is a simple operation. What happens to the blood pressure after demedullation?

Henry: We haven't done this. We are, however, studying the effects of adrenal denervation on tissue enzyme levels during social interaction.

References

AXELROD, J. (1971) Noradrenaline: fate and control of its biosynthesis. *Science (Wash. D.C.)* **173**, 598-606

BARNETT, S. A. (1963) *The Rat: A Study in Behaviour*, pp. 202-203, Aldine, Chicago

COCHRANE, A. L. (1969) Neuroticism and the discovery of high blood pressure. *J. Psychosom. Res.* **13**, 21

DAVIES, M. H. (1971) Is high blood pressure a psychosomatic disorder? *J. Chronic Dis.* **24**, 239-258

FOLKOW, B. & NEIL, E. (1971) *Circulation*, pp. 344-349, Oxford University Press, London

HARRIS, R. E. & SINGER, M. T. (1968) Interaction of personality and stress in the pathogenesis of essential hypertension. In *Hypertension vol. 16: Neural Control of Arterial Pressure* (Proceedings of Council for High Blood Pressure Research), pp. 104-114, American Heart Association, New York

HENRY, J. P. & CASSEL, J. C. (1969) *Am. J. Epidemiol.* **90**, 171-199

HENRY, J. P., STEPHENS, P. M., AXELROD, J. & MUELLER, R. A. (1971) Effect of psychosocial stimulation on the enzymes involved in the biosynthesis and metabolism of noradrenaline and adrenaline. *Psychosom. Med.* **33**, 227-237

MASON, J. W. (1968a) A review of psychoendocrine research on the pituitary–adrenal cortical system. *Psychosom. Med.* **30**, 576-607

MASON, J. W. (1968b) A review of psychoendocrine research on the sympathetic–adrenal medullary system. *Psychosom. Med.* **30**, 631-653

REIMER, J. D. & PETRAS, M. L. (1967) Breeding structure of the house mouse *Mus musculus* in a population cage. *J. Mammal.* **48**, 88-99

ROBINSON, J. O. (1969) Symptoms and the discovery of high blood pressure. *J. Psychosom. Res.* **13**, 157-161

TIBBLIN, G. (1967) High blood pressure in men aged fifty. *Acta Med. Scand.*, suppl. 770

VON HOLST, D. (1972) Renal failure as the cause of death in *Tupaia belangeri* (tree shrews) exposed to persistent social stress. *J. Comp. Physiol.* **78**, 236-273

Influence of psychological variables on stress-induced pathology

JAY M. WEISS

The Rockefeller University, New York City

Abstract Recent studies with experimental animals have revealed the importance of psychological variables in the regulation of somatic stress reactions, particularly in the development of gastric lesions. The predictability, avoidability and escapability of a stressor were found to have considerable influence upon the severity of tissue pathology. The results have led to a theoretical model that describes how certain psychological factors are related to the development of gastric ulceration. The theory states that ulceration is a function of two variables: the number of coping attempts an animal makes and the informational feedback it receives from making the coping attempts. Experiments have been carried out which show that alterations in feedback from responding greatly increase or decrease ulceration. The theory also explains a well-known paradoxical finding, the 'executive monkey' phenomenon.

In this paper I shall explain some of the recent work done at the Rockefeller University on the problem of how psychological variables affect the development of certain types of pathology.

Much of what has been presented at the meeting so far summarizes the way the field of 'psychosomatic medicine' looked to me when I first became interested in it five or six years ago. As one might expect, I was first struck by the many exciting clinical observations which linked pathology and psychological processes. Through decades, even centuries, of medical practice, these data had been gathered with remarkable sensitivity and perceptiveness. Yet in the final analysis, no matter how compelling these case studies were, the results could not establish that there was any causal connection between psychological factors and somatic disorders; one could only conclude that certain forms of pathology seemed to occur together with various psychological events and/or personality characteristics. As a result, I found much scepticism as well, with many individuals rightfully questioning whether psychological factors were actually important in disease processes.

The answer to this question seemed to me likely to come from experimental rather than from observational study. The experimental approach permitted one to specify the conditions imposed on the organism so that one could be sure that a specific treatment did, in fact, lead to pathology. Surveying the experimental studies related to this question, I found two basic types. First, there were the studies carried out by pathologists and endocrinologists. Painstakingly, they had produced a wide range of pathological conditions in the laboratory. In these instances, one certainly could make unambiguous statements about the treatments leading to experimentally induced disorders. However, invariably these experiments were not set up to examine the influence of psychological variables so that the importance of the psychological factors in producing the disorders could only be conjectured. The second type of study was that which had been set up specifically to investigate the effect of some psychological variable. Usually carried out in man, these studies showed that emotional and/or cognitive states could affect somatic changes. But these studies produced small and/or transient changes in somatic functioning and did not demonstrate that such variables resulted in tissue pathology.

With this as a background, I therefore asked a basic question: could an experimental situation be constructed that would clearly show whether psychological variables could influence the development of pathology in an animal? As stated above, it was already known that animals could be exposed to stressors and would subsequently develop pathology. But it remained quite another matter to interpret the significance of psychological variables in producing this result. In fact, one had no way of knowing whether psychological aspects of the stressor condition had anything to do with such pathology or not! As an example, suppose an animal were made to swim for some period of time and the animal then developed pathology. What could one conclude? Surely the animal was frightened by this forced swim, by the danger of drowning. But the swim stressor also produced extreme muscular activity as well as other physical changes, such as temperature loss, depending upon the temperature of the water, and so on. Was the resultant pathology attributable to the fear the animal experienced or to some direct action of the stressor on physiological processes? Clearly, one could not know. From the point of view of one who wished to know about psychological factors, the problem with experiments that exposed animals to a stressor and examined the resultant pathology was that the effects of psychological factors simply could not be separated from the sheer physical impact of the stressor on the organism.

Fortunately it was possible to deal with this problem. The way I have attempted to handle it is exemplified by an early study on the effects of having control over a stressor (Weiss 1968). The experimental situation is shown in

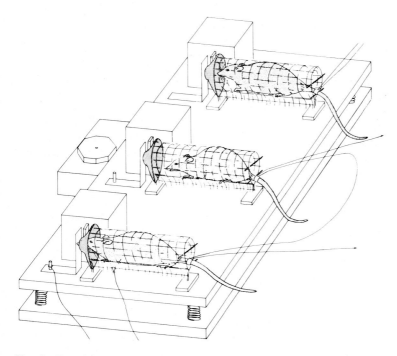

FIG. 1. Experimental apparatus showing the avoidance-escape (foreground), yoked (centre) and non-shock (rear) subjects. In addition to the tone preceding the shock, the platform on which the animals remained during the experimental session was vibrated (by means of a cam-see centre, left of figure) as part of the warning signal. (From Weiss 1968.)

Fig. 1. In this experiment, a rat was exposed to an electric shock which it could avoid and/or escape by touching its nose to a panel. A second rat was given exactly the same shocks but it had no control over them. Thus, the two animals received exactly the same physical stressor; they differed only in their control over the shock. In these circumstances, if a difference in pathology was observed between the two subjects, the difference could not be due to the physical stressor, which was the same for both subjects, but must be due to the psychological difference inherent in having control over the stressor as compared with being helpless. To assess the effect of the shock stressor itself, the experimental design also included a third animal which received no shock at all, but of course the principal concern was the difference between the two shocked subjects.

In experiments using this design, it is critical to control the shock carefully. To do this, I attached the shock electrodes to the animals, on their tails. This procedure eliminated the ability of an animal to cause alterations in the shock by his movements. Thus, jumping or rearing, which is normally effective in changing shock delivered through a grid floor, has no effect with fixed electrodes. The reason that this precaution is important is that animals in one psychological condition might perform movement patterns that are different from those performed by animals in another condition. If this occurs, the two groups will receive different amounts of shock, obviously invalidating the experiment. The fixed electrodes make this impossible. Fixed electrodes also have another advantage, since one can wire any number of electrodes *in series*, so that the matched animals in different conditions receive exactly the same duration and intensity of current.

In the early experiment shown in Fig. 1, the animals remained in the apparatus for 21 hours, given one trial each minute. Each trial consisted of presentation of a tone ten seconds before a shock. If the avoidance-escape animal touched the panel with its nose during the signal before the shock, the signal was terminated and neither it nor its helpless (called 'yoked') partner received shock on that trial. If the avoidance-escape animal failed to touch the panel during the tone and the shock occurred, it then had to touch the panel to terminate the shock for itself and its yoked partner. Thus, the avoidance-escape animal had control over the shock while its yoked partner received exactly the same shocks but was helpless.

The results are shown in Fig. 2. First, it is apparent that the animals able to avoid and escape shock developed less gastric ulceration than their helpless partners. But the more surprising result was the magnitude of the difference. While the avoidance-escape animals clearly developed more ulceration than did non-shock subjects, the yoked animals developed much more ulceration than either of these two groups. Thus, the results showed that simply receiving shock was not in itself particularly ulcer-producing; the more important variable was what the animal could do about the shock! I should add that I was quite sceptical of this finding initially but the same sorts of differences have emerged in every experiment I have done. This has occurred in experiments using different apparatuses and in ones where loss of body weight was measured rather than gastric ulceration. It also occurred when I studied the effects of predictable as compared with unpredictable shock (Weiss 1970). Therefore, I can only conclude that psychological variables are, in fact, the principal determinants of stress reactions in the experiments I have conducted.

In the initial experiments, the shock was always preceded by a signal so that the avoidance-escape animal had information to tell it when to respond. I wondered whether the benefit of being an avoidance-escape subject rather than a yoked subject depended upon this information imparted by the signal.

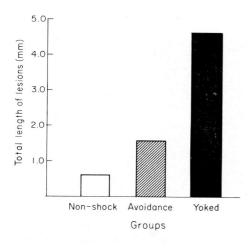

FIG. 2. The median of the total length of gastric lesions for the non-shock, avoidance-escape and yoked groups. Lesions in each subject were measured (in millimetres) and the total for each subject was computed; the median found in each group is shown. Also, it can be seen that a small amount of ulceration developed in non-shock animals, which resulted from the prolonged restraint and food and water deprivation during the experimental procedure.

To answer this question, an experiment was carried out to compare the effects of different signals preceding the shock (Weiss 1971a). In one condition, a single signal preceded shock as in earlier experiments; in a second condition, no signal preceded shock; and in a third condition, a series of different signals preceded shock, giving the animals in this condition even more information about when shock would occur than was available to the animals in the regular signal condition. In all conditions, a correct response by the avoidance-escape animal postponed the shock for 200 seconds. If the shock had begun, the response terminated it and the shock did not occur again for 200 seconds. Thus, avoidance-escape animals in all conditions had the same control over shock; they differed only in the signal-information which they received before the shock.

For these experiments, the subjects were placed into small cages, each cage having a wheel at the front of it. The correct response for an avoidance-escape subject was to rotate the wheel. A yoked animal was matched to each avoidance-escape animal and received exactly the same signals and shock as its avoidance-escape partner, but wheel-turning responses by the yoked subject had no effect on the shock. A non-shock subject was also included in each case.

The results are shown in Fig. 3. Regardless of the warning-signal condition, the avoidance-escape animals developed less ulceration than the yoked animals.

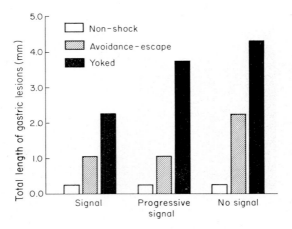

FIG. 3. The median of the total length of gastric lesions for the non-shock, avoidance-escape and yoked groups in each warning-signal condition. (From Weiss 1971*a*.)

Thus, the absence of a warning signal did not change the basic finding that being able to avoid and escape shock results in less pathology than does being helpless. Moreover, if one examines these results carefully, one can again see the primary importance of psychological variables in affecting gastric lesions. This is evident if one first notes the size of the difference between the avoidance-escape group in the signalled shock condition and the yoked group in the unsignalled shock condition. This large difference is due to psychological factors—to a difference in the ability to control shock and to predict (via a signal) the occurrence of shock. Now, if one notes the small difference that occurs between the avoidance-escape group in the signalled shock condition and any non-shock group, one can see that the occurrence of shock *per se* is not nearly as significant as are the above-mentioned psychological parameters.

Interesting as the main results of this experiment were, they initially provided me neither with an explanation for why effective coping responses reduce ulceration nor with any clue as to how I might alter conditions to mitigate this effect. However, when I carefully analysed the results, some interesting and unexpected findings emerged, which led to a simple theory.

First, I noted that the more responses an animal made, the more likely it was to have gastric lesions. This observation led to the first proposition of the theory: the more coping attempts, or responses, one observes, the greater is the ulcerogenic (ulcer-producing) stress. It is important to note that this does not say that behavioural coping responses cause ulceration; only that the amount of coping attempts and the amount of ulceration are positively correlated and therefore tend to rise together.

However, it was apparent that responding could not be the only variable functionally related to ulceration because some animals made many responses and did not develop ulcers. I then discerned that animals having little ulceration usually responded so as to terminate shocks or warning signals and thus received a great deal of information that they were 'doing the right thing'. Some weeks passed while I carried this messy concept around in my head, plaguing my colleagues with the prescientific revelation that animals did not develop ulcers if they received information telling them they were doing the right thing. Finally, I managed to define what I meant by this statement. I reasoned that information consisted of stimuli, so that the receipt of information meant the occurrence of stimuli. What kind of stimuli? If the stressful situation consisted of the stressor and stimuli associated with the stressor, then the 'right kind' of information consisted of stimuli that were not associated with the stressor. Thus, when an animal received information that it was 'doing the right thing', this meant that it made a response which was immediately followed by stimuli not associated with the stressor. The occurrence of such stimuli following a response I called the occurrence of *relevant feedback*. The amount of relevant feedback produced by any response could vary depending on the extent to which it produced stimuli that were not associated with the stressor. Thus, the second proposition of the theory emerged: the greater the amount of relevant feedback for responding, the less the ulcerogenic stress.

Therefore, two variables, responding and relevant feedback, are said to be related to ulceration. Ulceration will increase as the number of responses increases, and ulceration will decrease as the amount of relevant feedback from responses increases. Combining these two relationships produces a function, which is a plane, shown in Fig. 4a. From this plane one can predict the amount of ulceration that is expected to occur in any stressful situation by specifying the number of coping attempts, or responses, which the animal makes and the amount of relevant feedback that these responses produce. Fig. 4b shows how this is done. Given a hypothetical number of responses and amount of relevant feedback, the amount of ulceration that will result is specified by the height of the plane above the point where the number of responses and the amount of feedback intersect.

This theory first of all tells us why animals that are able to perform effective coping responses usually develop fewer ulcers than do helpless animals. Whenever a helpless animal makes a coping attempt, this response necessarily produces no relevant feedback because it has no effect on the stimuli of the animal's environment. Thus, if these animals make an appreciable number of

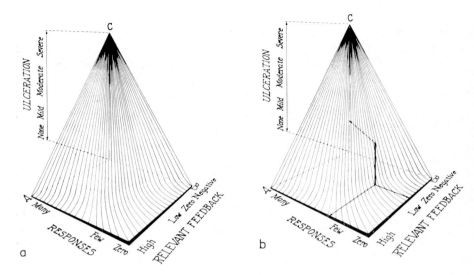

FIG. 4. On the left (*a*) is shown the three-dimensional figure which describes the proposed relationship between responses, feedback and ulceration. This relationship is a plane which shows how the two independent variables, responses and feedback, are related to the dependent variable, ulceration. On the right (*b*) is shown how this plane is used. Where a hypothetical number of responses and amount of feedback intersect, the amount of ulceration is determined by the height of the plane above this point. (For ease of reading this figure, responses and feedback are labelled across the axes in the foreground. These labels are customarily placed along the axes in the background which are parallel to the ones bearing the labels. It therefore should be noted that feedback designations apply to the axis from Point A to the intersection of the three axes, and response designations apply to the axis from Point B to the intersection.)

coping attempts, which many of them do, they will develop ulcers because the relevant feedback is zero. (Note in Fig. 4 that along the zero feedback coordinate, the plane rises sharply, denoting a sharp rise in ulceration, as responding increases.) Animals that have control in a stressful situation, however, do receive relevant feedback when they respond. In my experiments, for example, the avoidance-escape animals could terminate warning signals and/or shocks (thereby producing silence and the absence of shocks), so that their responses produced non-stressor stimuli. (Note in Fig. 4 that along feedback coordinates above zero, the plane shows less elevation, denoting less ulceration, than it does along the zero coordinate.) Thus, animals in control of a stressor can usually make a large number of responses and not develop ulcers because they normally receive a substantial amount of relevant feedback for responding.

Separate experiments have been carried out to test the theory directly. I

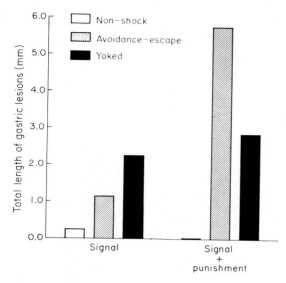

Fig. 5. On the left is shown the median total length of gastric lesions which developed in non-shock, avoidance-escape and yoked groups exposed to a stress condition in which shock was preceded by a warning signal. On the right is shown the amount of gastric lesions which developed in the same groups exposed to the same conditions except that a brief punishment shock pulse (negative amount of relevant feedback) was given to the avoidance-escape and yoked animals whenever an avoidance-escape response was made during the second 24 hours of the stress session. (From Weiss 1971*b*.)

first used the theory in an attempt to produce more ulceration in animals having control over shock than in helpless animals, a result I had not been able to obtain previously. The theory suggested that this would occur if relevant feedback could be made even lower than it is in the 'zero' relevant feedback, or helpless, condition. Therefore, the following experiment was done (Weiss 1971*b*). After avoidance-escape animals had spent 24 hours in the normal signalled avoidance situation, they were given a brief pulse of shock ('punishment') every time they performed the correct response. Thus, each avoidance-escape response now produced precisely the wrong kind of feedback stimulus—the stressor stimulus itself—making the amount of relevant feedback in this condition even lower than zero. This should, of course, produce severe ulceration. The results are shown on the right side of Fig. 5. One can see that the avoidance-escape animals in the 'negative' relevant feedback condition developed severe ulceration—more ulceration, in fact, than did helpless animals receiving the same shock. The bars on the left side of Fig. 5 show the effect of the normal signalled avoidance condition for comparison.

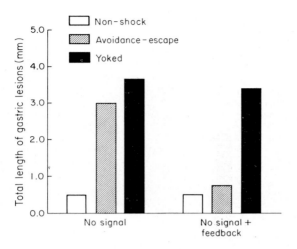

FIG. 6. On the left is shown the median total length of gastric lesions which developed in non-shock, avoidance-escape and yoked groups in a stress condition in which shock was not preceded by a warning signal. On the right is shown the amount of gastric lesions which developed in the same groups exposed to the same conditions except that a brief feedback signal (tone) was given to the subjects whenever an avoidance-escape response was made. (From Weiss 1971c.)

Having found that very low relevant feedback would cause severe ulceration, I conducted an experiment to determine if a high amount of relevant feedback could reduce and possibly eliminate ulceration in a stressful situation. For this experiment (Weiss 1971c), the unsignalled shock condition was used, since under this condition avoidance-escape animals will develop a considerable amount of gastric ulceration. The theory states that ulceration occurs in this condition because the relevant feedback for responding, while not zero, is nevertheless low. Relevant feedback is low because, without a warning signal being present, avoidance responses only postpone the shock without causing any alteration in the animals' external stimulus situation. As a result, the relevant feedback from such responses comes entirely from proprioceptive cues and not at all from the external environment. To attempt to increase the relevant feedback, a brief tone was added to the situation. This tone occurred every time the avoidance animal made a response. Since every response postponed the shock, the tone, which immediately followed the response, was never associated with the shock. Thus, the tone constituted an external stimulus event that was not associated with the shock, and was therefore excellent feedback.

The results of this experiment are shown in Fig. 6. On the left side is shown the ulceration which resulted in the normal unsignalled shock condition, while on the right side is shown the ulceration which resulted from the same condition but with the tone feedback stimulus added. It is important to note that avoidance-escape animals in both conditions made a similar number of responses and therefore received a similar number of shocks, so that the difference was not due to a difference in shock. We can see that the avoidance-escape animals which received the tone feedback stimulus showed less ulceration than did animals in any other avoidance-escape condition; in fact, they developed only slightly more ulceration than did non-shocked controls.

This theory has also enabled me to integrate a finding which was otherwise very puzzling. The finding is known as the 'executive monkey' phenomenon. In this striking experiment reported by Brady *et al.* in 1958, it was found that monkeys able to avoid an electric shock developed severe gastrointestinal ulceration and died, while helpless yoked animals apparently developed no gastrointestinal abnormalities. Of course this result is opposite to all the results that I have consistently obtained, and also does not agree with some experimental findings in human subjects (Champion 1950; Geer *et al.* 1970). Indeed, informed investigators have long considered that the 'executive monkey' phenomenon might be simply an anomaly since it was found in only four pairs of monkeys and had proved difficult to replicate. However, if one considers the executive monkey result in relation to the formulation presented above, the result seems readily understandable.

The 'executive' monkeys died of severe gastrointestinal ulceration while performing in an unsignalled-shock, or Sidman avoidance, condition. In this condition, each response postponed (avoided) shock for 20 seconds, but since there were no external signals, these responses produced no stimulus change whatsoever in the animals' external environment. As a result, the relevant feedback from avoidance responding was quite low, as has been explained previously. In addition to this, the number of responses made in this condition was extremely high. The avoidance schedule demanded a response at least once every 20 seconds and this condition was in effect for 12 hours a day for many days. This combination of high responding and low relevant feedback, which characterized the avoidance in the executive monkey experiment, is precisely the combination of circumstances that the theory predicts will produce severe ulceration.

Actually, the situation was even worse for the avoidance monkeys. They had, in fact, been chosen to be the avoidance subjects because they tended to respond at a high rate! Before the experiment was begun, the monkeys were divided into pairs, both animals were given a 2–4 hour avoidance pre-test, and the animal showing the better performance was made the avoidance subject

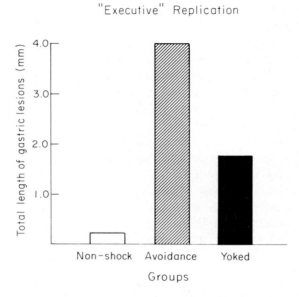

FIG. 7. The median total length of gastric lesions found in subjects which 'replicate' the selection factors and conditions of the 'executive monkey' experiment.

while the poorer performer was assigned to the yoked position. Thus, the avoidance animals, being high-rate responders, were from the start more likely to develop ulcers than their yoked partners, according to the present theory. Moreover, the avoidance monkeys responded at such a high rate that their yoked partners received only one or two shocks per hour, so that the yoked monkeys—even though they were in a zero feedback condition—probably made very few coping attempts because the situation for them was rather benign. Putting these facts together, one can understand why the avoidance animals developed severe ulceration while the yoked animals showed no apparent ill effects.

Finally, by using the foregoing principles, it has been possible for me to replicate, in a sense, the 'executive monkey' experiment with rats. First, I considered all of my rats that had been used in the unsignalled shock condition, which is the condition analogous to the one used in the 'executive monkey' experiment. Then, although my animals had been assigned to the avoidance-escape and yoked conditions randomly, I statistically selected all of those matched avoidance-escape and yoked pairs which, based on their overall responding throughout the experiment, had shown the same tendency toward high and low responding that was present in the monkey pairs. The results are shown in Fig. 7. It is apparent that the avoidance-escape animals in this population developed more ulceration than their matched yoked partners. Thus, I conclude that while the 'executive monkey' experiment represents a clearly atypical situation, it appears explainable by simple principles that are now coming to light.

ACKNOWLEDGEMENTS

The research described here was supported by U.S. Public Health Service grants MH 19991, MH 13189 and GM 01789.

References

BRADY, J. V., PORTER, R. W., CONRAD, D. G. & MASON, J. W. (1958) Avoidance behavior and the development of gastroduodenal ulcers. *J. Exp. Anal. Behav.* **1**, 69-72

CHAMPION, R. A. (1950) Studies of experimentally induced disturbance. *Aust. J. Psychol.* **2**, 90-99

GEER, J. H., DAVISON, G. C. & GATCHEL, R. I. (1970) Reduction of stress in humans through nonveridical perceived control of aversive stimulation. *J. Pers. Soc. Psychol.* **16**, 731-738

WEISS, J. M. (1968) Effects of coping responses on stress. *J. Comp. Physiol. Psychol.* **65**, 251-260

WEISS, J. M. (1970) Somatic effects of predictable and unpredictable shock. *Psychosom. Med.* **32**, 397-208

WEISS, J. M. (1971a) Effects of coping behavior in different warning signal conditions on stress pathology in rats. *J. Comp. Physiol. Psychol.* **77**, 1-13

WEISS, J. M. (1971b) Effects of punishing the coping response (conflict) on stress pathology in rats. *J. Comp. Physiol. Psychol.* **77**, 14-21

WEISS, J. M. (1971c) Effects of coping behavior with and without a feedback signal on stress pathology in rats. *J. Comp. Physiol. Psychol.* **77**, 22-30

Discussion

Sachar: I should like to compliment you on a very elegant study. A few points may be of interest and may also broaden the discussion. First, the 'executive monkey' study (Brady *et al.* 1958) could never be replicated, and some of the features of your design may account for that. On the other hand, studies done with John Mason and replicated many times, using the free-shock paradigm, produced data on 17-hydroxycorticosteroid responses in monkeys that resemble your results (Sidman *et al.* 1962). The animal is trained to avoid a shock by pressing a lever every few seconds, and then a few random extra shocks are given to the animal *despite* his excellent performance. This generates a tremendous increase in 17-hydroxycorticosteroid secretion, much more than in the yoked control.

Your experiments also emphasize the crucial importance of the feedback information the animal is getting—the signals he actually receives—for the problem you mentioned of generating a psychological experiment that is free from contamination by physical stress, or in which physical stress is controlled for. Actually, the shoe is on the other foot. When one tries to study *physical* stress the problem of *psychological* contamination by these signals becomes tremendous. When Mason attempted to study the effect of cold or starvation on 17-hydroxycorticosteroid production he found that the monkey became exquisitely sensitive to signals. When the temperature was rapidly lowered the monkey responded to the signal that the temperature was falling rather than to the cold itself. So the experimenter has to reduce the temperature by half a degree every two hours to get a psychologically uncontaminated situation. The same happens with food; when a monkey is passed by and the other animals are fed, you are not dealing with starvation but with a monkey who is infuriated, shaking the cage. In order that the effects of starvation could be studied without concurrent psychologically stressful stimuli, the monkeys had to be fed pellets that looked like food. Your studies therefore have this methodological significance, as well as the exciting physiological findings.

Engel: The peculiar feature of the single executive monkey study was that the monkey cages were out in the corridor. That virtually replicated the conditions that Dr Weiss described: namely, the monkeys were getting all kinds of irrelevant feedback from activity around them.

I am excited by your study, because you may have succeeded in doing what nobody has done so far; that is, in setting up a design which corresponds closely to what we encounter clinically. In our experience the single most important correlate with disease onset is that before the disease becomes manifest the patient has gone through a period of 'giving up', with affects which Schmale has defined as helplessness or hopelessness (Schmale 1958, 1969; Sweeney *et al.* 1970). What I think you have done is to put what clinicians refer to as 'giving up' in the operational terms of a laboratory experiment, because giving up means that for the moment the person has, or feels he has, no solutions available and hence there is nothing he can do. Regardless of what he does or thinks (this may go on intrapsychically as well as in direct response to the environment) he gets no feedback which works. On the contrary, he gets what you call negative feedback; not only doesn't it work but it may make things worse. This is therefore a valuable contribution towards bridging the gap to our clinical observations.

Sandler: We (Kanter & Sandler 1955) gave a questionnaire, which included items relating to phobic anxiety, to patients with duodenal ulcer or functional dyspepsia and to a control group of patients who had been to a general practitioner. We found no difference in score on the phobic items between patients with functional dyspepsia and those with ulcer but both these groups had very high scores compared to the control group. We concluded that these two groups of patients consisted of people who were actually phobic about the situations they found themselves in (they were salesmen, executives and so on) but nevertheless forced themselves to go into those situations, and that this was correlated with the development of dyspepsia or peptic ulceration. There seems to be a parallel here with Dr Weiss's rats which couldn't predict when they would receive the extra shock and had a greater incidence of ulcer. In my view they must have been extremely anxious in comparison with the animals which were able to control the situation. I think that, from clinical experience, where safety-producing situations are available in a situation which causes anxiety, the amount of pathology that develops is consequently less.

Gray: Dr Weiss, how many responses did your yoked-control rats make? And why do they respond?

Weiss: They make many responses. I don't know why. I think the yoked rat is probably clawing at the wheel in an attempt simply to get out of the box. But the avoidance-escape rats turned the wheel more than the yoked or helpless rats because, in psychological terms, they received reinforcement for turning the wheel while the yoked rats did not.

Gray: Do you find a correlation in your yoked-control rats between the number of wheel-turns and the number of ulcers?

Weiss: Yes. We found a poor but significant correlation, within all groups and in all the various conditions, between the number of responses and the amount of ulceration, as our model would predict. An interesting result is seen in the experiment with high relevant feedback. All avoidance-escape animals are in the no-signal condition, similar to the situation of the executive monkey experiment. I consider this to be a condition with low relevant feedback. One group of avoidance-escape animals, however, received a tone after each response, producing high relevant feedback. Fig. 1 shows the number of responses and the amount of ulceration for all avoidance-escape subjects. In the normal, no-signal condition, where the feedback is low, the animals ulcerate in proportion to how much they respond. For the animals that had a feedback signal, the regression line is essentially flat. This study was made because the model predicts that however many responses the animal makes, if the relevant feedback is high enough he will not ulcerate, and that is precisely what happened.

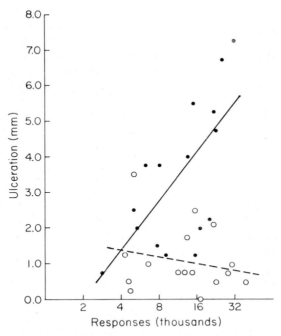

FIG. 1 (Weiss). The amount of ulceration as a function of the number of responses for avoidance-escape rats in a situation where there was no warning signal before shock. Half the subjects received a tone feedback signal after each response and half did not. o = Feedback tone (regression line — — —); • = No feedback tone (regression line ———).

Gray: This correlation within the yoked-control animals is very puzzling. I take it that by a 'response' you mean something other than the rat just moving some part of its body, because when a rat is not turning the wheel it's presumably always doing something, twitching an ear or swishing its tail or other more complex activities. 'Response', as you are using the word, can only be defined by some experimental contingency which has been attached to some specific part of the overall observed behaviour, otherwise the rat is continually making an indefinite number of different 'responses'. But only in the escape-avoidance group has such a contingency been attached to wheel-turning. The correlation between number of wheel-turns and degree of ulceration in the yoked-control group (for which a response is undefined) suggests, therefore, that this is a correlation, not between coping responses and ulceration, but between general activity and ulceration.

Weiss: For these experiments I defined response operationally, as how often the animal turns the wheel. What I wanted was a sample of the total number of coping attempts.

Gray: That is my point. How can the yoked-control rat be said to be making any coping attempts of any kind?

Weiss: He certainly is, although I accept that the number of wheel-turns is a better measure of the total number of coping attempts in the avoidance-escape group than it is in the yoked group, because the yoked animals may also do various other things which we don't measure. One of the weaknesses of the model is that we need a better measure of the very loosely defined variable of coping attempts. It's a useful parameter at present, as is relevant feedback, but we need a better conception of what these two things really represent and how we can measure them.

Gray: Do you envisage something central in the animal which is as it were saying 'I must try this out' and that wheel-turning in the yoked-control rat is simply a reflection of attempts to do *something* to his environment?

Weiss: If you take out the cognition, I agree! 'Coping attempt' only means an attempt of the yoked animal to deal with his environment in the stressful situation.

Gray: Did the number of responses in the yoked-control animals decline over time?

Weiss: Yes. But this occurs even in the avoidance-escape group.

Gray: Does it decline more in the yoked controls? I am puzzled by the behaviour of an animal that continues to turn a wheel although this is having no effect on the shocks it is receiving.

Hofer: There is one way of looking at this which is a little more parsimonious. Ader (1964) has shown in immobilization-induced ulceration that the point in the activity cycle at which you immobilize the rat considerably affects the number of ulcers obtained. The animals which are immobilized at their most active period develop most ulcers. You may have some relatively active animals and some relatively inactive ones and it is something built into the more active animals that makes for increased avoidance responses. The number of avoidance responses may just be an index of the overall activity level of these animals which in turn correlates with the incidence of ulceration, as in Ader's study.

Gray: That also fits with Brady's executive monkey result.

Weiss: Yes. I think we are sampling, under the category of coping attempt and its operational measurement by wheel-turning, some sort of central variable. If we knew precisely what it was, this would be what we should measure. The fascinating thing is what happens when relevant feedback is received. Our data suggest that it has an immediate effect on this system.

Storey: If animals are kept in a different type of experimental cage, say where the shock comes through the floor, what happens to the rats who can't make reinforced movements? Do their movements die away more quickly?

Weiss: We haven't used a grid floor because in this situation the rat isn't really helpless. He can avoid shock entirely if he hurls himself into the air; in addition, the electrical resistance of the back feet appears to be greater than that of the front feet and the rats learn to keep their front paws off the grid floor, and also to maximize the area of contact with a constant current shock source. To answer your question, towards the end of the experiment the rat is quite often planted with its front feet against the wall and its back feet wrapped as completely as possible round the grid bars.

Engel: I want to extend Dr Hofer's comments on Ader's experiments. Your rats are in the box for 48 hours and are able to move to some extent—they can turn over, for instance. What would be the effects of the diurnal activity cycle in this situation, particularly in the control rat? Did it show the usual periods of less activity, or inactivity alternating with activity? The rat that has to learn to turn the wheel has a different experience, if Ader's observations are correct, in its active phase from in its inactive phase. This would surely make a difference for the yoked rats as well.

Weiss: It probably would. Clearly there is an interaction of such variables. We put the lights on for 48 hours continuously. This doesn't eliminate the diurnal rhythm but it prevents the profound activity bursts that occur when the lights are switched on and off. We haven't measured cyclical changes in activity but we measured plasma corticosteroids at the end of the experiment and, for what it is worth, the level of plasma corticosterone correlates with the extent of gastric ulceration, which confirms the idea that steroid levels may be correlated with the genesis of ulceration (and possibly causal, from the studies in which injected steroids have produced ulceration) (Spiro & Milles 1960).

Sandler: I would like to suggest something about the turning of the wheel by the yoked-control rats who appear to turn it for no good reason, so to speak. Some time ago I put forward the hypothesis, on clinical grounds (Sandler 1960), that when a person is in a state of anxiety or lowered safety he will attempt to make repetitive movements, because the feedback of perceiving what is expected will result in an increase in his feeling of safety. In the situation you describe, the most controlled activity which the yoked-control rat could undertake is to turn the wheel. It provides him with a regular repetitive movement. Of course, it doesn't help very much. It seems to me that turning to an habitual, rather complicated mode of functioning, in the attempt to gain a feeling of safety, prompted this response in an anxiety-producing situation.

Hill: We began the meeting with simple models of the stimulus–response variety, and considered the possible number of responses and how to reduce them, as Dr Gray did with three systems. We have considered the possible central organization of such responses and their relationship to the emotional state, the peripheral physiological changes which accompany these changes, and more complex models involving social interaction between groups of individuals placed in association with one another under conditions which we call 'stress'. We are now considering the feedback mechanisms which are evident not only at physiological levels in the body, and how these might be conceived. Are they to be treated in terms of physical feedback systems, or in terms of the consequences of the meaning which the individual applies to the feedback signal? This also came up in the studies of the complex social interactions between mother and infant that Professor Denenberg described (p. 191). He wanted to make an analysis of the physical behaviour of the mother and baby, but as clinicians we can't help being concerned with the meaning of such feedback signals.

Sachar: Some psychoendocrine research bears on this point. The study of the adrenocortical response to stress has become a hallowed avenue of investigation in animals. This is not too great a problem when one studies a group of rats and presents them with a standard stressful stimulus. One can count on a good batting average in adrenocortical response. But when this has been studied in man, the responses are more variable and confusing. When one brings people into the laboratory and tries to stress them in various ways the adrenocortical response is more variable and less profound than in the experimental animal. What the animal model fails to take into account is the intervening variable of the buffering system of psychological defences and coping strategies that people use to assign meaning to the stimulus, serving to minimize the emotional and stressful impact of their environmental perceptions. This has been studied in the laboratory and also in very gruelling field situations. Dr Hofer took part in a study of parents of children dying of leukaemia (see below, p. 275). We have studied women who are awaiting biopsy for tumours of the breast and are uncertain about the outcome. These studies, as well as studies of pilots in Vietnam and soldiers undergoing the stress of basic training, show consistently that the majority of subjects show very little adrenocortical response but that a minority do. From interviews and clinical assessments one finds that most of the subjects have an extraordinary capacity to deny, to rationalize, to project and to intellectualize, and to cope effectively with the stress in this way. When the subjects are rated in terms of how well defended they are, those that are more poorly defended generally have the larger adrenocortical response; the very well-defended subjects (the majority of the subjects in all these situations) show little response.

Psychoendocrine studies have also shown that people experiencing the most severe emotional turmoil that human beings probably ever go through, namely the acute schizophrenic reaction characterized by intense panic and a sense of personal disintegration, show the kind of massive adrenocortical response that one sees in the helpless animal—tremendously high, but lasting for a few days only (Sachar *et al.* 1970). Then comes a point at which the patient suddenly forms a psychotic solution: 'I have it all figured out; this is all a plot and now I'm certain of the situation', and he organizes a fixed delusional system. Emotional turmoil promptly disappears and the adrenocortical response equally promptly returns to normal. When this 'defensive system' is challenged by the therapist the patient becomes temporarily uncertain of his position and shows a slight adrenocortical response, but in general the psychotic solution remains effective.

Finally, the psychosomatic implications. One might expect, if one subscribes to a 'hydraulic' hypothesis, that if these defences are operating in normal people and psychotics to minimize the affective response to stress, one would then see an intense discharge of the emotion along autonomic and endocrine pathways, in line with the idea of re-routing. That is, in the absence of affective response at the psychological level, one might expect to see a massive discharge in terms of other physiological indices of stress. But one does *not*. The psychological defence mechanisms minimize the stress response effectively both psychologically and physiologically and play a major role in physiological as well as psychological homeostasis (Sachar 1970).

Hill: What is the present position on the concept of conservation of psychic energy?

Sandler: Many psychoanalysts, including myself, do not subscribe to the 'hydraulic' model which treats psychic energy as if it were a fluid having to find its outlet. The concept goes back to the first phase of psychoanalysis and I subscribe to the view that what was viewed as 'discharge' of energy is a reduction in internally arising stimuli as a consequence of information feedback, and this is consistent with what we now know about the nervous system. The function of the defences would then be to reduce feelings of tension, on the basis of having found a solution, and to send back the information: 'you can be quiet now'. What you say, Dr Sachar, is consistent with my own way of thinking.

Engel: Dr Sachar has just referred to patients awaiting breast biopsy. Dr Greene and his associates in our group studied the complex and stressful situation of cardiac catheterization (Greene *et al.* 1970). As one would expect, subjects differed greatly in their responses. At first the investigators directed their attention to such categories as whether the subjects were anxious or calm or depressed and withdrawn. They then became aware of another factor, namely whether or not the patients were engaging with the team doing the cardiac catheterization. These authors measured plasma cortisol and growth hormone concentrations and found that cortisol was elevated in the subjects who were anxious but not in those who were calm or categorized as depressed, which included a tendency to withdraw. Growth hormone concentrations were low and did not rise in the calm or the depressed subjects; nor did they rise in patients who were anxious but who were interacting with the team—talking, asking questions and so on. On the other hand, growth hormone *was* increased among subjects who were anxious but not engaged. So there was an interesting dissociation between the two hormones: cortisol was raised and growth hormone lowered in anxious but engaged people; whereas both cortisol and growth hormone were raised in anxious, non-engaged people.

We also studied the effects on healthy volunteers of the BBC documentary film of the one-year follow-up after the disaster in Aberfan, a Welsh mining village. This film had profound effects on viewers and we therefore used it as an experimental device to evoke feelings of sadness (Frader *et al.* 1971). Here too we found that plasma growth hormone concentrations rose in subjects who felt sad at the times when they were experiencing sadness. My preliminary impression of the data is that cortisol does not rise simultaneously with growth hormone.

Weiss: I find it difficult (and the sort of data that Dr Engel has just presented is a part of my bewilderment) to handle the relationship between somatic disorders and emotions. I have difficulty in seeing consistent relationships between specific emotions and specific somatic–pathological responses. The formulation that arises directly from my experimental data does not emphasize any emotion as such as a primary variable. It talks simply about responses or coping attempts or whatever we want to say about the central state that the data suggest is there, and some sort of informational feedback variable. Of course, I hope the conception will improve. 'Emotion' may be somehow embodied in those particular variables. When an organism is 'anxious' for instance, the response rate tends to rise; so one might conceive of emotion fitting into my formulation in this way. But nothing in the conception demands that we think of the resulting pathology in terms of emotion. All it requires is that we think of it in terms of the number of responses or coping attempts and the informational feedback variable. As a consequence, I have tended to try to stay away from the idea of emotion.

There are suggestions from clinical data that such alternative approaches should be explored. Recently I re-read the literature published in the 1934–1954 period on the relationships between emotion and somatic illness, particularly studies of 'personality' types and peptic ulcer. Nearly everyone in the field agreed that 'ulcer-susceptible individuals' are hard-driving, intense people. This may not be true but it is certainly pervasive in the literature. Can this observation be related to high response rate? What is the relevant feedback that such persons experience? In general, can we approach this disorder from a point of view which does not emphasize emotion?

Hill: You have expressed an important position, that of the laboratory experimentalist, in contrast to the position of the clinician studying patients with psychosomatic disorders. How can you do anything with your model but observe the frequency of responses? And how could a clinician deal with 'frequency of responses'?

Gray: A lot turns on Dr Weiss's notion of the 'number of coping attempts'. I want to go back to this in connection with personality. The flaw in Brady's study on the executive monkeys was that he allocated them according to their own response rates in preliminary trials, and Dr Weiss, in his one true replication of this study, where he used an unsignalled Sidman avoidance schedule, did the same, allocating to the escape-avoidance group those rats that already had a high avoidance response rate. And he succeeded in reproducing Brady's results, which is very important. In other words, one could say that in Brady's experiment and in this replication of it, if you choose a subject with a pre-existing tendency towards a high response rate, you are choosing a subject with a high tendency towards ulceration. This was independently shown by Sines *et al.* (1963) in experiments in which rats selectively bred for high susceptibility to ulceration were subsequently found to be particularly good at avoidance learning. Ader's observations, mentioned earlier by Dr Hofer (p. 269), on the relation between activity and ulceration, may be part of the same basic phenomenon. Thus the correlation within each of Dr Weiss's groups of rats between number of responses and degree of ulceration may simply reflect the tendency for highly active animals (which are usually good at avoidance learning) to be particularly prone to ulcers. The mysterious notion of 'coping attempts' would then be superfluous.

Weiss: From the figure (p. 268) which shows ulceration and responding in the tone-feedback experiment it can be seen that both the group with the tone-feedback signal and the group without it had a similar range of responding— that is, both groups made a similar number of responses. So one can't explain that result by postulating two groups with different response rates.

Hinde: Dr Weiss has raised the question of whether we *need* to use the concept of emotion, and how far we can get without it. It seems to me that so long as one has (or is investigating) only one dependent variable, it will never be necessary to use an intervening variable (such as emotion). One of the main differences between clinicians and experimentalists is that clinicians are inevitably involved with many dependent variables and must therefore use intervening variables. Whether the intervening variable has anything to do with subjective experience is a separate issue, but it is likely that in dealing with the sorts of phenomena under discussion, the intervening variables that are useful, either clinically or to the experimentalist if he uses many different dependent variables, are likely to be related to the intervening variables that we use in everyday speech; that is, to emotion-type words.

Henry: Surely the mass of neurophysiological and clinical neurological work in animals and man has succeeded in establishing that certain regions of the mammalian CNS can be identified with certain broad functions. The limbic system and the hypothalamus and midbrain have been shown to be involved with emotion and with drives and consummatory responses (Ganong 1971). The association areas of the neocortex, which are so large in man that Washburn and Hamburg (1968) speak of them as a sociocultural brain, are involved in delayed responses, response preservation, and complex sensory discriminations and perceptions. It is these parts of man's cortex that give him the capacity to form cross-modal associations and to relate sensory, auditory and visual images using words and without employing limbic connections and emotional arousal.

Hofer: In the course of our study on parents of children with leukaemia, we found several exceptional subjects (Wolff *et al.* 1964). We studied two or three women with 'histrionic' personalities who managed to upset everybody by their apparent emotional reaction to the situation, but whose rates of urinary corticosteroid excretion were found to be quite low. One of these women gave us a chance to go further into the relationship of affect and adrenocortical function. Her corticosteroid excretion was low throughout the child's illness, but about a week before the child died she quietened down and became very much like some of the other women, who were tender with their children. In reacting to this woman we were more moved by her in that last week than before, and at the same time her corticosteroid excretion went *up*. It seemed to us that one can look at affect as display; even though it was perhaps experienced by this woman in the same way as by the other mothers, it served a different purpose in her CNS organization, namely to mobilize attention, perhaps to distract her from even more painful feelings which went with tenderness. Finally this defence was broken through when the reality of the child's imminent death confronted her. These sorts of unexpected findings suggest that emotion is still worth studying in psychoendocrine research.

Sleight: In your studies and those of Dr Sachar on stressed people in various situations, where most of the subjects had low plasma adrenocortical hormone levels and a minority had high ones, was there a higher incidence of previous 'psychosomatic illness' in the group with high steroid levels? Was there a basic difference in the way they responded to stressful situations, or is this too naive a way of looking at it?

Hofer: We found a tendency toward a greater number and variety of illnesses in parents with high corticosteroid excretion rates but the difference was not significant for the numbers compared (nine 'highs' and nine 'lows') (Hofer *et al.* 1972).

Sachar: We have no information about past history in our patients, but one particular case is interesting. We were studying the output of adrenocortical hormones of a man hospitalized with chronic schizophrenia and attempting to relate the adrenocorticoid and 'emotional' responses to various types of intervention. His father had died of malignant hypertension, so we knew that he had this genetic factor in his make-up. An acute personal crisis occurred and he responded with a temporary state of acute emotional turmoil with anxiety and panic. His output of adrenocortical hormones at that time soared, although previously normal, and his blood pressure rose to 200+/180 mmHg. When the personal crisis passed and he returned to his standard ways of doing things, adrenocorticoid output and blood pressure returned to normal. One might predict that this man is likely to develop hypertension in the future in response to emotional stress.

Donald: Emotion is difficult to measure, however. There are many possible ways of measuring it or its effect on the body. Some years ago we studied cardiac output by cardiac catheterization, and a woman with mild ulcerative colitis volunteered to undergo the procedure. She was known as the calmest person in the ward. Her resting cardiac output was about 12 litres, more than double the normal figure. We had no idea that this woman was in this state of tension. She still appeared perfectly calm when we catheterized her. It is difficult to be sure what you are measuring and what you are looking for.

Rutter: The measurement of emotions is certainly difficult but by no means impossible. Did you give the same attention to the methods used in observing this woman's emotions that you gave to the development of cardiac catheterization?

Donald: None of the team of about five reasonably intelligent physicians, who were selected as such, not as experimental physiologists, thought that this woman was under tension.

Rutter: That really isn't accurate enough. You would not accept the measurement of cardiac output by an intelligent physician just looking at the patient, would you? The same applies to emotions. One has to devise techniques for the purpose. Within limits, emotions can be assessed fairly reliably by means of questionnaires, interviews and other means (e.g. Rutter & Brown 1966). Although falling short of a satisfactory differentiation of emotions these measures are useful and of predictive value.

Donald: I agree, but do you not find that the pattern of what you are trying to measure varies in relation to what is apparently the same emotion?

Rutter: That is true to some extent. Individuals differ in the way their emotions are linked to physiological responses. There is also individuality in the way feelings are expressed in terms of tone of voice, facial expression and bodily movements but there is enough consistency for judgements on emotions to have fair validity.

Aitken: One of the intriguing questions for the clinician is that his observations can so frequently be explained in a different way from the most obvious. I was fascinated by Dr Ginsburg's observations on wolves because clinical evidence complements his observation that to become permanently tame, a wolf has to have experienced anxiety. The treatment of phobic disorders by psychotherapeutic interpretation is only effective if it produces an emotional response; and flooding—another treatment for phobias—is an experience of fear. Marks *et al.* (1971) found that patients seemed to learn control of their anxiety more effectively when treated by flooding than by desensitization.

Hill: Dr Marks now believes that the experience of fear is not always necessary for behavioural improvement in phobic patients, although it may have a facilitating function (Watson *et al.* 1971).

Rutter: Perhaps one ought to distinguish between the experience of no fear at all and the experience of only mild fear. Dr Marks's experiments suggest that the *amount* of fear bears no relationship to therapeutic outcome; you can diminish anxiety during the behavioural treatment of phobias by giving appropriate drugs and yet still get just as good a therapeutic effect. Whether that is the same as totally obliterating anxiety by using very high doses of drugs, as in Dr Ginsburg's studies, is another matter.

Gray: In this meeting we have been trying to bridge certain gaps. One that we haven't yet looked at is the gap between the brain experiments that Professor Fonberg and I described and experiments on the endocrine and autonomic nervous systems. I'll take Dr Weiss's ulceration experiments as a starting point.

It is known that there is a connection between corticosteroid output and peptic ulceration, and that the former is under the control of the hypothalamus via the release of ACTH from the anterior pituitary. Two very important higher nervous structures which influence hypothalamic control of ACTH release are the septo-hippocampal system that I talked about (pp. 95-116) and the amygdala, which Professor Fonberg discussed (pp. 131-150) (Schadé 1970). The former is inhibitory, the latter excitatory. I would like to suggest that the reason why Dr Weiss's experimental situations produced such extreme ulceration may not be unconnected with this scheme. First, his rats are giving an unconditioned response to shock. In my terms, this will involve activity in the amygdaloid fight/flight system, which will be excitatory with regard to corticosteroid release. Consider next Dr Weiss's irrelevant feedback and Professor Levine's finding (see pp. 281-291) that a departure from expectation in an unpleasant direction causes a release of steroids. Since, as I argued in my paper, it is this kind of event whose behavioural consequences are mediated by the septo-hippocampal system for behavioural inhibition, I suggest that Professor Levine's result arises because such unpleasant surprises turn off septo-hippocampal inhibition of steroid release. Thus the initial punishment and the irrelevant feedback in Dr Weiss's experiments are both likely to activate corticosteroid output, but by different routes. This is, of course, a highly speculative account, but all the details are open to experimental investigation.

Weiss: We demonstrated a correlation between the amount of ulceration the rats developed and the concentrations of plasma corticosteroids at the end of the experiment. This suggests that the amounts of corticosteroids which the animal can secrete endogenously are related to ulceration.

Sachar: I think the ulcerations are more likely to be related to a direct influence from the hypothalamus to the stomach, rather than to an effect of the increase of plasma corticosteroids.

Sandler: The behavioural experiments all relate to the perception of certain stimuli and experiences, and these must travel down neural pathways, so the higher centres must be involved.

Weiss: Of course the direct neural pathways from brain to gut are very important in ulceration but this does not rule out the possibility that the steroids are ulcerogenic.

References

ADER, R. (1964) Gastric erosions in the rat. Effects of immobilization at different points in the activity cycle. *Science (Wash. D.C.)* **145**, 406-407

BRADY, J. V., PORTER, R. W., CONRAD, D. G. & MASON, J. W. (1958) Avoidance behaviour and the development of duodenal ulcers. *J. Exp. Anal. Behav.* **1**, 69-72

FRADER, M., BARRY, C. J., SCHALCH, D. S. & ENGEL, G. L. (1971) Endocrine changes during experimentally induced sadness. I. Serum growth hormone (abstract). *Psychosom. Med.* **33**, 471

GANONG, W. F. (1971) Neurophysiologic basis of instinctual behavior and emotion. *Review of Medical Physiology*, 5th edn, pp. 173-185, Lange Medical Publishers, Los Altos, Calif.

GREENE, W. A., CONRON, G., SCHALCH, D. S. & SCHREINER, B. F. (1970) Psychologic correlates of growth hormone and adrenal secretory responses of patients undergoing cardiac catheterization. *Psychosom. Med.* **32**, 599-611

HOFER, M. A., WOLFF, C. T., FRIEDMAN, S. B. & MASON, J. W. (1972) A psychoendocrine study of bereavement. Part II. Observations on the process of mourning in relation to adrenocortical function. *Psychosom. Med.* in press

KANTER, V. B. & SANDLER, J. (1955) Studies in psychopathology using a self-assessment inventory. V. Anxiety, functional dyspepsia and duodenal ulcer: an investigation. *Br. J. Med. Psychol.* **28**, 157-166

MARKS, I., BOULOUGOURIS, J. & MARSET, P. (1971) Flooding versus desensitization in the treatment of phobic patients: a crossover study. *Br. J. Psychiatr.* **119**, 353-373

RUTTER, M. & BROWN, G. W. (1966) The reliability and validity of measures of family life and relationships in families containing a psychiatric patient. *Soc. Psychiatr.* **1**, 38-53

SACHAR, E. (1970) Psychological factors related to activation and inhibition of the adrenal cortical stress response in man. In *Progress in Brain Research*, vol. 32, *Pituitary, Adrenal and the Brain* (de Wied, D. & Weijnen, J. A. W. M., eds.), Elsevier, Amsterdam

SACHAR, E. J., KANTER, S. S., BUIE, D., ENGLE, R. & MEHLMAN, R. (1970) Psychoendocrinology of ego disintegration. *Am. J. Psychiatr.* **126**, 1067-1078

SANDLER, J. (1960) The background of safety. *Int. J. Psycho-Anal.* **35**, 91

SCHADÉ, J. P. (1970) In *Progress in Brain Research*, vol. 32, *Pituitary, Adrenal and the Brain* (de Wied, D. & Weijnen, J. A. W. M., eds.), pp. 2-10, Elsevier, Amsterdam

SCHMALE, A. H. (1958) Relationship of separation and depression to disease. A report on a hospitalized medical population. *Psychosom. Med.* **20**, 259-277

SCHMALE, A. H. (1969) Importance of life setting for disease onset. *Modern Treatment* **6**, 643-654

SIDMAN, J., MASON, J. W., BRADY, J. V. & THACH, J. S. (1962) Quantitative relations between avoidance behavior and pituitary–adrenal cortical activity in rhesus monkeys. *J. Exp. Anal. Behav.* **5**, 353

SINES, J. O., CLEELAND, C. & ADKINS, J. (1963) The behaviour of normal and stomach lesion susceptible rats in several learning situations. *J. Genet. Psychol.* **102**, 91-94

SPIRO, H. M. & MILLES, S. S. (1960) *New Engl. J. Med.* **26**, 286-294

SWEENEY, D. R., SCHMALE, A. H. & TINLING, D. C. (1970) Differentiation of the giving up affects, helplessness and hopelessness. *Arch. Gen. Psychiatr.* **23**, 378-382

WASHBURN, S. L. & HAMBURG, D. A. (1968) Aggressive behavior in old world monkeys and apes. In *Primates: Studies in Adaptation and Variability* (Jay, P., ed.), pp. 458-468, Holt, Rinehart & Winston, New York

WATSON, J. P., GAIND, R. & MARKS, I. M. (1971) Prolonged exposure; a rapid treatment for phobias. *Br. Med. J.* **1**, 13-15

WOLFF, C. T., HOFER, M. A. & MASON, J. W. (1964) Relationship between psychological defenses and mean urinary 17-hydroxycorticosteroid excretion rates. II. Methodological and theoretical considerations. *Psychosom. Med.* **26**, 592-609

Expectancy and the pituitary-adrenal system

SEYMOUR LEVINE, LARRY GOLDMAN* and GARY D. COOVER**

Department of Psychiatry, Stanford University School of Medicine, Stanford

Abstract The influence of changes in expectancies on the pituitary–adrenal system was examined in a series of experiments in rats. Using operant conditioning procedures it was demonstrated that extinction (non-reinforcement) following continuous reinforcement resulted in a marked increase in pituitary–adrenal activity. However, further experiments demonstrated that the pituitary–adrenal system can respond bi-directionally. Activation of this system is observed when the frequency of reinforcement is suddenly less than that obtained during training. Suppression is seen if reinforcement frequencies are suddenly greater than expected. These results are interpreted as consistent with the hope–disappointment dimension of Mowrer's theory.

Pituitary–adrenal responses during avoidance conditioning also demonstrate a reduction in the activation of this system when expectancies are developed and a reactivation when these expectancies are not fulfilled during extinction.

It is proposed that pituitary–adrenal activity may be suppressed when expectancies of reward are exceeded, while the failure to meet expectancies may be one of the primary environmental conditions which increases arousal and results in an increased secretion of ACTH from the pituitary.

Although the concept of stress has been in extensive use for at least three decades, its definition remains elusive. However stress is defined, there is little question that many affective states are accompanied by the hormonal events which have been so well described (Selye 1950). Thus, the pituitary–adrenal system is activated by physical injuries, other physiological events and pain, as well as aversive or threatening stimuli which do not actually cause physiological insult. Activation of the pituitary–adrenal system has also been

---

* *Address until October 1973:* Department of Anatomy, The Medical School, University of Birmingham, England.
** *Present address:* Department of Psychology, Northern Illinois University, De Kalb, Illinois 60115.

observed as a consequence of placing an organism in a novel environment (Friedman & Ader 1967; Levine & Treiman 1969). Although there have been extensive investigations of the affective states which are accompanied by the activation of the pituitary–adrenal system, most of these experiments have dealt primarily with aversive situations and the emotion of fear. Mowrer (1960) has proposed the emotion of 'hope', a positive motivational state which is elicited by situations previously paired with pleasure, analogous to the relationship between fear and pain. Furthermore, when this motivation of hope is aroused but not fulfilled (i.e. the expected reward does not occur) a state of disappointment or frustration results, which has both aversive (Adelman & Maatsch 1956; Wagner 1959) and energizing (Amsel 1958) properties similar to fear. Little experimental attention has been paid to this hope–disappointment dimension. We have recently been investigating the role of the pituitary–adrenal system in behaviours related to these emotional states. As these experiments progressed, the concept of failure of expectancies emerged as an important conceptual framework. The purpose of this present paper is to analyse the concept of stress along the dimensions of changes in expectancies, and to demonstrate that changes in reinforcement contingencies which fail to meet expectations (disappointment) result in an activation of the pituitary–adrenal system, while changes in expectancies leading to more reinforcement (elation) cause a rapid suppression of the pituitary–adrenal system.

Rats trained to press a lever for water on a continuous reinforcement schedule (CRF) showed an elevation of plasma corticosterone concentration as a consequence of extinction, while no such change occurred as a function of a reinforced session (Coover *et al.* 1971) (Fig. 1). These data suggest that frustration, here defined as the absence of a reinforcement occurring in a context where reinforcement is expected (Amsel 1958), does lead to pituitary–adrenal activation. It should also be noted that extinction also evokes in animals other responses which are best interpreted as emotional responses, such as biting the bar (Mowrer & Jones 1943) or attacking another animal if another animal is available (Ulrich & Azrin 1962).

Although the failure of expectancies emerged as the most reasonable interpretation of these data, it was also possible that implicit in changing from CRF to extinction, an element of novelty was introduced and that novelty itself could have caused all of the changes seen in pituitary–adrenal activity. However, if novelty were the primary causative event, then it would be expected that a shift from one reinforcement schedule to any reinforcement schedule which is different from that on which the animal has been performing over a long period of time, should lead to increased plasma corticosterone.

A series of experiments was undertaken which involved stabilizing an animal

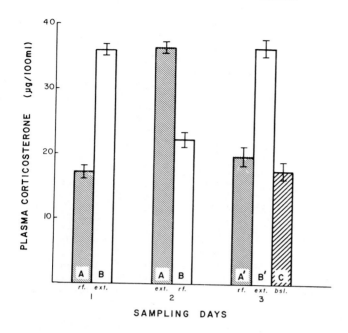

Fig. 1. Mean plasma corticosterone concentrations following 20-minute sessions of rein-forcement (rf.) and extinction (ext.). The rats were water deprived and trained to press a lever for water on a CRF schedule. On sampling day 1, group A was reinforced and group B extinguished. After five more sessions of CRF, group A was extinguished and B reinforced (sampling day 2). On sampling day 3, the treatments were again reversed, except that one-third of the rats of each group were sampled directly from their home cage at their usual testing time (group C), thus providing an estimate of pre-session, or basal (bsl.), plasma corticosterone concentration in water-deprived rats. (The vertical lines at the top of the bars indicate the standard error of the mean.)

on one reinforcement schedule and then shifting to a condition of either less frequent or no reinforcement, or more frequent reinforcement (Goldman et al. 1972). The results revealed two opposing effects on the pituitary–adrenal system of shifts in the amount of reward from that expected: an increase in plasma corticosterone resulted when a sudden decrease in the frequency of reward was presented and a decrease in plasma corticosterone was produced by an equally sudden increase in reward frequency. In one experiment animals were trained on a variable interval (VI) reinforcement schedule. On this schedule the animal is reinforced at an average of every 12 seconds but the reinforcement appears randomly between 7 and 17 seconds. Following a period of stabilization, these animals were shifted to either a condition of non-reinforcement (extinction) or continuous reinforcement. The results indicated

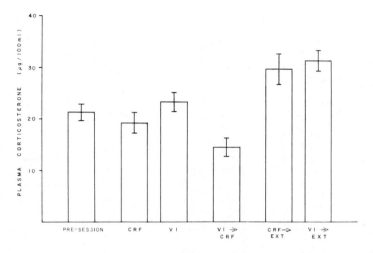

FIG. 2. Mean plasma corticosterone concentrations following normal (expected) sessions on CRF and VI, and sessions where there was a shift to a different schedule. All animals were first trained on CRF, and sampled after a reinforced (CRF) and a single extinction session (CRF → EXT), in a balanced design. They were then stabilized on a VI-12 schedule, and sampled after a reinforced session (VI) and a single session on CRF (VI → CRF) and extinction (VI → EXT), in a balanced design. All animals were also sampled directly from their home cage at the usual time of operant testing (pre-session). (Vertical lines represent standard error of the mean.)

(see Fig. 2) that after non-reinforcement there was the expected increment in plasma corticosterone. However, after a shift to continuous reinforcement there was a decrease in plasma corticosterone. The drop in plasma corticosterone observed after a shift from partial to continuous reinforcement is especially interesting, since there are few reports of rapid suppression of adrenal corticoids other than through electrical stimulation of certain brain areas (Mandell *et al.* 1963; Matheson *et al.* 1971). This decrease in plasma corticosterone concentration cannot be interpreted as a function of the increased water consumed on a CRF schedule. The animals shifted from VI to CRF were compared to animals that had been operating continuously on CRF. The plasma corticosterone values of the shifted animals are significantly below those of the non-shifted CRF animals, although the latter are actually consuming significantly more water than those animals shifted from VI to CRF.

Further experiments tended to confirm and extend these results, to indicate again that shifts which lead to less reinforcement or no reinforcement are capable of activating those systems which release adrenal corticoids and that shifts to higher reinforcement densities again lead to the suppression. In these

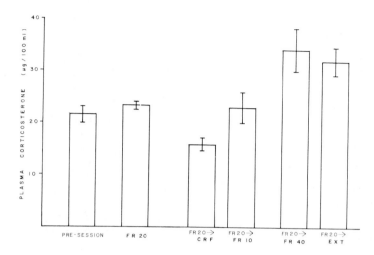

FIG. 3. The first two bars represent the mean plasma corticosterone concentrations for all animals sampled before (pre-session) and after (FR-20) a normal session of stabilized FR-20 responding. The last four bars represent the mean value for each of four subgroups after a shift from stabilized FR-20 to one session of either more frequent reward (CRF, FR-10) or less frequent or no reward (FR-40 and EXT). (Vertical lines indicate standard error of the mean.)

experiments animals were trained on a fixed ratio (FR) schedule which leads to reinforcement following a fixed number of bar presses. Thus, an animal was required to press the bar 20 times in order to achieve a single reinforcement. Once the animals were stabilized on this reinforcement schedule, they were shifted to either less reinforcement, that is, one reinforcement per 40 responses, or no reinforcement—extinction; or to greater reinforcement, that is, one reinforcement per 10 responses or reinforcement for every response (CRF).

Once again it was found (Fig. 3) that a shift to less reinforcement (FR-40) and extinction yielded a significant elevation of plasma corticoids, whereas shifting to CRF led to the suppression of adrenal corticoids. These results cannot be interpreted as simply due to the novelty of the new schedule, since shifts to more frequent reward did not activate the pituitary–adrenal system but suppressed it.

It is our conclusion that the pituitary–adrenal activation seen with extinction or reduced reward frequency is indicative of frustration. The term frustration is often used to refer to both the frustrating operation—removing or delaying the reward—as well as the emotional state thereby induced in the animal. In either case the pituitary–adrenal activation seen in the present experiment would properly be called a frustration effect, and could be interpreted along the disappointment dimension of Mowrer. The suppression of the pituitary–adrenal system with increased rates of reinforcement suggests that the pituitary–adrenal system is not simply activated by stress but can be affected bi-directionally. Thus, aversive stimulation and a reduction in reinforcement density—frustration—activates this system, while increasing reinforcement density—elation—can lead to a rapid decrease in pituitary–adrenal activity.

So far our hypotheses concerning expectancies and pituitary–adrenal activity have been based on shifts from one density of reinforcement to either higher or lower densities. The question remains as to whether or not we can observe activation of the pituitary–adrenal system with changes in expectancies that do not involve changes in densities of reinforcement. We investigated one situation which appears to meet these requirements.

If animals are trained on a predictable reinforcement schedule with fixed intervals (reinforcement every 45 seconds in this experiment), the behaviour of the animal in the operant situation exhibits the development of a temporal discrimination. After reinforcement there is a pause and the animal begins to respond as the interval approaches the time at which reinforcement normally would occur. The fixed interval (FI) schedule therefore is a predictable schedule during which the animal's behaviour demonstrates learning and discrimination. The variable interval (VI) schedule is best described as an unpredictable schedule with reinforcement occurring at both shorter and longer intervals than the average.

In the experiment to be described, two groups of animals were trained, one on a FI schedule and the other on a VI schedule. Although the density of reinforcements is essentially the same, the rate of responding is higher on the VI schedule, due to the fact that there is no post-reinforcement pause. Once the animals are stabilized on both the VI and the FI schedules, they are then shifted to the opposing schedule, VI animals to FI and FI animals to VI; or to state it another way, one set of animals is moved from an unpredictable to a predictable situation and the other animals are shifted from a predictable to an unpredictable situation. After a single shift session, blood was obtained for plasma corticosterone determinations. Examination of the behaviour indicated that on the day on which the shift was made, the density of reinforcement of the shifted animals was exactly the same, so that VI → FI animals received exactly the same number of reinforcements as FI → VI animals. However, an examination of the plasma corticoid concentrations indicated that while there was no change in those animals which were previously trained on VI and then shifted to FI, there was a significant elevation in those animals which were trained on FI and then shifted to VI (Fig. 4).

We propose that animals trained on a predictable FI schedule develop a set

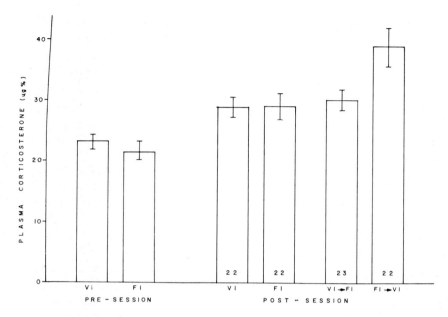

FIG. 4. Mean plasma corticosterone concentrations of water-deprived rats prior to (pre-session) and immediately following 20-minute operant sessions on variable interval (VI) and fixed interval (FI) reinforcement schedules (45-second interval), and after half of each group was shifted from their usual schedule to the other schedule (VI → FI or FI → VI). The number at the base of the bar is the mean number of reinforcements obtained by each group on the experimental day. (The vertical lines at the top of the bar graphs represent the standard error of the mean.)

of expectancies in relationship to the onset of reinforcement through constant repeated exposure to a situation in which a temporal discrimination is developed. When the set of predictable events is removed so that the expectancies are no longer present, this change in expectancy leads to an activation of the arousal system which subsequently increases pituitary–adrenal activity. Once again these data also fit within the framework of Mowrer's hypothesis of hope and disappointment. Changes from predictable to unpredictable events which thus increase ambiguity are sufficient conditions to cause affective states which are evidenced in increases in pituitary–adrenal activity. An animal which has been functioning in a random, ambiguous situation does not respond to a shift to a predictable situation since it has apparently not developed the concept of predictability within the given framework of the stimulus contingencies.

Investigators who have been working with the pituitary–adrenal system are acutely and aggravatingly aware of the lability of this system. To obtain resting or basal hormone levels extreme precautions have to be taken in order not to disturb the animal in even minimal ways. Most of the stimuli which activate these systems stem from changes in environmental events which are for the most part within the class of psychogenic stimuli. We propose that activation of the pituitary–adrenal system by environmental events which do not involve tissue damage can be accounted for by a two-stage model involving expectancies. Thus, either the lack of any previously established expectancies about the environment, or a change in expectancies, can result in an increased output of ACTH from the pituitary.

The processes involving neuroendocrine activation from lack of expectancies are best explained by a model elaborated by Sokolov (1960) to account for the general processes of habituation. The pattern of habituation is familiar. The subject is presented with an unexpected stimulus; he shows an alerting reaction. The physiological components of this reaction are well known—a general activation in the brain, decreased blood flow in the extremities, changes in the electrical resistance of the skin, and also an increase in circulating adrenal corticoids. If the stimulus is frequently repeated all of these reactions gradually diminish and eventually disappear, and the subject is said to be habituated, although it does appear that the pituitary–adrenal system habituates more slowly than the other observed reactions. Sokolov's model in essence is based on a matching system in the representation in the central nervous system of prior events whereby the organism is either habituated or gives an alerting reaction. This matching process is defined as the development of expectancies (Pribram & Melges 1969). Thus, the habituated organism has a set of prior events (expectancies) with which to deal with the environment and if the environment does not contain any new contingencies the habituated organism no longer responds with the physiological responses related to the alerting reaction. The activation of the pituitary–adrenal system by changes in expectancy is best accounted for in terms of the hypotheses presented in the hope and disappointment continuum of Mowrer.

Although we have discussed changes in expectancies in appetitive positive reward situations, there is evidence that modifications of pituitary–adrenal function also occur when expectancies are developed and changed during avoidance behaviour.

In a recent experiment (Coover *et al.* 1972) pituitary–adrenal function during shuttlebox avoidance learning was assessed by determining plasma corticosterone levels after the initial avoidance training session, after a session during the acquisition phase when 80% performance rate was initially attained, and after a session late in performance when avoidance learning was well stabilized.

Although there was a marked increase in pituitary–adrenal activity during the first avoidance session, which would be expected since the animals were receiving a high density of shocks, there was a slight but significant decrease in the post-session level between the initial and the first acquisition phase. However, once the animals were well stabilized there was a much larger decrease in pituitary–adrenal activity (Fig. 5). These data were interpreted as supporting the two-factor theory of avoidance learning (Rescorla & Solomon 1967). This theory proposes that there are two phases in avoidance learning—an initial classical conditioning phase in which the conditioned stimulus (CS) becomes a signal for shock, and an instrumental learning phase during which the animal learns to respond behaviourally to the CS. The high corticoid concentrations seen during the early stages of acquisition when the animal is not being shocked would tend to indicate the classical conditioning process whereby the CS has become a signal for the shock and is capable of eliciting a pituitary–adrenal response. However, during the later stage of avoidance there is a decrease in fear and arousal as the animals learn to predict and control the situations; that is, when the animal develops a set of expectancies about these stimulus contingencies.

The role of electric shocks in maintaining the avoidance behaviour is ambiguous. Increases in corticosterone concentration occurred during sessions when no shocks were received and the magnitude of the increases was not related to the number of shocks received or to the trials since the last shock. The acquired signal value of the CS is probably one important factor in the rise in corticosterone. Perhaps the very meaning of the electric shock changes once avoidance behaviour is acquired. At this stage shocks may play a positive role by aiding the animal in a process of learning predictability and control of the situation. Such learning reduces the stressfulness of the situation (Seligman & Meyer 1970; Weiss 1968). That shock is not the primary factor for the elevation of plasma corticosterone is further supported by data obtained during extinction of the avoidance response. A marked increase in pituitary–adrenal activity over previously stabilized values occurs during two types of forced extinction, (1) when the response is prevented and (2) when it is punished. During both kinds of forced extinction, avoidance and inter–trial responses cease, defecation increases, and a relatively large pituitary–adrenal response is reinstated. Thus, when the predictability and control that the rats had acquired no longer exist, an apparent increase in arousal and an increase in pituitary–adrenal function result.

We have hypothesized that one of the conditions that will activate the neuroendocrine mechanisms leading to subsequent release of ACTH is a change in expectancies developed during previously well-established behaviour. In the

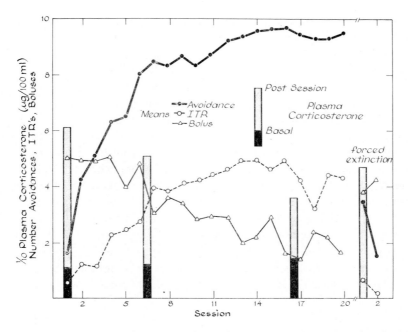

FIG. 5. Plasma corticosterone concentrations during two-way active avoidance learning. All rats were given 20 acquisition sessions of ten trials at one-minute intervals (CS-US interval = 5 seconds; US intensity = 0.5 mA). Blood samples were taken following the 1st, 6th or 7th, and 16th or 17th sessions. Pre-session (basal) samples were taken before training and 24 hours after the 5th or 7th and 15th or 17th sessions. A final session was given during which avoidance responses were punished (or blocked in a subsequent experiment), and plasma corticosterone concentrations were again determined after this session. The number of avoidance responses, inter-trial barrier crossing responses (ITR) and bolus droppings were taken on every session.

avoidance experiment, the disruption of ongoing avoidance behaviour, by blocking the response which had resulted in appropriate coping, was sufficient to reactivate the state of arousal which results in increased neuroendocrine responses, even though no shock was presented.

Unfortunately, neither the data nor the theoretical models presented solve the definitional problem of stress. Nor will they eliminate the current usage of this concept in psychological and psychiatric literature. We believe that we have presented a model based on environmental and cognitive factors which defines some of the parameters by which the information processed by the central nervous system is translated into the final common path of the hypo-thalamo–pituitary–adrenal system, to activate and suppress this system in the appropriate environmental circumstances.

ACKNOWLEDGEMENTS

This study was supported by Research Grant NICH&HD 02881 from the National Institutes of Health, ONR Contract N00014-67-A-0112-0009 and the Leslie Fund, Chicago. Seymour Levine is supported by USPHS Research Scientist Award 1-K05-MH-19936 from the National Institute of Mental Health. Larry Goldman is supported in part by Biological Sciences Training Grant MH 8304-06. Gary D. Coover is supported in part by USPHS Post-doctoral Research Fellowship 5-F02-MH-30312-02 (PS).

References

ADELMAN, H. M. & MAATSCH, J. L. (1956) Learning and extinction based upon frustration, food reward, and exploratory tendency. *J. Exp. Psychol.* **52**, 311-315

AMSEL, A. (1958) The role of frustrative nonreward in noncontinuous reward situations. *Psychol. Bull.* **55**, 102-119

COOVER, G. D., GOLDMAN, L. & LEVINE, S. (1971) Plasma corticosterone increases produced by extinction of operant behavior in rats. *Physiol. Behav.* **7**, 261-263

COOVER, G. D., URSIN, H. & LEVINE, S. (1972) Plasma corticosterone levels during active avoidance learning in rats. *J. Comp. Physiol. Psychol.* in press

FRIEDMAN, S. B. & ADER, R. (1967) Adrenocortical response to novelty and noxious stimulation. *Neuroendocrinology* **2**, 209-212

GOLDMAN, L., COOVER, G. D. & LEVINE, S. (1972) Bi-directional effects of reinforcement shifts on pituitary-adrenal activity. *Physiol. Behav.* in press

LEVINE, S. & TREIMAN, D. M. (1969) in *Physiology and Pathology of Adaptation Mechanisms* (Bajusz, E., ed.), pp. 171-184, Pergamon Press, Oxford

MANDELL, A., CHAPMAN, L., RAND, R. & WALTER, R. (1963) Plasma corticosteroids: changes in concentration after stimulation of hippocampus and amygdala. *Science (Wash. D.C.)* **139**, 1212

MATHESON, G. K., BRANCH, B. J. & TAYLOR, A. N. (1971) Effects of amygdaloid stimulation on pituitary-adrenal activity in conscious cats. *Brain Res.* **32**, 151-167

MOWRER, O. H. (1960) *Learning Theory and the Symbolic Processes*, Wiley, New York

MOWRER, O. H. & JONES, H. (1943) Extinction and behavior variability as functions of effortfulness of task. *J. Exp. Psychol.* **33**, 369-386

PRIBRAM, K. H. & MELGES, F. T. (1969) in *Handbook of Clinical Neurology*, vol. 3 (Vinken, P. J. & Bruyn, G. W., eds.), pp. 316-342, North-Holland, Amsterdam

RESCORLA, R. A. & SOLOMON, R. L. (1967) Two-process learning theory: relationships between Pavlovian conditioning and instrumental learning. *Psychol. Rev.* **74**, 151-182

SELIGMAN, M. & MEYER, B. (1970) Chronic fear and ulcers in rats as a function of the unpredictability of safety. *J. Comp. Physiol. Psychol.* **73**, 202-207

SELYE, H. (1950) *Stress*, Acta Inc., Montreal

SOKOLOV, E. N. (1960) in *The Central Nervous System and Behavior*, Transactions of the Third Conference, Josiah Macy Foundation, New York

ULRICH, R. E. & AZRIN, N. H. (1962) Reflexive fighting in response to aversive stimulation. *J. Exp. Anal. Behav.* **5**, 511-520

WAGNER, A. R. (1959) The role of reinforcement and nonreinforcement in an 'apparent frustration effect'. *J. Exp. Psychol.* **57**, 130-136

WEISS, J. M. (1968) Effects of coping responses on stress. *J. Comp. Physiol. Psychol.* **65**, 251-260

Discussion

Lader: What is the physiological significance of a rise in plasma corticosteroids? I presume these hormones are being used up peripherally and/or metabolized in the liver and a rise in plasma concentration may be due to increased production or decreased breakdown peripherally or both?

Levine: The utilization rate remains constant, as far as we know, and, of course, these hormones reach the brain in significant concentrations. We view this system as a sequence in which changes in or failure of expectancies lead to a complex set of Sokolov-type arousals, which also have built into them the neuroendocrine reflex, which leads to the rise in plasma ACTH and corticosteroids. Feedback to the brain from increased corticosteroids in plasma facilitates the extinction of those behaviours which are related to the set of situations in which the animal is involved, and this can lead to the extinction of 'freezing' responses and arousal responses. There is evidence that plasma corticosteroids have an inhibitory action on many processes in the brain.

Sachar: In our studies of response to stress in man (or change in expectancy, in your terms) the plasma ACTH concentration parallels plasma cortisol; the half-life of cortisol does not change in isotope studies. Since ACTH secretion parallels the burst of cortisol secretion, there must be a neuroendocrine mechanism mediating the response, but that raises problems for your theory, because ACTH and corticosteroids have opposite effects on extinction (de Wied *et al.* 1970).

Levine: In our experiments they are never secreted simultaneously. The peak plasma ACTH concentration precedes the peak corticosteroid output, which remains elevated for a much longer time.

Hofer: If you infused corticosterone at the point of extinction you might be able to answer part of Dr Sachar's question about the release of ACTH, which may occur before that of corticosterone.

Levine: There are several ways in which this could be analysed. You can block ACTH; you can implant cortisol in the median eminence. We haven't done this yet.

Gray: We have recently completed experiments on the extinction of a running response in which rats have been trained for positive reinforcement. Initially, we injected ACTH during extinction of the running response. All the previous literature led us to expect that this would enhance extinction. But we found that this procedure *retarded* extinction, and we have now repeated this finding three times (Gray 1971; P. Garrud, unpublished observations).

Sachar: Did you remove the adrenals? ACTH stimulates cortisol secretion in the intact animal.

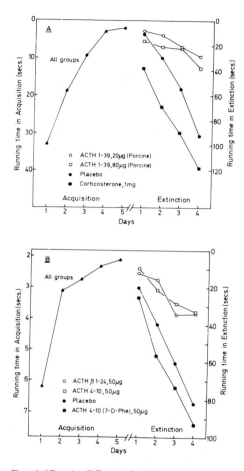

FIG. 1 (Gray). Effects of ACTH, corticosterone and ACTH-like peptides injected daily in extinction on running times during extinction of a food-rewarded running response in rats. Data from two unpublished experiments (A and B) by P. Garrud.

Gray: These were intact rats, which is why that finding on its own was uninterpretable. Garrud has gone on, still with intact animals, to study extinction in exactly comparable circumstances, injecting ACTH or corticosterone alone, or a fragment of the full ACTH molecule, ACTH 4-10. De Wied has suggested that this fragment only has effects on the brain and does not induce release of corticosteroids from the adrenal cortex. This seemed to be a good way to see whether our finding with the full molecule was due to an action of ACTH itself or of corticosterone. Garrud did the appropriate experiment and showed that corticosterone enhanced extinction and ACTH 4-10, like the full

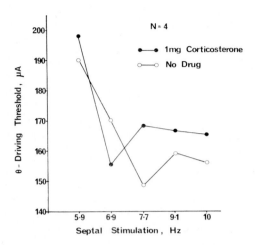

FIG. 2 (Gray). Effects of 1 mg corticosterone in 0.5 ml propylene glycol injected sub-cutaneously one hour before testing on the thresholds for septal driving of the hippocampal theta rhythm as a function of stimulation frequency. Average results from four male rats.

ACTH molecule, retarded extinction (Fig. 1). De Wied's group has reported similar findings in other behavioural situations (de Wied *et al.* 1970; van Wimersma Greidanus 1970). It seems that ACTH has one effect on behaviour, via a direct action on the brain, and corticosterone a different effect; the outcome must therefore depend on the exact balance between these two effects.

We are now investigating the action of these hormones on the septo-hippocampal system which I described (pp. 95-116). So far, our results indicate that corticosterone, in the behaviourally effective dose (i.e. the dose which produced more *rapid* extinction in Fig. 1), consistently lowers the threshold for production of a theta rhythm by septal stimulation selectively at a frequency of about 7 Hz (Fig. 2).

Weiss: Professor Levine, what happens if you just omit the shocks?

Levine: The problem then is to find the point at which the response is extinguished, because many animals keep on running if the shocks are omitted. It's not a gradual extinction. The animal continues to run and then suddenly stops, so one has to monitor each animal; we haven't yet done that. Our results are overall values for a population.

Gray: Your interpretation of your results is that you are dealing with change in expectation generally: I don't think the data support that. So far they seem to support only a mechanism for change from expectation in a direction which is unpleasant to the animal; plus perhaps one for response to punishment *per se*, as in the initial stages of avoidance learning (cf. my discussion of the two limbic mechanisms for control of corticosteroid release, p. 277). The only experiment which might be interpreted in the way you want is the one in which the rats were moved from a fixed interval to a variable interval schedule of reward. But this shift, even though the average density of reward is not reduced, does involve (until the rat learns that it is on a new schedule) some disappointed expectations of reward, namely the occasions when, at the termination of the fixed interval previously in operation, reward is not delivered. Thus the rise in steroid levels occasioned by this change in reinforcement schedule is not a critical test of the hypothesis that change from expectation in *any* direction is capable of producing such a rise. When the rats are changed from variable interval to continuous reinforcement there is certainly a change in expectation, but in a pleasant direction. And in these conditions you found the reverse of a steroid elevation.

Levine: There's a complication about that experiment. The problem is that the expectation *is* changed, but in order to train the rats initially, they are always trained on continuous reinforcement (CRF), so they have a past history of CRF. They are then shifted to the variable interval schedule; then we shift them back to CRF. We are now beginning to train the rats on high and low density reinforcement.

Weiss: 'Stress' is a very difficult subject to discuss in the context of this symposium. The whole concept of stress, if injected into the meeting on the level of mechanism, is not likely to help our understanding of the relationship between psychological processes and somatic disease. I say this not because it isn't very germane. Professor Levine has presented experiments which tell us about very important mechanisms, but these mechanisms are extremely complex and not yet well understood. To illustrate this complexity, we know that stress concerns not only the pituitary–adrenal system, which has been typically called the 'stress system', which is a great oversimplification. Other neuroendocrine systems are involved, including all the neurotransmitters in the brain—noradrenaline, as a neurotransmitter perhaps in the sympathetic nervous system, and the serotonergic and dopaminergic systems. Then one must consider the circulating peripheral catecholamines as well. All these enter into the mechanism by which the external signal is translated into a somatic response.

Engel: I feel equally concerned about the tendency to assume that the adrenocortical response necessarily has something to do with the development of somatic disease—that is, to invoke this as a psychosomatic mechanism. This is a unitary concept which has dominated our thinking since Selye and is too often brought in as *the* explanation. The pituitary–adrenal system is available for study because methods for measuring the hormones are available.

The correlations that have been demonstrated between stress and adrenocortical activation do not justify the assumption that this necessarily plays any role in such organic processes as develop in relation to stress. Quite different experimental designs will be necessary to test that thesis.

Sandler: I want to suggest that we distinguish conceptually between 'stress', as the external situation or the forces applied to the animal from the outside, and 'strain', which refers to the internal tensions or whatever disruptions occur within the animal as a consequence. Because experimental psychologists and physiologists can measure the external factors in a stressful situation they tend to equate this with the state of strain or inner disruption within the person or within the animal. It is important to distinguish internal and external tensions because such defence mechanisms as denial, rationalization and so on reduce the *strain* on the individual. They are successful coping mechanisms or adapting mechanisms.

Zanchetti: I would suggest further that we give up the use of the word 'stress'. I think it's a dangerous and useless word. It may seem useful because it is a unifying word, but it unifies our ignorance rather than our knowledge. It gives the false impression that we know much more than we really do about these stimuli and that a whole variety of stimuli can be grouped in a single category and one can therefore expect a single reaction, which is not so. It would be better to refer individually to the different stimuli and the different reactions.

References

DE WIED, D., WITTER, A. & LANDE, S. (1970) in *Progress in Brain Research*, vol. 32, *Pituitary, Adrenal and the Brain* (de Wied, D. & Weijnen, J. A. W. M., eds.), pp. 213-218, Elsevier, Amsterdam

GRAY, J. A. (1971) Effect of ACTH on extinction of rewarded behaviour is blocked by previous administration of ACTH. *Nature (Lond.)* **229**, 52-54

VAN WIMERSMA GREIDANUS, TJ. B. (1970) in *Progress in Brain Research*, vol. 32, *Pituitary, Adrenal and the Brain* (de Wied, D. & Weijnen, J. A. W. M., eds.), pp. 185-191, Elsevier, Amsterdam

Psychophysiological research and psychosomatic medicine

MALCOLM LADER

Institute of Psychiatry, University of London

Abstract The terms 'psychosomatic illness', 'psychosomatic medicine' and 'psychosomatic approach' are examined and found to be of limited scientific value. Such terms may even be counter-productive in diluting the eclecticism which is the strength of the psychosomatic concept. Psychophysiology is regarded as a laboratory discipline fundamental to psychosomatic research. It shares a common philosophical framework with the psychosomatic approach. Concepts such as arousal and response specificity have great heuristic value for psychosomatic research and enable a model of psychosomatic illness to be set up. Recent work on instrumental conditioning and feedback control of physiological measures suggests that effective therapeutic intervention in a range of psychosomatic conditions is now feasible.

The psychosomatic approach must use all the techniques of investigative medicine including epidemiological ones. Psychophysiological research could be carried out within an epidemiological frame work, for example, on immigrants. Whenever they are used, psychophysiological techniques should examine the relationships between functioning of all levels of the nervous system and peripheral physiological changes, normal and abnormal.

In this general paper, I shall examine the disciplines of psychosomatic medicine and psychophysiology, explore the relationship between them, and suggest some possible areas of research. Finally I shall discuss some of the possibilities for therapy, implicit in the psychophysiological research approach. My criticisms are intended to be constructive and I should stress that I approach the topic as a laboratory scientist seeking clarification of concepts and heuristic hypotheses. This is more rigorous and rigid than my use of existing concepts and hypotheses in my clinical practice. This is an opportune time to take stock because, whereas the area of psychosomatic medicine has lost its pristine promise, psychophysiological research is expanding and some useful theoretical guide-lines are emerging (Wittkower 1969).

PSYCHOSOMATIC ILLNESS

In the halcyon days of psychosomatic medicine certain illnesses were designated psychosomatic—bronchial asthma, essential hypertension, neurodermatitis, peptic ulcer, rheumatoid arthritis, thyrotoxicosis and ulcerative colitis (Schmale *et al.* 1970). Since then, many other conditions have been labelled psychosomatic, including diabetes mellitus, anorexia nervosa, obesity, psychogenic vomiting, abdominal pain, diarrhoea, irritable colon, coronary thrombosis, torticollis and writer's cramp. There is no general agreement on which illnesses are psychosomatic. No true definition, or even description, of psychosomatic illness has ever been proposed, the only common characteristic being the assumption that psychological factors play a major role in their complex, obscure aetiology (Lipowski 1968). On these grounds alone the term 'psychosomatic illness' has limited scientific value. Furthermore, the term is counter-productive, because designating some illnesses as psychosomatic implies that the remainder are not psychosomatic. Thus, the eclecticism of approach which is the strength of psychosomatic medicine is concentrated on only a minority of diseases and not brought to bear on the bulk of illness.

A second criticism of the concept of psychosomatic illness is that it implies more homogeneity with respect to aetiology than may, in fact, be justified. Many conditions labelled psychosomatic are mere syndromes and represent a range of conditions, from those in which physical factors predominate almost exclusively, through those in which both physical and psychological factors are important, to those in which psychological factors appear to strongly influence the clinical picture. For example, patients with torticollis range from those with obvious and constant neurological deficits to those whose conditions varied with psychological factors (Meares 1971; Meares and Lader 1971). Furthermore, the relative contribution of physical and psychological factors may vary at different stages of a disease. Again taking torticollis as an example, it may present with marked psychological precipitants, initially pursue a fluctuating course, then become more severe and constant until finally other neurological abnormalities, such as widespread dystonias, occur.

Psychosomatic medicine

If the concept of psychosomatic illness is too imprecise to be of much value, psychosomatic medicine is not definable as the study and management of psychosomatic illnesses. Could the concept of psychosomatic medicine be diluted to represent a vague entity without clear boundaries but containing certain core conditions about which all agree? Thus, psychosomatic medicine would be allocated a position lying between general medicine and psychiatry along an 'organic–psychogenic' continuum. However, this continuum itself reflects clinical convenience rather than any scientific criterion. The addition of an ill-defined area lying between medicine and psychiatry would only represent operational clinical organization.

Psychosomatic approach

Although neither psychosomatic illnesses nor psychosomatic medicine can be adequately defined, one could assert that the nub of the matter concerns the method of approach to ill people. Wolff (1970) has summed up this approach thus: 'The majority of illnesses are multi-factorial in origin and psychological and somatic aspects and their mutual interaction need to be taken into consideration in every patient who is ill'. These sentiments are admirable and unexceptionable but consist of little more than eclecticism regarding aetiology. Again, this could be counter-productive, since the existence of some practitioners rightly stressing such an approach could lessen the onus on other clinicians to assess all aspects of the patient.

This is only a minor criticism. The real problem is the difficulty in isolating and assessing such psychological factors, especially as the term 'psychological' is often taken to mean 'psychic' rather than 'behavioural'. Furthermore, there seems to be no unanimity about conceptualizing the way in which 'psychic' factors influence somatic processes. This is essentially a philosophical problem which needs either solution or successful evasion in order that a fruitful scientific approach can be adopted. Unfortunately, many advocates of the psychosomatic approach perpetuate a Cartesian dualist model. For example, one of the leading proponents of the psychosomatic approach (Engel 1967) states: 'The psychosomatic approach is concerned with the ways in which psychological and somatic factors interact in the whole sequence of events that constitute a particular disease experience'. Engel implies an 'interface' with a complex 'coding' between mind and body.

Psychosomatic research

The basic strength of psychosomatic concepts lies not in their application to clinical treatment nor in their philosophical implications but in the unique nature of the research which they foster. Lewis (1954) concluded: 'It is best to recognize that 'psychosomatic' refers to an ill-defined area of interest, with constantly changing boundaries, in which there are manifest relations between events best studied by psychological methods and events best studied by physiological methods'. That statement emphasizes the research aspects of the topic: the simultaneous study of at least two major aspects of human functioning. Most forms of clinical research rely heavily on the basic sciences, although the dependence is by no means solely one-way. Psychophysiology could fulfil a basic scientific role with respect to psychosomatic medicine in somewhat the same way that neurophysiology already does for neurology.

PSYCHOPHYSIOLOGY

Psychophysiology has been defined as 'the science which concerns those physiological activities which underlie or relate to psychic functions' (Darrow 1964). This is a wide definition and in practice certain aspects of both psychology and physiology have received most attention. The emotions have been the particular focus because they are accompanied by physiological changes, often very marked. This has isolated psychophysiology somewhat, because emotions have not been in the mainstream of either psychology or physiology, either in theory or experiment.

In practical terms, psychophysiology has become formalized in many centres as the recording on a polygraph of several physiological measures from the intact human while psychological variables are manipulated. The alteration in psychological variables can be either artificially induced in the laboratory or spontaneous changes in natural conditions; the latter include diseases. The measures used are autonomic, such as heart rate, forearm blood flow and palmar sweat gland activity; somatic, such as respiration and electromyogram; and 'central'—the electroencephalogram and its responses. Often, the physiological concepts used have been antiquated, mainly because most psychophysiologists, being basically psychologists, have received only desultory physiological training or none at all. For example, autonomic measures dominate psychophysiology with attempts to measure 'autonomic balance' or 'lability'. These approaches stem from the Eppinger-Hess concept of vagotonia–sympatheticotonia, discarded by physiologists 30 years ago.

I shall outline three areas where psychophysiology can contribute substantially to psychosomatic medicine: in sharing a common philosophical framework which evades problems of the mind–body conundrum; in providing concepts based on laboratory research; and in suggesting possible therapeutic procedures.

A philosophy for psychophysiology and psychosomatic medicine

Graham (1971) has stated: 'Psychosomatic medicine is clinical psycho-physiology, and there is no question in psychophysiology that does not have an exactly analogous counterpart in psychosomatic medicine'. Both disciplines can adopt an identical philosophy with respect to the mind–body relationship, namely the assumption of psychophysical parallelism. In this epistemological model psychic events and physiological events are parallel and simultaneous and neither can occur alone or produce direct effects one on the other. An interface between mind and body is assumed but it is regarded as both extensive and simple, although one cannot say whether this relationship differs fundamentally from, for example, the translation of physiological events into biochemical processes. By adopting parallelism, research in this area can sidestep the issue of the *mind–body* relationship because it is simplified to the point where it can be ignored and research can concentrate on the relationship between *behavioural* and *physiological* events. From the scientific standpoint there is no fundamental difference between the observation of avoidance of a phobic object, the noting of a facial expression of fear, the measurement of any increase in heart rate on a polygraph and the analysis of verbal reports. But the subjective changes presumed to relate to the verbal reports are epiphenomena not susceptible to scientific analysis, although, of course, of profound clinical significance (Kräupl Taylor 1972). Therefore, anxiety can never *cause* tachycardia but verbal reports of anxiety are usually accompanied by tachycardia, both being produced by the same stimulus. Psychological events are regarded as *responses*, not as stimuli as in other psychosomatic models.

Concepts in psychophysiology

There are several basic concepts in psychophysiology which have much relevance to the psychosomatic approach. They include responsivity, stress, arousal, response specificity, cognitive interaction and conditioning of physiological measures. Of these, I shall discuss two with relation to the psychosomatic research approach, namely arousal and response specificity.

The concept of arousal

Psychophysiology is much concerned with the translation of physiological changes into psychological terms. Ax (1964) has stated that psychophysiology examines the 'code' between psychology and physiology. Up to a point an empirical approach suffices; that is, groups of patients can be compared with respect to a range of physiological variables or the pattern of changes noted in those measures in response to stimulation. But eventually the findings need extrapolating into terms of central processes, firstly of a neurophysiological character; but, most important, they need to be translated into behavioural equivalents. It is a simplification to assume that the physiological variables in some way assess a specific emotion such as hostility, either qualitatively in terms of its idiosyncratic nature or quantitatively in terms of its intensity. Although the experiencing of any emotion is regularly accompanied by increased levels of many physiological indices, a whole range of intense affects, such as rage, panic, ecstasy and revulsion, are all accompanied by such changes. Some differentiation in the physiological response patterning which accompanies different affects such as anxiety and anger has been noted and some contrasts found (Ax 1953; Bernick et al. 1971; Schachter 1957), but the differences were not marked. Subtle differences might be expected to occur, as it would be maladaptive for stereotyped response patterns to result after stimulation of differing affect-producing properties. The physiological needs of a 'fight' response are very different from those of 'fright' or 'flight'.

As an interim method of handling these problems the concept of 'arousal', 'activation' or 'energy mobilization' has been developed (Duffy 1962; Malmo 1959). This concept is of most use when it refers to a behavioural continuum ranging from deep sleep to lighter stages of sleep, to drowsiness and an unalert state, through to usual working levels of alertness and wakefulness. Higher levels of arousal are accompanied by disquiet, edginess and uneasiness and then by affective states such as anxiety, anger, disgust, pleasure and resentment. At the upper extreme of the continuum are the over-aroused states such as terror, horror, revulsion, rage and ecstasy. Thus, the concept of arousal is inserted as a construct between the physiological measures and the concomitant affect. Inasmuch as heightened arousal is a necessary condition for the experience of an emotion, any physiological measure will reflect the emotional intensity. Before changes in a physiological measure can be confidently ascribed to changes in the level of any particular emotion such as anxiety, self-reports and assessments of overt behavioural changes must be consistent.

If the different physiological measures were all indicators of one common level of arousal, high correlations between the measures across subjects would be expected. In general, inter-correlations of this type have been uniformly low, a finding which has led to the questioning of the validity of the concept of arousal as a unitary factor. The concept has been divided on an anatomical basis into many components, such as 'autonomic' arousal and 'cortical' arousal.

In this context, it is interesting to note that Sherrington, and especially Head (1925), put forward the concept of 'vigilance' of the central nervous system to refer to its degree of integrative function and preparedness; vigilance was not seen as a unitary factor in the organism but was applicable to anatomical or functional divisions of the central nervous system, as in 'vigilance level of the spinal cord'.

There are several reasons why close relationships between various physiological measures may not be found. There is often a tendency for psychophysiologists to become so bemused with the psychological implications of their measures that they overlook the physiological aspects. For example, the physical conditions of the experiment must not vary, since they profoundly affect many physiological measures; for example, skin blood flow is dependent on the ambient temperature. Also the measures differ in their ranges so that one measure, such as vasoconstriction, may have reached an extreme point and no longer be reactive whereas another, such as the electromyogram, may still be capable of showing marked changes in level.

Clear distinctions are necessary between the use of physiological measures to compare putative arousal levels between individuals, within individuals on different occasions, within individuals on the one occasion under different conditions, and repeated readings in each subject under a fixed condition. Too much is expected of physiological measures as indicators of arousal level: they are most worthwhile in assessing changes within a subject when the experimental conditions are altered, for example, by asking a resting subject to do difficult mental arithmetic (Mathews & Lader 1971).

The concept of response specificity

This concept is crucial to psychosomatic medicine because it provides a theoretical springboard for the notion that the degree of vulnerability of the physiological systems of the body varies from subject to subject (Lipowski 1968). More important, there are experimental data to support this view.

In the first form of response specificity, termed 'intra-stressor stereotypy', each subject shows a similar pattern of response to a repeated stimulus situation. For example, in one individual a marked heart-rate response and a minimal electromyographic response might be recorded to a stimulus and the same preponderance of heart-rate response will occur whenever the stimulus is repeated. The hypothesis is supported by the results of two studies which showed the patterns of autonomic responses to repeated stimuli to remain stable (Lacey 1950; Lacey & VanLehn 1952). In two further studies (Lacey *et al.* 1952; Lacey & Lacey 1958), an extension of the concept was attempted by examining the patterns of response to different stimulation procedures. Some subjects responded with reproducible patterns ('inter-stressor stereotypy') but others were more variable. Schnore's (1959) experiments supported Lacey's findings but Wenger *et al.* (1961) claimed that the similarity between the stimuli used and their temporal proximity could account for the similarities of response.

Davis (1957) proposed a different model and showed that response patterns were related more to the type of the stimulus than to the idiosyncrasies of the subject. This is termed 'situational stereotypy'. Other investigators have concluded that both individual and stimulus factors are important in determining the pattern of a response (Engel 1960; Engel & Bickford 1961). More recently, Lacey (1967) proposed that different somatic processes have different roles to play in the execution of different types of behaviour: in other words, situational stereotypy is acknowledged to be important. This certainly corresponds with general physiological principles regarding the adaptive and integrative nature of bodily responses.

A related principle, also of direct relevance to psychosomatic research, is that of 'symptom specificity'. This states 'that in psychiatric patients presenting a somatic complaint, the particular physiological mechanism of that complaint is specifically susceptible to activation by stressful experience' (Malmo *et al.* 1950). A group of patients was divided into those with head and neck pains and those with cardiovascular complaints; the latter patients were found to have higher mean heart rates and heart-rate variability, while the other subgroup had higher mean electromyographic levels in the neck muscles (Malmo & Shagass 1949). Support comes from Sainsbury & Gibson's (1954) study in which they divided their anxious patients into a group complaining of headache and a group with aching of the limbs or rheumatic pains. The group with headache had higher frontalis tension, while the latter group had higher forearm muscle activity.

Specificity has been a key concept in psychosomatic medicine for a long time although the nature of the specificity has been disputed. Alexander's (1950) theory postulates that 'physiological responses to emotional stimuli, both normal and morbid, vary according to the nature of the precipitating emotional state'. When correlations between psychological events and particular psychosomatic conditions have been attempted, ambitious aetiological theories have been constructed with subsequent disillusionment with the whole concept of 'specificity'. The psychophysiological concept of patterns of response depending partly on the stimulation situation and partly on individual idiosyncrasies allows more flexibility in the experimental approach to the whole problem of specificity in psychosomatic medicine, because the examination of

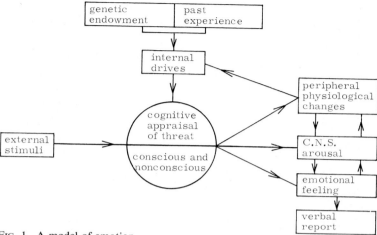

FIG. 1. A model of emotion.

the relationship between psychophysiological responses and psychosomatic illnesses can be attempted at a more fundamental level. However, it need not elucidate the psychological or personality factors (traits, emotions, attitudes, defences, ego-strength and so on) which are supposed to be related to particular psychosomatic conditions, because the relationships between psychophysiological responses and personality factors are themselves tenuous.

A synthesis

From these concepts and from the experimental data underlying them a model of the psychophysiological basis for psychosomatic symptoms can be tentatively proposed (Fig. 1). The extrapolation from the laboratory to real life is always perilous, but this model at least enables one to collate the available information, to highlight the inconsistencies and to suggest further areas of research. The model is derived from many people's ideas and work and represents a consensus rather than an original exposition.

The first element in the model is the physical and social environment which impinges on the subject in the form of stimuli. These stimuli may be unconditioned or may have been secondarily conditioned. They interact with intra-individual factors such as personality traits and previous learning and produce in some degree a non-specific arousal state. Clues in the environment are interpreted by the subject and the interaction between this cognitive information and the arousal results in a specific emotion being experienced. The interactions between sensory stimuli and individual factors may occur in consciousness or, presumably, at the subconscious symbolic level. In the former case, the emotional experience will appear to the subject to be appropriate to the environmental situation or, if inappropriate, the reasons for the irrationality will be apparent. Conversely, if the interaction takes place at a symbolic level the emotion may appear irrational. These interactions govern both the intensity and the quality of the affect.

Physiological changes occur as concomitants to the emotion. Four factors can be invoked to explain differing individual patterns of response: (1) The emotion produced depends to some extent on the particular person's previous experiences, and physiological patterns vary according to the emotion. (2) Differences between individuals in response to affectively neutral stimuli are marked and should be no less variable than responses to emotionally evocative stimuli. (3) The intensity of the response varies from individual to individual and various systems of the body will be differentially involved at the various levels of response. (4) Awareness of peripheral autonomic changes varies from system to system so that differential feedback could occur.

This stimulus–response model provides a basic paradigm for the psychosomatic approach. Environmental influences of a severe, chronic or abnormal nature interact with factors in the subject such as personality, previous experience, expectations and attitudes, and result in a high arousal state, which if of sufficient intensity is accompanied by an emotion. Even if an emotion is not evoked, physiological changes will still occur. These changes may be morbidly severe in one particular system of the body if the factors enumerated above lead to excessive responses in that system.

A second element in the model is loss of adaptation. Under conditions of high arousal the subject is much less able to adapt to a continuing or repetitive stimulus. Once a high level of arousal has been attained the condition tends to become self-perpetuating, as adaptation becomes negligible and untrammelled rises in physiological activity can occur (Lader & Mathews 1968). It should be noted that the responses induced are normal in quality but abnormal in intensity and duration. In time, the function of the bodily system showing the largest responses becomes impaired, anatomical changes are superimposed and a 'psychosomatic illness' appears.

Experimental strategies

As outlined earlier, there is some experimental support for this general model.

Physiological changes in high arousal states have been studied in detail and each subject shows some idiosyncrasies of pattern of response: adaptation is slow in intense arousal states; cognitive clues are important in the elicitation of emotion. This model also suggests that emotions are responses to stimuli and not stimuli in their own right producing physiological abnormalities, although feedback processes are not precluded.

Physiological mechanisms have been examined experimentally in patients with psychosomatic illnesses. For example, respiratory function can be assessed under various conditions of stressful stimulation in asthmatics (Purcell & Weiss 1970). Abnormal patterns or amplitudes of physiological measures have been found in such patients with psychosomatic conditions, but interpretation is difficult. Pathological changes in the affected organ could be secondary to the psychosomatic condition, not causal to it. Similarly, abnormal responses in other systems could be due to emotional changes following the physical symptoms, rather than reflecting a general psychophysiological imbalance. Firm evidence of this type would only be obtained if there was an invariant relationship between the abnormal physiological measures and the degree of pathology during cycles of exacerbation and remission.

An alternative approach is the epidemiological one (Scotch & Geiger 1962). The psychophysiological research approach could with advantage be combined with the epidemiological in prospective studies, such as the large-scale screening of thousands of normal people. This technique of screening well populations has been used to some extent (Whitby 1968), but to be of use for psychosomatic complaints new techniques need to be developed. Thus, a range of physiological measures would be assessed in the normal population under laboratory conditions of rest and during stressful stimuli. A longterm follow-up would then be mounted to note changes in the life circumstances of the probands and to detect psychosomatic illnesses. Unfortunately, such a study would be very expensive and wasteful because of the small numbers of people falling ill with any one complaint. Despite the large amounts of useful normative information which would accrue, such a study is not economically viable.

The problem is essentially to narrow the search to the population at risk. One could concentrate on a selected group of the initially screened population, such as those with the highest gastric acidity. The probability of illness is still fairly low and one might miss important factors because present data are still so scanty.

An alternative is to study a population at risk because of changes in life-events. For example, recently bereaved individuals, in whom the incidence of illness is known to be high, have been studied (Parkes 1970). Unfortunately, there are ethical problems of intrusion into private grief and the follow-up itself, if it were intensive and sympathetic, might afford some support and actually lessen the incidence of subsequent pathology. Another population at risk is immigrants (Groen 1971), and here the problems of mounting a prospective psychophysiological study are not insuperable. Immigrants to a new country should receive a health check anyway, especially if their living conditions have been substandard in their country of origin, and if the new country has advanced, free medical services the follow-up becomes almost automatic. A study of this type would still be expensive but not prohibitively so and the results would be important.

THERAPEUTIC INTERVENTION

The third topic which I shall outline briefly concerns the possibility of therapeutic intervention. In this sphere, too, psychophysiology has suggested important new methods of influencing abnormal physiological systems, using instrumental conditioning techniques or feedback of information.

Autonomic conditioning

Autonomic responses were formerly believed to be only conditionable using classical, Pavlovian conditioning techniques (Kimble 1961) but studies from both the Russian and American literature have recently suggested otherwise. The most impressive evidence comes from some elegantly controlled animal experiments by Miller and his associates who have modified autonomic responses using operant conditioning techniques (Miller 1969). Thus, thirsty dogs were trained to decrease or increase their salivation rate by giving them water as a reward for the appropriate spontaneous response. Using various reinforcers, the heart rates of rats were accelerated or decelerated, their intestinal activity was increased or decreased, their glomerular filtration rate and renal blood flow augmented or reduced, their electroencephalograms increased or decreased in voltage, their gastric or tail blood flow raised or lowered, or their blood pressures increased or decreased. Each physiological response could be modified independently of the others and one ear of a rat could even be made to vasodilate without affecting the other.

In studies of human subjects the results have been equivocal. Alterations in levels of autonomic activity have been induced with schedules of instrumental reinforcement and both blood pressure and heart rate can be controlled (Engel & Hansen 1966; Shapiro *et al.* 1970; Schwartz *et al.* 1971). It is not clear whether this control is true instrumental conditioning or whether it is mediated by cognitive and somatic intervention, such as respiration changes, muscle tensing or imagining various scenes (Katkin & Murray 1968). We tried to examine this problem rigorously by attempting to condition the galvanic skin responses differentially on the two sides of the body, and were unsuccessful (Whittome & Lader 1972).

Whatever the mechanism, the ability to teach patients to control their physiological responses using reinforcement or feedback may be a powerful therapeutic tool. For example, patients have been able to lessen the incidence of their premature ventricular contractions (Weiss & Engel 1971) and their headaches (Budzynski *et al.* 1970).

CONCLUSION

Psychophysiology could play as important a role in psychosomatic medicine as physiology does in general medicine. That it does not yet do so is partly due to the relatively inchoate state of the discipline itself, but is mainly attributable to the different philosophical framework, non-scientific approach and excessive claims made by some enthusiastic advocates of the psychosomatic approach. This approach still seeks chimaeric connections between psyche and soma and believes that emotions 'cause' bodily changes.

The psychosomatic approach must use all the techniques of contemporary investigative medicine. The epidemiological and sociological approaches must not be neglected (World Health Organization 1964), but the basic biological sciences have still not been fully applied to psychosomatic problems. When it is so used, psychophysiology should examine the relationships between the functioning of the nervous system at all levels and peripheral physiological changes, both normal and abnormal. Man is both the most intelligent and the most emotional of animals and it is fitting that the former faculty be used to study the latter phenomenon.

References

ALEXANDER, F. (1950) *Psychosomatic Medicine*, Norton, New York

Ax, A. F. (1953) The physiological differentiation between fear and anger in humans. *Psychosom. Med.* **15**, 433-442

Ax, A. F. (1964) Goals and methods of psychophysiology. *Psychophysiology* **1**, 8-25

BERNICK, N., KLING, A. & BOROWITZ, G. (1971) Physiologic differentiation of sexual arousal and anxiety. *Psychosom. Med.* **33**, 341-352

Büdzynski, T., Stoyva, J. & Adler, C. (1970) Feedback induced muscle relaxation: application to tension headache. *Behav. Ther. Exp. Psychiat.* **1**, 205-210

Darrow, C. W. (1964) Psychophysiology, yesterday, today, and tomorrow. *Psychophysiology* **1**, 4-7

Davis, R. C. (1957) Response patterns. *Trans. N.Y. Acad. Sci.* **19**, 731-739

Duffy, E. (1962) *Activation and Behavior*, Wiley, New York

Engel, B. T. (1960) Stimulus-response and individual-response specificity. *Arch. Gen. Psychiatr.* **2**, 305-313

Engel, B. T. & Bickford, A. F. (1961) Response specificity. Stimulus-response and individual-response specificity in essential hypertensives. *Arch. Gen. Psychiatr.* **5**, 478-489

Engel, B. T. & Hansen, S. P. (1966) Operant conditioning of heart rate slowing. *Psychophysiology* **3**, 176-187

Engel, G. L. (1967) The concept of psychosomatic disorder. *J. Psychosom. Res.* **11**, 3-9

Graham, D. T. (1971) Psychophysiology and medicine. *Psychophysiology* **8**, 121-131

Groen, J. J. (1971) in *Society, Stress and Disease*, vol. 1, *The Psychosocial Environment and Psychosomatic Diseases* (Levi, L., ed.), pp. 91-109, Oxford University Press, London

Head, H. (1925) The conception of nervous and mental energy. II. Vigilance: a physiological state of the nervous system. *Br. J. Psychol.* **14**, 126-147

Katkin, E. S. & Murray, E. N. (1968) Instrumental conditioning of autonomically mediated behavior: theoretical and methodological issues. *Psychol. Bull.* **70**, 52-68

Kimble, G. A. (1961) *Hilgard and Marquis' Conditioning and Learning*, Appleton-Century-Crofts, New York

Kräupl Taylor, F. (1972) A logical analysis of the medico-psychological concept of disease. Part 2. *Psychol. Med.* **2**, 7-16

Lacey, J. I. (1950) Individual differences in somatic response patterns. *J. Comp. Physiol. Psychol.* **43**, 338-350

Lacey, J. I. (1967) in *Psychological Stress: Issues in Research* (Appley, M. H. & Trumbull, R., eds.), pp. 14-37, Appleton-Century-Crofts, New York

Lacey, J. I. & Lacey, B. C. (1958) Verification and extension of the principle of autonomic response-stereotypy. *Am. J. Psychol.* **71**, 50-73

Lacey, J. I. & VanLehn, R. (1952) Differential emphasis in somatic response to stress. An experimental study. *Psychosom. Med.* **14**, 71-81

Lacey, J. I., Bateman, D. E. & VanLehn, R. (1952) Autonomic response specificity and Rorschach color responses. *Psychosom. Med.* **14**, 256-260

Lader, M. H. & Mathews, A. M. (1968) Physiological basis of desensitization. *Behav. Res. Ther.* **6**, 411-421

Lewis, A. J. (1954) Aspetti di medicina psicosomatica. *Recent Prog. Med.* **16**, 434-453

Lipowski, Z. J. (1968) Review of consultation psychiatry and psychosomatic medicine. III. Theoretical issues. *Psychosom. Med.* **30**, 395-422

Malmo, R. B. (1959) Activation: a neuropsychological dimension. *Psychol. Rev.* **66**, 367-386

Malmo, R. B. & Shagass, C. (1949) Physiologic study of symptom mechanisms in psychiatric patients under stress. *Psychosom. Med.* **11**, 25-29

Malmo, R. B., Shagass, C. & Davis, F. H. (1950) Symptom specificity and bodily reactions during psychiatric interview. *Psychosom. Med.* **12**, 362-376

Mathews, A. M. & Lader, M. H. (1971) An evaluation of forearm blood flow as a psychophysiological measure. *Psychophysiology* **8**, 509-524

Meares, R. (1971) Features which distinguish groups of spasmodic torticollis. *J. Psychosom. Res.* **15**, 1-11

Meares, R. & Lader, M. H. (1971) Electromyographic studies in patients with spasmodic torticollis. *J. Psychosom. Res.* **15**, 13-18

Miller, N. E. (1969) Learning of visceral and glandular responses. *Science (Wash. D.C.)* **163**, 434-438

PARKES, M. (1970) in *Modern Trends in Psychosomatic Medicine* (Hill, O. W., ed.), pp. 71-80, Butterworths, London

PURCELL, K. & WEISS, J. H. (1970) in *Symptoms of Psychopathology. A Handbook* (Costello, C. G., ed.), pp. 597-623, Wiley, New York

SAINSBURY, P. & GIBSON, J. G. (1954) Symptoms of anxiety and tension and the accompanying physiological changes in the muscular system. *J. Neurol. Neurosurg. Psychiatr.* **17**, 216-224

SCHACHTER, J. (1957) Pain, fear, and anger in hypertensives and normotensives. A psycho-physiological study. *Psychosom. Med.* **19**, 17-29

SCHMALE, A. H., MEYEROWITZ, S. & TINLING, D. C. (1970) in *Modern Trends in Psychosomatic Medicine* (Hill, O. W., ed.), pp. 1-25, Butterworths, London

SCHNORE, M. M. (1959) Individual patterns of physiological activity as function of task differences and degree of arousal. *J. Exp. Psychol.* **58**, 117-128

SCHWARTZ, G. E., SHAPIRO, D. & TURSKY, B. (1971) Learned control of cardiovascular integration in man through operant conditioning. *Psychosom. Med.* **33**, 57-62

SCOTCH, N. A. & GEIGER, H. J. (1962) The epidemiology of rheumatoid arthritis. *a.* A review with special attention to social factors. *J. Chronic Dis.* **15**, 1037-1087

SHAPIRO, D., TURSKY, B. & SCHWARTZ, G. E. (1970) Differentiation of heart rate and systolic blood pressure in man by operant conditioning. *Psychosom. Med.* **32**, 417-423

WEISS, T. & ENGEL, B. T. (1971) Operant conditioning of heart rate in patients with premature ventricular contractions. *Psychosom. Med.* **33**, 301-321

WENGER, M. A., CLEMENS, T. L., COLEMAN, D. R., CULLEN, T. D. & ENGEL, B. T. (1961) Autonomic response specificity. *Psychosom. Med.* **23**, 185-193

WHITBY, L. G. (1968) Well-population screening. *Br. J. Hosp. Med.* **1**, 79-91

WHITTOME, V. J. & LADER, M. H. (1972) Operant G.S.R. conditioning: an attempt to condition differentially the two sides of the body. *J. Psychosom. Res.* **16**, 421-424

WITTKOWER, E. D. (1969) A global survey of psychosomatic medicine. *Int. J. Psychiatr.* **7**, 499-516

WOLFF, H. H. (1970) in *Modern Trends in Psychosomatic Medicine* (Hill, O. W., ed.), pp. 298-311, Butterworths, London

WORLD HEALTH ORGANIZATION (1964) Psychosomatic disorders. *W.H.O. Tech. Rep. Ser.* no. 275

Discussion

Hinde: Your model needs to take into account the various components of the nervous system. These include physiological and cognitive as well as neural factors.

Sandler: And one might add adaptive coping and defensive responses.

Aitken: Two other components—genetic make-up and previous learning—are in the past and therefore temporarily distinguished from cognitive factors which are in the present.

Hinde: We seem to have been talking about unpleasant rather than pleasant emotions, the implication being that in the model we are limiting emotional states mostly to those associated with high arousal. You specifically mentioned affective states such as anxiety, anger, disgust, and you did include pleasure, and also ecstasy, but the majority of the emotions mentioned were unpleasant.

Lader: This may be more a theoretical than a practical objection. Subjects viewing comedy films have similar catecholamine responses to those of subjects shown disturbing films (Levi 1972), so I think the intensity of the arousal is important, not the quality.

Hinde: Can't an emotion be associated with low arousal?

Lader: I am suggesting that 'arousal' is a substrate on which an emotion is grafted.

Sandler: The depressive mood (as distinct from depressive illness) is associated with low arousal, and includes a feeling-state—in other words, an 'emotion'.

Lader: Depressive *illnesses* are very complex. Our experimental results suggest that the important thing in depression, as far as peripheral physiology, and perhaps the EEG as well, is concerned, is whether there is psychomotor retardation or agitation or both. If retardation is present, the physiological measures themselves are so altered that they can no longer be used as indicators of central arousal (Lader & Wing 1969; Noble & Lader 1971*a,b*).

Engel: I think we should also distinguish conservation–withdrawal, which is a state of reduced arousal in a physiological sense and not necessarily always experienced as a depressive mood; it may equally well be experienced simply as fatigue.

I agree with Dr Lader in questioning the usefulness of adhering to the terminology of psychosomatic illness or psychosomatic disease and I have earlier proposed that our concern should be with elucidation of the psychosomatic *factors* in disease (Engel 1967). Here I am thinking in terms of the interface between events, experiences or disturbances which can be identified and expressed in psychological and/or behavioural terms, and processes that lead ultimately to tissue or organ pathology of one sort or another. Furthermore, I don't feel that it is helpful to substitute the word 'psychophysiology' for 'psychosomatic factors', because the term psychosomatic, awkward as it is, at least has the merit of being associated with a concept of a somatic disease—that is, the presence of pathological changes in tissues or in organs, about which pathologists would be in agreement. I am differentiating here such organic states from what are in effect either the physiological concomitants of affects or biological defence patterns. I further distinguish conversion symptoms, which are somatic symptoms expressing ideas or fantasies (Schmale 1969). Ulcerative colitis, leukaemia or a myocardial infarction would be examples of the first. Palpitation, sweating, fatigue or vomiting may be concomitants of affects or biological defences, while pain, paralysis or a feeling of being unable to breathe may be conversion symptoms. Hyperventilation is a reaction to the conversion symptom of breathlessness and leads to hypocapnia as a consequence of blowing off carbon dioxide. Hypocapnia in this example I regard as a complication of conversion (Engel 1968, 1970). Dr Lader's model stops well short of this. It tells us only that there is an intimate relationship between mental or psychological events (systems for regulating behaviour, if you wish), and changes in the body. It doesn't tell us how the bodily changes which we measure, often determined by the techniques that happen to be available rather than by what is in fact relevant, really occur. It doesn't help us to answer, for example, Dr Weiss's question of why his rats develop ulcers. Why not something else? Why only in the lower, acid-secreting part of the stomach? How do you explain the ulcers that develop in the non-secretory (rumenal) part of the stomach of the rat under different experimental conditions?

Lader: I am reacting against the classical psychosomatic approach, which is to think in terms of an interface between the psyche and the soma. This may be clinically valid but scientifically it is sterile, because one cannot use scientific methods to investigate such an interface. Substituting that system of epistemology called 'parallelism', one assumes that the relationship between psyche and soma is extremely simple (even though it may be very extensive) and one can 'dismiss' the psyche and follow a psychophysiological approach which investigates the relationship between behavioural events and somatic events.

Engel: The implication in that approach is that there is a direct pathway to the development of somatic pathology, without reference to the different tissues that are affected.

On the issue of parallelism, I agree that one cannot jump from one frame of reference to another, but I would also argue that in order to conceptualize what constitute meaningful events for the individual in whom a somatic disturbance occurs, it is necessary to use psychological data; that is, to get information from and about the person who is sick or at risk. This has to be done retrospectively first, in order to construct hypotheses. You are then in a position to move in either of two directions, though both have their drawbacks. One is to set up a prospective study; you indicated one kind of difficulty with prospective studies. Another difficulty is that you have to wait until the appropriate circumstance occurs or recurs. Clinical science is by its very nature naturalistic, not experimental, in the sense that nature (or society), not the investigator, provides the critical circumstance. At least that is so when one is studying disease in man. The other direction is to go to the experimental psychologist who may give some clues about what constitutes at least a parallel situation in animals. Dr Weiss's study is an example and one, incidentally, which is an exception to the general rule that most so-called 'stress' experiments have had little resemblance to what occurs in the real life of man, or of the rat for that matter. Too few experimental psychologists have bothered to work enough with clinicians who are knowledgeable about the settings in which human disease develops.

Hill: Dr Lader, can we clarify your theoretical position on this? You described the psychophysical parallel with the soma and said that emotion as experienced was to be treated as an epiphenomenon—something outside your system, not involved in the responses. But you also said that the cognitive appraisal, in the light of the past or of the situation arising from the inputs, was inside the system and thus is an intervening variable. Is that right?

Lader: I used the word epiphenomenon because it is a familiar term but the correct term for the intrapsychic experience is 'noumenon'. The cognitive factors need not necessarily be experienced consciously, but there is an appraisal.

Hill: In human terms, the cognitive appraisal presumably involves the appraisal of the meaning of events and the consequences which might follow from this or that course of action?

Lader: One has to assume a symbolic interaction at times, because in clinical practice and in lay experience one observes irrational emotions—that is, emotions which cannot be explained on the available overt evidence.

Sandler: I disagree with this view, because all we know are subjective experiences. Even in the most precise scientific experiments we are still dealing with sense data when we read dials or make measurements. So the noumena are the assumed real world; the stimuli we assume to exist are not known except through subjective experience.

Dr Engel, why can't we move from one frame of reference to another, if we know that we are doing so? Surely we use a frame of reference according to what our business is, and we become hamstrung and muscle-bound intellectually if we try to remain within one frame of reference only, using it to encompass things occurring at these different levels.

Engel: I meant that we can't move directly from one frame of reference to another in the sense of interchanging terms or concepts or of ascribing causality: we can only deal with covariance. Certain environmental events or psychological experiences coincide with or are followed by certain bodily changes. We cannot say, for example, that repression 'causes' cardiac acceleration or use 'regression', a psychological term, to refer to physiological events. Further, psychological data are arbitrary constructs of the investigator which have no independent existence, unlike the entities we measure by physiological or biochemical means. Thus, the data an investigator collects from a patient during psychosomatic or psychophysiological research fall into two classes. There are raw behavioural or psychological data—what the patient is saying, how he looks, changes in his facial expression, bodily movements, the sequence of sentences or sequence of associations. Simultaneously the investigator is measuring certain physiological or biochemical parameters, or is concerned with the subsequent development of a pathological somatic process. But his psychological categories are his own abstract constructs. They may be constructs that many people agree on; for example, there is certainly general agreement in this symposium that there is a category of psychological phenomena that we call emotion or affect or feeling. We may also speak of cognitive processes, or about 'relating' behaviour, or intrapsychic processes, defences, coping mechanisms and so on. But actually all these psychological processes not only do not exist as entities; they all are going on at once, so to speak. Hence, though it seems clear that there is a parallelism (to use that term now) between a manifest affect, for example, and changes in biochemical or physiological parameters, one has no way of knowing that the affect is the significant variable contributing to, much less responsible for, the biochemical change. It may have been some other aspect of the behaviour which one didn't happen to record or wasn't interested in.

A physiological measurement may, however, allow for a certain kind of dissection of the psychological categories. I referred earlier (p. 272) to Greene's finding that some anxious people during cardiac catheterization showed a rise in plasma growth hormone concentrations and others did not (Greene *et al.* 1970). When he included whether or not these anxious patients were engaging with others in the laboratory, he was able to show that the covariance was with the degree of relating and not with the interpreted anxiety *per se.* Investigators not interested in or not aware of the 'relating' type of behaviour would have concluded that growth hormone secretion had an inconsistent association with anxiety. Or if the series had been small and not representative they might have had a preponderance of anxious–relating or anxious–non-relating people and have drawn the wrong conclusion.

Gray: If one of Dr Weiss's escape-avoidance yoked-control rats that developed ulcers went to his doctor, would the doctor not need some word to distinguish this kind of ulcer from viral influenza? And if it's not 'psychosomatic', won't it have to be some other word? Dr Weiss's experiments clearly showed that the key variable producing the ulcers was the behavioural situation in which the animal found itself. It didn't seem to have much to do with the sorts of things usually regarded as the main causative agents of diseases like tuberculosis or pneumonia. I am not saying that there are no psychological factors in determining who gets worse pneumonia or who suffers most from tuberculosis, but the balance of factors is usually very different in the two cases.

Engel: The determination of disease is far more complex than you imply.

There are quantitative as well as qualitative factors in respect to both the environmental influences and host resistance. For example, Dr Weiss confined his rats for 48 hours in his experimental situation. If the rats had been confined for six hours, a much smaller number would have developed ulcers. If a different strain or species had been used, again the results would have been different. His experiment was intentionally designed to study behavioural factors and he deliberately set out to make that the overriding factor, just as Koch selected the most susceptible animal and the most certain route of administration to prove the relationship between the tubercle bacillus and tuberculosis. But in the everyday life of rats and men the development of gastric ulcer or tuberculosis is determined by multiple factors. A particular factor (restraint or tubercle bacilli) may determine the kind of process that will develop but will not alone determine why or when it develops, even among those exposed to the pathogenic factor.

Gray: You may not produce an illness until you have given a sufficient number of bacilli, but this doesn't mean that the bacillus is not the causative agent in an infectious disease.

Engel: It depends what you want to take as the 'cause'. Let me describe a 'new' disease and examine the 'cause'. This disease is characterized by painful redness and blistering of the skin. Now, what you think of as the 'cause' may depend on what information you have. If you appreciate that the lesion occurs only in exposed areas of the skin and only after exposure to the sun you will call it 'sunburn' and say the rays of the sun are the 'cause'. But an epidemiologist may demonstrate in a large population that the more pigmented people are, the less likely they are to develop this disease. Hence no amount of exposure to sun will produce the disease in some people while others who tan will lose their susceptibility upon recovery. The biochemist demonstrates that this pigmentation is related to the ability to form melanin and the geneticist will prove that to a large extent this capacity is genetically determined. Hence someone might argue that the disease is 'caused' by a deficient capacity to form melanin and even refer to it as a biochemical or a genetic disease, like phenylketonuria, which only becomes manifest upon ingestion of phenylalanine. But a psychologically oriented investigator may call attention to behavioural factors which lead poorly pigmented persons to expose themselves unnecessarily to the sun (comparable to rats restrained too long developing gastric ulcers). Such concepts of 'cause' are archaic remnants of misapplied Newtonian physics, whereas this area requires a field theory approach. I cannot think of *any* disease where it is justified to ascribe the aetiology to a single factor. The only thing one can say about the tubercle bacillus, for example, is that it is responsible for the specific pathology of tuberculosis; whether, when, and how tuberculosis develops in any individual is a function of multiple factors. Ader has shown that the tendency of mice and rats to develop clinical disease in response to a variety of viruses and other pathogenic agents depends on the nature of current and/or previous life situations and that one cannot predict for any single agent what the direction of the effect will be (Ader 1970).

Henry: In preliminary work we find a great increase in the incidence of breast tumours in female mice of the CBA strain exposed to the altered social stimuli that are associated with removal of the young. Mammary adenoma is a condition that has not commonly been associated with psychological factors. But as work in neuroendocrinology and neurophysiology advances, the neuro-humoral mechanisms by which the 'psyche' or brain can influence the rest of the 'soma' or body become more clearly identified. Extensive and sustained changes in vascular resistance and hormonal levels, together with altered autonomic nerve impulse traffic, force us to consider the role of the CNS even in conditions such as Cushing's disease (Gifford & Gunderson 1970), chronic interstitial nephritis (Henry *et al.* 1971) and prostatic hypertrophy (Steele *et al.* 1971) . At the same time there are good reasons to question the use of the word 'psychosomatic', because it can so easily be thought of as implying a dualism of psyche and soma.

Aitken: Dr Lader pointed out two dangers in the use of the term 'psycho-somatic'. Firstly, if we teach students that only certain diseases are psycho-somatic, we encourage the wrong attitude, because psychological factors are relevant in some degree to the distress experienced in all diseases. Secondly, if we believe that psychological factors can *produce* disease, we may be going beyond the evidence, and hence permit the danger of future disillusionment. That essential hypertension, for example, may be found more commonly in certain types of personality has been mentioned (pp. 242, 248) but is the evidence valid? What is *not* in doubt is that psychological factors can con-tribute to the nature of the symptomatology and the mode of presentation in the sick role (Robinson 1969). Here, use of the word psychosomatic should be less contentious.

Hill: Would anyone like to define what is meant by 'psychological factors'?

Weiss: I have used the term so I can at least give my working definition of it. By 'operation of psychological factors' I mean the arrangement of sensory stimuli which in and of themselves do not usually elicit somatic stress responses, and which can, in different arrangement, produce different effects in the animals. I completely restrict it to external stimuli. This is a purely behaviour-istic and possibly rather shallow way of looking at it, but it is simply my operational definition. I agree with Dr Henry that you cannot make a good separation between external or sensory on one hand and somatic on the other, because a stimulus is not a stimulus until it gets inside the organism. I can only say that when we use the term 'psychological', we are trying to define an area roughly so that we can communicate in a rather general way.

Hill: Emotions are not psychological factors, then?

Weiss: Not in my experiments.

Hinde: Neither, according to this definition, are psychological differences between individuals, which lead to their responding in different ways to the same stimulus.

Levine: A stimulus is not a stimulus unless the apparatus exists in the brain to do something with it. If you give the same stimulus to a hippocampectomized animal and to an intact one they don't respond in the same way. In a sense the operated animal does not process the information about that stimulus.

Henry: There is good evidence that the mammalian nervous system has certain gross functional subdivisions. Dr Lader's model might be strengthened if one assigned certain of his functions to appropriate regions. Thus his non-specific 'state of arousal' is associated with the reticular formation; his 'physiological changes', such as those involved in cardiovascular and respiratory regulation, are primarily hindbrain. His 'drives' and subjective experience of specific emotion would suggest limbic system activity, and previous learning sets appear to be connected to the association areas in the temporal and parietal cortex.

Levine: I wish it were as simple as this!

Sachar: We have to make certain decisions for the purpose of the meeting. If we are talking about what 'psychological factors' contribute to the development of somatic diseases, we can make distinctions. There should be some illnesses in which the psychological contribution is trivial, and others in which it is large and significant. Then we could clarify what we mean by 'psychological factors'. Here again we could include a whole unmanageable range of behaviours, including the man who becomes preoccupied with his business affairs and walks in front of a truck, or the man who lies too long in the sun. But the aim of this meeting is to consider those psychological factors which specifically include emotional responses, and to ask whether the pattern of responses that we call 'emotional' can contribute in a significant way to the susceptibility to or exacerbation of certain somatic disease states. While that still leaves a very large mire to get tangled in, it does allow us for purposes of this symposium to rule out some of these other matters.

Donald: We must be careful in interpreting these differences entirely as differences in the behaviour of people's minds or of the CNS. An example of how wrong one can be is that for many years many shrewd clinicians described two groups among people with acute or chronic respiratory failure, usually chronic bronchitics who were acutely ill with pneumonia. They spoke from their experience of 'fighters' who were manifestly breathing with great difficulty but battling to remain alive and 'non-fighters' who floated gently away and died without any apparent dyspnoea or distress. In the last fifteen years it has been shown that the 'fighters' had, in fact, fairly normal Pco_2 levels, their ventilatory response remained normal and they continued to ventilate even although they were suffering from severe dyspnoea. The 'non-fighters' have now been shown to be people who had been given oxygen at high Pco_2 levels. They were, in fact, narcotized by carbon dioxide, they were underventilating and died quietly, often on high oxygen. What was an obvious division of a random population into 'fighters' and 'non-fighters' in fact was describing two different physiological situations. All one can conclude from this is that we must beware of filling in the gaps in our knowledge with this type of false interpretation.

Engel: A good model to illustrate how somatic pathology may develop by virtue of an interaction between a psychophysiological stress response and a pre-existing defect, either genetic or acquired, is the adrenogenital syndrome. This involves a genetic defect in the biosynthesis of adrenal steroids which results in a relatively greater proportion of androgenic steroid being secreted relative to cortisol. Bush & Mahesh (1959) reported a young woman with such a defect who had a sudden onset of hirsutism. She had an identical twin sister who demonstrated the same defect in steroid biosynthesis but had no significant hirsutism. The hirsute girl had been in an upset emotional state whereas her twin was tranquil. One can postulate that the patient had the usual pituitary–adrenal cortical stress response but because of this defect in the biogenesis of cortisol she secreted excessive androgenic steroids and developed hirsutism as a consequence. Her twin, not under stress, has so far remained unafflicted. If and when she is stressed she too may develop the manifest syndrome.

References

ADER, R. (1970) The effects of early life experiences on developmental processes and susceptibility to disease in animals. In *Minnesota Symposia on Child Development* (Hill, J. P., ed.), vol. IV, pp. 3-35, University of Minnesota Press, Minneapolis

BUSH, J. & MAHESH, V. B. (1959) Adrenocortical hyperfunction with sudden onset of hirsutism. *J. Endocrinol.* **18**, 1-25

ENGEL, G. L. (1967) The concept of psychosomatic disorder. *J. Psychosom. Res.* **11**, 3-9

ENGEL, G. L. (1968) A reconsideration of the role of conversion in somatic disease. *Compr. Psychiatr.* **9**, 316-326

ENGEL, G. L. (1970) Conversion symptoms. In *Signs and Symptoms* (MacBryde, C. M. & Blacklow, R. S., eds.), 5th edn, pp. 650-668, Lippincott, Philadelphia

GIFFORD, S. & GUNDERSON, J. G. (1970) Cushing's disease as a psychosomatic disorder: a selective review of the clinical and experimental literature and a report of ten cases. *Perspect. Biol. Med.* **14**, 169-221

GREENE, W. A., CONRON, G., SCHALCH, D. S. & SCHREINER, B. F. (1970) Psychologic correlates of growth hormone and adrenal secretory responses of patients undergoing cardiac catheterization. *Psychosom. Med.* **32**, 599-614

HENRY, J. P., ELY, D. L., STEPHENS, P. M., RATCLIFFE, H. L., SANTISTEBAN, G. A. & SHAPIRO, A. P. (1971) The role of psychosocial factors in the development of arteriosclerosis in CBA mice: observations on the heart, kidney, and aorta. *Atherosclerosis* **14**, 203-218

LEVI, L. (1972) Sympathoadrenomedullary responses to 'pleasant' and 'unpleasant' psychosocial stimuli. *Acta Med. Scand.*, suppl. 528, 55-73

LADER, M. H. & WING, L. (1969) Physiological measures in agitated and retarded depressed patients. *J. Psychiatr. Res.* **7**, 89-100

NOBLE, P. J. & LADER, M. H. (1971a) Depressive illness, pulse rate and forearm blood flow. *Br. J. Psychiatr.* **119**, 261-266

NOBLE, P. J. & LADER, M. H. (1971b) Salivary secretion and depressive illness: a physiological and psychometric study. *Psychol. Med.* **1**, 372-376

ROBINSON, J. O. (1969) Symptoms and the discovery of high blood pressure. *J. Psychosom. Res.* **13**, 157-161

SCHMALE, A. H. (1969) Somatic expressions and consequences of conversion reactions. *N.Y. State J. Med.* **69**, 1878-1884

STEELE, R., LEES, R. E. M., KRAUS, A. S. & RAO, C. (1971) Sexual factors in the epidemiology of cancer of the prostate. *J. Chronic Dis.* **24**, 29-37

Emotions and heart diseases

GÖSTA TIBBLIN, BODIL LINDSTRÖM and SUZANNE ANDER
Department of Medicine, University of Göteborg

Abstract　The relationship between cardiovascular changes, emotions and heart diseases is analysed. It is evident that we are working with a two-way system. From our studies in Göteborg we suggest that the perception of bodily sensations can be linked to cardiovascular diseases.

It is familiar to anyone who has flushed with embarrassment, sweated with anxiety, or felt his heart pounding while physically at rest, that emotions can bring about changes in the cardiovascular system. We also know that the cardiovascular system can contribute to emotions, but from the clinical point of view the fact that emotions may be caused by heart diseases seems to have been neglected. This review will follow four lines, as shown in Fig. 1.

CARDIOVASCULAR CHANGES

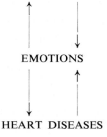

EMOTIONS

HEART DISEASES

FIG. 1

The literature on this subject is enormous. David Jenkins (1971) could summarize over 160 papers dealing only with the psychological and social precursors of one disease—coronary artery disease. Our aim here is to deal only with knowledge which the busy clinician could actually use in the course of his daily work.

EMOTIONS INFLUENCING THE CARDIOVASCULAR SYSTEM

It has been demonstrated that psychogenic stimuli may be accompanied by measurable changes in pulse rate, blood pressure, stroke volume and cardiac output (Grollman 1929; Hickam *et al.* 1948). We are accustomed to consider the effects of such stimuli in terms of overt behaviour such as fear, anxiety and rage. However, Burch & de Pasquale (1965) have shown that many stimuli from outside which influence the circulation may be unnoticed by the patient. The orienting reflex, which is initiated by any change in the subject's environment that arouses a questioning reaction, can be produced by extremely mild stimuli and still result in profound peripheral vascular responses. For example, the ringing of a telephone in the distance may produce a reduction in the volume and rate of digital inflow secondary to constriction of digital blood vessels. They have also shown that environmental stimuli can increase the venous tone in an isolated venous segment to a great extent. Stuart Wolf (1966) has pointed out that the diving reflex can elucidate the relation between emotion and the cardiovascular system. The elements of the oxygen-conserving diving reflex have been identified as follows: bradycardia, decreased flow of blood to the skin and viscera, fall in blood pH, and a rise in lactic acid, CO_2 and potassium in the plasma. In man the reflex is subject to considerable modulation by higher centres of the brain. Stressful situations were found to be capable of initiating the reflex without immersion of the face in water. Thus the bradycardia of vasovagal fainting was shown to be accompanied by slower respiration and a rapid rise in lactic acid and potassium concentrations. The reflex may be inhibited, facilitated or even induced in response to symbolic stimuli—words or events with emotional significance to the individual concerned.

CARDIOVASCULAR CHANGES INFLUENCING EMOTIONS

Stuart Valins (1970) has shown that peripheral body changes can be viewed as determinants of emotions. Bodily changes evoke cognitive processes which influence our subjective and behavioural reactions to emotional stimuli. Valins provided subjects with false information about their bodily reactions and studied the effects of this information on their subjective reactions to emotional stimuli. Slides of female nudes were shown to a group of males while they heard heart-like sounds that they thought were coming from themselves, but which were prerecorded. One group heard an increase in their heart rate in relation to five slides, and no change to five other slides. A second group heard a decrease in response to five of the slides and no change to five others. The effect of the false information about heart rate was assessed using measures of the subjects' attraction to the nudes. The data from the various measures were all quite similar. Nudes to which subjects heard their heart rate change, whether an increase or decrease, were liked significantly more than nudes to which they heard no change in their heart rate. In other words, subjects were oriented toward liking the nudes to which their hearts had reacted.

Lacey & Lacey (1970) have studied the autonomic nervous system and how the afferent inputs from the thoracic cavities back to the brain act and their effects on brain function. We know that increases in heart rate and blood pressure cause many electrophysiological changes. The EEG shows signs of an inhibited cortex. Zanchetti and his collaborators (Bartorelli et al. 1960) have produced evidence that an increase in cardiovascular feedback can inhibit such cortical activities as sham rage. Lacey & Lacey (1970) think that the temporary hypertension and tachycardia observable in acute emotional states (and in aroused behaviour of all sorts) may not be the direct index of so-called 'arousal' or 'activation' they are so often considered to be. Instead they may be signs of the attempt of the organism to calm down the turmoil produced inside the body by appropriate stimulating circumstances. They have also suggested that one important effect of cardiovascular activity on behaviour is to 'gate' environmental inputs and motor outputs into and out of the central nervous system, in that elevations in blood pressure and heart rate may in appropriate circumstances produce a kind of 'stimulus barrier' and that decreases in heart rate and blood pressure may produce a more permeable 'stimulus barrier'.

EMOTIONS INFLUENCING HEART DISEASES

In his review of psychological and social precursors of coronary artery disease Jenkins (1971) summarizes by saying that status incongruity (for example, high income and low education), social mobility, anxiety and neuroticism, life dissatisfactions and a coronary-prone behaviour pattern (competitiveness, dedication to work, urgency about time and inability to relax), are all factors which precede coronary artery disease. Do these behavioural risk factors raise the chances of coronary artery disease by elevating traditional risk factors, or do they work through other mechanisms, such as catecholamines? This also raises the question whether these psychosocial variables are specific for coronary artery disease or also act in other severe diseases or death in general.

The necessity of changing one's adaptation creates dissatisfaction, an unpleasant situation that might be experienced as stress. Kits van Heijningen & Treurniet (1966) observed that rejection by a loved person, a setback in work or a loss of prestige often preceded the clinical occurrence of coronary artery disease. Russek (1967) found that prolonged emotional strain associated with job responsibility preceded the attack of coronary artery disease in 91 of his series of 100 young patients. Bruhn *et al.* (1968) describe the 'emotional strain' resulting from frustrating longterm struggles with persisting life problems as often preceding death from coronary artery disease.

Can grief kill, and kill through the heart? Parkes *et al.* (1969) studied a total of 4486 widowers of 55 years of age and older. They followed them for nine years after the deaths of their wives. Of these men, 5% died during the first six months of bereavement—40% above the expected rate. Half of these deaths were from heart disease. It is possible that bereavement acts as an aggravating or as a precipitating factor in coronary artery disease.

EMOTIONS IN HEART DISEASES

John Hunter (1728–1793) was aware that emotion is a threat to the patient with heart disease. He once stated that his life was 'in the hands of any rascal who chose to annoy and tease him'. He died, as you may know, while attending a board meeting at St George's Hospital.

The occurrence of angina pectoris during sleep has long been of interest to the clinician. Nowlin *et al.* (1965) could show that most episodes of nocturnal angina were associated with REM sleep which preceded the electrocardiographic changes. The general characteristics of the dreams which preceded an awakening with chest pain tended to fall into two categories: those involving strenuous physical activity and those involving the emotions of fear, anger or frustration. REM sleep is characterized by increases in blood pressure, respiratory rate, cardiac irregularities and catecholamines. It is also quite likely that fatal cerebrovascular accidents and myocardial infarction may be precipitated by the autonomic storm of REM sleep. Perlman *et al.* (1971) conducted a controlled survey of 105 patients admitted to hospital in congestive heart failure, and they found that 'acute emotional events' occurred in the three days preceding hospitalization in 49% of them. Such events occurred in only 24% in a matched control group. The events seen most frequently were: violent arguments (14%), actual or threatened separation from family members (13%), and anxious change or threat of change in routine circumstances (5%).

The precise mechanism by which psychological factors mediate bodily changes is obscure. The course of events might be as follows: with emotional stress, the adrenals are stimulated to release adrenergic catecholamines and glucocorticoids. As the catecholamines increase the need of the myocardium for oxygen, the normal heart compensates by augmented coronary blood flow. In myocardial insufficiency there may be failure of augmentation resulting in myocardial hypoxia. This, in turn, causes depletion of cardiac magnesium and potassium and an increase in sodium content, a condition to which the adrenal glucocorticoids contribute. The electrolyte imbalance aggravates the hypoxia, thereby creating a vicious circle. This imbalance disturbs cardiac conduction and contractility with consequent likelihood of arrhythmia, severe myocardial ischaemia or congestive heart failure. Burch has pointed out that psychogenic reflexes may be responsible for a peripheral venous constriction (Burch & de Pasquale 1965). As approximately 80% of the circulating blood volume is contained within the venous system, a large increase in systemic venous return may cause acute pulmonary oedema in patients with severe cardiac disease, and also sudden death.

Wolf (1966) speculates that the oxygen-conserving diving reflex may contribute to sudden death in angina pectoris and myocardial infarction. The association of intense anxiety or fear with an anginal attack or infarction might thus accentuate or even initiate the reflex. The bradycardia, the rise in blood potassium and the slight acidification of the blood together with the local products of ischaemia increase the likelihood of fatal arrhythmia.

HEART DISEASES INFLUENCING EMOTIONS

A cardiac arrest is a sudden and frightening experience which calls forth a variety of defence mechanisms. Denial of the event or its consequences was found to be the most important of these mechanisms in a study by Druss & Kornfeld (1967). The survivors of the cardiac arrest maintained an unperturbed front, but they had intense dreams of violent death. This type of dream was not reported by the groups of patients who had myocardial infarction without cardiac arrest.

The denial of fear is commonly found in coronary care units. In many cases it means an unusual ability to deny being frightened rather than to accept the fear at face value. Fear or reasonable concern is so appropriate for myocardial infarction patients that its total absence is peculiar.

The second most common emotional reaction to myocardial infarction is depression. Dependence problems have been reported. Both emotional and biological changes have been reported when patients were transferred from the coronary care unit. Dependence problems are related to discharge from the hospital. Dominian & Dobson (1969) could show that ten times more patients without outpatient appointments after the hospital stay were re-referred to the hospital, than were those of a similar group which had an appointment arranged. This indicates one way of dealing with this problem.

During the recovery process psychological response mechanisms are of great importance. A common view is that during the acute phase of a heart disease fear dominates the picture. Physical restriction usually gives rise to feelings of helplessness, vulnerability and depression. As the recovery process proceeds, different types of response patterns come into play. Initial depression and dependency disappear as the patient regains confidence and self-mastery. Sometimes, however, dependency responses become permanently established. In some instances a cardiac illness can be more disabling by superimposing a cardiac neurosis on the original disease.

STUDIES IN GÖTEBORG

In Göteborg, Sweden, a Heart Control Programme has been established in cooperation with the World Health Organization. It includes population studies, preventive trials and the medical care of more than 1000 myocardial infarction patients (Ander *et al.* 1971; Wilhelmsen *et al.* 1972). It has been possible to confirm that three months after myocardial infarction, the patients have significantly more symptoms related to anxiety, exhaustion, depression and irritability than do a control group from the population of Göteborg. Among the myocardial infarction patients more suicides occurred than expected. One of our interests has been to study the reporting of symptoms in different categories of subjects with and without heart diseases.

A random sample of men, born in 1919, who took part in a population study which was also a screening examination for individuals at high risk for developing myocardial infarction, were asked 30 questions regarding nervous and somatic symptoms. Angina pectoris was defined according to the criteria of Rose and Blackburn (1968). In order to study how persons with high blood pressure report symptoms, those with overt diseases including angina pectoris were excluded and the remaining 517 subjects were divided into two groups: above and below a systolic blood pressure of 175.

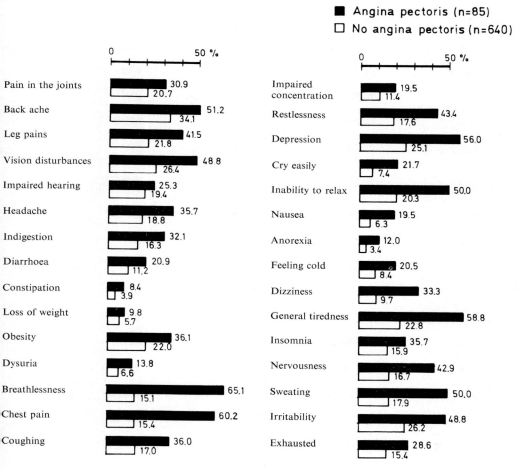

FIG. 2. The percentage of symptoms in male subjects with angina pectoris.

RESULTS

In this sample of men born in the same year there was a striking difference in reporting symptoms between the subjects with angina pectoris and those without. On all questions the angina pectoris group reported about twice as many symptoms as the others. The hypertensive group did not differ from the non-hypertensive group except for a trend to report fewer somatic symptoms (Figs. 2 and 3).

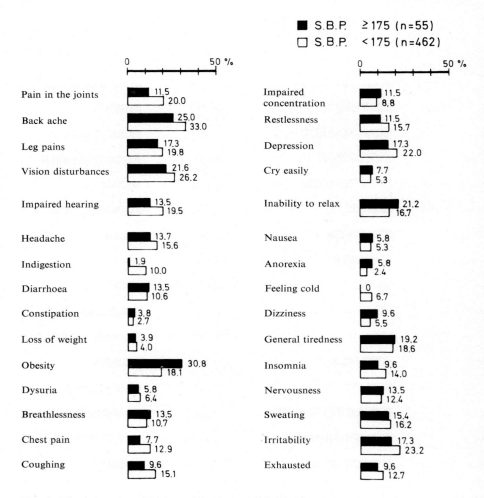

FIG. 3. The percentage of symptoms in male subjects with high blood pressure.

In Tables 1 and 2 the results are presented in another way. Subjects with angina pectoris and with hypertension are grouped according to the numbers of somatic and nervous symptoms they report. It is evident that subjects with angina pectoris are found in the groups with many symptoms, while the hypertensives are found in the groups with few symptoms.

A relationship is shown in Fig. 4 between reporting somatic symptoms and nervous symptoms. The marked squares indicate the median for nervous symptoms in different groups of somatic symptoms.

TABLE 1

Frequency of angina pectoris and hypertension in subjects with different numbers of somatic symptoms

Number of somatic symptoms	Number of subjects (N = 725)	% with angina pectoris (N = 85)	% with high blood pressure ($\geqslant$ 175) (N = 55)
0	113	2.6	10.6
1-2	288	5.5	10.7
3-4	180	11.6	4.4
5-6	75	29.3	1.3
7-8	37	35.1	5.4
9-	32	34.4	3.1

TABLE 2

Frequency of angina pectoris and hypertension in subjects with different numbers of nervous symptoms

Number of nervous symptoms	Number of subjects (N=725)	% with angina pectoris (N = 85)	% with high blood pressure ($\geqslant$ 175) (N = 55)
0	269	2.6	11.5
1-2	179	8.9	6.7
3-4	118	22.0	5.1
5-6	66	9.1	1.6
7-8	38	29.0	5.3
9-10	37	32.4	5.4
11-	18	44.4	5.5

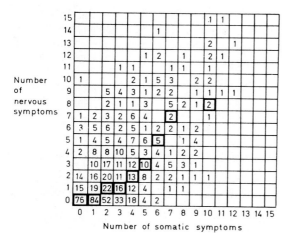

FIG. 4. The relationship between nervous and somatic symptoms.

DISCUSSION

The findings in the present study confirm what we have found in earlier population studies using a limited number of questions in an oral examination, namely, that subjects with angina pectoris report more other symptoms, both somatic and nervous, than do a group without angina pectoris. Hypertensive subjects have a tendency to under-report symptoms.

It is unlikely that the angina pectoris patients report all kinds of symptoms because of severe somatic disability. Nearly all the subjects were working full time. According to our view, the explanation might lie in a difference in the perception of bodily sensations. The strong correlation between reporting somatic symptoms and nervous symptoms supports this. The tendency for the hypertensive subjects to under-report symptoms may also be explained by a change in perception. A hypertensive and a normotensive group were shown films depicting one good and one bad doctor–patient relationship. In an interview afterwards, the hypertensive subjects denied seeing any difference between the two different types of behaviour of the doctors (Sapira *et al.* 1971).

The work of Lacey & Lacey (1970) may also be relevant here. They suggest that an elevation of blood pressure and heart rate may in appropriate circumstances produce a kind of stimulus barrier. The result of such a barrier could be that bodily sensations are less often perceived and therefore not reported.

Differences in the reporting of body sensations must be of importance in the evaluation of the diagnosis, treatment and prognosis of the patient. It is of special interest to study subjects who have a tendency to under-report or deny symptoms. Probably we have here a group of patients who are difficult both to diagnose and to treat.

From the clinic we know that there are both silent myocardial infarctions and silent peptic ulcers. A huge problem is sudden unexpected death. Can differences between subjects in perceiving body sensations explain some of the mechanisms behind these types of diseases?

References

ANDER, S., LINDSTRÖM, B., TIBBLIN, G., ANDERSSON, E. & SANNE, H. (1971) Psykosociala faktorer vid hjärtinfarkt. *Läkartidningen* **68**, no. 33

BARTORELLI, C., BIZZI, E., LIBRETTI, A. & ZANCHETTI, A. (1960) Inhibitory control of sino-carotid pressoceptive afferents on hypothalamic autonomic activity and sham rage behaviour. *Arch. Ital. Biol.* **98**, 308-326

BRUHN, J. G., McCRADY, K. E. & DU PLESSIS, A. (1968) Evidence of 'emotional drain' preceding death from myocardial infarction. *Psychiatr. Dig.* **29**, 34

BURCH, G. E. & DE PASQUALE, N. P. (1965) Methods for studying the influence of higher central nervous centers on the peripheral circulation of intact man. *Am. Heart J.* **70**, 413

DOMINIAN, J. & DOBSON, M. (1969) Study of patients' psychological attitudes to a coronary care unit. *Br. Med. J.* **4**, 795

DRUSS, R. G. & KORNFELD, D. S. (1967) The survivors of cardiac arrest. *J. Am. Med. Assoc.* **201**, 75

GROLLMAN, A. (1929) The effect of psychic disturbances on the cardiac output, blood pressure and oxygen consumption in man. *Am. J. Physiol.* **89**, 584-588

HICKAM, J. B., CARGILL, W. H. & GOLDEN, A. (1948) Cardiovascular reactions to emotional stimuli: effect on cardiac output, A-V oxygen differences, arterial pressure and peripheral resistance. *J. Clin. Invest.* **27**, 290-298

JENKINS, C. D. (1971) Psychological and social precursors of coronary disease. *New Engl. J. Med.* **284**, 307

KITS VAN HEIJNINGEN, H. & TREURNIET, N. (1966) Psychodynamic factors in acute myocardial infarction. *Int. J. Psycho-Anal.* **47**, 370-374

LACEY, J. L. & LACEY, B. C. (1970) Some autonomic-central nervous system interrelationships. In *Physiological Correlates of Emotion* (Black, P., ed.), pp. 205-227, Academic Press, New York & London

PARKES, C. M., BENJAMIN, B. & FITZGERALD, R. G. (1969) Broken heart: a statistical study of increased mortality among widowers. *Br. Med. J.* **1**, 740-743

NOWLIN, J. B., TROYER, W. G. JR, COLLINS, W. S. *et al.* (1965) The association of nocturnal angina pectoris with dreaming. *Ann. Intern. Med.* **63**, 1040-46

PERLMAN, L. V., FERGUSON, S., BERGUM, K., ISENBERG, E. L. & HAMMARSTEN, J. F. (1971) Precipitation of congestive heart failure: social and emotional factors. *Ann. Intern. Med.* **75**, 1

ROSE, G. A. & BLACKBURN, H. (1968) *Cardiovascular Survey Methods* (*W.H.O. Monogr. Ser.* 66), World Health Organization, Geneva.

RUSSEK, H. I. (1967) Role of emotional stress in the etiology of clinical coronary heart disease. *Dis. Chest.* **52**, 1-9

SAPIRA, J. D., SCHEIB, E. T., MORIARTY, R. & SHAPIRO, A. P. (1971) Differences in perception between hypertensive and normotensive populations. *Psychosom. Med.* **33**, 239-250

VALINS, S. (1970) The perception and labeling of bodily changes as determinant of emotional behaviour. In *Physiological Correlates of Emotion* (Black, P., ed.), pp. 229-243, Academic Press, New York & London

WILHELMSEN, L., TIBBLIN, G. & WERKÖ, L. (1972) A primary preventive study in Gothenburg, Sweden. *Prev. Med.* **1**, no. 1-2

WOLF, S. (1966) Sudden death and the oxygen-conserving reflex. *Am. Heart J.* **71**, 840-841

Discussion

Gray: Did you use any kind of questionnaire to measure personality in your different groups?

Tibblin: Yes, but the results are not yet complete. We used Eysenck's Personality Inventory and a Swedish personality inventory (Marke Cecarec).

Gray: It is often assumed in psychosomatic medicine and research that differences in what I would regard as personality factors—that is, differences between two groups of people which are found to be associated with a difference in the incidence of the disorder in question—are part of the mechanism whereby the disease has occurred. But of course, as with all correlations, this need not be so. It could simply be that people of a certain personality type (say, people who tend to report a lot of symptoms) are *also* predisposed towards the disorder being looked at (say, angina pectoris), with no direct mechanism linking the personality factor and the disorder.

Ginsburg: A person with angina pectoris, for example, may become more conscious of all his other symptoms. Could your hypertensive patients be divided into those who knew they had hypertension and those who did not know, and would this make a difference to the results?

Tibblin: This is the line of reasoning that we follow too. People reporting a lot of symptoms seem also to report things like being in conflict much more often than those who are not reporting bodily sensations. We know that people under treatment have many more symptoms than people not receiving treatment but it would not be technically easy to divide our hypertensive subjects into two groups according to whether they know they have high blood pressure or not.

Sachar: Dr Ginsburg's point is relevant to the problem of studying people with established illnesses. We have few markers to tell us in advance who is going to fall ill and so most research in this area is done on people who already have established illnesses, like ulcerative colitis or peptic ulcer. Once such an illness exists it has such an enormous impact on the personality and on one's perceptions of sensations that one becomes preoccupied with one's stomach or feeding or whatever, depending on the illness. If a man knows that he has hypertension and is at the mercy of the first scoundrel who makes him angry, as Dr Tibblin quoted, he becomes acutely sensitive to these issues and this will show up in psychological tests. The methodological problem in such studies is to try to separate (*a*) the psychological response to illness from (*b*) personality traits that may independently coexist with the predisposition to the illness and from (*c*) psychological traits which may actually predispose to the illness itself. There are these three possibilities. The way to avoid this problem is to try to define markers in order to identify the subjects at risk in the population and then do prospective studies—an enormous enterprise.

Tibblin: We have a good indicator, namely metabolic and physiological changes. I mentioned our prospective study of men born in 1919, where we have found good indicators of disease—raised haematocrit, cholesterol, triglycerides and blood pressure. According to our model these indicators can be regarded as mechanisms, because they reflect wear and tear on the organism. Behind these mechanisms could be psychosocial changes.

Reichsman: Was there any correlation between the *duration* of anginal symptoms in your population and the reporting of the other symptoms, not related to ischaemic heart disease?

Tibblin: Unfortunately we haven't such data.

Engel: Dr Gray is correct that it is improper to make any aetiological or causal association between the demonstrated personality type and the disease. On the other hand it is worth keeping in mind that the identification of particular dynamic personality features allows one to make predictions of what kinds of life situations may prove stressful. Clinically, these are useful intervening variables to be aware of. Dr Tibblin, did you differentiate between patients with angina pectoris and patients who had a myocardial infarction without angina pectoris?

Tibblin: The sample was taken from a random population, and the number of cases of myocardial infarction in such a population sample is low. Patients without angina pectoris but with myocardial infarction report fewer symptoms, so this over-reporting seems to be linked to angina pectoris.

Sandler: People who completed neuroticism questionnaires before and after psychoanalysis had higher scores afterwards than before, which suggests that the thresholds for *reporting* such things as being anxious about crossing the road or going across open spaces were much lower than before psychoanalysis. This is relevant to the clinical examination of patients, if the clinician uses leading questions; he has preconceptions and asks questions which draw the patient's attention to symptoms. This may be a source of bias in studies using questionnaires and also in clinical work.

Aitken: People come to doctors because of symptoms, not because of what happens in their coronary arteries, and this reminds us as clinicians that we have just as much a duty to treat symptoms as to lower the serum cholesterol. At present, much more effort is being put into finding ways of lowering serum cholesterol concentrations than into alleviating the multitude of symptoms, often in systems other than the cardiovascular system. Dr Tibblin's data make us ask what makes people susceptible to a variety of *symptoms*. This question is just as valid as what makes people susceptible to coronary artery disease.

Errors have been perpetrated by neglecting this. Specific symptoms have been attributed to mild anaemia, and have been copied into generations of textbooks; but these symptoms are now known to relate more to mood disturbance than to haemoglobin concentration (Robinson & Wood 1968). Similarly for many of the symptoms attributed to hypertension, the blood pressure is less relevant than mode of presentation in the sick role (Robinson 1969).

Tibblin: I agree. Reporting many symptoms in our study did not mean that the subjects were somatically sick but that they had a lot of personal trouble.

We shouldn't look just at one symptom, but see how many other symptoms exist and whether behind all the symptoms is a family crisis or a job crisis, and not so much treat the symptoms as treat the crisis—the life situation.

Henry: There is some evidence that the mechanism by which angina pain is produced differs anatomically from the mechanism in patients with myocardial insufficiency without pain. It has been suggested that in angina pectoris there is arteriosclerosis of small intramural vessels which retain the capacity to change calibre. In such cases, autonomic responses can induce vasoconstriction within a myocardium whose blood supply is already inadequate due to arteriosclerosis (Nellen *et al.* 1971). Results obtained from free-moving baboons with flow probes in the coronary arteries show that the coronary vascular bed does indeed constrict in response to emotionally arousing stimuli (Vatner *et al.* 1971).

Rutter: Dr Sachar pointed out the difficulty, once a disease is established, of knowing whether emotional upset caused the physical disorder or whether the physical handicap led to emotional disturbance. This problem makes it extremely difficult to determine the role of emotions in the initial causation of physical disease. This handicaps the planning of preventive services, but it is not necessarily the most important question in the treatment of patients. They are likely to be less interested in the theoretical question of why they became ill in the first place than in the practical question of what will make a difference to whether they will get better, remain ill or have a recurrence. That requires a different strategy, as Professor A. Querido (1959) showed. Psychosocial factors have been found to be important predictors of the course of chronic and recurrent diseases once these are established (e.g. Rutter 1963). These psychosocial factors have not necessarily led to the disease in the first place but they are crucial from the point of view of the course of the patient's illness, and of patient care.

Donald: The hypertensive group is a difficult one because the patients are usually taking strong drugs which are interfering with their autonomic systems in all sorts of ways, centrally and peripherally. These are psychotropic drugs as well, often with very bizarre effects, and therefore a normal group given these drugs would be different in many ways from the control group not on drugs. This is an added difficulty in doing personality tests in hypertensives.

When we talk about psychosocial pressure, and Dr Tibblin's studies have shown that life changes (divorce, separation or losing a house or a job) may be followed by morbidity, the crisis may have been the earliest sign of organic or psychological ill health with loss of efficiency, and is itself an early component of the disease process.

Zanchetti: Most hypertensive people do not feel themselves to be sick people, but when they come to be treated they become conscious of being ill, which is another reason for their symptoms increasing.

Wolff: In a large group of people with high plasma cholesterol concentrations some are likely to have familial hypercholesterolaemia. If in your study, Dr Tibblin, you find an individual with raised plasma lipids, do you investigate the abnormality in greater detail? And did you find any instances of familial hypercholesterolaemia? Are the specimens of blood obtained in the fasting state? Otherwise it is not possible to interpret triglyceride levels.

Tibblin: In the prospective study the lipids were measured in the fasting state. We looked for a number of hyperlipaemic diseases and found one patient with clear-cut manifestations of hyperlipaemic disease. I don't think this single case blurs the picture.

Sifneos: I agree with Dr Sachar about the importance of having and reporting symptoms. We have been particularly interested in the *form* in which the symptoms are reported, which varies a great deal in different groups of patients. For example, there are some individuals who suffer from various psychosomatic diseases and who have difficulty in talking about their emotional reactions to anxiety-producing situations. We recently compared 25 patients who suffered from a variety of psychosomatic diseases with 25 controls. By a margin of better than two to one the psychosomatic group showed evidence of constriction of emotional functioning, a poor fantasy life, and a striking inability to find appropriate words to describe this feeling (Sifneos 1972). If these observations are correct, how can one explain such a difficulty? Is it possible that we are dealing with a congenital absence—an agenesis—of emotion, on a neuroanatomical basis, or could such patients have some defect in the amygdala like the dogs described by Professor Fonberg? Or are we dealing with a neurophysiological defect or neurochemical deficiency? Or is this a developmental difficulty along the lines of Dr Hofer's observations? Finally, is our familiar psychoanalytic explanation of the use of denial of emotions the best way to understand such behaviour? The problems encountered by these patients are striking. The question to us is whether the psychosomatic disease contributes to the aetiology of these emotional reactions or the other way round. What is the personality of these particular patients like before the onset of the illness? Some subjects without psychosomatic diseases show these difficulties and some patients with psychosomatic diseases do not. Will the former group of patients eventually develop psychosomatic illness?

Hill: What is your evidence that patients with these various diseases and an inability to express or feel emotions were like this before they were identified as suffering from the diseases?

Nemiah: We have external, corroborative statements from relatives that these patients never seemed to be bothered by anything, that they never complained or became angry.

Rutter: We should not go too far in considering what neural mechanisms might mediate the lack of emotions until we know whether the observation is valid. At the moment all we have is an interesting hypothesis. Until there has been a systematic study of these patients with so-called psychosomatic diseases, in which comparison is made with an adequate control group matched on appropriate variables, we do not even know if lack of emotion is associated with the diseases, let alone whether the supposed lack preceded or followed the disorder.

References

NELLEN, M., DECK, W. & SCHRIRE, V. (1971) Angina pectoris and normal coronary angiography. *S. Afr. Med. J.* **45**, 437-438

QUERIDO, A. (1959) Forecast and follow-up: an investigation into the clinical, social and mental factors determining the results of hospital treatment. *Br. J. Prev. Soc. Med.* **13**, 33

ROBINSON, J. O. (1969) Symptoms and the discovery of high blood pressure. *J. Psychosom. Res.* **13**, 157-161

ROBINSON, J. O. & WOOD, M. W. (1968) Symptoms and personality in the diagnosis of physical illness. *Br. J. Prev. Soc. Med.* **22**, 23-26

RUTTER, M. (1963) Psychosocial factors in the short-term prognosis of physical disease: 1. Peptic ulcer. *J. Psychosom. Res.* **7**, 45-60

SIFNEOS, P. E. (1972) The prevalence of alexithymic characteristics in psychosomatic patients. In *Proc. 9th European Conference on Psychosomatic Research*, Vienna, Karger, Basel, in press

VATNER, S. F., FRANKLIN, D. F., HIGGINS, C. B., PATRICK, T., WHITE, S. & VAN CITTERS, R. L. (1971) Coronary dynamics in unrestrained conscious baboons. *Am. J. Physiol.* **221**, 1396

Emotional disturbances before and after subarachnoid haemorrhage

PETER STOREY

St George's Hospital and Springfield Hospital, London

Abstract   The role of emotional factors in the precipitation of subarachnoid haemorrhage (SAH) was studied retrospectively in a personally conducted follow-up of 291 patients, and from a case-note study of 203 patients. It seemed clear that emotional turmoil could be followed immediately by SAH, especially in patients with no evidence of aneurysm or angioma on cerebral angiography. These findings were supported by smaller prospective studies in which the role of emotional factors and of life events in the preceding weeks was studied before it was known whether or not the patient had an aneurysm. There is also evidence that those without vascular malformation were more prone to affective disorders before and after the SAH.

The incidence of depressive states after SAH in the whole series is described and some of the personality and organic factors involved are considered. Rupture of posterior communicating artery aneurysms, which lie lateral to the hypothalamus, is particularly often followed by persistent depression.

Subarachnoid haemorrhage (SAH) is an illness in which blood escapes into the subarachnoid space—that is, into the cerebrospinal fluid which bathes the surface of the brain and spinal cord. In about half the patients there is a berry aneurysm of the circle of Willis; in about 10% there is an angioma or other vascular malformation; and in the others no gross abnormality is shown on cerebral angiography, although microaneurysms may be present similar to those found in hypertensive cerebral haemorrhage. The annual incidence of SAH is about six per 100 000 of the population; it is most common between 40 and 60 years of age; and about 35% of those admitted to hospital are alive six months later. There must be between 2500 and 5000 new survivors in England and Wales each year.

It is accepted that strokes can occur in paroxysms of rage or other strong emotion, presumably because of a sudden rise in blood pressure, but I started a follow-up study of SAH without any interest in its precipitation and without asking any questions about that aspect. After a time I realized that some patients, and their relatives, attributed the illness to emotional factors.

In the first series of 261 patients (Storey 1967) seen at follow-up six months to six years after the SAH, I was told of four very dramatic and two less dramatic episodes of precipitation (Storey 1969). These were all in women, although 43% of the series were men; and five of the six had normal angiograms, although only 30 of the 261 patients in the series had normal angiograms.

The cases were briefly as follows:

(1) A woman of 40 years who had her stroke when she opened the door to a policeman, who told her that her friend and neighbour had been found dead, hanging in the lavatory.

(2) A woman of 49 years who was watching on television the first flight of a new plane, of which her son was a crew member, when it exploded. (In fact, he was off sick that day.) Her stroke occurred within seconds of the disaster. (This was the only aneurysm case.)

(3) A woman aged 35, having treatment for an anxiety state, who had her stroke when her husband told her he knew of her adultery, and would divorce her.

(4) A woman aged 50 who was told on the telephone that her son had been badly injured in a road accident. She became anxious and panicky, and had her stroke about three hours later.

The less dramatic cases were:

(5) A woman who had nursed her husband as he died of cancer, and had an SAH in the last few hours of his life.

(6) A woman of 47 years, troubled for years by obsessional thoughts of sex and obscene words, developed an anxiety state after some sexual experience she could not bring herself to describe, and had her SAH three days later, in a state of great anxiety and tension.

There were several other spontaneously described emotional precipitants, but none of them was so clearcut in the timing.

Not only were those with normal angiograms more liable to describe dramatic emotional precipitants for the bleed, but they had significantly more often had treatment for an affective disturbance (mainly drugs from their general practitioner in the more distant past). There is therefore no suggestion in this material that the physical illness is in any way an 'alternative' to psychological distress.

The next 30 patients I followed up were all women with aneurysms, and I enquired carefully about emotional precipitants. In only one case did this seem important, in a woman who had an SAH at the height of a fierce quarrel with her stepson.

I next studied the neurological folders of 102 patients with and 101 without aneurysms after admission to hospital for SAH, taking cases before 1960 to exclude possible reactions to monoamine oxidase inhibitors, introduced for the treatment of depression. This showed that the cases with normal angiograms were significantly more often unmarried; that physical activity was less often involved in the onset; and that they more often had psychiatric symptoms afterwards (not quite significant).

So far, the studies had been entirely retrospective, so Dr R. Penrose and I carried out a blind prospective study by interviewing the relatives of 56 patients admitted for SAH before the results of angiography were known (Penrose & Storey 1970). Table 1 shows some of our results for the reported emotional state.

TABLE 1

Reported emotional state

	Aneurysm		Normal angiograms		Total
	Female	Male	Female	Male	
Normal	26	10	1	3	40
Some distress	6	2	0	0	8
Marked distress	4	0	2	1	7
Major turmoil	0	0	1	0	1
Totals	36	12	4	4	56

The χ^2 tests used in Tables 1, 2 and 3 were applied to groups separated after the data were examined. In other words, the separation was chosen to maximize the statistical significance. It was pointed out during the meeting that this may alter its validity, and the significance may be less meaningful.

In Table 1 'some distress' means a state of worry, anxiety or depression of fairly ordinary degree—business worries, marital disharmony, and so on—described as not unusual for the patient.

'Marked distress' included the following: a woman who was reading again the obituary notice of her son as the anniversary approached; a woman who had just received a letter from a school saying that her son had been stealing; a woman very angry with her daughter for coming in late; a woman trying to prepare for a farewell speech to an organization for which she had worked for fifteen years; a woman arranging for her dog to be put down by a vet; and a woman whose husband had recently left her being told by her daughter that she too did not like her.

The one case of major turmoil was a woman who had just been told that her husband had died, after a few hours of mounting anxiety and distress.

If Table 1 is simplified, men and women are considered together, and those with normal mental states or some distress are compared to those with marked distress or major turmoil, there is significantly more emotional disturbance in patients with normal angiograms ($\chi^2 = 7.194$; 1 d.f.; $P < 0.01$: Yates correction for small numbers). It is a pity that more patients with normal angiograms were not studied, as such small numbers can never be really satisfying despite the statistical manoeuvre. However, this blind study confirms the findings made in the retrospective follow-up and in the neurosurgical case-note study.

Forty-four of the same group of patients have been studied by Dr Penrose using the Brown-Birley Life Events schedule, originally used in studies of the onset of schizophrenia (Brown & Birley 1967). This is a detailed structured interview, modified here because relatives were being questioned, as the patients are not usually well enough for such an interview and may indeed be unconscious. Table 2 shows the results.

TABLE 2

Percentage of patients and controls experiencing 'life events' in three-week periods before subarachnoid haemorrhage

	Three-week periods				
	12	9	6	3	
Control group (N = 325)	19%	19%	19%	19%	
Aneurysms (N = 27)	24% (6)	20% (5)	24% (6)	28% (7)	
Normal angiograms (N = 17)	18% (3)	30% (5)	24% (4)	48% (8)	Illness

If Table 2 is reduced to a 2 × 2 table, then $\chi^2 = 6.147$; $P < 0.02$; and in the three-week period before the SAH there is a significant increase in the number of life events in those with normal angiograms.

In summary, there is evidence from both retrospective and immediate studies of patients with SAH that those with normal angiograms more often have some emotional disturbance just before the bleed, and more often have upsetting life events in the preceding three weeks, than those with aneurysms. There is also a suggestion that they have been more often affectively disturbed in the past, and they more often seem to have treatment for psychiatric symptoms afterwards. This last point is touched on again later.

EMOTIONAL DISTURBANCE AFTER SUBARACHNOID HAEMORRHAGE

Emotional disturbances after SAH were studied in 261 patients, nearly all seen in their homes, in 242 cases with a relative as added informant.

Depression was rated as absent, mild, moderate or severe, ignoring the first six months after the bleed. The judgment was subjective, but most of the depressed patients had had some treatment.

TABLE 3

Severity of depression and CNS signs after subarachnoid haemorrhage

	Depression rating				
	Absent	Mild	Moderate	Severe	Total
CNS signs absent	121	12	12	3	148
CNS signs present	71	19	18	5	113
Total	192	31	30	8	261

Simplified, $\chi^2 = 11.748$; 1 d.f.; $P < 0.001$.

Overall 69 patients (26%) were rated as depressed—11% mildly, 12% moderately and 8% severely. There were several important factors, of which brain damage (as demonstrated by CNS signs) was the most important, as shown in Table 3. Interestingly, the group with no aneurysms, who often have emotional precipitants of the bleed, suffer from anxiety and depression afterwards without much in the way of CNS signs (Fig. 1). These patients without aneurysms seem to form a special group, with labile emotions and, presumably, labile blood pressures.

Of the patients with aneurysms, depression was most common in those with posterior communicating artery aneurysms, rupture of which we know interferes with the fine perforating vessels to the hypothalamus. The differences are not statistically significant, but the depressive states were longer and relatively more severe in the group with aneurysm of the posterior communicating artery. Four of the patients complained of alterations in temperature sensitivity in that they felt continuously warm, and had prolonged menstrual disturbances. However, they did not present a more 'endogenous pattern' of depression, as far as I could see.

There were some striking differences in the depressed patients with and without brain damage. These are summarized in Table 4. Those without brain damage are generally more vulnerable and neurotic-seeming, low in energy, high in anxiety and reserved or withdrawn. They are in fact the sort of people who are prone to become depressed anyway, but in some the SAH

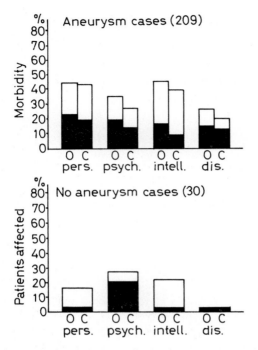

Fig. 1. Psychiatric symptoms in patients with and without aneurysms. Open columns, mild disability. Filled columns, moderate and severe disability. O, operated cases; C, conservative treatment. Pers., personality impairment; psych., psychiatric symptoms; intell., intellectual impairment; dis., physical disability.

is followed by very prolonged depressive states, so that their life is very different afterwards. In some, as I mentioned, it seemed that hypothalamic damage might be significant.

TABLE 4

Comparison of depressed patients with and without brain damage after subarachnoid haemorrhage

	Brain damage	No brain damage
Previous personality 'energy'	High (52/136)*	Low (17/125)
Anxiety	Average*	High
Outgoingness	Average*	Low
Previous history of depression	Slight	Marked
Sex	Equal numbers of men and women	Nearly all women

* Statistically significant.

Those patients who were both depressed and brain damaged were different in temperament from and significantly more often described as 'energetic' than those who were brain damaged and not depressed. Perhaps this is because more energetic and active people suffer relatively more from their disabilities and loss of function than do others.

To return to the question of the onset of SAH, we have no explanation of why the patients with normal angiograms should have more emotional precipitants than those with aneurysms. Probably emotional and vascular instability occurs with equal frequency in those with and without aneurysms, but the aneurysm predisposes to haemorrhage on physical exertion. As there are so many more people in the world with normal angiograms, we are perhaps seeing that selected group who are vulnerable enough to bleed when emotional turmoil raises the blood pressure.

References

BROWN, G. & BIRLEY, J. L. T. (1967) Crises and life changes and the onset of schizophrenia. *J. Health Soc. Behav.* **2**, 203-214

PENROSE, R. & STOREY, P. B. (1970) in *Proc. 8th European Conf. on Psychosomatic Research* (Pierloot, R.A., ed.), pp. 321-325, Karger, Basel

STOREY, P. B. (1967) Psychiatric sequelae of subarachnoid haemorrhage. *Br. Med. J.* **3**, 261-266

STOREY, P. B. (1969) The precipitation of subarachnoid haemorrhage. *J. Psychosom. Res.* **13**, 175-188

Discussion

Donald: You didn't mention migraine, Dr Storey, which is surprising.

Storey: Migraine was significantly more common in patients with aneurysms of the posterior communicating artery than in those without aneurysms. Most migraine is cured after the subarachnoid haemorrhage.

Zanchetti: Is there an additional cause for the increased number of cases with depression after the aneurysm? I imagine that many of these patients were already hypertensive and untreated before the aneurysm. A lot of medication is then given for hypertension, and it is this drug treatment that gives rise to depression. Reserpine, for example, is known to induce depression.

Storey: I found no relationship between hypertension and depression, except that neurological damage was more common in the hypertensives.

When that was allowed for the hypertension was not related to depression, so this was probably not caused by the medication.

Fonberg: I am pleased by Dr Storey's results because they support our findings that the hypothalamus is involved in the syndrome of depression. Did you observe any psychotic symptoms?

Storey: No. One patient without neurological damage had a schizophrenic illness about a year after her haemorrhage. She made a good recovery from the schizophrenia, which didn't seem to be related to the haemorrhage. But in a group of 291 people one would expect one or two cases of schizophrenia. There were three manic depressives. One had been both manic and depressive before the haemorrhage; the other two had markedly cyclothymic temperaments. So there was no association with psychosis.

Hill: Do you wish to emphasize a causal relationship between aneurysm of the posterior communicating artery affecting the hypothalamus and the occurrence of depressive illness?

Storey: The numbers are not sufficient to be definite but patients with aneurysms in this region have a much longer and more severe illness; I am still seeing two people who first came to my attention during that study, who still become depressed about ten years later.

Hill: Are there any recorded cases of small focal lesions in this area of the hypothalamus producing depression?

Storey: I don't know of any. It is an area which everybody feels is related to depression, but this is not established.

Engel: Dr Storey's report is complementary to our own studies on ischaemic strokes in some respects but not in others (Adler *et al.* 1971). We too found a low incidence of association between the very dramatic emotional episode and ischaemic stroke; in only two out of a series of 35 strokes did this kind of event immediately precede the stroke. On the other hand, there may be some problems in your study as regards the sensitivity of the instruments that you are using. I don't know about the interview technique you used; ours is open-ended and also explores the personality structure more, and has allowed us to be rather precise in identifying the kinds of life situations which would be most likely to be significantly disturbing for these people. I suspect that with more sensitive techniques the difference you report between patients with and without aneurysm would decline, though the finding that an intense emotional experience has special significance in the cases without aneurysm may prove valid.

However, my two most dramatic and uncanny cases in which emotional crises were associated with subarachnoid haemorrhage both did have aneurysms. A 17-year-old boy collapsed and died at 6 a.m. on June 4, 1970, from what post-mortem examination revealed to be a rupture of an aneurysm of the anterior communicating artery. Exactly one year earlier, at 5.12 a.m. on June 4, 1969 his older brother had died, a few hours after a car crash. The family had heard the boy stirring in his room around 5 a.m., earlier than he usually arose (Engel 1971). The other patient, whom I never reported, was a man of 46 years who had a subarachnoid haemorrhage due to a ruptured aneurysm subsequently demonstrated at surgery. His father had died at age 46 on the same date in the same hospital, also from a subarachnoid haemorrhage after a quarrel with the patient, then a boy of 15 years of age. Thirty years later this man found himself impelled to provoke a quarrel with his teenage son, the day before his haemorrhage. The dates were verified from the father's old hospital record.

Gray: I found Dr Storey's results extremely interesting, but I wonder why he chose to measure personality, anxiety, depression and so on the way he did. Psychologists have developed and standardized a large number of tests to measure these things: there is almost a supermarket into which you can walk and pick out the test you need. The advantage of using such standardized tests is that, if it gives you any results, you can relate these to others previously or subsequently obtained with the same test. It seems unnecessary to measure anxiety or a tendency to depression by an unstandardized questionnaire. It's not harder to use a standard questionnaire; it's easier.

Storey: I did take expert advice. One problem was time; the interviews could only be about two hours. Secondly, many of these patients are severely brain damaged; many are dysphasic and a few are aphasic. They are being followed up years after the event. I didn't know of any questionnaire which I could use with a relative of the patient, not the patient himself, which would describe his personality some years previously, before a stroke.

Gray: I accept this. But I would also like to raise again the more general question of whether the relation seen between the personality description on the one hand and the disorder on the other is causal in either direction or is a joint function of some other variable, such as the constitutional make-up. One way to tackle this problem is to use questionnaires which are known to relate to personality description. I have been struck by the lack of such data from the clinicians here. Instead, we have discussed observations at interview and descriptions from relatives of the sort of personality that goes with this or that disorder. I can see that you have difficulties in applying standardized questionnaires to your population, but these difficulties don't apply in other contexts.

Storey: The problem is that the questionnaires are not relevant to many of the ideas thrown up by clinicians.

Gray: You cannot know this in advance. It may be that, in say Dr Tibblin's study, the correlation between complaints of cardiac pain and the tendency to report many other symptoms is part of the general personality make-up. If one gave these people a few standardized questionnaires one would rapidly find out whether that possibility is real or not.

Aitken: Personality questionnaires have not been validated for individual patients. It is true that a group of neurotic patients can be distinguished at a high level of statistical significance from a group of healthy people, but the variability within the group is extensive. For example, the manual of the Eysenck Personality Inventory (Eysenck & Eysenck 1964) provides data from which it can be calculated that the mean score for neurotic patients lay only at the 87th percentile of scores obtained from the general population. Validity can only be judged empirically, and studies have not yet been done comparing the results from a personality questionnaire like the Eysenck Personality Inventory with another index, such as clinical assessment. With a few asthmatics ($N = 12$), we determined that two raters only assessed manifest anxiety with a correlation coefficient of 0.23 as the index of reliability. Once the numbers had increased to $N = 88$, the correlation coefficient increased to 0.60. The correlation coefficient for this clinical assessment of anxiety with the Taylor Manifest Anxiety Scale score was only 0.33 where $N = 88$, though it had been 0.52 when $N = 12$. Clearly the validity of one or other measure was poor and the reliability of the clinical assessment far from satisfactory (Aitken *et al.* 1969; K. Hope, unpublished findings 1972). Nevertheless the findings available from both questionnaire and clinical methods of assessment are of interest. It must be clearly recognized that they are different measures and that neither is more or less appropriate for the purpose of personality description than the other. Dr Storey chose clinical assessment, and as a clinician I understand the reasons for his choice. However, I would have liked to have heard more about the reliability of his data. I know no colleague who relies on the scores from a personality questionnaire like the Eysenck Personality Inventory to judge the personality of a patient under treatment.

Gray: My point is not that you need a questionnaire to prove that you are dealing with a particular clinical disorder, but that questionnaires or other standardized measurements are essential for the communication of research results.

Hill: We would all agree about the value of standardized questionnaires and clinical observations.

References

ADLER, R., MACRITCHIE, K. & ENGEL, G. L. (1971) Psychologic processes and ischemic stroke (occlusive cerebrovascular disease). I. Observations on 32 men with 35 strokes. *Psychosom. Med.* **33**, 1-29

AITKEN, R. C. B., ZEALLEY, A. K. & ROSENTHAL, S. V. (1969) Psychological and physiological measures of emotion in chronic asthmatic patients. *J. Psychosom. Res.* **13**, 289-297

ENGEL, G. L. (1971) Sudden and rapid death during psychological stress. *Ann. Intern. Med.* **74**, 771-782

EYSENCK, H. J. & EYSENCK, S. B. G. (1964) *Manual of the Eysenck Personality Inventory*, University of London Press, London

Metabolic and behavioural correlates of obesity

JOEL GRINKER and JULES HIRSCH

The Rockefeller University, New York

Abstract Adult humans and animals regulate food intake and caloric expenditure to maintain a fixed body weight. Studies of adipose cellularity and behavioural responses to weight reduction support the contention that body weight regulation exists in obesity. The number of adipocytes is determined early in life and is unchanged by later dietary manipulations. In contrast, adipose cell size can be influenced by events occurring at any time. Adult obese individuals with juvenile-onset of obesity have an increased cell number; those with adult-onset have an increased cell size. Weight reduction produces a decrement in cell size, but not in cell number. Juvenile-onset patients experience behavioural disturbances during and following weight reduction: symptoms of depression, fatigue and anxiety, and distortions in timing perception and body image. Adult-onset patients do not experience these symptoms.

Another approach to the problem of how men and animals maintain body weight is to examine the influence of metabolic or 'internal' cues and sensory or 'external' cues on eating behaviour. There are no differences between obese and normal weight subjects in taste sensitivity but there are marked differences in preference for sucrose. Obese subjects show a pronounced aversion for strong concentrations of sucrose, whereas normal weight subjects prefer moderate concentrations. A significant correlation exists between preference rating and adipose cell number: the greater the cell number, the more negative the preference ratings. Current experiments are aimed at uncovering additional correlations among the behavioural and metabolic components of obesity.

The term 'psychosomatic' describes a state in which physiological and psychological variables are correlated. A disorder is not usually regarded as 'psychosomatic' when either physiological or psychological factors alone highly predict its occurrence, but is more properly termed psychosomatic when nearly equal involvement of both physiological and behavioural components is approached. Obesity should be considered in this perspective. Is it primarily a response to emotional problems, is it mainly the result of a metabolic or chemical defect, or is it some blend of these factors?

The major hypothesis presented here is that obesity is a disorder of the mechanisms which control body weight. Body weight in the normal organism is an equilibrium state achieved by the balance between food intake and energy expenditure and subject to a variety of controlling forces. A constant proportion of body weight is stored as fat. In man, such storage normally constitutes 15% of body weight or a month's supply of calories. Several studies provide examples of the resistance of body weight to permanent change. Forced-fed or starved adult rats become appropriately anorexic or hyperphagic with the resumption of *ad libitum* food intake (Cohn & Joseph 1962; Corbit & Stellar 1964; Hoebel & Teitelbaum 1966). Prison volunteers subjected to an enriched diet and a controlled activity regime gain only 25% of body weight and promptly adjust food intake and return to their initial body weights when overfeeding is discontinued (Sims *et al.* 1968).

Obesity is likewise an equilibrium state. The mechanisms regulating body weight can be considered as a hierarchy ranging from cognitive and social factors through sensory and taste components to cellular and metabolic components. A series of studies of these various factors which regulate the level of fat storage in man and animals as well as the effects of weight reduction on the obese equilibrium state will be discussed.

ADIPOSE TISSUE MORPHOLOGY

The size of the adipose tissue depot is a function of the number and size of the adipose cells. The number of adipocytes is determined early in life and is unchanged by later dietary manipulations. This finding of a fixed number of adipocytes may be an important factor in the regulation of adult body weight. Several experiments on the development of adipose tissue cellularity in normal and obese animals are summarized below.

Growth and development of animal adipose tissue

Johnson *et al.* (1971) and Johnson & Hirsch (1972) have demonstrated the influence of genetic factors on adipose cellularity in several strains of obese rats and mice. Obesity was accomplished primarily through an increase in adipose cell size at three different depots: epididymal, retroperitoneal and subcutaneous. Cell number was clearly stabilized early in the animal's life (by 15 weeks in rats, 6 weeks in mice). The Zucker obese rat and the *ob/ob* mouse proved exceptions since obesity was also associated with increases in cell number in some adipose sites and cell number was still increasing at 26 weeks. Knittle & Hirsch (1968) have shown that the number of adipocytes can be affected by early nutritional manipulations. Newborn rats were permanently stunted when reared in an artificially large litter. After weaning, when the animals had unlimited access to food, the stunted animals remained thinner than the animals raised in small litters. Adipose tissue was composed of a reduced number of smaller sized cells in the stunted animals.

These findings suggest that adipose cell number may be primarily determined by events operating early in life; in contrast, adipose cell size can be influenced by events occurring at any time. Thus, adult rats overfed on a high fat diet can be made extremely obese; adult rats underfed by an acute starvation can be made dramatically thin and in both cases, there are no changes in cell number, but only in cell size. Similarly, when animals are made obese by ventro-medial hypothalamic lesions or by injections of gold thioglucose, adipose tissue storage is achieved through marked adipocyte hypertrophy but without change in cell number (Hirsch & Han 1969; Johnson *et al.* 1971; Johnson & Hirsch 1972).

Growth and development of human adipose tissue

Similar results are found in studies on humans. Obesity produced experimentally in man was achieved solely by an increase in adipose cell size (Salans *et al.* 1971). When subjects returned to their regular diets, both weight and cell size returned to normal. Although in moderate obesity fat cell hypertrophy is highly correlated with the excessive weight, in severe obesity the degree of excessive weight is best correlated with the number of cells rather than the size (Hirsch & Knittle 1970; Bjorntorp 1972). Severely obese adult patients have an approximately threefold increase in adipose cell number and weight reduction is accomplished exclusively by a shrinkage of adipocytes to below average cell size (Hirsch & Knittle 1970). Table 1 presents mean cell size and number from normal weight individuals, obese individuals and reduced obese individuals. A classification made on the basis of age at onset of obesity shows that obesity of individuals with juvenile-onset (before age 12) appears to be primarily a hyperplastic disorder (increased cell number), while obesity of adult-onset (after age 19) appears primarily hypertrophic.

The obese individual cannot change the number of adipose cells through dieting. The individual with a large number of adipose cells may thus be 'programmed' for a higher level of adipose storage. The application of external forces to reduce weight would be in conflict with internal forces which maintain

TABLE 1

Size and number of adipose cells of normal weight, obese (juvenile and adult-onset) and reduced obese subjects (mean ± s.e.m.)

	Cell size*	Cell number**
Normal weight N = 5	0.6651 ± 0.0674	26.83 ± 1.76
Juvenile-onset obese N = 9	0.9051 ± 0.0559	85.41 ± 6.97
Adult-onset obese N = 4	0.9822 ± 0.1376	62.01 ± 4.21
Reduced obese*** N = 19	0.4555 ± 0.0525	62.96 ± 5.32

* microgrammes of lipid/cell.
** × 10^9
*** Each subject had lost approximately 50 kg.

the obese weight. We know that normal weight individuals experience a variety of disorders when undergoing experimental starvation (Keys *et al.* 1950). Weight reduction for the obese may be achieved only at the expense of similar changes in behaviour.

BEHAVIOURAL CONSEQUENCES OF WEIGHT REDUCTION

A general summary of our findings so far would be: juvenile-onset obese individuals undergoing weight reduction experience a variety of behavioural changes including distortions in time perception, errors in estimation of body image and depressive and anxious symptoms (Glucksman & Hirsch 1968; Glucksman *et al.* 1968; Glucksman & Hirsch 1969). In contrast, adult-onset obese individuals experience none of these disorders (Grinker *et al.* 1973a, b). The behavioural changes are the result of longterm weight reduction rather than the immediate result of food deprivation since these changes persist with isocaloric refeeding and acute starvations of 48 hours do not produce any changes.

Affective changes

Early explorations of the response to weight reduction among juvenile-onset subjects suggested that while these subjects experience periods of conflict and turmoil, no one neurotic or personality trait was common to all. In fact, individual responses bore a striking similarity to those reported for normal

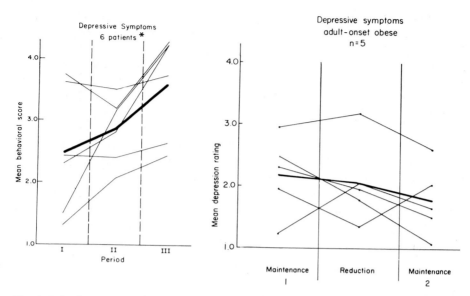

FIG. 1. Behavioural rating scale scores of depression for six juvenile-* and five adult-onset obese subjects. Juvenile-onset subjects (onset before age 12) are shown on the left and adult-onset subjects (onset after age 19) are shown on the right. Ratings were made during periods of weight maintenance and weight reduction. (On left graph, maintenance: I, III; reduction, II.) Heavy lines represent mean ratings.

weight individuals experiencing starvation (Schiele & Brozek 1948; Glucksman & Hirsch 1968). A quantitative means of measuring affective change by a behavioural rating scale was designed. Ratings were made independently by observers after brief interviews. Results from the first group of juvenile-onset obese patients showed primarily a moderate depression with some associated anxiety. This depression persisted after weight loss.

The reactions of a small group of adult-onset obese subjects were studied thereafter. These subjects were equivalently obese and had the same duration of obesity as the juvenile-onset group. There was no increase in depressive affect measured by behavioural ratings or by self-administered rating scales. Fig. 1 shows behavioural ratings of depression for individual juvenile and adult-onset obese subjects.

Body image

Several of the juvenile-onset obese subjects manifested concern with their changing body size during the course of interviews. Some continued to feel obese in spite of marked weight loss. These image disturbances were studied separately by a quantitative procedure. Subjects were presented with a projected image of themselves and by means of an anamorphic lens attachment were able to make themselves more or less 'obese'. They were asked to adjust their image to their 'correct' size at many intervals during and after weight reduction. Juvenile-onset obese subjects made increasingly larger errors in size estimation as they lost weight and after weight reduction they greatly overestimated their body size (Glucksman & Hirsch 1969). Stunkard & Mendelson (1967) and Stunkard & Burt (1967) conducted extensive interviews with obese adults and reported that major disturbances in body image perception occurred only in those with juvenile-onset obesity. Preliminary data from our laboratory indicate that adult-onset obese subjects slightly underestimate their size throughout hospitalization, in sharp contrast to the overestimation of body size found in the juvenile-onset group.

Time perception

Variations in metabolism have been found to affect the perception of time (Hoagland 1933). We developed a series of studies to determine whether the metabolic and affective changes produced by weight reduction would be reflected in changes in timing perception (Grinker *et al.* 1973a). Before, during and after weight reduction obese subjects listened to a tape recording of sounds of varying durations. Subjects were instructed to compare their concept of a given temporal unit (one or three seconds) with the durations of the recorded tones. The durations varied from 0.1 to 1.9 seconds with a mean of one second on the first set and from 0.3 to 6.0 seconds with a mean of three seconds on the second set. In this way an estimate was made of the subjects' internal concept of one and three seconds; a score of less than one second (or three seconds) would indicate an internal clock slower than real time and a higher score or overestimation would indicate a more rapid internal clock. After weight reduction, juvenile-onset obese subjects underestimated the duration of the standard intervals. Fig. 2 shows the judged durations for juvenile- and adult-onset obese subjects during the maintenance and reduction periods of hospitalization as well as data collected from normal weight subjects. Adult-onset obese subjects did not show changes in time perception.

The underestimation of these brief intervals by juvenile-onset obese subjects indicates a slowing of the internal clock. This finding corresponds with the findings of increasing depression and fatigue experienced by these patients with

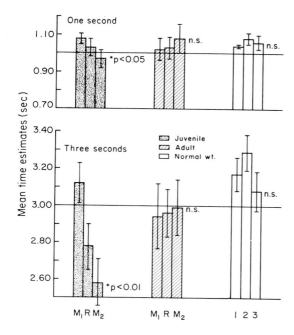

Fig. 2. Estimates of the duration of one and three clock seconds by 9 juvenile-onset obese, 5 adult-onset obese and 13 normal weight subjects during hospitalization. Values represent mean and s.e.m.; M_1 and M_2 are the initial and final maintenance periods; R is the reduction period for obese subjects. *P values obtained by Student t test for correlated means.

weight loss. Fig. 3 shows the degree of correlation between affective responses (depression) and perceptions of the three-second time interval.

The alterations in timing perception and the correlated changes in affect might well be an expression of the biological consequences of weight reduction. The response of the juvenile-onset obese subject may represent a pattern of energy conservation aimed at maintaining homeostasis of fat storage. The absence of these changes in adult-onset subjects again suggests that age of onset is an important variable in describing the nature of obesity.

COGNITIVE AND SENSORY COMPONENTS IN THE REGULATION OF FOOD INTAKE

The examination of the various elements which control the regulation of body weight must eventually involve direct studies of food intake. It is well known that when the equilibrium point for body weight is changed by lesions

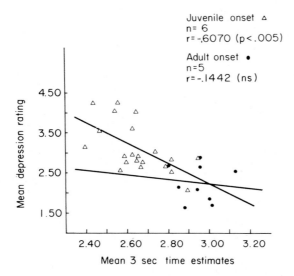

FIG. 3. Correlation of depression ratings and three-second time estimates for juvenile-onset and adult-onset obese subjects during longterm hospitalization for weight reduction. Each point represents the average depression and time perception score of all juvenile or adult-onset subjects on each trial. Note that the adult-onset subjects show no significant changes in timing perception or depression during hospitalization; consequently the measure of correlation is low. The data support the contention that juvenile- and adult-onset subjects represent two distinct populations.

in the ventro-medial hypothalamus in rats, a variety of behavioural changes occur. The palatability and availability of food become dominant determinants of eating behaviour (Miller *et al.* 1950; Teitelbaum 1955). The animals with lesions are generally described as more finicky; they eat more for 'taste' than for 'calories' (Jacobs & Sharma 1969). Adulteration of the food with quinine leads to a far greater suppression of intake in these animals than in non-lesioned animals.

Unlike lesioned animals, genetically obese animals will appropriately adjust their food intake for calories. Genetically obese animals will continue to work on a high fixed ratio reinforcement schedule while lesioned animals will cease to work (Greenwood *et al.* 1971). The genetically obese Zucker rat and its normal weight littermate will adjust food intake for caloric dilution whereas lesioned animals will not.

The 'taste versus calories' paradigm has been applied to man. There are a number of studies which attempt to show that the obese person is more insensitive to 'internal' cues for eating behaviour than the non-obese and thus more susceptible to 'external' cues. Relative overeating by moderately obese subjects occurs when food is freely available and attractive—prominently displayed in front of the subject, shells removed from nuts, particularly tasty 'French' ice cream and so on, and relative undereating when food is unattractive or when effort is required to obtain the food—unshelled nuts, food placed at some distance in the refrigerator, or ice cream adulterated with quinine (Schachter *et al.* 1968; Nisbett 1968*a*, *b*; Schachter 1971). The authors have interpreted these results as indicating that the obese suffer from a learning deficit; that is, internal cues for food intake or satiety were never appropriately integrated (Bruch 1961, 1969; Schachter 1967). These data may be interpreted in other ways. The obese might have strong internal drives for food intake which they must continuously deny and hence disregard their internal signals; or the obese may be concerned with and ashamed of their obesity and consequently attempt to control their eating by responding only to stimuli which are socially appropriate. Thus, the obese subjects eat the amounts implicitly designated in the experimental design.

Sensory factors

The hypothesis that the obese individual is unable to respond to internal physiological cues has been tested by several investigators. Stunkard & Koch (1964) have shown that normal weight individuals tended to report hunger in the presence of gastric motility and no hunger when the stomach was quiescent. Obese individuals did not show this correlation; women tended to deny hunger in the presence of gastric motility and men tended to exaggerate by reporting hunger even when gastric motility was not present. The hunger reports of the obese appeared to be more the result of response biases, than of the presence or absence of gastric motility. Stunkard & Fox (1971) have shown that the perception of gastric contractions by obese subjects could be improved with training, but the improved perception of gastric motility had no effect on the control of body weight. After longterm monitoring of hunger sensations, they concluded that gastric motility exercises a weak influence on hunger sensations and that obese subjects are not significantly different from those of normal weight.

Direct observations on the ability of human subjects to regulate food intake have been made. Hashim & Van Itallie (1965) have reported that obese individuals would maintain body weight when given standard hospital diets, but lost weight when provided only with a bland liquid formula. They further reported that adult obese women failed to adapt intake when systematic changes in caloric concentration of the diet were made (Campbell *et al.* 1971).

Adolescent obese boys were better able to adjust intake to changes in caloric density. Normal weight males were able to maintain weight and adjust intake when the nutritive density of the liquid diet was changed. This study is difficult to interpret since normal weight women were not studied and there was no systematic control of the propensity of obese women to attempt weight loss. We have experienced difficulty in maintaining obese patients on standard hospital food diets at the Rockefeller University Hospital. Patients hospitalized for obesity tend to lose weight even when 'dieting' is contrary to instructions.

Others have emphasized the difficulties that animals and men have in regulating food intake after caloric dilution or intragastric or intravenous loading (Janowitz & Hollander 1955; Jordan *et al.* 1966; Stellar 1967; Spiegel 1971). Walike *et al.* (1969) reported that oral preloads depressed intake, but not sufficiently to keep subjects from overeating. A recent study of longterm regulation (ten days) reported that although obese and non-obese males were able to maintain body weight on all-liquid diets they did so with 'incomplete' caloric adjustment; they consumed a greater volume of the low calorie diet, but still consumed more calories of the high calorie diet (O. W. Wooley 1971). All subjects had agreed not to gain or lose weight during the experiment. Spiegel (1971) reported that when cognitive cues were removed by making subjects drink from a tube attached to a hidden reservoir, subjects adjusted slowly to changes in caloric density; most subjects required four to six meals. In another study glucose, mannitol and saline were given intravenously to normal weight subjects and subsequent hunger sensations and food intake measured (Grinker *et al.* 1971*a*). Although subjects rated themselves as less hungry after intravenous glucose than after saline or mannitol, they did not decrease their food intake. These studies suggest that the role of habitual cues and cognitive factors is of major importance in controlling the food intake of normal weight individuals.

Cognitive factors

Several recent studies emphasize the importance of cognitive factors in controlling intake. Nisbett & Storms (1972) reported that obese and normal weight subjects were equivalently influenced by the social conditions under which food was served. The number of crackers eaten by subjects was influenced by the amounts eaten by an experimental confederate. In a recent, carefully designed study, cognitive feedback about the caloric value of liquid preloads was controlled; the actual nutritional value and the apparent caloric value were separately manipulated (S. C. Wooley 1972). In addition, all subjects (obese and normal weight males and females) participated in all conditions. All ate less and reported feeling fuller after the apparently high calorie drink. The actual number of calories consumed had no effect on subsequent food intake.

An increasing number of studies, some of which are described above, indicate that a simple 'external-internal' cue hypothesis is not sufficient to account for the observed differences in food intake between obese and normal weight individuals. It is possible that the 'external' behaviour of the obese individual is specific to the testing situation.

TASTE PARAMETERS

The increased taste reponsiveness of the obese observed by Nisbett (1968a) and Schachter (1971) could be a function of differences in taste sensitivity or threshold, response bias or even taste preference. A series of experiments on taste parameters using appropriate psychophysical procedures are summarized here.

Using a criterion-free signal detection procedure, we found no differences between obese and normal weight subjects in their ability to detect low concentrations of sucrose (Grinker et al. 1972). With signal detection, it is possible to separate the true detectability or threshold for sucrose from the criterion or willingness to say 'yes' or 'no' when confronted with any given concentration. Since the obese were purported to be particularly influenced by external factors, an experiment was designed to manipulate criterion by the addition of a tasteless, red vegetable dye. The decision criterion for sucrose (as measured by a 'yes-no' procedure) was uninfluenced by the colouring. However, in another experiment using a magnitude estimation procedure, all subjects rated suprathreshold solutions of sucrose coloured red as more sweet than colourless solutions of the same concentration. From these experiments, we concluded that the taste parameters of obese and normal weight individuals could be equivalently influenced by visual cues. We next examined taste preference, a more complex measure of appetitive behaviour.

Taste preference

Taste preferences for sucrose and salt were measured in obese and normal weight subjects by two procedures: paired comparisons (forced-choice between two solutions) and hedonic ratings (ratings of pleasantness, for each solution

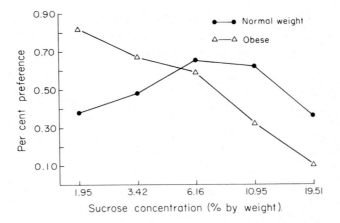

FIG. 4. Sucrose preferences of 22 obese and 13 normal weight subjects using the paired comparisons procedure. Sucrose concentrations ranged from 1.95% to 19.51% and were maintained at 34°C. Percentage preference is a function of the number of times a solution was chosen over all other solutions.

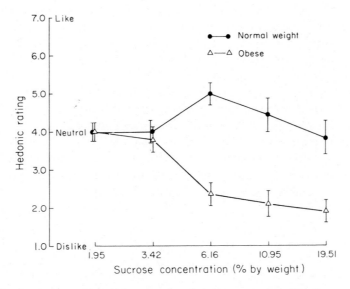

FIG. 5. Hedonic ratings of sucrose (1.95% to 19.51% at 34°C) by 10 obese and 13 normal weight subjects. The attractiveness of the solutions was rated on a scale from one to seven.

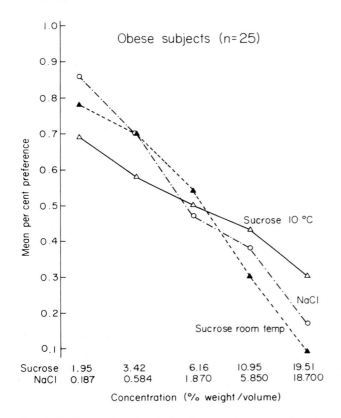

FIG. 6. Preference for salt solution (at room temperature) and sucrose (at room temperature and at 10°C). Percentage preference represents the number of times a concentration was preferred over all other concentrations.

separately). The two procedures gave concordant results. Sharp differences emerged between the obese and non-obese subjects (Grinker *et al.* 1971*b*) (see Figs. 4 and 5). Normal weight subjects rated most solutions neutral and preferred the concentrations of medium strength (6.1% and 10.95%) to the other concentrations. For the obese, a different preference pattern emerged: the higher the concentration of the solution the more unpleasant it was rated and the lower the frequency of choice. These differences in taste preference between obese and normal weight subjects seemed to be specific for a sweet taste. Our obese subjects also showed a strong aversion for increasing salt concentrations (0.187% to 18.7% sodium chloride solution). We have repeated these experiments with another group of obese subjects. Again, obese subjects showed a pronounced dislike for salt, a pattern which is shown by normal

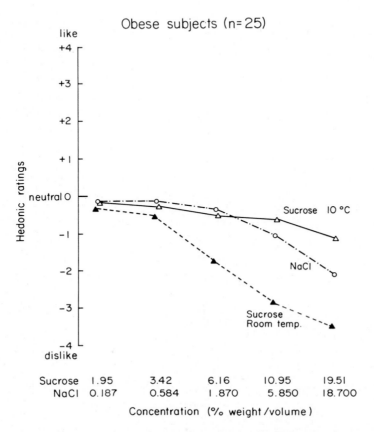

FIG. 7. Hedonic ratings of salt solution (at room temperature) and sucrose (at room temperature and at 10°C). The attractiveness of the solutions was rated on a scale from +4 to −4.

weight subjects, and a strong dislike for sweet solutions, a pattern which is not shown by the majority of normal weight subjects (Pfaffmann 1961). Thus, the obese have a selective aversion for 'sweetness'. Figs. 6 and 7 show hedonic ratings and paired comparisons for salt and sucrose at both room temperature and 10°C. The colder temperature served only to flatten the negative preference function.

Since subjects might well deny a preference for sweet solutions in a laboratory situation, our next series of experiments correlated the preference pattern with intake. Subjects were asked to drink as much or as little of a given solution as they wished after first tasting it. Ten minutes later, subjects rated the pleasantness of the solution and estimated its sweetness. Fig. 8 shows that

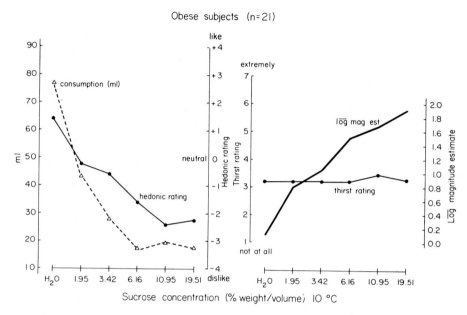

Fig. 8. Hedonic ratings, consumption (ml) and magnitude estimates of sweetness as a function of sucrose concentration. Solutions presented included water and ranged from 1.95% to 19.51% sucrose. Thirst ratings (on a scale from one to seven) were made before consumption. After a ten minute consumption period, estimates of sweetness (expressed as mean logarithmic estimates) and preference (on a scale from +4 to −4) were made.

consumption parallelled preference ratings precisely. Subjects liked water and disliked all the sweet solutions. In an effort to ensure a minimum consumption, subjects were required to go without food or drink for the immediately pre-ceding two hours. Note that although thirst ratings showed a moderate degree of thirst and remained constant throughout the experiment, consumption was solely influenced by the subjects' preferences.

The effects of an internal signal

It is possible that the metabolic state of an individual can affect his sucrose preference. Previous work has shown that normal weight subjects experience sweet solutions as unpleasant when tasted after a glucose load (Cabanac et al. 1968). This indicates that internal signals may modify taste pleasantness in normal weight subjects. Obese subjects did not reduce the rated attractiveness of solutions (Cabanac & Duclaux 1970). We repeated this experiment with

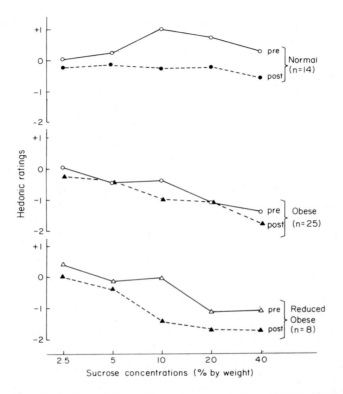

FIG. 9. Hedonic ratings of sucrose concentrations (2.5% to 40%) before and after oral glucose loads by normal weight, obese and reduced obese subjects. Ratings were made on a scale which ranged from +2 to −2.

one group of obese subjects before weight loss, one group of obese subjects after moderate weight loss and a group of normal weight subjects. After an overnight fast, subjects rated five suprathreshold concentrations of sucrose and were then given an oral glucose load (loads were normalized by calculating the dose on the basis of lean body mass plus a 15% allowance for normal body fat). One hour later, subjects again rated the five sucrose concentrations. Fig. 9 shows that the normal weight group and the reduced obese group made significant decrements in the rated attractiveness of the sucrose solutions. Obese subjects who had not begun weight loss did not respond to the oral glucose load. One explanation of this phenomenon might be that the obese individual is initially unwilling to attend to this physiological signal. However, once weight reduction has begun, it is physiologically possible to 'listen' to these stimuli.

Feeding patterns

An examination of the role of both 'taste' and 'calorie' factors in food regulation can best be made by continuously monitoring food intake. Stunkard *et al.* (1955, 1959) have classified eating abnormalities into three distinct types: eating without satiation, binge eating occurring at times of stress and the 'night eating syndrome'. We have found that this last pattern of eating at night is common among our severely obese individuals. They are typically anorexic in the morning and hyperphagic in the evening, engaging in large, continuous afternoon and evening meals or large midnight snacks following their regular dinner. Obese animals may also show disturbances in meal patterns. Le Magnen (1967) and Richter (1927) have demonstrated the sensitivity of continuous meal pattern analysis for uncovering the factors influencing the initiation and termination of feeding. Rats generally eat seven to ten discrete meals a day and over 50% of these are in the 12 hours of darkness. This light–dark cycle disappears from the eating patterns of hyperphagic ventro-medially lesioned animals (Kakolewski *et al.* 1971; Becker & Kissileff 1971). Lesioned animals eat more than normal animals by taking in constant amounts through-out the 24 hours. Genetically obese Zucker rats observed in our laboratory display a feeding pattern similar to that of ventro-medially lesioned animals (Becker & Grinker, unpublished data). The main variable contributing to the greater food intake of the obese animals is the absence of the light–dark periodicity; they eat the same number of large meals during the day as in the night. Although the intake of normal weight animals is the same as that of the Zucker obese in the night portion of the cycle, the intake of the normal animal drops off in the normally inactive light portion of the cycle.

CONCLUSION

The relative equivalence of significant metabolic and behavioural findings in human obesity supports the conclusion that this is a psychosomatic disorder. Adult men and animals tend to maintain a fixed body weight and a constant proportion of body fat by a continuous process of adjustment and regulation. The factors governing weight equilibrium are partially established early in life and appear more difficult to change with growth and development. Studies in our laboratory have shown that obese subjects have an increased adipose cell number which persists after weight reduction. Weight reduction leads to depression, a slowing of internal time and increasing errors in evaluating body size. Both cellular and behavioural changes occur primarily among juvenile-

onset obese. These individuals are also different from normal weight individuals in taste preference. Normal weight subjects showed the greatest
liking for the 6.16% sucrose concentration while obese individuals strongly
disliked this solution. In fact, a significant correlation exists between
preference ratings and adipose cell number, such that the more negative the
preference ratings, the greater the cell number ($r = -0.4274$; $P < 0.02$). Adipose
cell number and percentage overweight are highly correlated. The correlation
between hedonic ratings and cell number exists even when body weight is held
constant (partial $r = -0.3416$; $P < 0.06$). Current experiments are aimed at
discovering additional correlations among the behavioural and metabolic
components of obesity.

The therapeutic implications of our research are as follows. Successful
treatment will depend on the age at onset of obesity as well as severity and
duration. Weight loss for the juvenile-onset obese induces a 'starvation-like'
state. With few exceptions, all will succumb to the pressure towards equilibrium and regain the lost weight. Because of this poor prognosis, weight
reduction might be an unrealistic objective and perhaps should be vigorously
pursued only with those severely obese patients with juvenile-onset obesity who
have severe medical complications. Nutritional counselling, psychotherapy
and behaviour modification are now commonly recommended treatment
procedures. Psychotherapy may be particularly useful for the juvenile-onset
patient in helping him to accept and understand his obesity. Behaviour modification or the learning of control over the external determinants of food intake
may be somewhat useful (Stuart 1967), but such treatment can only help to
bolster the individual in his battle against a body weight permanently 'set' at
a higher level.

ACKNOWLEDGEMENTS

This work was supported in part by Research Grants HD-03719 and 02761
from the National Institutes of Child Health and Human Development and
Grant RR-00102 from the General Clinical Research Centers Program of the
Division of Research Resources, National Institutes of Health, Bethesda.

References

BECKER, E. E. & KISSILEFF, H. R. (1971) Abrupt changes in meal pattern following ventro-
    medial hypothalamic lesions. Eastern Psychological Association, Annual Meeting.
    (abstract)

BJORNTORP, P. (1972) Disturbances in the regulation of food intake. Obesity: Anatomic and physiologic-biochemical observations. In *Advances in Psychosomatic Medicine* (Reichsman, F., ed.), **7**, Karger, Basel

BRUCH, H. (1961) Conceptual confusion in eating disorders. *J. Nerv. Ment. Dis.* **133**, 46-54

BRUCH, H. (1969) Hunger and instinct. *J. Nerv. Ment. Dis.* **149**, 91-114

CABANAC, M. & DUCLAUX, R. (1970) Obesity: Absence of satiety aversion to sucrose. *Science (Wash. D.C.)* **168**, 496-498

CABANAC, M., MINAIRE, Y. & ADAIR, E. (1968) Influence of internal factors on the pleasantness of a gustative sweet sensation. *Commun. Behav. Biol.* Part A, I, 77-82

CAMPBELL, R. G., HASHIM, S. A. & VAN ITALLIE, T. B. (1971) Studies of food intake regulation in man. Responses to variations in nutritive density in lean and obese subjects. *New Engl. J. Med.* **285**, 1402-1407

COHN, C. & JOSEPH, D. (1962) Influence of body weight and body fat on appetite of 'normal' lean and obese rats. *Yale J. Biol. Med.* **34**, 598-607

CORBIT, J. D. & STELLAR, E. (1964) Palatability, food intake, and obesity in normal and hyperphagic rats. *J. Comp. Physiol. Psychol.* **58**, 63-67

GLUCKSMAN, M. L. & HIRSCH, J. (1968) The response of obese patients to weight reduction: A clinical evaluation of behavior. *Psychosom. Med.* **30**, 1-11

GLUCKSMAN, M. L. & HIRSCH, J. (1969) The response of obese patients to weight reduction: III. The perception of body size. *Psychosom. Med.* **31**, 1-7

GLUCKSMAN, M. L., HIRSCH, J., McCULLY, R. S., BARRON, B. A. & KNITTLE, J. L. (1968) The response of obese patients to weight reduction: II. A quantitative evaluation of behavior. *Psychosom. Med.* **30**, 359-373

GREENWOOD, M., JOHNSON, P. R., CRUCE, J. A. F., QUARTERMAIN, D. & HIRSCH, J. (1971) Is the ability to regulate food intake impaired in genetic obesity? *Fed. Proc.* **30**, 527 (abstr.)

GRINKER, J., COHN, C. K. & HIRSCH, J. (1971a) The effects of intravenous administration of glucose, saline and mannitol on meal regulation in normal weight human subjects. *Commun. Behav. Biol.* **6**, 203-208

GRINKER, J., SMITH, D. V. & HIRSCH, J. (1971b) Taste preferences in obese and normal weight subjects. *Proceedings of the IVth International Conference on the Regulation of Food and Water Intake*, Cambridge, England (abstract)

GRINKER, J., HIRSCH, J. & SMITH, D. V. (1972) Taste sensitivity and susceptibility to external influence in obese and normal weight subjects. *J. Pers. Soc. Psychol.* **22**, 320-325

GRINKER, J., GLUCKSMAN, M., HIRSCH, J. & VISELTEAR, G. (1973a) Time perception as a function of weight reduction: A differentiation based on age at onset of obesity. *Psychosom. Med.* in press

GRINKER, J., HIRSCH, J. & LEVIN, B. (1973b) The affective responses of obese patients to weight reduction: A differentiation based on age at onset of obesity. *Psychosom. Med.* in press

HASHIM, S. A. & VAN ITALLIE, T. B. (1965) Studies in normal and obese subjects with a monitored food dispensing device. *Ann. N. Y. Acad. Sci.* **131**, 654-661

HIRSCH, J. & HAN, P. W. (1969) Cellularity of rat adipose tissue: Effects of growth, starvation and obesity. *J. Lipid Res.* **10**, 77-82

HIRSCH, J. & KNITTLE, J. L. (1970) Cellularity of obese and nonobese human adipose tissue. *Fed. Proc.* **29**, 1516-1521

HOAGLAND, H. (1933) The physiological control of judgments of duration: Evidence for a chemical clock. *J. Gen. Psychol.* **9**, 267-287

HOEBEL, B. G. & TEITELBAUM, P. (1966) Weight regulation in normal and hypothalamic hyperphagic rats. *J. Comp. Physiol. Psychol.* **61**, 189-193

JACOBS, H. L. & SHARMA, K. N. (1969) Taste vs. calories: Sensory and metabolic signals in the control of food intake. *Ann. N. Y. Acad. Sci.* **157**, 1084-1125

JANOWITZ, H. D. & HOLLANDER, F. (1955) The time factor in the adjustment of food intake to varied caloric requirement in the dog: A study of the precision of appetite regulation. *Ann. N. Y. Acad. Sci.* **63**, 56-67

JOHNSON, P. R. & HIRSCH, J. (1972) Cellularity of adipose depots in six strains of genetically obese mice. *J. Lipid Res.* **13**, 2-11.

JOHNSON, P. R., ZUCKER, L. M., CRUCE, J. A. F. & HIRSCH, J. (1971) Cellularity of adipose depots in the genetically obese Zucker rat. *J. Lipid Res.* **12**, 706-714

JORDAN, H. A., WIELAND, W. F., ZEBLEY, S. P., STELLAR, E. & STUNKARD, A. J. (1966) Direct measurement of food intake in man: A method for the objective study of eating behavior. *Psychosom. Med.* **28**, 836-842

KAKOLEWSKI, J. W., DEAUX, E., CHRISTENSEN, J. & CASE, B. (1971) Diurnal patterns in water and food intake and body weight changes in rats with hypothalamic lesions. *Am. J. Physiol.* **221**, 711-718

KEYS, A., BROZEK, J., HENSCHEL, A., MICKELSEN, O. & TAYLOR, H. L. (1950) *The Biology of Human Starvation*, University of Minnesota Press, Minneapolis

KNITTLE, J. L. & HIRSCH, J. (1968) Effect of early nutrition on the development of rat epididymal fat pads: Cellularity and metabolism. *J. Clin. Invest.* **47**, 2091-2098

LE MAGNEN, J. (1967) Habits and food intake. In *The Handbook of Physiology*, section 6, *Alimentary Canal*, vol. 1, *Control of Food and Water Intake* (Code, C. F., ed.), pp. 11-30, American Physiological Society, Washington, D.C.

MILLER, N. E., BAILEY, C. J. & STEVENSON, J. A. F. (1950) Decreased 'hunger' but increased food intake resulting from hypothalamic lesions. *Science (Wash. D.C.)* **112**, 256-259

NISBETT, R. E. (1968a) Taste, deprivation and weight determinants of eating behavior. *J. Pers. Soc. Psychol.* **10**, 107-116

NISBETT, R. E. (1968b) Determinants of food intake in human obesity. *Science (Wash. D.C.)* **159**, 1254-1255

NISBETT, R. E. & STORMS, M. D. (1972) In *Cognitive Alteration of Feeling States* (London, H. S. & Nisbett, R. E., eds.), Aldine, Chicago

PFAFFMANN, C. (1961) The sensory and motivating properties of the sense of taste. In *Nebraska Symposium on Motivation, 1961 IX* (Jones, M. R., ed.), University of Nebraska Press

RICHTER, C. P. (1927) Animal behavior and internal drives. *Q. Rev. Biol.* **2**, 307-343

SALANS, L. B., HORTON, E. S. & SIMS, E. A. H. (1971) Experimental obesity in man: Cellular character of the adipose tissue. *J. Clin. Invest.* **50**, 1005-1011

SCHACHTER, S. (1967) Cognitive effects on bodily function: Studies of obesity and eating. In *Neurophysiology and Emotion* (Glass, D. C., ed.), pp. 117-144, Rockefeller University Press and Russell Sage Foundation, New York

SCHACHTER, S. (1971) Some extraordinary facts about obese humans and rats. *Am. Psychologist* **26**, 129-144

SCHACHTER, S., GOLDMAN, R. & GORDON, A. (1968) Effects of fear, food deprivation and obesity on eating. *J. Pers. Soc. Psychol.* **10**, 91-97

SCHIELE, B. C. & BROZEK, J. (1948) Experimental neurosis resulting from semistarvation in man. *Psychosom. Med.* **10**, 31-50

SIMS, E. A. H., GOLDMAN, R. F., GLUCK, C. M., HORTON, E. S., KELLEHER, P. C. & ROWE, D. W. (1968) Experimental obesity in man. *Trans. Assoc. Am. Physicians (Phila.)* **81**, 153-169

SPIEGEL, T. A. (1971) Regulation of caloric intake in man. *Proceedings of the IVth International Conference on the Regulation of Food and Water Intake*, Cambridge, England (abstract)

STELLAR, E. (1967) Hunger in man: comparative and physiological studies. *Am. Psychologist* **22**, 105-117

STUART, R. B. (1967) Behavioral control of overeating. *Behav. Res. Therapy* **5**, 357-365

STUNKARD, A. J. (1959) Eating patterns and obesity. *Psychiatr. Quart.* **33**, 284-295

STUNKARD, A. & BURT, U. (1967) Obesity and the body image: II. Age at onset of disturbances in the body image. *Am. J. Psychiatr.* **123**, 1443-1447

STUNKARD, A. J. & FOX, S. (1971) The relationship of gastric motility and hunger. *Psychosom. Med.* **33**, 123-134

STUNKARD, A. J., GRACE, W. J. & WOLFF, H. G. (1955) The night-eating syndrome. A pattern of food intake among certain obese patients. *Am. J. Med.* **19**, 78-86

STUNKARD, A. & KOCH, C. (1964) The interpretation of gastric motility 1. Apparent bias in the reports of hunger by obese persons. *Arch. Gen. Psychiatr.* **11**, 74-82

STUNKARD, A. & MENDELSON, M. (1967) Obesity and the body image: I. Characteristics of disturbances in the body image of some obese persons. *Am. J. Psychiatr.* **123**, 1296-1300

TEITELBAUM, P. (1955) Sensory control of hypothalamic hyperphagia. *J. Comp. Physiol. Psychol.* **48**, 156-163

WALIKE, B. C., JORDAN, H. A. & STELLAR, E. (1969) Preloading and the regulation of food intake in man. *J. Comp. Physiol. Psychol.* **68**, 327-333

WOOLEY, O. W. (1971) Long-term food regulation in the obese and non-obese. *Psychosom. Med.* **33**, 436-444

WOOLEY, S. C. (1972) Physiologic versus cognitive factors in short-term food regulation in the obese and non-obese. *Psychosom. Med.* **34**, 62-68

Discussion

Ginsburg: Did you have any artificial sweetener as control, and if so, did it make any difference as against natural sugars?

Grinker: We have used saccharine; it makes no difference. The tasting procedure is that the subjects sip and spit: they never swallow anything.

Donald: Did you test any more subtle tastes than sugar? In other words, was there a gourmet population among the subjects, or are they just quantitatively abnormal?

Grinker: Since the composition of adipose tissue reflects the nature of ingested fat, it is possible to draw some conclusions about diet from a comparison of the adipose tissue of obese and normal weight subjects. There are no significant differences between the two groups (Hirsch 1965; Hirsch & Goldrick 1964), suggesting that in the long run obese individuals eat the same proportion of fats, carbohydrates etc. as individuals of normal weight. In our tasting experiments, our subjects show a pronounced dislike for the sweet tasting solutions. However, they report that they take sugar in their coffee. Several studies (Nisbett 1968; Price & Grinker 1972) find that both obese and normal weight subjects eat more of foods they like (ice cream and crackers, respectively) than foods they dislike, but that the intake of obese subjects is more responsive to their preference.

Levine: Have you looked at any other threshold changes of the sensory apparatus? The adrenocortical hormones lower several sensory thresholds, including taste (Henkin 1970). It might be worth looking at other thresholds in your obese patients; the abnormality may not have to do with food alone.

Grinker: Bear in mind that we did not find differences in taste threshold; that is, taste sensitivity, using both sucrose and sodium chloride, did not differ between obese and normal weight subjects. We have tried a variety of psychophysical measures. We have looked at simple and disjunctive reaction time, both visual and auditory, and we find no differences between obese and normal weight subjects.

Sachar: Something implicit in your data might be made explicit. If the people with juvenile-onset obesity are fat primarily through an increase in cell number, and they reduce by 100 lb, the cell number doesn't change, so their fat cells are shrunken cells when they have lost weight. This change in cell size below what the normal person has then coincides with the onset of depression and the persistence of their images of themselves as being fat. Is that right?

Grinker: Yes. We have particularly tried to correlate metabolic and behavioural changes. Certainly these findings suggest that obesity represents an equilibrium state for these juvenile-onset patients and that weight reduction induces a 'starvation-like' state. It should therefore surprise no one that the prognosis for maintaining weight loss is extremely poor.

Sachar: This suggests that such patients in some way 'sense' their shrunken, starvation-type fat cells, despite a normal maintenance diet, and respond psychologically to that.

Ginsburg: Your 'set-point' hypothesis suggests an interaction between a genetic constitution and early experience. Would you like to comment on that?

Grinker: The cellular development of adipose tissue was evaluated in a cross-sectional study with normal weight children from birth to 13 years (Hirsch & Knittle 1970). Cell size shows a three-fold increase from birth to age six, with little or no change between ages six and 13 years. Cell number, however, shows a rapid three-fold increase by one year and a more gradual increase up to puberty. But neither cell size nor cell number reach adult values by puberty. Thus, it is not clear at what age adipose cellularity becomes fixed. One suspects that nutritional influences would have some effect up to this point.

However, a recent study in our laboratory suggests that nutritional manipulations do not always produce clearcut results (Johnson, Stern, Greenwood & Zucker, unpublished findings 1972). Total cell number and size in lean Zucker rats can be manipulated by raising the animals in small or large litters (three to four or 12 to 18 pups). This effect of under-nutrition was originally shown by Knittle & Hirsch (1968) in Sprague Dawley rats. In the genetically obese Zucker rat, however, total cell number and size can be influenced by over-nutrition (small litters) but cannot be manipulated by under-nutrition (large litters). This would suggest some invariant baseline.

Jerry Knittle (1971) is studying obese children. He feels that by age six years there are already three distinct populations, one with increases in cell number and in cell size, one with increases primarily in cell size and one with increases primarily in cell number.

Ginsburg: If you take some index of cell number, for example, does that provide the set-point, or do you have some other way of estimating it from your physiological data? Evidently there is an equilibrium, as you described it, that sets the weight at some point above what it normally should be, and then behavioural mechanisms and other mechanisms, even in spite of diet and motivation, tend to keep it there. Have you any ideas on the mechanisms by which the homeostat is set high?

Grinker: Factors known to influence body weight include calorie intake and energy expenditure (see Hirsch 1972). I would expect that adipose tissue also plays a part in this regulation, but I don't know how.

Gray: In view of the fact that ventro-medial hypothalamic lesions in the rat may have different effects depending on the sex of the animal (Valenstein 1968), have you looked for or found any sex differences? Were there sex differences in your two groups?

Grinker: There were no sex differences in studies of the behavioural responses to weight reduction. The numbers of male and female subjects were approximately equal in the longterm studies of weight reduction in hospital. The population that is referred to the Rockefeller University Hospital has a preponderance of women, especially in the juvenile-onset obesity group. We are currently examining the data on cellularity for sex differences.

Hofer: What happened when rats were raised in smaller litters than normal? Can you produce adults with an abnormally large number of fat cells, indicating that some early experience can determine the number of fat cells?

Grinker: Both the lean and the obese Zucker rat showed increases in total cell number when raised in litters of four compared to the standard litters of eight. The experiment was set up in a parametric design, using litters of four, eight and 12–18 pups.

Levine: There are complications about comparing enlarged rat litters with reduced litters of four pups. A lot goes on as well as the underfeeding. But in a litter that has been increased to 18 pups there is a whole range of size, so apparently some pups consistently get to the nipples and stay at normal weight. So within a single litter one can compare a group of pups of normal weight and a group of runt pups, and that would be a more appropriate comparison than the large and small litters.

Grinker: This would certainly be another method. I wonder whether the larger animals might not be genetically different *ab initio*? One would not have the control of randomly selecting animals to be under- and overfed.

Wolff: Dr Charles Brook in our department has studied adipose cell size and number in obese children (Brook *et al.* 1972), and our data are in agreement with Dr Grinker's. In our study the children with an increased number of adipose cells had already become obese during the first year of life. These children were also of above average height, their skeletal development was advanced and puberty tended to start early. These findings suggest that over-nutrition during infancy leads to an increased rate of multiplication not only of adipose cells but also of cells in some other tissues. When obesity has its onset later in childhood the rate of cell multiplication does not appear to be affected. Like Dr Grinker, we found that adipose cell number is not increased in obesity which has its onset in adult life; and we also agree that weight loss tends to be accompanied by a decrease in the size but not the number of adipose cells. We have also studied the fatty acid composition of adipose tissue and find that in obese children the percentage of palmitoleic acid is increased. This finding suggests increased lipogenesis from carbohydrate and supports the suggestion that these children eat an excess of carbohydrate.

Sandler: Dr Grinker's results make one question some of the psychoanalytic hypotheses about obesity. From a psychoanalytic point of view one would have said that people who are overweight are orally fixated and get greater gratification through eating, probably starting in the first or second year of life. In a situation which causes strain later on they return to these earlier modes of gratification and as a consequence become overweight. This may become rather like an addiction. From Dr Grinker's results, if the number of cells is determined genetically, there may be a vicious circle; the children one regards as orally fixated for psychological reasons may, to some degree, be genetically predestined to be orally fixated. One would imagine that they, or their bodies, wouldn't want to go through life with shrivelled cells in order to reach a normal weight, so there would be something within their metabolism which would lead them to eat more. It would be interesting to study the range of cell numbers in neonates or very young infants, using needle aspiration techniques, and to follow up these studies to see if there is a correlation later in life with the earlier findings.

Wolff: I know of no studies which show an increased number of adipose cells in the newborn infant.

Levine: There are experimental ways of producing heavier infants at birth, at least in rats; if one uterine horn is tied off the litter is cut in half and the pups born are 25–30% heavier than normal. The problem could be investigated in this way.

Grinker: This would be an interesting procedure and would provide a prenatal nutritional manipulation.

Ginsburg: Your data suggest that the patients retain an exaggerated image of their body size after they have lost weight. Is it possible that they have used this obese body image as a defence against life situations, which breaks down when they lose weight? Might this be a psychological component in their returning to the higher weight, as against your set-point hypothesis, which would be a physiological component?

Grinker: This takes us to the issue of correlation again. Once people are obese, it is hard to know whether certain behaviours are merely correlated with obesity or are an adaptation to it. Since obese people have made a long-term adjustment to the obesity they may use it defensively and have unreal expectations about what will happen to them when they lose weight. One cannot exclude that.

Ginsburg: Could this be another hypothesis, in addition to the set-point hypothesis, or would it exclude the latter?

Grinker: Certainly it is possible that psychodynamic components play a role in the maintenance of a fixed body image. But I do not think it is particularly useful to invoke the existence of a defensive strategy as an explanation of why the obese regain their lost weight.

Sifneos: In the self-assessment of depression, how do your patients perceive or describe depression?

Grinker: We did not have a category of depression on the rating scale. Instead we grouped certain adjectives (regretful, sad, sorry) into a category we called depression (see Nowlis 1965).

Sifneos: I understand that there are certain obese individuals who confuse anger and hunger, and when they are angry they overeat. Have you any evidence that this is the case?

Grinker: We have no evidence linking anger and eating. Our patients report that they are more likely to eat when tense or bored. Certainly we know that they are likely to have difficulties with weight reduction during any period of emotional stress.

References

BROOK, C. G. D., LLOYD, J. K. & WOLFF, O. H. (1972) *Br. Med. J.* **2**, 25-27

HENKIN, R. I. (1970) The effects of corticosteroids and ACTH on sensory systems. In *Progress in Brain Research*, vol. 32, *Pituitary, Adrenal and the Brain* (de Wied, D. & Weijnen, J. A. W. M., eds.), pp. 270-294, Elsevier, Amsterdam

HIRSCH, J. (1965) Fatty acid patterns in human adipose tissue. In *The Handbook of Physiology*, section 6, *Adipose Tissue*, pp. 181-189, American Physiological Society, Washington D.C.

HIRSCH, J. (1972) Discussion. In *Advances in Psychosomatic Medicine* (Reichsman, F., ed.), 7, 229-242, Karger, Basel

HIRSCH, J. & GOLDRICK, B. (1964) Studies on composition and metabolism of adipose tissue in man. In *Fat as a Tissue* (Rodahl, K., ed.), pp. 314-328, McGraw-Hill, New York

HIRSCH, J. & KNITTLE, J. L. (1970) Cellularity of obese and nonobese human adipose tissue. *Fed. Proc.* 29, 1516-1521

KNITTLE, J. L. (1971) Childhood obesity. *Bull. N.Y. Acad. Med.* 47, 579-589

KNITTLE, J. L. & HIRSCH, J. (1968) Effect of early nutrition on the development of rat epididymal fat pads: cellularity and metabolism. *J. Clin. Invest.* 47, 2091-2098

NISBETT, R. E. (1968) Taste deprivation and weight determinants of eating behavior. *J. Pers. Soc. Psychol.* 10, 107-116

NOWLIS, V. (1965) Research with the mood adjective check list. In *Symposium on Affect, Cognition and Personality* (Tompkins, S. S. & Izard, C. E., eds.), pp. 352-389, Springer, New York

PRICE, J. & GRINKER, J. (1972) The effects of the degree of obesity, food deprivation, and palatability on eating behavior of humans. Presented at Eastern Psychological Association Annual Meeting (abstract)

VALENSTEIN, E. S. (1968) In *The Neuropsychology of Development* (Issacson, R. L., ed.), pp. 1-39, Wiley, New York

The treatment of psychopathology in bronchial asthmatics

R. C. B. AITKEN, A. K. ZEALLEY and C. G. BARROW

Department of Psychiatry, University of Edinburgh

Abstract Sixty-eight patients with bronchial asthma were selected at random from registers of diagnosed cases. These—and an additional 14 patients referred to psychiatrists (the authors)—were examined for psychopathology, along with control subjects. Investigations included the use of psychometric tests, clinical assessment of personality traits, and psychophysiological examination.

There was virtually no evidence that the distribution of psychopathology in the randomly selected cases differed from that found in the general population; there was evidence of more psychopathology and more severe pulmonary disorder in the psychiatrically referred cases. No relationship could be discerned between the amount of psychopathology and the severity of pulmonary disorder in the randomly selected series.

Forty of these cases were divided into four groups of similar severity of asthma. Two of the groups had higher scores than the median on combined psychometric tests and two of the groups had lower scores. The patients were assessed fortnightly during a three-month period. One group in each pair received intensive psychiatric treatment, based on behaviour therapy principles, for one hour on each of ten occasions during the second month.

For those with higher psychometric morbidity scores, clinical ratings of 'anxiety severity' and of 'asthma severity' fell significantly more during the observation period, but this was irrespective of whether or not intensive psychiatric treatment was given. The rate of spontaneous fluctuations in skin resistance improved likewise. The psychiatric treatment allayed a tendency for ventilation volume to increase between successive occasions of measurement. At three-month follow-up, more of the patients who were treated intensively felt improved, both with respect to anxiety and to asthma symptoms.

It is concluded that anxious asthmatic patients benefit from regular contact with a psychiatrically orientated therapeutic team. It looks as if this contact need be little more than minimal, i.e. sufficient only to make clinical observations.

As psychiatrists, we were interested in investigating the effect of psychiatric management on a physical disease. For various reasons we selected bronchial asthma for study, a paradigm of a 'psychosomatic condition'.

Before starting, we required to know the nature of the psychopathology associated with the condition. Before accepting the findings of previous studies, we wished to be sure that the observations had been made on a sample of patients truly representative of the disease. Zealley (1971) had shown that inattention to this principle biased the results. Secondly, we insisted that the observations had been made with methods known to be reliable, sensitive and valid; or if these were in doubt, that evidence of attention to these considerations had been given. This meant that the observations had probably been made on matched control subjects also, preferably on some both with and without psychopathology. Lastly, we required that the methods of investigation had been comprehensive. Where both psychopathology (e.g. anxiety) and pulmonary pathology (e.g. asthma) can produce altered physiology (e.g. hyperventilation), it seemed important that this sort of contingency should also have been considered. As the clinical rating of personality assessment seems so different from that obtained by psychometric tests, we wished both methods to have been included in the assessment procedure.

Sadly, but not surprisingly, we did not find reports in the literature on investigations fulfilling these criteria. Studies by Rees (1956) and Leigh & Marley (1967) came closest, but they had been orientated more toward the aetiology of bronchial asthma, rather than toward a description of the psychopathology found in such patients. The authors of both these studies concluded that the disease was multifactorial in aetiology and pathogenesis.

Our work began with a study designed to obtain more information using methods fulfilling our stated criteria (Zealley *et al.* 1971).

PHENOMENOLOGICAL STUDY

Method

Sixty-eight patients with bronchial asthma were selected at random from registers of such diagnosed cases. The majority were matched for age, sex and social class with either a normal or a neurotic control subject. In addition, 14 patients with bronchial asthma who had been referred to us for psychiatric treatment were investigated similarly.

All subjects completed a selection of psychometric tests of personality, and were interviewed comprehensively for the assignment of personality traits. In addition several psychophysiological and pulmonary function measurements were made. The reliability of all observations was known, as was the sensitivity of the tests to detect abnormality in the control groups, which were selected to be bipolar for neurotic psychopathology.

Results

Preliminary findings were reported at a previous Ciba Foundation symposium (Aitken *et al.* 1970), and more fully at a meeting of the Royal Society of Medicine (Zealley *et al.* 1971).

On virtually all the scales of the psychometric tests (Taylor Manifest Anxiety Scale, Eysenck Personality Inventory and Foulds' Hostility and Direction of Hostility Questionnaire), the mean of the random asthmatics lay close to that which has been found from samples of the general population. The only exception was for females with mild asthma, whose mean neuroticism score on the Eysenck Personality Inventory was statistically significantly higher.

What was of more fascinating importance was that the scores obtained from the asthmatics spanned the entire range of those obtained from the normal and neurotic control subjects. Furthermore, the distribution of these scores was quite unrelated to an index of asthma severity.

Slightly more of the asthmatics were ascribed the trait 'underconfident' than the 'normal' controls, but for all other personality traits the prevalence did not differ from that found in the 'normal' controls. This contrasted with the high prevalence of neurotic personality traits found in the 'neurotic' controls.

Similar findings were obtained for both heart rate and ventilation volume. The means did not differ from those of the 'normal' controls, but the ranges were extensive, some patients having a tachycardia of 125 beats/minute and some hyperventilating at 15 litres/minute.

The prevalence of neurotic psychopathology and of severe asthma was higher in the small group of patients specifically referred to us for psychiatric treatment. More of them had 'unstable', 'hysterical' or 'dependent' traits on clinical personality assessment, and their mean score on the Taylor Manifest Anxiety Scale score was higher. More of them were being treated with corticosteroids.

Conclusions

There was virtually no reason to conclude that the prevalence or nature of psychopathology in patients with bronchial asthma differed from that found in people without the disease. Far from being a negative finding, this has demonstrated clearly that some of these patients had extensive neurotic disorder, just as some were remarkably stable. We concluded that patients with both bronchial asthma and neurotic psychopathology deserve psychiatric treatment just as much as neurotic patients without bronchial asthma, and with an expectation of gaining relief from superadded emotional distress. As anxiety can be associated with hyperventilation, which itself increases resistance to breathing and hence may induce bronchospasm, alleviation of anxiety could influence the pathogenesis of the respiratory disorder.

TREATMENT STUDY

In view of the evidence that some of the asthmatics suffered from neurotic disorder, with the specific and relevant physiological response of hyperventilation, treatment of anxiety on behaviour therapy principles seemed indicated. Promising results from a small trial were reported by Moore (1965).

Method

Forty of the previously investigated patients participated in a trial of treatment. They were divided into four groups of similar asthma severity. Two groups had higher scores than the median on psychometric tests, and two had lower scores than the median. All patients attended fortnightly for assessment during a three-month observation period. In addition, one group in each pair received intensive psychiatric management given on ten occasions during the middle month. This included relaxation training, ideational desensitization and breathing against resistance applied in an external airway, in practice rather like desensitization to an unpleasant but relevant stimulus. Positive transference was encouraged and tranquillizers were prescribed when thought appropriate. Reduction in hyperventilation was an aim of treatment.

Results

A brief summary of preliminary findings is given in Table 1. The groups with high 'psychometric emotionality' showed a reduction in the clinical rating of anxiety severity and of asthma severity. These groups also had a significant reduction in the rate of spontaneous fluctuations in skin resistance. Psychiatric treatment reduced the tendency for ventilation volume to increase between successive occasions of measurement; and it produced a drop, nearly reaching significance, in the Taylor Manifest Anxiety Scale scores.

At follow-up between three and nine months later, 50% of patients in the groups receiving psychiatric treatment felt that symptoms either of anxiety or

TABLE 1

Effect of 'psychometric emotionality' and psychiatric management on indices of psychopathology and pulmonary pathology

	'Psychometric emotionality' groups				Management groups			
	High	Low	F	P	Psychiatric treatment given	Observations only	F	P
Psychopathology								
Clinical rating of anxiety severity (0-4 scale)	−0.4	−0.1	4.73	0.05	−0.3	−0.2	–	N.S.
Taylor manifest anxiety scale score	−1.0	−0.9	–	N.S.	−1.9	0	3.43	N.S.
Skin resistance: spontaneous fluctuations (rate/min)	−1.5	−0.3	9.44	0.01	−1.0	−0.7	–	N.S.
Pulmonary pathology								
Clinical rating of asthma severity (0-4 scale)	−0.4	0.3	5.78	0.02	−0.1	0.1	–	N.S.
Forced expiratory volume in one sec (litres)	−0.09	−0.22	1.15	N.S.	−0.08	−0.23	1.76	N.S.
Ventilation volume (litres/min)	0.62	0.65	–	N.S.	−0.55	1.82	10.2	0.01

The values are the changes between the mean scores obtained on three occasions *before* treatment and on three occasions *after* treatment (two occasions for the Taylor Manifest Anxiety Scale scores). The F values were calculated from analyses of variance (df = 1 and 36). On no occasion was there a significant interaction between the main effects. N = 20 in each group for comparison of a main effect. N.S., not significant.

of asthma had been better in the period following the study than in a similar period beforehand: this contrasted with only 15% of those who had not received such intensive treatment.

Conclusions

Patients with bronchial asthma and also patients with high 'psychometric emotionality' have benefited by attendance at a psychiatric clinic relatively independently of the intensity of treatment. Hyperventilation was reduced by intensive treatment. At follow-up, patients reported benefit both in asthma and in anxiety.

It is logical that if a patient has both significant pulmonary pathology *and* psychopathology, he should receive appropriate treatment for both conditions.

If the problem is proneness to anxiety, it is likely to occur with bronchospasm. There is reason to believe that the anxiety response can be ameliorated by psychiatric treatment, with resulting improvement in the distress deriving from both emotional and pulmonary causes.

ACKNOWLEDGEMENTS

The authors are grateful to Dr I. W. B. Grant and Professor K. W. Donald for permission to investigate and treat patients under their clinical charge. They also thank Dr S. V. Rosenthal for assistance in the investigation of these patients. We express our appreciation to Professor G. M. Carstairs for provision of laboratory facilities. This work was supported by the Medical Research Council and the Mental Health Research Fund, to whom we are indebted.

References

AITKEN, R. C. B., ROSENTHAL, S. V. & ZEALLEY, A. K. (1970) Some psychological and physiological considerations of breathlessness. In *Breathing: Hering-Breuer Centenary Symposium (Ciba Found. Symp.)*, pp. 253-267, Churchill, London
LEIGH, D. & MARLEY, E. (1967) *Bronchial Asthma: a Genetic, Population and Psychiatric Study*, Pergamon Press, Oxford
MOORE, N. (1965) Behaviour therapy in bronchial asthma: a controlled study. *J. Psychosom. Res.* **9**, 257-276
REES, L. (1956) Physical and emotional factors in bronchial asthma. *J. Psychosom. Res.* **1**, 98-114
ZEALLEY, A. K. (1971) Bronchial asthma: a problem attributable to sampling when establishing its psychopathology. *Psychother. Psychosom.* **19**, 37-46
ZEALLEY, A. K., AITKEN, R. C. B. & ROSENTHAL, S. V. (1971) Personality and bronchial asthma. *Proc. R. Soc. Med.* **64**, 13-17

Discussion

Nemiah: Did any of your patients have other psychosomatic disorders, such as duodenal ulcer or rheumatoid arthritis? And if so, did they tend to fall in the low-emotionality part of the psychometric scale?

Aitken: The numbers in the study were quite small (68 patients) but there was no evidence that asthma went along with any other so-called psychosomatic disease.

Sachar: These data illustrate an interesting methodological point, that from objective indices there was no evidence of improvement of the asthma associated with the period of intensive psychiatric treatment. On the other hand, as you emphasized, you used a lot of suggestion and used the positive transference as much as possible, so that when you ask the patients afterwards whether they think the treatment did them any good, it's not surprising that most should say that it did. This is probably an effect of the transference which you encouraged.

Aitken: I agree that this explanation is possible, but there is no way to distinguish it as the correct cause of the improved self-reports.

Donald: One word of caution: the respiratory tests one uses are a crude measure of improvement. The major disease is in the very small airways which do not affect these tests, so there may still be a lot of continuing disease or functional disturbance. Although these tests have proved that the patient is aware that his expiratory flow rate has improved in his major airways, he is not aware of what's going on in the small airways. So it is a relatively crude test of total behaviour of the disease. An asthmatic may have an almost normal forced expiratory volume and yet the oxygenation of the arterial blood may be extremely low, down to a Po_2 of 40 or 30 mmHg.

Hill: Self-reporting of changes in asthmatics is a very poor indicator of improvement. I was involved with Dr Albert Mason in a small trial some years ago in which hypnosis was reported by the patients to produce a great improvement, but the actual figures of the ventilation exchange were not affected. But their relatives who kept diaries thought that the amount of asthma and the amount of distress was less.

Aitken: We too have some evidence on this. Sixteen patients also marked a visual analogue scale (10 cm line; Aitken 1969) each day when they blew a peak expiratory flow rate meter. All but one of the correlations were positive and over half were statistically highly significant. In other words, generally, subjective reports were detecting what was happening in the lung as revealed by the peak expiratory flow rate.

Reichsman: Your finding that the Taylor Manifest Anxiety Scale scores of the asthmatic patients were just about within the range of scores for the general population surprises me, because asthma is such an anxiety-provoking disease, irrespective of how you formulate its pathogenesis in an individual patient. It is striking how anxious these patients are—if not about anything else, about the illness itself.

Donald: Were these people who had been attending an asthma clinic previously or were they new patients? If they had been attending for some time and getting treatment or reassurance, this may have decreased their anxiety.

Aitken: The patients were selected from registers of asthma cases and we were aware of the significance of choosing them in this way. Zealley (1971) has reported changes in psychometric scores related to frequency of clinic attendance. A few of our patients may have attended the hospital clinic only once, and that some years previously. It appears that the majority of patients with asthma in Edinburgh are recorded on these registers on account of this initial referral.

Henry: Mathé & Knapp (1971) have made preliminary observations indicating that asthmatics have a diminished production of adrenaline during both stress and control periods. Their results indicate very significant differences from normal people in the catecholamine response to a given stimulus, despite the fact that they appeared to be just as emotionally aroused by the stressors. These were mental arithmetic performed for 30 minutes under criticism and time pressure, and a disturbing film showing burn accidents and treatment. They speculate that young asthmatics have either a neurohumoral defect or a sort of reversed fight–flight response with curbing of the stress-meeting mechanisms.

References

AITKEN, R. C. B. (1969) Measurement of feelings using visual analogue scales. *Proc. R. Soc. Med.* **62**, 989-993

MATHÉ, A. A. & KNAPP, P. H. (1971) Emotional and adrenal reactions to stress in bronchial asthma. *Psychosom. Med.* **33**, 323-341

ZEALLEY, A. K. (1971) Bronchial asthma: a problem attributable to sampling when establishing its psychopathology. *Psychother. Psychosom.* **19**, 37-46

General discussion

MODELS FOR MULTIDISCIPLINARY RESEARCH ON EMOTION

Sandler: It is appropriate to open a discussion into the conduct of an enquiry into the emotions and their consequences with a quotation from Kaplan, who says: '....We have come to recognize every concept as a rule of judging or acting, a prescription for organizing the materials of experience so as to be able to go on about our business. Everything depends, of course, what our business is ... A concept as a rule of judging or acting is plainly subject to determination by the context in which the judgement is to be made or the action taken' (1964). This quotation is extremely relevant to our discussions, for the problem of meanings and definitions is an important one—for example, the way in which each of us, in relation to his business and to his own theoretical system, uses such terms as emotion. As I personally see it, emotion has a double aspect, including bodily changes as well as feelings. Others see it in a different way. For example, in the interpretation of Professor Levine's experiments in which the rats were changed from variable reward to continuous reinforcement (p. 283), I would say that the regularity of response was linked with a feeling of safety and the irregularity with a reduction in the feeling of safety, and that this could account for the results. His interpretation, quite legitimate, is a different one. In the same way, psychological stimuli as I see it represent conscious or unconscious changes in the sensorium, rather than being 'external'. Models, as I have suggested by using the quotation from Kaplan, are related to our business, whether we are engaged in clinical investigation or in psychological or physiological theorizing. (It is interesting how often the aims of our work are related to the techniques we have at our disposal, whether they be techniques of measurement or techniques of influencing our experience.) It is important to realize that models are different and that this is as it should be. If we were to try to find a simple integrated model which we would all agree on, not only would it take many years but the model would be so large and unwieldy that science would sink under the weight of it. The function of discussion at such a symposium is to interact, to accept that we have different models, to apply our different points of view, knowing they are different, to present our results accordingly and to allow these results to affect our own thinking. They may not affect our model and our theory but they may affect the application of the model. For example, Dr Grinker's results (pp. 349-369) affect my own ideas about fixation, in the sense that from the psychoanalytic point of view it may be that the child seeks out his own fixation points to a greater degree than might previously have been supposed. This sort of interaction can be extremely valuable.

Rutter: I agree with Dr Sandler that different models have different purposes, but I would add that not all models are equally good or equally appropriate.

COMMUNICATION BETWEEN CLINICIAN AND EXPERIMENTALIST

Engel: At interdisciplinary conferences involving clinicians and basic scientists an extraordinary difficulty in discourse commonly emerges along with a clear, whether acknowledged or not, adversary posture, in which each vigorously defends his own methods and models and attacks those of the other. This is usually ascribed to lack of understanding of each other's disciplines. While this is certainly so, I believe that the differences in the nature of the materials with which each of us deals and the radically different strategies required to study them are more crucial (Table 1). Clinicians deal with patients; basic scientists deal with animals or 'subjects'. Those who have never taken care of patients, that is, who are not physicians, will find it difficult to appreciate how much this professional and ethical responsibility determines both the limitations and the advantages of *clinical* research. For the primary strategy of clinical research has to be that of *naturalistic* observation, in contrast to that in basic research, which is primarily *experimental*. Neither, of course, is purely so. As clinical scientists we are presented with situations over which we have little or no control. We had little to do with the conditions responsible

TABLE 1 (Engel)

Materials and strategies used by clinicians and basic scientists

	Clinician	*Basic scientist*
Material:	Patients	Subjects, animals
Strategy:	Naturalistic	Experimental
Role:	Doctor–patient	Control, mastery
Data:	Too much, reduction necessary	Circumscribed, controlled

for the object of our study becoming a patient and we are constrained not to do anything not in the patient's interest. To pursue scientific study we look for situations which happen to exist in which we can make observations or measurements and from which we can generate hypotheses to be tested by further observation, measurement or intervention. The laboratory-based scientist, in contrast, begins with an hypothesis and proceeds to design experiments to test the hypothesis, experiments in which he tries to determine the conditions and material most suitable for his purposes.

Another important difference is that clinical research is done within the framework of the doctor–patient relationship, which is unique from both sides. The very fact of being a patient relating to a physician leads the patient to provide the physician with categories of information which are often not accessible to the experimentalist working with a 'subject'. The professional role is also an interpersonal and interactional one. To a large extent the investigator is part of the experiment and proper design often requires an observer of the physician–patient dyad if complete information is to be obtained (Engel et al. 1956). The basic scientist, by contrast, has relative control over his material and manipulates it at will, though even he must take into account relationships, at least with higher animals and human subjects.

There is also a major difference in the nature of the data. Those of the basic scientist are relatively circumscribed at his pleasure: he can exclude what he is not interested in. A hundred years ago much physiology was done with the pithed animal; in other words, the nervous system was then considered a source of interference. Some experimentalists today regard psychological phenomena in the same light; they think they could do more interesting experiments if only they could get rid of the mental apparatus. The clinician-scientist cannot exclude any ongoing process except by ignoring it; patients cannot be pithed. As a result the clinician must deal with an enormous amount of data presented to him by his patient-subjects, much of which may not be germane to his interest.

How can we clinicians handle this excess of information and reduce it to terms we can communicate to our basic science colleagues? We deal with what we see people do and say, what we can invoke in them by interview or testing procedures or by making certain kinds of demands on them. And whether we acknowledge it or not, our conclusions are inevitably influenced, often crucially, by data we never report, indeed sometimes never even realize had influenced us. This is a major problem for methodology.

The crux of the matter, well illustrated in this symposium, is that our laboratory-based colleagues demand that we apply the laboratory-designed experiment to what are more properly categorized as field conditions or experiments of nature. We seem old-fashioned because much of our research remains at the hypothesis-developing stage. We on the other hand criticize them for performing 'unnatural' experiments, testing hypotheses not derived from situations that exist in nature. But this is exactly where we should be working together, for many of our hypotheses cannot be tested on patients, but will require experimentation. This is particularly so in the elucidation of psychosomatic mechanisms. We provide the data upon which to model natural situations; the basic scientists design the experiments that fit the model to test the hypothesis.

Rutter: I think that Professor Engel overestimates the differences between the clinical approach and the basic scientific approach. Clinical research is not necessarily purely observational; nor is basic research necessarily experimental. Scientists studying animal behaviour do not always use the experimental method, and in the human field epidemiologists do not do so either. Conversely, clinicians use the experimental method whenever they carry out a controlled trial of treatment. Indeed, one could argue that any treatment is a type of experiment, in that it involves systematically altering one variable to determine the effect on another, which is the essence of the experimental method.

NATURAL EVENTS AND EXPERIMENTAL RESEARCH

Ginsburg: Dr Sandler has reintroduced feeling into the symposium, and in this respect I feel that I belong more among the clinical practitioners, although my patients may be slightly peculiar. In purporting to study overt behaviour, whether in a patient or an animal, we infer affect from the observed behaviour. When I observe a slinking wolf who is trembling and salivating, I say that he is afraid and anxious. I submit that the basis for my inference is much the same as that of the clinician with respect to his patients.

When I manipulate the wolf's environment and (if I am successful) bring about a modification of his behaviour, I am acting like the psychiatrist who fits his observations of the patient into his clinical taxonomy, and both practises his art and tests his hypotheses in attempting to alter behaviour. At this level we do not need to talk about affect. We can each measure intercorrelated physiological and molecular events but, however well they are correlated with the changing behaviour, they are not the same as either the affect or the behaviour. I must still infer subjectively that the animal is anxious, whether I know his serotonin levels or not. Nevertheless, to deal with affect at this level, both for the clinician and for the experimentalist, *is* a scientific approach, providing we can use this concept to frame hypotheses which can then be tested. In the work I presented earlier (pp. 163-174), I found it impossible to formulate an adequate hypothesis without involving the notion that one has to work with the naked affect of fear or anxiety in the animal in order to bring about a lasting behavioural change.

With respect to wildness, which includes a very low threshold of response when it occurs, I infer that the homeostat or set-point is at a level in the wild animal that is adaptive for it, and at different but also adaptive levels in domestic animals and in man. The physiological mechanisms that control this homeostat exist as part of our evolutionary legacy. My hypothesis is, therefore, that the mechanisms involved in the extreme anxiety and wariness of the wild animal are identical with those underlying similar behaviour in man and that the behaviours are homologous. This hypothesis can be tested. Because a physiological event has happened in the same way in man and Canid, does not, of course, mean that it is perceived, felt or interpreted in the same way. This is another whole area for investigation.

Hinde: I think you are in danger of falsifying by oversimplifying when you compare wolves to people and imply that it is merely a matter of a difference in setting the homeostat of the wildness response to novelty. Species are very different from each other and one cannot make jumps from one species to another by superficially abstracting symptoms in this way. Razran (1971) has shown very beautifully the increase in the complexity of learning up phyletic levels. I am chary of the biologist or comparative psychologist who wants to neglect the fact that human beings are different from wolves and that the role of the emotional states, in whatever way you like to interpret that, can only be compared when you have abstracted to the right level.

Ginsburg: I hope I am not making glib analogies. I am suggesting the hypothesis that at the level of the emotions and arousal, the degrees of freedom for man are not significantly greater than for wolves (except for the secondary associations that man can make), and that the underlying mechanisms are the same. I maintain that this hypothesis can be tested, which includes the possibility of disproving it, and that the behavioural results from our laboratory constitute evidence in its favour.

Levine: The problem for many of us who are trained in psychology in the laboratory is that we rarely observe animals in the field. This can be a revelation, in that the responses that the animal demonstrates in its natural environment are not the kinds that it shows in the laboratory. And similarly, the questions one asks in the laboratory are not the kind of questions that can be asked in a natural environment, because one cannot, and does not want to, intervene in the natural environment. The issue really is this: how can one elucidate the mechanism? I cannot get at mechanisms by looking at either patients or animals in the naturalistic situation. But I can get an enormous amount of information which gives me clues to the kinds of questions I can ask about mechanisms.

Engel: This is the central problem of our research strategy: to devise means for the exchange of information between those working in clinical or naturalistic settings and those in laboratory settings.

Sandler: There is a fundamental difference between man and the lower animals used in research that is relevant to the production of psychosomatic illness. In the lower animals a behavioural response is not normally inhibited. It is a fairly direct response. In man, the mental apparatus can inhibit and restrict action to a much higher degree, very often to a trial or sample action or thought, as described by both Piaget and Freud. There exist covert responses and certain feeling signals connected with these; warnings, if you like, that the action may result in a greater state of pain or have other unfortunate consequences, or that alternative actions may result in the obtaining of greater pleasure. These will therefore be facilitated and allowed to proceed to overt action. This is a fundamental distinction. There is an 'animal' part of the human being and a controlling part; we have to take into account the covert aspects of human mental functioning when we relate it to experimental work. To give a clinical example: someone's mother-in-law comes to visit. This arouses a response of aggression and anger. The person's conscience may be such that he doesn't permit himself to act aggressively or to feel his anger; or having felt it he pushes it back. He has to live with this anger for a long time. If he feels helpless and hopeless in the face of the situation, he may have a conservation–withdrawal reaction; he might get depressed because he can't do anything about it; or he might develop a psychosomatic symptom, if we believe that pent-up emotion (to go back to an earlier psychoanalytic frame of reference) gives rise to psychosomatic disturbances. He might become paranoid or develop a hysterical symptom. In the step between animal and man we have to take into account this checking and controlling system, and the difference between what is manifest in behaviour and experience on the one hand and what is latent in the form of trial responses on the other. It is at the level of trial responses that we can probably bridge the gap more easily than at the level of the manifest response.

A DEVELOPMENTAL EXPERIMENTAL MODEL OF INDIVIDUAL DIFFERENCES

Denenberg: We began the meeting with some excellent examples of individual differences. Dr Nemiah talked about two cases of abnormal response to the emotional trauma of loss, profoundly different in their clinical manifestations. Dr Sandler talked about the mental apparatus, which refers to the way a particular individual turns on and turns off certain sets of behaviour, attitudes and so on. The problem for the clinician, as I understand it, is to try to explain individual differences: why do certain individuals behave in one way and others, given the same stimulus events, in another? The problem for the experimentalist is the very different one of how to reach general laws which apply to all individuals regardless of their idiosyncratic characteristics.

The problem for all of us now is, how do we meet? I suggest one way of meeting: to understand individual differences one has to know the developmental history of the organism (Denenberg 1970). Before we can explain why Madame D. acted in the way she did, we need to find out about the early developmental history, and her genetic make-up.

I would like to introduce another model—the developmental experimental model—to help us. One task for those of us doing research with animals in a developmental context is to create 'personalities', in the sense that we can by experimental manipulations create animals of low emotionality, high learning ability and capacity for survival in distressing situations (Denenberg 1969; Denenberg & Whimbey 1968). One way for experimentalists and clinicians to come together is for those of us who have such animal models to get suggestions from those who have the rich clinical material. I know that some of the things I can do with my animals in their early life will modify the animal's capability to respond to stress, for example. By the use of a developmental model, we can begin to bring together the power of observation of the clinician with the rigour of the experimentalist.

Rutter: I agree with Professor Denenberg and regret that we have not spent more time considering developmental issues, both the expression of normal emotions and the pathogenesis of emotional disturbance itself. It is curious that we have discussed most aspects of physiology, emotion and psychosomatic illness, except the determinants of emotions in human beings which some might consider the central theme. In this connection there are advantages to the study of children, partly because the emotional situation is somewhat less complicated in childhood, and partly because one can study the development of emotions directly rather than having to rely on retrospective reconstruction of the past by adult patients.

PENSÉE OPÉRATOIRE AND CONSERVATION–WITHDRAWAL: POSSIBLE
NEUROPHYSIOLOGICAL MECHANISMS

Henry: Dr Nemiah and Dr Sifneos have suggested (1970) that *pensée opératoire* may be associated with lack of connection and communication between the limbic system, which is the substrate of emotion, and those regions in the neocortex underlying the capacity for critical evaluation and the creation of complex systems of association. Nauta has recently discussed (1971) the functional significance of the major tracts that place the frontal lobe in a reciprocal relationship with these two great functional realms, namely with the telencephalic limbic system and with the newly developed parietal and temporal regions of the cerebral cortex involved in the processing of visual, auditory and somatic sensory information. Perhaps persons whose environment has been such that they have not sufficiently exercised one or the other or both of these pathways during their early years are predisposed to deficiencies in later life.

The values on which any particular sociocultural environment places a premium may help to determine which functional realm preponderates. D. F. Benson's work on aphasia (personal communication) suggests that man's unique capacity for cross-modal review of sensory perceptions depends on the integrity of the new association areas of the 'sociocultural brain', in particular, on the angular and the second temporal gyrus. These regions give him the power to review the various modalities, such as sound, touch and visual sensations, as they relate to words and abstract concepts—that is, as they contribute to the flow of technical or operational thought. Such activity can go on without emotional arousal and may represent an important anatomical locus of the processes of *pensée opératoire*.

On the other hand, fantasy and affect-laden patterns are probably based on the limbic system, for they are associated with the species- and self-preservative activities connected with territory, with the search for shelter, food and water, and with parent–child, male–female and social hierarchical considerations. Nauta points out that the activation of such responses largely involves the alternative fronto-limbic pathways. In this view, the frontal cortex becomes the critical junction zone between the environmentally dependent patterning activities of the sociocultural brain and the environmentally stable systems of the limbic circuits.

The emotionally charged symbols—the dogmas, beliefs and idea systems of man's societies—find expression in various rites of passage and fixed cultural practices. It is proposed that the frontal cortex may play an important role in the effective use of these socially determined response patterns as coping mechanisms. Katz *et al.* (1970) have shown that the rise in plasma levels of 17-hydroxycorticosteroid in women waiting to undergo biopsy of a breast tumour is inversely related to the effectiveness of their ego defences. These authors comment that projection, denial with rationalization, fatalism and prayer and faith are important defence patterns. These are socially determined responses and they control the extent to which the situation is perceived as threatening and in consequence permitted to arouse the sympathetic–adrenal medullary and pituitary–adrenal cortical control mechanisms. Elsewhere I have proposed that animals use such symbols as well as men and referred to a deficiency in the capability as a state of dys-symbolia (Henry 1967). This appears related to Nemiah and Sifneos's view of *pensée opératoire* as 'a failure to discern the qualities of emotion' and to Nauta's proposal of relative 'interoceptive agnosia' in states of frontal cortical deficiency as 'an impairment of the subject's ability to integrate certain information from his internal milieu with the environmental reports provided by his neocortical processing mechanisms'.

The testable hypothesis which emerges is that sustained disturbances of neuroendocrine balance with pathophysiological consequences may be more frequent in those faced with psychosocial stimuli who suffer from a deficiency in either or both of these systems. A preponderance of fronto-temporo-parietal activity may be related to *pensée opératoire* or extraversion and a preponderance of fronto-limbic activity to conservation–withdrawal or introversion—a balanced and effective operation of both modes being needed for optimally adapted behavioural and neuroendocrine responses.

CLINICAL RESEARCH STRATEGY

Zanchetti: The best way I could contribute to this discussion is to suggest how I, as a physician interested in arterial hypertension, could test the hypothesis that essential hypertension may originate through psychological mechanisms. What sort of facts would be needed to support this hypothesis? We already know that an increase in blood pressure can be produced from direct stimulation of the brain (Ranson & Billingsley 1916; Karplus & Kreidl 1927). We would like to know whether the relevant areas of the brain are also connected with behaviour, and this we also know (Hess 1949; Abrahams *et al.* 1960). We now want to know whether, by stimulating these brain areas, we can obtain prolonged, self-perpetuating changes in blood pressure, because hypertension is a prolonged self-perpetuating set of reactions. This point is not yet proved: for instance, the rats whose hypothalami were stimulated by Folkow & Rubinstein (1966) developed a hypertension which lasted for several weeks but declined when stimulation was interrupted. We would also like to know the converse, whether behaviour can raise blood pressure; for example, the kinds of behaviour I described in my paper do not raise the blood pressure very much. Instrumental conditioned behaviour has been shown to increase

blood pressure (Forsyth & Harris 1970; Herd *et al.* 1971), but here again we
lack evidence that this is self-perpetuating. After the stimulus was discontinued
pathology was shown in one monkey only (Benson *et al.* 1970). However, the
model Dr Henry presented (pp. 225-246) appeared more successful, probably
because it concerns a more complex and meaningful behaviour than just
pressing a lever. Using this model he could obtain a sustained increase in
blood pressure and vascular and organ pathology, as in hypertension in man.
But here is another important question: are there specific behaviours for inducing on the one hand, say, a raised blood pressure and on the other a peptic
ulcer, or does the same behaviour produce either type of damage? In the latter
case, which seems more probable, what are the peripheral factors which interact and make one animal respond with a rise in blood pressure and another
with a peptic ulcer? I know of no studies on this problem, though convenient
approaches can be easily seen. For example, strains of rats with genetically
determined hypertension have now been bred. It would be interesting to know
if irreversible hypertension can be produced in such a rat with behavioural
stimuli more easily than in ordinary strains.

But what can the physician himself do? I think that psychologists, psychiatrists and physicians should together try to develop much finer clinical tests of
behaviour. There are now several multidimensional tests that could be developed
or applied to study and define better the different psychological dimensions of
the patients (Zill 1972). One could take a large population with essential
hypertension and compare it in various ways with a group with secondary
hypertension, or see whether the population of essential hypertension patients
contains a significant number of patients showing particular psychological or
behavioural patterns and then compare any patterns that do emerge with
behavioural patterns in other diseases. Essential hypertension is a complicated
disease because of the effects of secondary vascular damage. Therefore, investigation might be conveniently concentrated on young subjects at the beginning of the disease, as well as on the children of hypertensives who are
known to be more liable to develop hypertension than normals.

Sleight: A clinician has not the expertise to design epidemiological or
psychological studies to examine the psychological factors involved in hypertension. One has cases where one tries to control a patient's blood pressure
and doesn't succeed until some 'stressful' situation disappears; a man may
eventually get his professorship and his blood pressure is thereafter easier to
control. These individual factors are important but they are difficult to control
experimentally and will be missed in large epidemiological studies. Clinicians
and experimental psychologists must work together in studying these sorts of
problems.

Aitken: I would like the meeting to tackle the issue of research strategy and tactics. In medicine several common diseases of unknown aetiology (such as bronchial asthma), which are characterized by morbidity rather than mortality, have symptoms that can also be due to other causes, notably anxiety. We now have relatively effective treatments for anxiety, but inadequately effective treatments for the pathology of these diseases. We have been discussing principally the strategy of looking at the particular mechanisms of the disease processes. I suggest that it should be equally respectable to look at their management. It is of course appropriate to look for fundamental causes, but this should not be at the expense of alleviating symptoms. For example, information now available on rehabilitation after myocardial infarction indicates that the success of this is as much related to absence of associated mood disturbance as to extent of coronary artery disease (Nagle *et al.* 1971). A good outcome of surgery for peptic ulcer is as much related to a low anxiety level of the patient as to anything that the surgeon might do (Small *et al.* 1969). Diminished life expectancy for those on chronic haemodialysis is as much related to increased hostility as to renal pathology (Daly 1969).

In our study of asthma (pp. 375-380) we found a number of people with severe psychopathology who were only receiving treatment for their pulmonary pathology. Only in the last few years have textbooks stopped relating the symptoms of hypertension or anaemia to blood pressure or haemoglobin concentration. These symptoms have now been shown to have little to do with hypertension or anaemia but to be related more to neurotic disturbance (Robinson 1969; Robinson & Wood 1968).

I suggest that people working in experimental psychology who are directing their students towards the respectable mechanistic type of research should consider directing them also to the tactical study of symptomatology. It is commendable to concentrate on mechanisms, because undoubtedly that should ultimately bring about the elucidation of the problems, but if more attention were paid to the simpler, more tactical methods of treatment an enormous amount of suffering could be relieved.

Weiss: I earlier questioned the usefulness of the concept of emotion in relation to somatic disease (p. 273). One reason why it is hard to get away from this concept is that we scientists as people are dominated by our thoughts and perceptions, and we perceive emotions very saliently. But if we consider the entire amount of 'behaviour' going on within us as organisms, including responses at the molecular level, we realize that the total activity within the organism is vast compared to the small amount available to us through consciousness. The information processed in our conscious thoughts and perceptions is relatively minuscule compared to the total amount of information processed in our bodies. Yet because thoughts are what are available to us through sensation and consciousness, and are so vivid, we tend to focus on them and build our theories of behaviour on them. When we see a frightening animal and run, we think we do so because we are frightened; that is the dominant sensation we have. We consequently frame our theory about why we run in terms of this predominant feeling of being frightened. But thoughts and intense feelings may be misleading in terms of the important variables which go into producing the running response. This is even more true when one tries to explain the extraordinary 'behaviours' within our body, and I include here events on a molecular level as well as gross skeletal behaviour. If we think only in terms of the sensations which to us are most salient we are sampling only a small part of the total processes probably going on and are likely to be wrong in our theories.

Hofer: As Dr Weiss says, there is a seductive danger in focusing on emotions, in that they become explanations and distract our attention from looking in a more detailed way at what is going on. On the other hand, the advantage in paying attention to emotions is that they can tell us something about central neural *states*. We can deduce something about the state of an animal only by observing its behaviour; in man, verbal behaviour is also available, adding a new dimension to our knowledge of a person's central state. We know that physiological processes are exquisitely sensitive to the state of the organism. We can see this by comparing the heart rate responses of a person during REM sleep, non-REM sleep, wakefulness and the excited state. Heart rate or almost any physiological response one chooses is extraordinarily state-dependent. This is where looking carefully at emotions gives us an added dimension in studying psychophysiological relations in man.

Hill: Professor Hinde earlier referred (p. 5) to Ryle's distinction between causes and reasons or dispositions; and in those terms there would be an equation between the animal's state in the different phases of sleep and the predisposition. In Ryle's example, it was jealousy that 'made' A hit B.

Engel: The discussion emphasizes the extent to which we neglect the primary data. Much of our discussion about emotions has sounded *as if* emotions could be considered in some substantive sense. What is the information one uses to make judgments when one is studying human beings? One devises a technique of interview which one tries to refine to avoid putting words into the patient's mouth or influencing what he says. The patient then talks and behaves; you listen and record what he says and does. These records constitute the primary data, a set of verbal and non-verbal material. I contend that this material is indivisible except in terms of the arbitrary constructs of the observer, who for his own purposes elects to group together certain characteristics of the material under such headings as emotion, cognitive performance, perception, object relations, drives, fantasies and so on. The investigator examines the relationship, if he is doing a psychophysiological study, between this material and the changes in some measurable physiological or biochemical parameter, which is usually two-dimensional: that is, it either goes up or goes down or remains unchanged. If he is an 'emotions' man, he may find that it seems to go up during the display of some particular emotion, say, fear. That may or may not be a valid correlation. Earlier (p. 272) I cited Greene's study of cardiac catheterization and the differential response of growth hormone and cortisol in anxious patients ('anxious' already is an interpretation of a set of data of the type I have just described) who were engaging as compared to anxious people who were not engaging with the people around them. Those two psychological parameters split the results. That is a warning that when we work with this kind of material we are dealing with a different kind of system from the one the behaviourists use. It is an indivisible system on the psychological side; it is a divisible system on the physiological–biochemical side.

Sandler: I don't think we can ever reach essential, intrinsic primary data; we have only our perceptions of what's going on and these are inevitably coloured by factors within ourselves. There comes a point where a certain amount of what one might call cognitive dissonance occurs, where information from other areas makes one look again, to try to re-interpret, to re-recognize or to reconstitute our perceptions of the data we are dealing with, and perhaps to reconstitute our theories. A symposium of this sort may cause us to do so, but we all initially perceive the data according to our own dispositions and our own theories.

Donald: One way to bridge the gap might be to study the people who do not become ill under extreme stress: the man who doesn't get his chair and hates his mother-in-law, has financial difficulties and so on, yet remains well, is normotensive, has no coronary artery disease and no indigestion and is totally healthy. Such people really must have something! They are successful organisms. What protects them from their emotions and the damage these are supposed to do to the body? This model has not been studied enough, either by experimentalists or by clinicians.

Sachar: The rigour of follow-up and carefully controlled studies of disorders classified as psychosomatic leaves much to be desired. There is no evidence that would satisfy the rigorous observer that psychoanalysis and psychotherapy have a significant effect on the clinical course of at least the original seven illnesses that Alexander defined, although during this meeting we have rejected those as *the* psychosomatic illnesses.

Sifneos: I agree with Dr Sachar and I would like to amplify this point by giving you a historical account. When I was directing the Psychiatric Clinic of the Massachusetts General Hospital it was easy to see that the clinic population could be divided into two main categories. The majority of the patients were self-referred, psychologically sophisticated young people. They were verbal, had easy access to their emotions and had a rich fantasy life. They had specific complaints and for all intents and purposes one could call them neurotic. They responded reasonably well to psychotherapy of short duration.

Having attended the Ciba Foundation Symposium on *The Role of Learning in Psychotherapy* in 1968 I was able to apply what I learned from the experimental psychologists and behavioural scientists at that meeting to the patients whom I have just described, with some success.

It was as a result of this experience that, one year later, I suggested a symposium on emotions. I had hoped that the exploration of the physiology of emotions would provide a baseline for the understanding of my second and smaller group of patients who were very different from the neurotic ones, and whose difficulties both John Nemiah and I have already mentioned. Mary B. is a typical example of these patients, some of whom suffer from one or two psychosomatic diseases, as she did. If one compares the description of a complaint of depression, for example, by these patients, with a similar complaint from the patients in the neurotic group, one is struck by the dissimilarity in the ways in which these two groups of patients talk about this specific symptom (Sifneos 1967). The former complained about physical sensation such as pain, muscle twitches and so on, as well as about insomnia. When they were asked to describe their thoughts while they were unable to sleep they had difficulty in remembering them and usually they said that they did not have any. In contrast, the depressed patients of our large neurotic group described endlessly their guilt feelings or their emotions of sadness about the loss of a loved one. They usually attributed this inability to sleep precisely to the presence of 'too many thoughts'. Another observation about the first group of patients was the presence of *pensée opératoire* originally described by Marty & de M'Uzan (1963; Marty *et al.* 1963). These patients also showed a striking inability to label or describe their emotions, as I have mentioned previously. For example, when asked what feelings or thoughts they would have if they saw that a car was coming at them at 90 mph, some patients would talk about being exhilarated or uneasy and offer similar completely inappropriate responses, instead of labelling the feeling as fright or panic. In addition these patients tended to act rather than think, and they had difficulty in communicating with the interviewer. Many of them were extremely dull. I wondered if the physiological understanding of their emotional difficulties might contribute more to the development of more useful therapeutic interventions than the psychological treatments which are available to them at present. Having attended this meeting I am doubtful whether I can offer to such patients in Boston any hope for a new kind of assistance. Despite this fact, however, during this symposium I have gathered a lot of valuable information and I am optimistic that the basic scientists who work with animals can help the clinician-observers. We have presented some observations on human beings. These observations may not be very precise or very well controlled, and may even appear as only interesting hypotheses which you may want to dismiss as too speculative, but this is all that we can offer you at present. Before you return to the safety of your laboratories, however, you may want to think about the development of treatments which may help to alleviate these patients' suffering; and they do suffer a great deal. I appreciate Dr Gray's caution to us not to rush into cutting off the dorso-medial amygdala or the lateral amygdala in man but the sad fact remains that at times we may be tempted to do just this, when we are confronted with a seriously disturbed violent individual whose actions are destructive to himself and to others, and who has failed to respond to all our conventional forms of therapy.

Nemiah: It was probably naive of us to come with the questions that Dr Sifneos has just raised and that I asked at the beginning of the meeting. It appeared to me then that nobody listened to us and that as the symposium progressed we received no answers. Instead, a whole variety of seemingly unrelated subjects were discussed, and our frustration mounted as it became clear that we were not going to find answers in the work of people whose investigations were not really relevant to our clinical problems. And yet one should not conclude from this that the symposium has been a failure—far from it! Over the past three days I have come to know several investigators whose work is indeed germane to the kinds of clinical enigmas with which Dr Sifneos and I are concerned. This will, I think, be the beginning of future collaborative work among us. That is the measure of a truly fertile meeting— the establishment of new professional relationships that will grow and be productive long after the meeting itself is forgotten. In that sense, our symposium has been a successful and satisfying adventure.

References

ABRAHAMS, V. C., HILTON, S. M. & ZBROŻYNA, A. (1960) Active muscle vasodilatation in the alerting stage of the defence reaction . *J. Physiol. (Lond.)* **154**, 491-513

BENSON, H., HERD, J. A., MORSE, W. H. & KELLEHER, R. T. (1970) Behaviorally induced hypertension in the squirrel monkey. *Circ. Res.* **26-27**, suppl. 1, 21-26

DALY, R. J. (1969) Hostility and chronic intermittent haemodialysis. *J. Psychosom. Res.* **13**, 265-273

DENENBERG, V. H. (1969) Animal studies of early experience: some principles which have implications for human development. In *Minnesota Symposium on Child Psychology* (Hill, J., ed.), vol. 3, pp. 31-45, University of Minnesota Press, Minneapolis

DENENBERG, V. H. (1970) Experimental programming of life histories and the creation of individual difference. In *Miami Symposium on the Prediction of Behavior: Effects of Early Experience* (Jones, M. R., ed.), pp. 61-91, University of Miami Press, Coral Gables, Florida

DENENBERG, V. H. & WHIMBEY, A. E. (1968) Experimental programming of life histories: toward an experimental science of individual differences. *Dev. Psychobiol.* **1**, 55-59

ENGEL, G. L., REICHSMAN, F. & SEGAL, H. (1956) A study of an infant with a gastric fistula. I. Behavior and rate of total hydrochloric acid secretion. *Psychosom. Med.* **18**, 374-398

FOLKOW, B. & RUBINSTEIN, E. H. (1966) Cardiovascular effects of acute and chronic stimulations of the hypothalamus defence area in the rat. *Acta Physiol. Scand.* **68**, 48-57

FORSYTH, R. P. & HARRIS, R. E. (1970) Circulatory changes during stressful stimuli in rhesus monkeys. *Circ. Res.* **26-27**, suppl. 1, 13-20

HERD, J. A., MORSE, W. H., KELLEHER, R. T. & GROSE, S. A. (1971) Cardiovascular functions during operant conditioning procedures. In *Cardiovascular Regulation in Health and Disease* (Bartorelli, C. & Zanchetti, A., eds.), pp. 33-41, Cardiovascular Research Institute, Milan

HENRY, J. P. (1967) Behavioral biology: an interdisciplinary study of potential interest to sociologists. *et al.* **1** (2), 7-10 (Winter 1967) (University of Southern California publication)

HESS, W. R. (1949) *Das Zwischenhirn: Syndrome, Lokalisationen, Funktionen*, Benno Schwabe, Basel

KAPLAN, A. (1964) *The Conduct of Inquiry*, Chandler, San Francisco

KARPLUS, J. P. & KREIDL, A. (1927) Gehirn und Sympathicus. VII. Ueber Beziehungen der Hypothalamuszentren zu Blutdruck und innerer Sekretion. *Pflügers Arch. Gesamte Physiol.* **215**, 667-670

KATZ, J. L., WEINER, H., GALLAGHER, T. F. & HELLMAN, L. (1970) Stress, distress and ego defenses: psychoendocrine response to tumor biopsy. *Arch. Gen. Psychiatr.* **23**, 131-142

MARTY, P. & DE M'UZAN, M. (1963) La pensée opératoire. *Rev. Fr. Psychoanal.* **27**, suppl., 345-356

MARTY, P., DE M'UZAN, M. & DAVID, C. (1963) *L'Investigation psychosomatique*, Presses Universitaires de France, Paris

NEMIAH, J. C. & SIFNEOS, P. E. (1970) Affect and fantasy in patients with psychosomatic disorders. In *Modern Trends in Psychosomatic Medicine* (Hill, O. W., ed.), pp. 26-34, Appleton-Century-Crofts, New York

NAGLE, R., GANGOLA, R. & PICTON-ROBINSON, I. (1971) Factors influencing return to work after myocardial infarction. *Lancet* **2**, 454-456

NAUTA, W. J. (1971) The problem of the frontal lobe: a reinterpretation. *J. Psychiatr. Res.* **8**, 167-189

RANSON, S. W. & BILLINGSLEY, P. R. (1916) Vasomotor reactions for stimulation of the floor of the IVth ventricle. III. Studies in vasomotor reflex arcs. *Am. J. Physiol.* **41**, 85-90

RAZRAN, G. (1971) *Mind in Evolution: an East-West Synthesis of Learned Behavior and Cognition*, Houghton Mifflin, Boston

ROBINSON, J. O. (1969) Symptoms and the discovery of high blood pressure. *J. Psychosom. Res.* **13**, 157-161

ROBINSON, J. O. & WOOD, M. W. (1968) Symptoms and personality in the diagnosis of physical illness. *Br. J. Prev. Soc. Med.* **22**, 23-26

SIFNEOS, P. E. (1967) Clinical observations on some patients suffering from a variety of psychosomatic diseases. *Acta Medica Psychosomatica* (Proc. 7th European Conf. on Psychosomatic Research, Rome)

SMALL, W. P., CAY, E. L., DUGARD, P., SIRCUS, W., FALCONER, C. W. A., SMITH, A. N.,

McManus, J. P. A. & Bruce, J. (1969) Peptic ulcer surgery: selection for operation by 'earning'. *Gut* **10**, 996-1003

Zill, N. (1972) Behavioral testing for cardiovascular studies in laboratory animals and man. In *Neural and Psychological Mechanisms in Cardiovascular Disease* (Zanchetti, A., ed.), Il Ponte, Milan, in press

Summing-up

SIR DENIS HILL

Institute of Psychiatry, University of London

The symposium has been concerned with the nature of emotion and the emotional state, the central and peripheral physiological changes associated with it and the relations between these and so-called psychosomatic disease. We now realize that this word carries no specific meaning and scientifically has proved counter-productive. We are prepared to say that we are concerned with the role of psychological factors in influencing somatic disease, but we have different opinions about what psychological factors are. Have they anything to do with the internal state of the individual? Are they, as Dr Weiss suggested, a function of the relationship between environmental stimuli? Or are they both, as most clinicians would hold? We were also warned by Professor Hinde that we should not all be using the word 'emotion' in the same sense. Some deny that there are pleasant emotions, or that emotion can be a function of the internal state alone; for them the emotional state is always a function of the individual's response to environmental events, that is to say, always a function of his behaviour. Emotion as experienced is, in this context, an unnecessary epiphenomenon of the central nervous system. For others and particularly those concerned with clinical research the emotional state is conceptualized more often as dependent upon a large series of inputs, from other systems of the CNS and from other bodily activities as well as from the environment.

It depends on our field of interest and study how we use the word. When studying the phenomenon of emotion in animals whose modes of communication we do not understand, we necessarily restrict the range of emotional phenomena to overt behaviour and bodily correlations. In man we cannot do this without denying our essential humanity for we are aware of the feeling-states which we call emotions in ourselves and we detect them in one another, and their disorder in our patients.

Much confusion in the past has arisen from the way in which the role of emotion as the feeling-state has been conceptualized. Without committing the category mistake we cannot view the feeling-state aspect of emotion as the prime mover or cause of behaviour, yet surely it is an important aspect or manifestation of that which is. If all behaviour is seen as an aspect of adaptation, then the emotional state is one manifestation of a central integrative activity of the organism, and its quality or character and its intensity are functions of that very complex state.

Dr Gray treats emotions as states of the CNS produced in it by reinforcing events in the environment and associated either in the present or in the rat's past behaviour with punishment or non-reward. He postulates there are three emotional states and three systems within the CNS serving them, leading to behaviour involving either approach, inhibition or fight–flight activity. In this concept the emotional state of the CNS is a function of the consequences of environmental stimuli or events and only of this, except of course that there is some variability in the intensity of response between animals. Such differences are explained on a genetic basis by making the intellectual jump from rat to man and imputing to the former the temperamental dimensions which H. J. Eysenck has described for the latter. It is, of course, true that emotional and non-emotional strains of rats and mice can be identified and breed true.

We have heard from clinicians who are concerned with the manifestations of emotion in man and who conceive it not only as a CNS state, producing profound bodily changes—muscular, autonomic and humoral—and changes in behaviour, but also as a 'feeling' or state of affect, privately experienced but variably so, and variably expressed verbally. Both Dr Nemiah and Dr Tibblin have drawn attention to the importance of this variability in human disease and psychiatric illness. There may be no direct concordance between the autonomic, humoral, perceptual and behavioural associations of the emotional state in the CNS and the intensity of the feeling-state as experienced by the subject. Evidence for different types of dissociation has been provided by the clinical examples of Dr Nemiah, by the studies on cardiovascular patients by Dr Tibblin—both at the experiential level—and by the deprivation studies of Dr Hofer at the physiological level.

It is not only psychoanalysts, like Dr Sandler, who would give to the quality and the intensity of feeling-state the central role in the determination of behaviour, and it matters little whether this feeling-state is conceptualized as an intervening variable such as anxiety (Hinde) or arousal (Lader) or as a state of tension in the ego or mental apparatus (Sandler). Dr Sandler, who has most usefully reviewed the history of the role of emotion in psychoanalytic theory, speaks of a mental apparatus and a physical apparatus. The former is a psychological system, whose only information is experiential—that is, it is concerned with judgments based on the meaning of events—and the latter is a physical apparatus concerned with bodily changes. The mental apparatus, Dr Sandler told us, functions to maintain feeling homeostasis, and in infancy and in normal functioning the mental and physical apparatuses operate in step to maintain homeostasis in both.

There is, however, here a logical trap into which I do not think Dr Sandler has fallen, but the danger of which cannot be ignored. Professor Hinde warned us about it. Anyone who has read Gilbert Ryle's *The Concept of Mind* (1949) must accept the fallacy of the category mistake which the traditional concept of Cartesian mind–body dualism with the idea of interaction between non-physical mind and physical CNS implies. Such a concept is logically not tenable. To the learning theorist, mind and therefore the feeling-states which are called emotions are regarded as useless and ineffective epiphenomena of the CNS. If that part of the CNS concerned with the emotional state, say the limbic system, continuously emits, as it were, mental events into consciousness we have the so-called identity theory—or the concept of psychophysical parallelism, to which Dr Lader subscribes. Some professional philosophers (e.g. Beck & Holmes 1968) can produce logical arguments against it. It is odd to say the least that efficient brains 'just cannot help producing useless consciousness'. Logically there are convincing arguments against both Cartesian dualism and epiphenomenalism yet Professor Hinde suggests that a compromise between the two concepts is impossible. While we must accept that a non-physical entity, mind or feeling, cannot influence the CNS, the other view which regards the whole of mental life and subjective experience as irrelevant is hardly acceptable. It does not do justice to facts of clinical experience.

How does Dr Sandler escape from the dilemma? And does he do it? 'The development and functioning of the psychological apparatus is a function of the nervous system', Dr Sandler told us, 'but it can be conceived of as a separate system of the body, functioning in interaction with other bodily systems and with the environment'. Its main function is to receive information from many inputs, environmental, and from inside—the drive forces expressing needs, the cognitive appraisal of any situation in the light of the present and the past, the memory store—and its job is to maintain homeostasis in the feeling-state, to so adapt behaviour to provide a sense of well-being and safety. The gaining of pleasure and the avoidance of unpleasure are secondary to this. But does restoring homeostasis, physical and mental, provide an adequate framework for understanding human behaviour? How far would human civilization have got if the main objective of man was to maintain homeostasis? Moreover, where is this most important part of the CNS found? Although aware of the dangers of neurologizing, I put forward the large non-specific thalamocortical system for this role. If so, it replaces Dr Gray's particular black box—the medial hypothalamus which he calls 'the decision mechanism'.

Dr Gray considers that the three emotional states to which the behavioural repertoire of the rat can be reduced are subserved by three anatomically distinct limbic systems, operating through a common pathway upon which the medial hypothalamus is situated. Professor Fonberg's experiments using dogs suggest how this neuronal substratum of the emotional state may operate. The behaviour antitheses of approach and inhibition or withdrawal, with their associated emotional states, which are of course matters of inference, although her dogs certainly looked sad, can be manipulated by surgical destruction of different parts of the amygdaloid nuclear complex and of the lateral and medial hypothalamic nuclei. Since the behavioural effects of destruction of one part of the amygdala complex can be reversed by destruction of the other—and the same applies to the different nuclear groups of the hypothalamus—the conclusion seems warranted that the emotional status and the overt behaviour are the resultant of inhibitory and excitatory processes mutually interacting between these cellular masses. It is surely of interest that the dog deprived of both parts of his amygdala becomes again a normally friendly adapting animal. But we still do not know how 'normal' a dog is, deprived of its amygdaloid nuclear masses. To what extent is its adaptive behaviour modified by the operations? Is it still capable, for example, of exhibiting the experimental neurosis?

These interesting studies by Professor Fonberg raise further issues about the nature—the restricted or more comprehensive nature—of the emotional state. To what extent is the emotional state dependent, not only upon the vagaries of a threatening, punishing or rewarding environment, but also upon internal factors of quite another sort? We have heard evidence to suggest that the internal responses which affect the total behaviour of the individual, whether animal or man, and over long periods of time, can be altered as a result of circumstances which cannot be called directly threatening or punishing, although they might, in Dr Gray's terms, be called 'frustrating non-reward'.

It is evident that there is another source of input to the emotional system, and one which determines the emotional state of the individual. Many, particularly experimental psychologists, have denied that the satisfaction of biological needs, for which we conceptualize a series of drives, gives rise to a positive emotion—that is, that pleasure is an emotion. There is no doubt, however, that the non-satisfaction of these needs gives rise to an unpleasant feeling-state in man and that there is evidence of profound alteration in the behaviour and the autonomic and humoral status of animals who are deprived, who are prevented in one way or another from gratifying those needs. The mechanisms upon which the very adverse effects of depriving an animal or human are dependent, which have been known and recorded for many years, are still unclear, but the work of this symposium has thrown light upon them. Dr Hofer, studying early maternal deprivation in the infant rat, and making a careful analysis of the responses, provided evidence that the overt behavioural responses and the effects on the heart are mediated by distinct and different neural mechanisms. Dr Hofer's work makes the point very clearly that the varied and diverse responses to a deprivation experience do not reflect a common and single reactive process. Indeed by appropriate manipulation, one type of response can be demonstrated to occur without the other. Dr Hofer has reminded us that in man we are accustomed to thinking of the emotional and physical components of the psychosomatic response as following from a single process—in man, the processing of information from a variety of inputs. If dissociations in the behavioural and physiological responses to maternal deprivation in the infant rat can be demonstrated, may we not be on the track of understanding the *physiological* mechanisms responsible for the *psychological* dissociations which are evident in man's psychiatric and psychosomatic disorders—the important phenomena to which Dr Nemiah and Dr Tibblin drew our attention?

Dr Engel has described a condition of conservation-withdrawal, which he believes can be detected in virtually every species of animal, and which is evoked in circumstances in which coping with an adverse environment has become impossible or unrewarding. This behavioural response of relative immobility, quiescence and unresponsiveness to the environment is very similar, as described, to the behavioural inhibition in Dr Gray's rats and the withdrawn, unfriendly and unresponsive dogs in whom Professor Fonberg had destroyed the dorso–medial amygdala. Dr Engel suggests that as a universal phenomenon in so many species, conservation–withdrawal is a biological mechanism serving regulatory and restorative functions—that is, it has a homeostatic function. But it is not clear what is conserved, what is restored by the behaviour. We must infer the intervening variable of the feeling-state and its need for safety. Dr Engel suggests, as others have done, that conservation–withdrawal can best be conceptualized in terms of the reciprocal excitatory and inhibitory functions of the nervous system and the multiple feedback loops between cortex, limbic system, hypothalamus and the reticular system.

The work of the symposium has suggested that the emotional state of the individual, both as a feeling-state and as a complex, multiple, physiological behavioural response, is essential to any model concerned with psychosomatic processes. As an intervening variable it can be described either in psychological terms of experience or in terms of the behaviour associated with it, or in terms of the physiological changes accompanying it. The latter, Dr Tibblin suggests, may affect the emotional state by negative feedback, which thus provides a regulating adaptive function for the physiological changes as well as the conventional defensive role. Dr Lader postulates that an essential aspect of the emotional state is the level of non-specific arousal of the organism, arousal being conceived as a continuum at the extreme of which various feeling-states, pleasant or unpleasant, occur. All adaptive behaviour must be associated with some degree of arousal. In man it is a condition of consciousness. At moderate levels of arousal the behaviour is adaptive; at extreme levels it is maladaptive. Presumably it may become self-perpetuating by positive feedback. Whether emotion is or is not elicited in the feeling-state, physiological changes always occur, and just as the physiological effects of arousal are not unitary, all measures not being affected equally, so the peripheral humoral and autonomic effects vary from one individual to another and between different systems or parts of a system in the same individual. Evidence from psychophysiological research on normal people and in mentally disturbed patients supports this view.

Substantial evidence of the pathogenic consequences of chronic high arousal, of continued evocation of the emotional state, has been produced. The effects seem particularly evident in the field of cardiovascular pathology, and this has been the most readily studied and has the greatest relevance to morbidity and mortality in man. Dr Storey has shown that emotional turmoil can be followed by subarachnoid haemorrhage, even when there is no local pathology in cerebral vessels, and in those patients mood disorders both before and after the cerebral accident are particularly likely to occur. The relation between social stimulation, adverse social circumstances and deprivation of social interaction, and physical illness has been a constant theme in the literature.

Man is primarily a psychosocial animal and a major field of his adaptational activity is with his social environment. No less than with wild forms of life he is dependent for survival upon the development of social bonds. Dr Ginsburg has drawn attention to the relevance of studies showing how social bonds are formed in the wild, and manipulated under laboratory conditions, to the problems of human adaptation. There is a biologically determined invariant pattern of response to certain environmental novelties, including strangers of the same species. A requirement of bond formation is the overcoming of the fearful or anxious emotional state which is part of that response. In this sense therefore Dr Ginsburg suggests that the anxious emotional state in the face of certain social stimuli is a behavioural legacy from the evolutionary past.

The elegant experimental work of Dr Henry and his colleagues draws together the relevance of social ethological studies, the conceptualization of the organization of integrative processes in the limbic system (the work of Dr Gray and Dr Fonberg), the question of stress and the inability of the individual to escape or combat threatening situations, and finally the relevance of this to physical disease. By using different strains of mice, differentiated by their degree of timidity, reactivity and social capacity, Dr Henry has demonstrated the consequences of constitutional differences for the cardiovascular changes and changes in catecholamine synthesis which accompany stress, and how these are mediated through the sympathetic–adrenomedullary system.

In mice sustained emotional arousal, due to social confrontation which the animals can neither escape from, nor cope with, can be lethal, and death is consequent upon cardiovascular changes. Sustained high blood pressure is evident and serious arteriosclerotic disease supervenes. Can we extrapolate the lessons learnt from mice to men? Dr Henry thinks we can.

Dr Weiss, using a different experimental model of restrained rats and studying gastric pathology, found that the greater the number of responses the animals had to make, the greater the pathology. On the other hand, and this has significant consequences for therapeutics, the greater the *relevant feedback* signals, the less the pathology. In this context, 'relevant feedback signals' are identified as those *not associated* with the stressor signals.

One of the impressive things that has emerged from this symposium is our realization of the ubiquitous character of the emotional state. Every system of the body would seem to be involved. An important and challenging question is the role of feedback signals from all these systems in reducing or enhancing the excitability in the central integrative processes regulating the level of the emotional state, promoting adaptive behaviour, restoring disturbed homeostasis, and protecting against pathology.

If it is evident that there is no 'specificity' of physiological pattern with different emotional states, described by their feeling-states, it is useful to look at the proposition that there may be 'situational specificity'—that is, that physiological patterns can be correlated with the form of adaptive behaviour which is the response. This is the conclusion which seems justified by Professor Zanchetti's work. The physiological pattern of muscular blood flow relates to the stimulus situation and the particular behaviour in which the animal is engaged. The careful analysis of clinical, pathological, psychological and social data in man has established, in my view, that potentially lethal physical disease can result from the physiological and humoral disturbances associated with chronic emotional turmoil—an aspect of the coping adaptive process in adverse circumstances. But since we cannot treat man as an experimental animal, we can only observe, monitor and measure the phenomena of disease as they occur in nature. What we have heard at this symposium justifies our hopes that the experimental study of animal behaviour will provide us with necessary understanding of the mechanisms which bring such diseases about, and so ultimately lead to their control.

It is surely a truism that man must now learn how to control his destiny, and this means his own behaviour, in order to survive. If we have advanced an understanding of the very complex problems of our behaviour—including our destructive and self-destructive behaviour—we have not wasted our time at this symposium. I am reminded of something written by the late Aldous Huxley. To paraphrase what he said: 'my rat's brain serves my rat's purposes, and my dog's brain my dog's purposes, but my own brain is something different. Who can say what my purposes are? I myself do not know'.

References

RYLE, G. (1949) *The Concept of Mind*, Hutchinson's University Library, London
BECK, L. W. & HOLMES, R. L. (1968) *Philosophic Inquiry: an Introduction to Philosophy*, 2nd edn, Prentice-Hall International Inc., London

Index of contributors

*Entries in **bold** type indicate papers; other entries are contributions to discussions*

Indexes compiled by William Hill

Subject index